Cases on
Information Technology
Management in Modern
Organizations

Jay Liebowitz
George Washington University

Mehdi Khosrowpour
Pennsylvania State University at Harrisburg

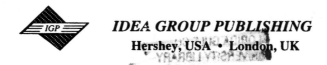

IDEA GROUP PUBLISHING
Hershey, USA • London, UK

Senior Editor:	Mehdi Khosrowpour
Managing Editor:	Jan Travers
Copy Editors:	Beth Green
Printed at:	BookCrafters

Published in the United States of America by
    Idea Group Publishing
    701 E. Chocolate Avenue
    Suite 200
    Hershey PA 17033-1240
    Tel: 717-533-8845
    Fax: 717-533-8661
    E-mail: jtravers@idea-group.com
    Website: http://www.idea-group.com

and in the United Kingdom by
    Idea Group Publishing
    3 Henrietta Street
    Covent Garden
    London WC2E 8LU
    Tel: 71-240 0856
    Fax: 71-379 0609

Library of Congress Cataloging-in-Publication Data
Liebowitz, Jay, 1957-
        Cases on information technology management in modern organizations
        /Jay Liebowitz, Mehdi Khosrowpour.
            304 pp. - (Series in information technology management)
        Includes bibliographical references and index.
        ISBN 1-878289-37-3 (pbk.)
        1. Information technology---Management--Case Studies.
        I. Khosrowpour, Mehdi 1951- . II. Title. III. Title: Information technology
management in modern organizations. IV. Series.
        HD30.2.L53 1997
        658.4'038--DC21   97-3865
                                                                        CIP

British Cataloguing in Publication Data
A Cataloguing in Publication record for this book is available from the British Library.

IDEA GROUP PUBLISHING

Hershey, PA, USA • London, UK

Series in Information Technology Management

The surge in information technology during the latter part of the 20th century has forced organizations to meet its challenges with an increased use and management of information resources. This series takes an in-depth look at trends, current practices, and problem resolution in information technology management and offers you a first-class source for expanding the reader's knowledge in this ever-growing field.

Books in this series:

- **Cases on Information Technology Management in Modern Organizations (Jay Liebowitz and Mehdi Khosrowpour)**
- **Collaborative Technologies and Organizational Learning (R. Neilson)**
- **Information Systems Outsourcing Decision Making: A Managerial Approach (L.A. de Looff)**
- **Information Technology and Organizations: Challenges of New Technologies (Mehdi Khosrowpour)**
- **Management Impacts of Information Technology (Edward Szewczak)**
- **Managing Information Technology Investments with Outsourcing (Mehdi Khosrowpour)**
- **Business Process Change: Reengineering Concepts, Methods and Technologies (Varun Grover and William Kettinger)**
- **Reengineering MIS: Aligning Information Technology and Business Operations (Kevin Coleman, Jim Ettwein, Clelland Johnson, Dick Pigman and Deborah Pulak)**
- **Organizational Information Systems and Technology Innovation and Diffusion (upcoming) (Tor Larsen and Eugene McGuire)**
- **The Virtual Workplace (upcoming) (Magid Igbaria and Margaret Tan)**

For more information, or to submit a proposal for a book
in this series, please contact:
Idea Group Publishing
1331 E. Chocolate Avenue
Hershey, PA 17033-1117
Tel: 1/800-345-4332 or 717/533-8845
Fax: 717/533-8661
E-mail: jtravers@idea-group.com
Website: http://www.idea-group.com

Author guidelines also available at http://www.idea-group.com

Other IDEA GROUP Publishing Books

Excellent additions to your library!

Cases on Information Technology Management in Modern Organizations

Table of Contents

Preface

As information systems educators, professionals, and students, we can learn best from the experiences of others. Successes and failures from others can help the information systems community to further develop and flourish. An effective means for conveying these experiences and lessons learned is through case studies.

Technology advances in our modern global society have lead to changing organizational needs. The result is a new set of challenges to organizations as they integrate technology into all functions and activities of the modern organization. Today's manager must be alert to opportunities afforded and, in fact, cannot solve problems without knowledge about both technology and total company processes.

Cases in Information Technology Management in Modern Organizations is a compilation of original cases that describe information technology related issues, problems, and experiences for greater management of IT in modern organizations. We are very fortunate to have refereed contributions from many active researchers, educators, and practitioners in the information systems field. The cases are both domestic and international and cover a cross-section of various information technology projects at universities, industry, and government. The primary objective of this book is to provide a means to examine experiences of organizations who have addressed prevailing issues in the technology revolution.

Each case has been carefully refereed by four reviewers (including the editors). The cases have been developed using the following standardized format:

- **Executive Summary**—Overview of the case and issues discussed.
- **Background**—Background on the history of the organization, type of business, products/services provided, management structure, financial status, strategic planning, organizational culture, economic climate, etc.
- **Setting the Stage**—Description of the status quo technique being used before the project was initiated and players involved.
- **Project/Case Description**—Overview of the project, technology concerns, management and organizational concerns.
- **Current Status of the Case/Project**—"What actually happened with the case/project.
- **Successes and Failures**—Discussion of successes and failures related to case/project.
- **Epilogue and Lessons Learned**—Discussion of technology, management and organizational lessons learned.
- **Questions and References**—Listing of five questions for discussion

(answers are supplied with the brief instructor's manual upon book adoption).

   With each case structure being fairly homogeneous, teaching and usage of these cases are greatly facilitated. This book is specifically geared for an undergraduate MIS course or an introductory MIS course at the MBA or MS level. Many of the current IS cases in existing books are either very voluminous or sparse in detail. *Cases in Information Technology Management in Modern Organizations* is a compromise between both ends of the spectrum, producing a meaningful and tractable set of case studies. At the end of each case is a liter of questions to stimulate class or case study discussion.

   The book consists of 21 cases authored by more than 40 IT researchers and managers. The cases deal with a variety of IT issues such as Planning for Information Systems, Human Side of Information Systems, End User Computing, Global Information Technology management, Organization Policies and Culture, Systems Design and Methodology and Communications and Networking. The cases in this book represent organizations in manufacturing and service industries and government organizations in the United States as well as in other nations.

   We hope you and your students can benefit from this book. We value your comments and feedback so we can plan for future volumes of this book. Please direct your questions and suggestions to either Mehdi Khosrowpour (M1K@PSU.EDU) or Jay Liebowitz (jayl@gwis2.circ.gwu.edu). We look forward to hearing about your comments and suggestions.

Acknowledgments

   Putting together a book of this level requires a tremendous effort and hard work. We greatly appreciate the valuable help from the authors and our reviewers for their excellent contributions to this book. We also greatly appreciate the assistance of managing editor, Ms. Jan Travers and our copy editor, Ms. Beth Green, at Idea Group Publishing. And of course, without the strong support of our families—Janet, Jason and Kenny Liebowitz and Beth Peiffer, this book would never be possible.

Jay Liebowitz
Mehdi Khosrowpour
January, 1997

Cases on
Information Technology Management
in Modern Organizations

Business Process Reengineering	Emerging & Innovative Technologies	Software Engineering Tools and Technologies	Planning for Information Systems	Health-Care Information Systems	Communications & Networking	Decision Support Systems	Human Side of Info Tech	Organization Politics & Culture	Government Organizations	Manufacturing Industries	Service Industry	End User-related Issues	Information Technology Management Issues	Global Information Technology Management	Systems Design & Methodology
			✗			✗		✗		✗			✗		✗
	✗		✗		✗		✗				✗		✗		✗
						✗		✗	✗				✗		
✗							✗	✗			✗	✗	✗		
				✗				✗			✗		✗	✗	
			✗	✗						✗			✗	✗	✗
			✗		✗		✗			✗					✗
			✗							✗			✗	✗	✗
✗			✗							✗					✗
			✗		✗						✗	✗	✗		✗
			✗		✗		✗				✗		✗		✗
			✗		✗			✗			✗	✗	✗		✗
			✗		✗	✗	✗	✗			✗	✗	✗		✗
			✗		✗	✗		✗			✗		✗	✗	✗
			✗		✗			✗			✗	✗	✗		
			✗		✗			✗			✗		✗		✗
		✗	✗		✗				✗			✗	✗		✗
✗		✗			✗			✗		✗			✗	✗	✗
✗			✗				✗	✗	✗			✗			✗
✗		✗			✗		✗		✗			✗	✗	✗	✗
			✗				✗			✗		✗	✗		✗

Chapter 1

Introducing Expert Systems at The Corporation*

Jay Liebowitz
George Washington University

Executive Summary

This case study highlights the concept that the "management" of the technology is usually the limiting factor causing the demise of a project rather than the "technology" itself. This real case study involves creating an awareness of a new technology within the company (hereafter named "The Corporation") and trying to start a (much needed) project using this technology. The technology in question here is "expert systems."

An expert system is a computer program that emulates the behavior of an expert in a well–defined domain of knowledge. At The Corporation, a few key top management executives thought that an expert system could be used to help The Corporation in configuring its minicomputer systems. The Corporation enlisted the help of a consultant to develop a feasibility study of using expert systems for configuration management at The Corporation.

In doing so, an awareness of expert systems technology was created throughout the company in almost all divisions—customer service, sales, marketing, finance, information systems, manufacturing, etc. The hidden agenda of the consultant was to start an expert systems project for configuration management at The Corporation, if the feasibility study deemed it worthwhile.

The case study describes many of the hurdles that had to be jumped, and shows the importance of understanding the corporate culture of the organization, especially in the difficult times of mergers and acquisitions, economic downturns, and tough competition. Let's now see how the case unfolds.

Background on the History of the Organization

The Corporation (a pseudonym) is a manufacturer of minicomputer systems who acquired a larger company in the same line of business. The Corporation manufactures a variety of computer

*"The Corporation" is being used to protect the name of the organization. Please use the following for a web-based version of this case: http://cac.psu.edu/~gjy1/case

families for use in real time simulation, software development, computer architecture research, and a host of other applications. The Corporation, a $280 million company, has about 900 employees at its corporate headquarters and about 200 employees at its manufacturing plant.

Over the recent years, downsizing and outsourcing have been dominant strategies used in The Corporation. A sense of uneasiness plagued many of the employees as they were unsure of whether their jobs were protected, as many of their colleagues were receiving pink slips. Those whose jobs were valued remained, but were troubled with large workloads due to the reduction in force.

A critical component of The Corporation's operations is configuration management. Configuration management, or more appropriately configuration control, refers to configuring the hardware (and software) correctly for a customer's order. The Corporation wanted to improve the number of times it took to correctly configure an order. About 90 percent of the computer configurations were done incorrectly the first time, and it would normally take about 12 times to correctly configure the order. The vice president of development (who was quickly let go after the acquisition) and the vice president/general manager of manufacturing and customer service wanted to explore the feasibility of developing a Configurator using expert systems technology. The Configurator would configure an order and provide a quotation correctly the first time.

By having such a system, it was thought that the amount of time spent in contracts/configuration control could be reduced, thereby freeing up time for manufacturing to build the customer's system and ship within the delivery date. Additionally, an automated Configurator could facilitate the creation of forecasting reports, improve customer relations, and provide timely and accurate configuration information out into the field to the analysts and sales representatives. It was also felt that an expert system may be a good vehicle for building up the corporate memory of the firm so that valuable knowledge and experiential learning would not be lost.

In the following sections, a discussion of how an awareness of expert systems technology was created within The Corporation will be made. However, due to mainly organizational reasons, the development and implementation of an expert configuration system were never realized.

Setting the Stage

Getting Started

The first step in getting an expert systems project started is to create an awareness of expert systems technology. Fortunately, at The Corporation, the vice president of development and the vice president/general manager of manufacturing and customer service had some familiarization with

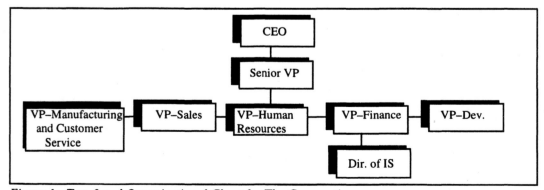

Figure 1: Top–Level Organizational Chart for The Corporation

expert systems and they thought that it would be useful to see how expert systems technology could help improve The Corporation's operations. They then hired a consultant specializing in expert systems to write a feasibility study on if and how expert systems could be used in configuration management at The Corporation.

The initial step of creating an awareness of expert systems technology was already made easy because some top management executives were backing the study. This top level, champion support helped to pave the way for this study. Unfortunately, however, the vice president of development (the main champion) left the company about a week after the consultant arrived. This was due to the acquisition, and all the former top management officials were now replaced with top management from the acquiring company. This event was not a major hindrance because the other sponsor of the project (i.e., the vice president/general manager of manufacturing and customer service) was a supporter of this feasibility study effort. Although, the main champion of the effort (i.e., the former vice president of development) was lost, and the new vice president of development did not seem to be interested in the value of expert systems. An awareness and understanding of expert systems still had to be created within the organization at all operating levels.

In order to permeate this notion of expert systems throughout the company, it was necessary to use a variety of methods to achieve this goal. These methods included: a top-down approach, a bottom-up approach, and an introductory seminar approach.

Project/Case Description

Top-Down Approach

In order to develop the feasibility study, the company's operations had to be understood and this involved speaking with top management at The Corporation on down through the various departments (customer service, manufacturing, engineering and development, sales, marketing, information systems, finance, etc.). In studying the organizational chart of The Corporation, the consultant realized that there was not a vice president of information systems, which is a rarity for a computer-oriented, high technology firm. Instead, the traditional, conservative hierarchy was used whereby the director of information systems reported to the vice president of finance. This realization would later come back to haunt the effort.

By having the support of some top management executives, it was rather easy to gain access to other individuals in the company in order to make them aware of this study and expert systems. In speaking with the various individuals throughout The Corporation, the thrusts of the conversations were to determine what their needs were if an expert configuration system were built and what practices and policies at The Corporation would have to change to successfully build and use an expert configuration system. The 35 individuals who were interviewed felt comfortable in that their comments would be incorporated into the feasibility study which would be sent to all top management officials. In essence, they felt ownership in the study.

An essential player in this effort was the proposed expert if an expert configuration system would be built. It was also important to obtain the input and advice from this expert in regards to the need in having such an expert system. Additionally, it was important to gain the expert's support, so that this project wasn't forced upon her. There really was only one expert who had been around long enough to understand the configurations of the different product lines. She was severely overworked, and would welcome an aid to assist herself and her staff in the configuration management/control area. The expert was kept abreast of the work during this feasibility study effort, so that there would be no surprises at the end of this study.

Another innovative idea to create a better awareness of expert systems at the top management level was to circulate a pad to each top management executive with each page of the notepad embossed with the saying "Artificial Intelligence/Expert Systems are for Real at The Corporation." This approach was borrowed from a similar technique applied by the expert systems manager at 3M Corporation. As top management would use these pads to write short notes, they would constantly be reminded of expert systems.

Bottom-Up Approach

Not only was a top-down approach used in gaining user support, but also a bottom-up method was utilized. This bottom-up approach involved working with the actual users of the proposed expert configuration system in order to obtain their views and requirements in having such a system. The consultant and a member of the information systems department at The Corporation took the 3 day real-time sales/analysts training course. Most of the configuration analysts and sales representatives at The Corporation in the real-time market were gathered during this course. We were able to have a round table discussion with about 16 analysts (the primary users of the expert configuration system) and also speak with several sales representatives (secondary users). The analysts were very interested in the project, and offered valuable comments and insights. Additionally, as an outgrowth of our meeting, four analysts from throughout the country were designated to assemble a list of their requirements for having an expert configuration system. This information was very helpful in formulating the feasibility study.

Almost everyone in the company was very excited about the prospects of having a better way of configuring orders. The consultant and members of the information systems department were particularly cautious to make sure that expectations were kept under control.

Introductory Seminar

Another way which was used to create an awareness of this project and expert systems throughout the company was to offer an introductory seminar on artificial intelligence/expert systems to key individuals at The Corporation. This hour presentation served to boost the interests of those who attended, and helped to better familiarize themselves with expert systems technology and applications. Descriptions of expert configuration systems used by competitors stimulated increased interest in keeping up with the competition via expert systems. Even though the attendance at this seminar was less than expected, we were able to gain further support for this project.

Technology, Management, and Organizational Concerns

The Feasibility Study and Requirements Document

After interviewing the many individuals throughout The Corporation and performing an analysis of the results, the feasibility study was written and sent to all top management executives. The feasibility study included the following sections:

Executive Summary
1.0 Does a Need Exist for Developing an Aid for Facilitating The Corporation's
      Configuration Management Function
2.0 Can Expert Systems Technology Solve the Configuration Need
         2.1 Survey of Expert Systems for Configuration Management

2.2 Can Expert Systems Technology be Used at The Corporation

3.0 Alternatives for Using Expert Systems Technology for The Corporation's Configuration Management

4.0 Cost/Benefit Analysis and Risk Assessment

5.0 Building an Expert System Prototype for Configuring a Specific Product Line at The Corporation

6.0 Recommendations and Next Steps

7.0 References and Appendices

As part of the feasibility study, a thorough survey of existing expert configuration systems worldwide was included. It showed that major companies had been successfully using expert systems for configuration management. This gave confidence to The Corporation's officials to see that expert systems have been proven technology for successful use in configuration management activities. A separate summary of the recommendations based upon this feasibility study was also circulated to top management.

Other groundwork was laid to "set" the stage. A functional requirements document for an expert configuration system was prepared and sent to top management. This document included:

1.0 Purpose of Expert System

2.0 Reference Documents

3.0 User Information

4.0 Functional Requirements

    4.1 Database Access

    4.2 User Interface

    4.3 Input/Output Content

    4.4 Control Structure (Inference Engine)

    4.5 Knowledge Representation

    4.6 Hardware

5.0 Documentation

6.0 Training

7.0 Maintenance Requirements

By preparing this document, it showed top management that we had gone one step further by generating requirements for an expert configuration system, instead of merely stating that it is feasible to build an expert configuration system at The Corporation. Also, we lined up a local company who had expertise in developing expert configuration systems for developing the proposed expert configuration system at The Corporation and providing technology transfer in order to better acquaint the information systems staff on expert systems. We also spoke with a major, local university to provide some education/courses on expert systems on-site at The Corporation to designated individuals. We also had the support of the expert to go ahead with this project.

The Final Approval from Top Management

The stage was set and a meeting had been scheduled with top management in order to get the go-ahead on developing the expert system. We quickly learned that "timing" is a critical part in making any business decision made. Unfortunately, the meeting was cancelled due to emergency budget planning sessions, and it became apparent that it would be difficult to reschedule this meeting with top management. We even tried to hold a videoconference between top management in two locations, but only half of the management attendees could be available. Additionally, the project's approval became clouded with other timing issues, such as a transition in information systems management and then a new company-wide hiring freeze. During this time, the (then current) director of information systems said that he had certain signing authority and he would sign for the funds to develop the expert systems prototype. Four days before signing off, a new chief information officer (CIO) was hired to ultimately replace the previous director of information systems. The consultant and Information Systems staff briefed the new CIO on the proposed expert configuration system, but the CIO felt that other priorities were perhaps higher. Even the vice president of manufacturing (one of the original advocates of the study) said that although the company was doing configuration poorly, at least it could be done whereas other important areas were not being done at all. Coupled with these events, The Corporation was trying to cut back new projects in order to help ensure profitability for the company.

"What Actually Happened" with the Project

What did these events mean to the expert configuration system project? Principally, the decision to go-ahead with the project was delayed until new management felt comfortable in funding new projects and aligning their priorities. Management said that they would revisit and reconsider this expert configuration system project in four to six months. This never happened due to other perceived priorities by top management. Additionally, staff turnover and firings had increased in order to reengineer the company and control costs.

Poor business decisions continued to plague the company. The former Director of Information Systems of The Corporation had heard from colleagues still at The Corporation that the new CIO agreed to buy a million dollar software package, only to find out later that it was incompatible with The Corporation's hardware.

Successes and Failures

What can be learned from this case study? First, obtaining top management and user support are critical elements to the success of a project, especially one involving a new technology. Integral to gaining this support is the ability to create a thorough awareness of the technology (e.g., expert systems) within the company. This awareness, especially at the upper levels of management in the company, should help in gaining the financial and moral support from top management in order to go ahead with the project. Recognizing the internal politics, organizational culture, and external climate of The Corporation are essential elements where the development team must have strong sensitivity.

Another important lesson learned is to strongly involve the expert(s) and users in helping to gain support for the expert system project. In this case, the expert (who was the only person who knew the different product lines for configuration) should have been used in a more vocal capacity in order to urge top management that the company needs this expert configuration system for productivity, training, and longevity purposes. If the expert were to leave the company, the configuration task would be extremely difficult to perform due to the lack of expertise in The Corporation in knowing the various product lines and associated configurations. This fact should have been emphasized more to top management in order to further convince them of the need for such a configuration system.

A potential major flaw in introducing expert systems to The Corporation may have been the chaotic state of the company. With firings, staff turnover, reengineering, and cost control measures rampant within the company, it would be difficult to introduce a new technology, like expert systems, within the firm. Even though the use of an expert system for configuration management was being marketed by the development team as a good business decision, there were too many other priorities that needed immediate attention by top management. Perhaps it would have been better to have stimulated interest in the project after the initial chaos had settled. There were too many high priority items on the platter for top management that needed attention.

Epilogue

The birth of a new technology at The Corporation (namely, expert systems) is slowly emerging. It took about three months from the first time the words "expert systems" were uttered at The Corporation to the time it took to saturate top management with the notion of expert systems. The best outcome of this project was creating an awareness of expert systems throughout the company. The Corporation took this important first step in bringing expert systems technology to the company. The hybrid approaches used to get the project underway at The Corporation were very successful in terms of introducing expert systems technology to The Corporation's employees and management.

Knowing the corporate climate and culture was an important lesson learned from this experience. Having an appreciation for the organizational structure, internal politics, organizational barriers, and possible resistance to change were key concepts that should have been appreciated more than just understanding the technology. Also, trying to implement a new technology in a chaotic environment (due to the recent acquisition and resulting restructuring of The Corporation) was a difficult task indeed.

This case study hopefully illuminates some useful techniques that other companies may use to create an awareness of expert or intelligent systems within the organization for eventual expert/ intelligent system funding and support. A critical concept is a thorough appreciation for understanding the "management" of the technology versus just the technology itself. After all, without careful attention to these matters, the project may be a technical success but a technology transfer failure.

Questions for Discussion

1. Since The Corporation was in a chaotic environment due to the acquisition of a large company, was it worthwhile to try to introduce a new technology into The Corporation under these trying times?

2. How could the consultant gain better support from the new vice president of development and the vice president of manufacturing?

3. What could have been done differently to have been able to get the expert system prototype project funded?

4. In what ways could the domain expert in configuration control have helped more in trying to get the expert system funded?

5. How could the users of the eventual expert system (i.e., sales representatives and configuration analysts) have been more active in order to get the expert configuration system project started?

References

DeSalvo, D. and J. Liebowitz (eds.) (1990), *Managing Artificial Intelligence and Expert Systems*, Prentice Hall/Yourdon Press, New Jersey.

Lee, J.K., J. Liebowitz, and Y.M. Chae (eds.)(1996), *Proceedings of the 3rd World Congress on Expert Systems*, Cognizant Communication Corp., New York.

Liebowitz, J. (ed.) (1994), *Worldwide Expert System Activities and Trends*, Cognizant Communication Corporation, New York.

Kerr, R.M. (1992), "Expert Systems in Production Scheduling: Lessons from a Failed Implementation," *Journal of Systems Software*, Vol. 19, Elsevier Science, New York.

Turban, E. and J. Liebowitz (eds.) (1992), *Managing Expert Systems*, Idea Group Publishing, Harrisburg, PA.

Selected Bibliography

International Society for Intelligent Systems/James Madison University (1995), *Developing Your First Expert System CD ROM*, PO Box 1656, Rockville, Md 20849.

Lee, J.K., J. Liebowitz, and Y.M. Chae (eds.) (1996), *Proceedings of the Third World Congress on Expert Systems*, Cognizant Communication Corp., Elmsford, New York.

Liebowitz, J. (Ed.)(1990), *Expert Systems for Business and Management*, Prentice Hall, Englewood Cliffs, NJ.

Liebowitz, J. (1992), *Institutionalizing Expert Systems: A Handbook for Managers*, Prentice Hall, Englewood Cliffs, NJ.

Liebowitz, J. (ed.) (1994), *Worldwide Expert System Activities and Trends*, Cognizant Communication Corporation, Elmsford, New York.

Turban, E. and J. Liebowitz (eds.)(1992), *Managing Expert Systems*, Idea Group Publishing, Harrisburg, PA.

Chapter 2

Montclair Mutual
Insurance Company

William H. Money
George Washington University

Executive Summary

Alan Rowne must plan and implement a number of information system (IS) upgrades at Montclair Mutual Insurance Company. This is a complex task given the evolving nature of IS developmental techniques, variety of vendor supplied tools and software, and industry organizational imperatives to modify the operations of firms to improve efficiency. He is concentrating on a decision to recommend either upgrading his present system or acquiring a new environment with new development tools. A new system development environment would offer Montclair Mutual Insurance Company the opportunity to develop information systems with strong system integration and interfacing capabilities that promise a high return on investment. This case presents data concerning the choices among information system development strategies, tools, systems which could be selected for upgrade or development, and implementation decisions for an insurance company facing a dynamic business environment.

Background

Montclair Mutual was founded by community members of the Maryland farming area around Silver Hills, Maryland. The firm was originally formed (140+ years ago) to provide insurance (fire) for farms and buildings in the developing Maryland countryside. The company seeks to provide a high level of security and comfort to its policy holders in its commercial, residential, and farm insurance businesses. The annual report presents the firm's single guiding principle: to provide affordable reliable insurance for all policyholders; and to carefully balance assets against liabilities; strictly control administrative expenses; maintain a consistently high level of policyholder service; build customer confidence; and business growth in the years to come.

The company offers highly competitive insurance products in the seven major areas listed in table one below. Table two presents the premiums and direct losses by state. Table three shows the business results for the previous five year period.

The MIS Environment

Alan Rowne is the Vice President of Information Systems at Montclair Mutual Insurance Company. He's facing a changing MIS environment and corporate pressure for performance improvements. He must decide what to recommend in order to address a number of systems development goals. His believes his broad options are to either apply the Systems Development Life Cycle (SDLC) methodology to upgrade the accepted mainframe systems used by the company for many years; or select and apply a new set of CASE tools, prototyping methodology, and database models to implement a new client server system.

The attractive new system components found in the client server environment are physically smaller machines that do not require specialized water cooled and air cooled facilities. When compared to a mainframe, the systems may house equivalent or greater amounts of CPU processing capability,

Policy Type	% of Total Premiums	% of Losses Paid
Automobiles	27	32
Homeowners	21	26
Commercial Multiple - Peril	11	9
Workers Compensation	16	14
Farm Owners	8	12
Fire and Allied - Inland Marine	7	5
General Liability & Products Liability	9	2

Table 1: Direct Premiums by Type

State	% of Direct Premiums	% of Losses Paid
Maryland	51	52
Virginia	22	17
North Carolina	17	21
District of Columbia	4	3
Delaware	4	5
Pennsylvania & West Virginia	2	2

Table 2: Direct Premiums and Losses by State

	1	2	3	4	5
Admitted Assets	67.4	75.3	80.7	84	87.8
Direct Premiums Written	46.7	49.6	57.6	64.6	65.7
Surplus	25.9	29.9	29.7	29.5	24.3
Direct Losses Paid	21.9	23.5	24.5	32.2	34.5

Table 3: Five Year Growth (Millions)

disk space, network connectivity and memory at significantly reduced costs. The CASE and database tools in the systems marketplace are advertised to have broad functionality covering input required during the design of information systems, diagramming techniques, design specification components which can produce code when fed into code generators, and testing and debugging tools to speed the acceptance and testing of software.

Alan believes the cost of running a mainframe to support Montclair Mutual's system requirements is becoming unacceptable. He is well aware of the need to perform a feasibility assessment of all the costs and benefits of any new applications of technology since he has a technical undergraduate economics degree, work background as a financial analyst, and a masters degree in information systems from a large nearby university. A simple example of the apparent cost differences between the two options can be seen by comparing the cost of disk drives for a mainframe and a server. Disk drives that originally cost over $100,000 can be purchased for as little as several hundred dollars on a PC. It also appears that direct support costs such as power, cooling, specially prepared floor space, operating system licenses, mainframe systems support (from the manufacturer), and maintenance charges are combining to make the mainframe uneconomical for Montclair Mutual. However, Alan is not convinced that the client server environment will produce savings in indirect expenses since various trade studies have argued that there are significant hidden personnel, software, training, and networking costs involved in supporting a client server system. An additional disadvantage attributed to the mainframe systems used by Montclair Mutual is that the mainframe monthly maintenance costs have typically increased linearly as premium volumes increase. Modifying the system to add a new company, business unit, or line of insurance that is not provided by a wholly owned subsidiary (if a merger or corporate purchase were to occur) would require significantly higher new licensing fees and higher software support payments.

The decisions to be made are complex and have long term implications. The recommendations must all be presented to the Chairman and President Mr. J. David Adams and approved by the executive committee of the firm (consisting of the chairman, senior vice president, chief financial officer, vice president information systems, vice president marketing, vice president underwriting, and vice president claims).

The flow of information in the company is primarily hierarchical and sequential. The information flow supports a mainframe system geared for production activities, and is not oriented toward the production of management information. The actions on a policy application and potential acceptance are initiated in the mail room where the mail is opened, sorted, and routed to appropriate locations for action. A policy application is first directed to an underwriting team for review of completeness, resubmitted to an agency if incomplete, prepared for entry into the system (with completed or corrected data), and then entered into CICS screens when all data are complete. Simple editing is then initiated, error lists are reviewed and corrected, and the policy revolves through in-baskets until it is ready for scanning into the system as digitized paper. The 10 day long process makes it difficult to track new business (the life blood of the company according to the President). Policies frequently have many errors, rejections, and corrections before they are approved. Error lists are continually maintained and updated to try to improve policy acceptance rates.

The systems used to implement the flow of information are best exemplified by a Policy Administration System (PAS) which supports policy/claims on an IBM 4381 mainframe, and a Direct Billing System (DBS). PAS is poorly structured; requires many manual codes, contains no data models, and has limited capability for rapid business or rule changes that are required when new and enhanced products are introduced by the firm. It does contain a stable database which has required very few changes or modifications for some time. However, Montclair is also being driven to consider alternative solutions because PAS will not operate when the year 2000 is reached. Date related programs and routines used for calculations and processing that will not work after the year 2000 are imbedded in PAS. The DBS is a full featured mainframe billing system that requires more system resources and support than the entire policy system (with a large monthly maintenance charge of $3,500). It is very risky to change the DBS, so modifications are only undertaken after completing extensive development and testing.

The systems must be coordinated by the "administrative staff" within Montclair Mutual through the imposition of rules, procedures, and behavioral standards that govern the client, policy, and charges for specific features in a policy, etc. Additional issues such as payment structures, discounts available to customers, advertising, sales techniques, and agent relationships are determined by state legislation and the "market environment" of the industry, but implemented by the business units of the firm.

Alan has identified several approaches to the problems presented by these old systems. Some of the approaches include: restructure the old systems into a tool based application (without rebuilding the systems); rebuild some or all of the applications to conform to new data definitions and business models based upon enterprise data modeling; do not convert any system to new client server technology, and build a bridge to the old systems using new technologies and data models; scrap everything and start over with an entirely new system; and purchase currently available new systems and/or replacement products that can be integrated into the organization's current environment. Alan believes the analysis of which approach to take cannot be a simplistic assessment such as: does a system or subsystem work (leave it alone if it does), and does it incur high maintenance cost (restructure or rebuild if it does). Alan knows that the old systems can't be converted easily or supported forever; but he also knows its safe to assume that some old systems (if not all) will continue to be critical to the firm because even with their quirks and problems they must meet the ongoing business needs for the foreseeable future (or until completely effective replacements can be provided).

Role of Information Systems Department (ISD)

The role of the ISD at Montclair is to implement the strategic systems plan, and to collect, store, and provide access to the organization's data when it is required. Company databases and shared applications are funded through common overhead mechanisms, and corporate development projects must be supported by users who are members of cross functional business teams.

Alan is authorized to maintain a staff of 19 in the ISD. At present, this number includes an assistant manager, five programmer - analysts, four operators, one personal - microcomputer specialist, a project coordinator, two senior programmer - analysts, one systems programmer - database administrator, and two administrative employees. The staff is carefully supplemented (as needed) by responsive vendors who can provide additional reliable technical support.

Alan's management philosophy is to provide a work environment that is mentally stimulating to all ISD employees. He attempts to involve all of the staff in designing, building, and implementing successful products. The ISD staff is viewed as a special resource within the company. This group has a intra-company reputation of being very successful in bringing up new mainframe systems and modifications while maintaining existing ones. They also have an in-depth knowledge of the company and its products, and are of exceptional value at Montclair.

Setting the Stage

Alan has identified four business limitations of the current system. First, there is significant information loss in the method used to store data. Many data elements such as children's names, ages, alternative phone numbers, previous addresses, and other predictors that may be used to track and identify credit or actuarial risks by experienced risk analysts and underwriters simply stay in the older systems' files. (As an example, agents know that individuals who may be poor risks are likely to change many things on their applications to a insurance firm; however, work phone numbers, home phone numbers, and old addresses will frequently remain the same on an application. These identifying variables could enable the firm's underwriters to link the high risk applicants to other policies or claims that have been made against the company.)

A major file, the policy record, has grown extremely large over a long period of time with address fields with differently defined field lengths because it contains duplicate data that is stored in other records (Agent, Customer, Mailing Address and Policy Mailing address records). The data has to be changed in several locations when an address change for a customer is received. Separate customer address change requests are required to trigger changes to automobile, umbrella, boat, or jewelry policies.

Secondly, poor storage techniques require that large fields be maintained to store data (and remain blank if data doesn't exist). The attributes of the data stored in these field are relatively inaccessible because they can not be searched for specific values or conditions.

Thirdly, data terms and rules for action are translated into numbers and letters (codes) used to implement processing in the mainframe information system. This prevents the firm from updating profiles (and possibly selling add-on policies with increased premiums) of preferred customers who may now own homes with fireplaces and higher risk wooden (shingle) roofs, or pursuing new marketing strategies as the customer base demographics changes. From a marketing perspective, this also prevents searches which could identify inconsistencies in the insurance of a customer. This would mean that one individual could have extremely high insurance coverage on a very valuable home, and limited coverage on an automobile. However, the company is unable to approach the agent for the insured to determine if the coverage on the autos should be increased, and an umbrella policy offered to the customer to cover very large risks above the limitations on the combined house and auto policies.

Fourthly, the current system offers only a limited ability to manage the flow of information, and improve the service levels and performance of the individual departments. As an example, if an insured requests an increase in insurance coverage, the company first needs to locate a folder. The request for the policy/folder must be sent to the vault, and frequently the policy is "somewhere else", believed to be in transit, or missing (removed by someone from another department). The policy may have been sent to accounting, claims, or to someone's desk where it will remain in a drawer, stack of papers, or filing cabinet until their work is finished. Minimally effective tracking systems require manual entry of data from all the user locations. The constant updates required by the tracking systems are never fully complied with by employees. This confusion and complexity results in interdepartmental conflicts, customer frustration with the service delays, and possible errors because only one person can have the folder with the policy history at one time (to prevent loss of critical information or errors in the underwriting decisions related to coverage, claims, or the addition of insurance riders).

Project Description

Potential Goals of New Systems

Alan believes he has to use this opportunity to construct a corporate data model to demonstrate the highly interdependent characteristics of Montclair's data and business relationships to the firm's various business units. Many complex information exchanges exist among the different departments (underwriting, claims, record storage (vault), and data entry/MIS) which have been assigned specific portions of the policy sales and management task. A new database model could use the policy entity as a central reference point for managing policy work, policy benefits, and all customer data. Coverage would be tracked to the basic data obtained from the policy. This major change could reduce the number of policy attributes because the stored data would be more concise. The new data model could also contain one customer number that may have multiple associated policies or policy numbers. For example, the customer number would associate the multiple customer addresses with dates to link changes in addresses with the appropriate policy data.

Alan is unsure of the rest of the modeling effort. However, he believes that the logical relationship could maintain an association between a policy and a customer number. The customer number would subsequently maintain an associated mailing address for that specific time. It even appears that similar processing logic could be used in managing the relationships for the coverages associated with a given policy. The business problem is that policies can be endorsed or changed many times during the policy term (and this has enormous implications for corporate liability). It is critical for Montclair business units to know what coverage was in force at a given time. Entities must be established to store the effective and expiration dates for each specific coverage and endorsement. In addition, the most current coverage with the coverage's effective and expiration dates identified for the last change in the policy must be maintained at some location. Singular relationships such as policy-address for one customer are easily understood by employees. However, if a customer purchases a second policy the same customer number is used again, and the address already stored is utilized by the system. If one assumes that the third, fourth, and other policies are obtained by the same customer more significant advantages are obtained. Even if a new policy is mailed to a different address (business, home, bank trust department, etc.), the entity policy address would be established. In that case, it would be used by the system logic as the default address unless it is not present. These detailed data dependent relationships are particularly important to the organization in the multiple policy business discount area. The current system has made it difficult to track multiple policies owned by one insured. Policies are purchased at different times or with variations in the name of the applicant (use of initials or middle names, etc.). The data are not always available for the agent (and different agents may have sold the policy to the owner). The present impact of this problem is twofold. The customer is overcharged; and, the state insurance department fines the company for discrimination and failing to follow its filed underwriting guidelines (a direct loss of profit for the firm).

Alan hopes there will be far fewer policy changes and missing address errors with this basic type of processing logic. He also hopes to address coverage concerns, readily compute correct discounts, and reduce incorrect charges. However, using all of this new logic would possibly introduce significant business and procedural changes for the business units, and many employees could find it difficult to accept that their unit is no longer exclusively in control of modifications to its data. In a survey of insurance systems to assess the options, Alan has reviewed the wide variety of available computer systems and software products. Lists of Property & Liability Insurance Systems available in the industry contain over 20 different systems available from more than a dozen different companies. The systems in the insurance area are written in many different languages with COBOL (for mainframe systems) being very common. Alan is concerned that the available commercial systems could use different data definitions, languages, databases and processes to implement the work of the organization. The risk is that the differences in the system databases used to store the data may ultimately require that the systems maintain contrasting data models, define the semantic meaning of the data differently, use conflicting values for specific information or cases, or implement incompatible data storage formats.

Current Status: Upgrade Assessment

There are a number of system and subsystem upgrades that could be included in any new system. The potential upgrades can be grouped into four major areas: data capture; operations and flow management; decision making (expert systems); and data storage and output.

Data Capture

Alan is considering recommending the acquisition of a screen development tool to use in building a new "front end" for all data entry. He has seen a tool called Powerbuilder from Powersoft. This package sits on top of a relational database (Oracle is used at Montclair) and could interface to a CASE tool. However, he has no personal experience with a GUI development environment, and wonders about its interfacing capabilities. He has been told that valid English term choices can be displayed for use during data entry. This would be an enormous change from the currently used codes associated with categories, policy types, and customer data.

Operations and Flow Management

He is also assessing tools to design and maintain an effective flow of information. The GUI front end screens could possibly be event driven, and enable one to enter data, present one with options based on this data, and perform consistency checks. In this way, the flow of data could be channeled at the time of entry by establishing selections available to the input staff based upon previous data value entries.

A system that controls the work would have to be very complex unless some tool or program can be found to support the development of this part of the system. It must establish mailboxes, define processing routines, set timing and triggers for the execution of routines, maintain comments, and construct forms to be used in systems processing, and effectively route images and files throughout the organization. Optional features include assigning a priority to the work, and placing the new business policy which requires review or approval/rating on the top of the list of items that must be handled in the underwriter's mailbox. The underwriter would have the ability and responsibility to act on the policy. It could be accepted, have comments placed on it in the file, or have an extract of the data sent to the CICS system where the data could be held in a staging area. Processing may also be impacted if an Optical Disk Storage System used for many years could be expanded using a window product with customized GUI screens. The optical image's goals would be to overcome the limits on the accessibility of the policy data. Currently, one department is able to locate and maintain control of a customer's file. What's needed is for the accounting department to have an image of the policy folder and all associated data on the screen while a claims representative is analyzing a claim. Multiple departments should be able to obtain a printed copy of the documents in the folder. Some newer optical systems may also maintain a "sticky note" or margin-comment capability that permits extensive comments or references to be associated with the information in the folder. This would permit the staff to document actions, note missing information, alert other department to problems, and even make comments on folders that are protected by special security levels. (Notes about jewelry or possessions of priority customers are only available to specific departments or underwriters at Monclair.)

The obvious benefits from integrating and even expanding the optical storage of information include speeding up the customer service activities of the organization, and reducing the telephone "tag" that develops between the company, customer, and sales agent regarding a policy. With an optical storage subsystem there would be no repetitive editing of the data entered into the system that would force one to call back to the agent or customer to obtain more information.

Decision Making (Expert Systems)

Another option for upgrading the system is to address the underwriting decision making area with an expert system. Alan recently viewed a vendor product written in C. It might be customized with the company's underwriting rules. (It can be purchased with some five hundred pre-developed business rules for one specific insurance line of business.) This product operates in a OS/2 environment and uses DB2/2 as its relational database. Documentation for the system includes the rating information, underwriting manual, business rules for the company, filed ratings guidelines, and procedural manuals.

An expert system could replace the previous edit reports with system edits of inputs against the rules that are filed (with the state insurance commission) in the organizations underwriting guidelines. The rules would have to be incorporated into the screens used to collect the policy data. The expert system would attempt to rate a policy, and if it is not rated and accepted by the company, automatically refer the policy to an underwriter for further review and analysis. The analysis could possibly follow an exception rule, and only if the policy cannot be accepted would it be referred to the electronic mailbox of an underwriter (if the underwriters permit the introduction of this new process).

Data Storage and Output

Alan's view is that a client information file is potentially the primary source of management information. It could control all policy processing and still be a central file for other applications. Using this file, the company could develop increased managerial "what-if" capabilities that could be derived from the database and environmental information available to the business. As an example, "what-if" questions might include: what would be the impact of an increase in insurance deductibles for hurricane storm paths in particular regions of southeastern states? Similar questions might be developed for coverage limitations. The company would then be able to calculate the lost premiums from the increased deductible, and balance them against the eventual reduced payment and processing costs for not handling the smaller claims for less significant damages.

Organizational Impacts

The planning of the firm must account for many organizational and business unit impacts associated with the complex changes contemplated.

Changes to Decision Rules and Process Improvement

The data corporate decision rules are now captured and recorded only by storing agreed to definitions or terms, and making these definitions available (via hard-copy memos) to all individuals in the company. This may be a problem for the company because the underwriters appear to disagree when presented with similar rating data. In effect, anything that creates standard data would create a more level playing field for the customer. One would then be able to obtain concurrence on a specific policy risk, or rating problem. Definitions would be documented for the policy questions and associated with the data that has been gathered from the customer. However, it is unclear if the underwriters will accept this new alternative. They may actually prefer the more ambiguous alternative and higher levels of discretion permitted when clear rules do not exist.

Training

A new system could radically change the training requirements of the data entry processors by eliminating the uses of arbitrary codes to represent field values, and by eliminating the need for data entry processors having to learn which codes to use under what circumstances. This training requirement has long been a problem during periods of clerical turnover. It is clear that experienced data entry personnel using the current procedures rapidly complete the entry of policy data. However, personnel with these requisite skills are difficult to acquire, train, and retain in the organization (since there is no career path for this highly specialized task). The system for training is now 3-4 months of training in codes, error messages, and data handling procedures. This could be significantly changed (hopefully reduced). Clerks would not have to memorize codes and information that would be presented to them on their screen.

This type of overall organization change is not without risk. The organization must be cautious of this change in operations and personnel. A future problem might develop if the highly trained underwriters are not present and future environmental shifts occur. New or less prepared staff underwriters might not have the experience to adjust the rules in an expert system to modify the criteria used to evaluate an application. This could be a cause for concern if the organization was required to change rules that are based on specific underwriting criteria rather than rules that are based on business or economics criteria.

Implementation Concerns

The question of "how" to implement any new system is also facing Alan. Decisions to implement changes have to be both strategic and incremental. The timing of the change must also be appropriate to the company's business success. Large investments cannot be expected in or after years where the company experiences significant losses. In addition, a high level of business and technical cooperation must be present between IS staff and the operating units. The tools, including the CASE, GUI front end, database, expert system, business rules, and optical scanning and storage capability all appear to be equally important. Finally, price is also a critical issue. The high cost of mainframe tools could make the adoption of a mainframe based CASE system far less advantageous than a less powerful client server CASE tool. However, the personnel and organizational costs of a new system or subsystem must be factored into any assessment and recommendation.

Epilogue

Alan firmly believes the company must remain flexible and able to make business decisions to respond to internal and external market demands and opportunities as quickly and economically as possible. This has been operationalized to mean that the firm's underwriters must be efficient and effective (not that clerical staff must be reduced as much as possible). The Montclair Mutual information system should not be a limiting concern in implementing this broad business goal. This goal implies that the company must be able to integrate multiple systems without specific system platform or contractual restraints. The client server platform appears to be the best platform for overall system integration, maximum flexibility, responsiveness, and cost savings.

The company has initiated the development of a full enterprise data model. The premise of this model is that all data for the company is defined and stored only once. Hopefully, this will eventually eliminate the various problems with the same information being in multiple places in various forms. A strong foundation for this model is relational database technology that provides the firm with better and faster access to information while enabling new applications and changes to be implemented at reduced costs.

Alan narrowed Montclair Mutual's options, and recommended rebuilding some (eventually all) of the applications to conform to new data definitions and business models based upon enterprise data modeling; and to building a bridge to some of the old systems using new technologies. The ISD has now developed the Maryland private passenger auto program primarily on a client server platform with the final feed of surcharge information to the mainframe policy system. The system is designed to use an Oracle relational database; Powerbuilder, for input screens; a workflow package; PC DocuMerge; and rating diskettes to produce a product that meets the specifications developed by a personal insurance lines task force. Alan believes the employees will like the new PCs, large color screens, and easy data entry expected with this new system. The design and development work has gone more slowly than expected. No implementation date has been set.

Questions for Discussion

1. Identify criteria to be used to assess the recommendation.

2. What complex decision making approach is required?

3. Describe the information flow and problems in the policy approval process.

4. Describe the firm's system procedures and coordination methods.

5. What are the limitations of the current system's data and information flows?

Recommended Student Case Assignments

1. Develop a Proposal for the Executive Committee and the President of Montclair Mutual.

2. Design the ISD organization structure which will best support the proposal you have developed for Montclair Mutual. Include job descriptions of individuals assigned to any project development work, and reporting relationships of any new hires or consultants required by the proposal. In addition, identify any special training required and the costs of the training.

3. Prepare a Development Schedule, Work Plan and Cost Estimate for all proposed development.

4. Prepare a data model with appropriate entities and attributes for the customers of the company.

5. Conduct a survey of potential commercial system development tools and options. Develop criteria appropriate to Montclair Mutual, and select a suite of tools appropriate for use on the development projects proposed.

Chapter 3

Better Army Housing Management Through Information Technology

Guisseppi A. Forgionne
University of Maryland, Baltimore County

Executive Summary

The Department of the Army must provide its personnel with acceptable housing at minimum cost within the vicinity of military installations. To achieve these housing objectives, the Army often must enter into agreements for the long-term construction of onpost housing or the leasing of existing offpost housing. A decision technology system, called the Housing Analysis Decision Technology System (HADTS), has been developed to support the construction or leasing management process.

The HADTS architecture is based on a combination of database, econometric, heuristic programming, mapping, and decision support techniques. Its deployment has enabled the Department of the Army to realize significant economic, management, and political benefits. Future enhancements, motivated by the challenges from the current system, promise to increase the power of HADTS and to further improve the Army's ability to manage its housing assets.

Background

The Department of the Army's Corps of Engineers is responsible for housing personnel at, or near, division installations. For the past twenty years, the Corps' Installation Management Office has administered the housing program. This office has a Chief of Housing, three functional managers, and a support staff of 10 technical specialists and 5 secretaries at its suburban Washington, D. C. (Fort Belvoir, Virginia) headquarters.

At headquarters, management plans housing policies, develops procedures to implement the plans, and then communicates the procedures to the housing managers at each Army installation. Such policies, procedures, and actions are audited by Department of Defense, Government Accounting Office, and other government agencies for compliance with existing laws, regulations, and guidelines. Since audit reports can significantly influence available funding, the Army typically is very responsive to auditor suggestions on housing management policy and practice.

Installation housing managers collect data pertinent to the planning process, communicate the data through various information systems to headquarters, implement headquarters-developed procedures, and administer onpost assets. Traditionally, these installation managers have been given much discretion in exercising their responsibilities. Moreover, headquarters has relied heavily on installation managers' input in formulating housing policies, procedures, and practices.

Figure 1 gives the organizational chart relevant to Army housing management. Currently, managers in this organization control $55 billion worth of onpost housing assets. The annual budget is $12 million for managing these assets and the associated housing programs.

Setting the Stage

At any Army installation, the projected supply of available government housing may be insufficient to meet the personnel demand expected at the site. Policy requires unaccommodated personnel to seek acceptable private rentals in the installation's predefined Housing Market Area (HMA). If the expected stock of private rentals in the HMA will be insufficient to eliminate the onpost housing deficit, the Department of the Army will enter into agreements for the construction of onpost housing or the leasing of existing offpost housing. Government policy and regulations require the Army to economically justify any leasing request with a Segmented Housing Market Analysis (SHMA).

SHMA Process

During a SHMA review, installation housing managers first compute the onpost deficit and forecast the private rental stock available to meet military housing needs. Next, they estimate the military's market share of the private stock and compute the number of adequate rental dwelling units available in the local market to offset any onpost deficit. The result is the gross military deficit, or the number of personnel that do not have adequate housing onpost or in the private market (Forgionne 1992).

The gross military deficit is reported by bedroom count (BC) for personnel in each of the twenty-one Army grades (ranks). There is a separate (grade by bedroom count or 21 x 6 = 126) matrix for unaccompanied (called UPH) and family (denoted AFH) personnel. Some cells in the housing deficit matrixes may show surpluses. In the interest of minimizing construction or leasing, Army policy is to offset deficits in other parts of the matrixes with these surpluses. Offsetting results in a final housing deficit, and this deficit becomes the basis for making construction or leasing requests.

Data Management

Much of the relevant onpost data needed for the SHMA process are captured, stored, and can be retrieved through Army information reporting systems. However, the onpost data were not organized into the variables needed to perform the SHMA process. Required offpost data originally were collected, captured, and recorded manually, and in an often sketchy manner, during the SHMA process. Typical offpost data sources included banks, local realty boards, public utility commission reports and statistical abstracts, state statistical abstracts, and vendors of local housing market

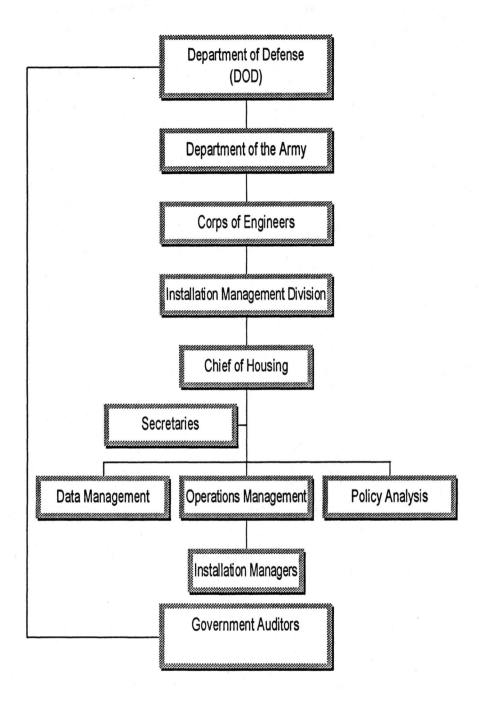

Figure 1: Army Housing Management Organization

statistics.

The original SHMA review was supported by a spreadsheet computer program that received pertinent data, helped managers perform the offsetting computations, and reported the deficit results. There was little (if any) sharing of information between the Army information reporting systems and this spreadsheet program.

Report Writing

The spreadsheet used to support the SHMA process generated a series of reports on market conditions and on projected Army housing deficits for the specified installation. Deficits were reported by grade and by the groups of grades needed to conform with the housing construction and leasing categories specified by Department of Defense policies (Forgionne 1991b). The original reports, however, did not give a detailed breakdown of the offsetting operations and computations. Such a categorization would: (a) be useful for Army officials seeking to evaluate alternative housing deficit reduction policies and (b) provide the policy implication information communicated by these officials to installation managers.

While the original SHMA process projected the number of private rentals available to reduce onpost housing deficits, the system did not locate the rentals. The original process also did not display characteristics about the available rental properties. Such spatial and attribute data would greatly enhance the Army housing managers' ability to implement leasing directives.

Auditor Concerns

In the Army's original approach, the prices and quantities of rentals were determined separately. Government auditors noted that, in this approach, prices will not change to eliminate any imbalances between demand and supply in the private market. Consequently, the Army's original approach can generate inaccurate projected quantities for some market segments.

As noted by government auditors, the potential difficulty could be avoided by determining the prices and quantities that equate demand and supply (clear the market) for private rental housing in pertinent market segments. These market-clearing quantities represent the number of rentals that will be available to consumers (including military personnel) at market-clearing prices in the long run on average.

Auditors also were dissatisfied with the Army's estimation of market share — the ratio of personnel renting offpost to total private rental stock. The original SHMA process assigned a single subjectively projected Army share to all market segments and estimated the market-clearing quantities independently of this share. In practice, the Army's share will be determined in conjunction with (rather than separately from) the market-clearing quantity and rent. Military personnel in distinct market segments (bedroom counts) likely will obtain different shares of the market-clearing quantities.

Technical Complexity

The complexity of the original SHMA process required installation housing managers to complete an ardent five-day training program that: (a) acclimated participants with the extensive SHMA documentation, (b) illustrated the complex and labor-intensive SHMA operations and computations, and (c) demonstrated proper documentation procedures. After this training, the managers still had trouble completing the analysis accurately, and they complained constantly about the complexity of the original SHMA process.

The technical complexities created many expenses. Training involved contractor fees, installation managers' opportunity costs, and other expenses that totaled approximately $250,000 per five-day program. On average, another $50,000 was spent in performing the data gathering, economic analyses, offsetting computations, and reporting and documentation activities involved in the actual SHMA review.

Project Description

The technical, management, and organizational difficulties induced senior Army officials to seek ways of: (a) improving the SHMA's economic analyses and (b) simplifying and automating key segments of the SHMA process. These officials sought support for the econometric analyses mandated by the government auditors, the complex computations involved in the SHMA, and the report writing necessitated by Department of Defense policies. A decision technology system, called the Housing Analysis Decision Technology System (HADTS), was developed to provide the desired support (Forgionne 1991a). This system was developed iteratively, using the Adaptive Design Strategy (ADS), by two researchers working in conjunction with affected Army executives (senior housing managers).

HADTS Components

HADTS integrates the functions of a Geographic Information System (GIS), an Executive Information System (EIS), and a decision support system called the Housing Analysis System (HANS). The GIS is delivered through ATLAS/GIS software, while the EIS and HANS are delivered through the SAS System for Information Delivery. Figure 2 shows the relationships between these HADTS components.

As Figure 2 illustrates, the GIS extracts Census data, creates Housing Market Area (HMA) maps, and displays user-specified market conditions on the maps. The EIS extracts HMA market conditions from the GIS and installation housing characteristics from Army information systems, captures the extracted data, and forms the database needed to perform the HANS analyses and evaluations. HANS utilizes econometric and heuristic programming models to compute the results displayed on the housing deficit reports.

HADTS Architecture

To conserve resources and to meet the needs of the Department of the Army's personnel, HADTS is made available through an easy-to-use computer system that can be readily used at headquarters, the major Army commands (MACOMs), or the military installations by nontechnical persons. Figure 3 gives a conceptual architecture of HADTS.

Inputs

HADTS has a data base that captures and stores spatial and attribute data for the HMAs and relevant onpost data. Spatial data includes longitude and latitude coordinates that are used to draw the HMA maps and features on the maps, including city and census tract boundaries, bodies of water, highways, streets, the installation's location, and the location of available rental properties. Attribute data consists of: (a) the socio-economic variables needed to perform HANS's deficit analyses and (b) housing characteristics of interest to Army housing managers.

The socio-economic variables include the HMA's total population, land area, average population

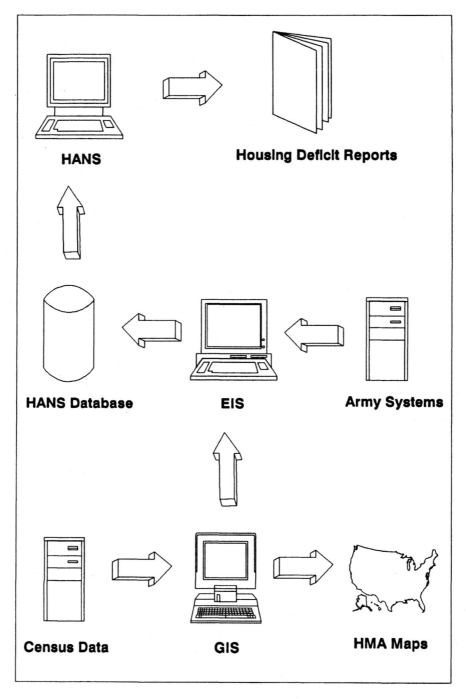

Figure 2: Housing Analysis Decision Technology System (HADTS)

age, average years of schooling, median house value, average travel time to work, median household income, total precollege school enrollment, average family size, the number of males, total housing stock, and vacancy rate. Housing characteristics include median rents and rental housing quantities categorized by bedroom count. Relevant onpost data consists of the elements needed to estimate housing requirements, government owned and controlled assets, personnel renting offpost, installation populations, and effective military demand dollars (housing allowances).

There is also a model base that contains statistical procedures, location formulas, data conversion rules, the upgraded econometric model, and the upgraded deficit reduction heuristics. The statistical procedures are used to categorize attribute data within the HMAs and to calculate summary statistics for the economic variables and housing characteristics within the HMAs. Location formulas, proprietary within ATLAS/GIS, are used to convert U.S. Census Bureau TIGER (Topologically Integrated Geographic Encoding and Referencing) degrees into HMAs.

Data Conversion Formulas. Data from existing Army information systems are not in the format needed to perform HADTS's analyses and evaluations. Predefined rules are used to convert the raw Army data into the needed HADTS formats. One set of formulas converts the extracted socio-economic and military characteristic data into the variables needed for HANS's analyses, evaluations, and reports. Some of these variables become inputs into HANS's econometric analyses, and such analyses output (project) available private (offpost) housing by grade and bedroom count. A second set of formulas transforms the remaining variables into projected housing requirements and government owned and controlled (onpost) housing by grade and bedroom count.

Econometric Model. HANS's econometric model includes quantity and market share components. The quantity component uses equations formed by senior Army housing managers' judgment, economic housing theory (Blackley and Ondrich, 1988; Goodman, 1988; and Turnbull, 1989), and regression analysis to forecast market-clearing supplies and rents for rental housing by bedroom count in the installation's HMA. Additional theory (Carruthers, 1989; Kaplan and Berman, 1988; and Turnbull, 1988), judgment, and statistical methodologies developed the market share equations that forecast the Army shares of the market-clearing rental quantities.

Multiplying the estimated market-clearing supplies by the predicted market shares gives the offpost rentals that will be available to Army personnel by category (unaccompanied or family), grade, and bedroom count. Army requirements less government owned and controlled assets less available offpost rentals give the unreconciled deficits/surpluses that can be anticipated by grade for each BC.

Deficit Reduction Heuristics. A heuristic programming model automatically reassigns (offsets) deficits and surpluses among BC and grades in accordance with the latest DOD policies, rules, and regulations, first using available offpost rentals and then using government owned and controlled assets. Such computer-assisted assignments are designed to improve decision making for this complex managerial problem (Adelman, 1992; Benbasat and Nault, 1990; and Silver, 1991).

Processing

The decision maker (a military housing executive or staff management assistant) uses computer technology to perform housing analyses and evaluations with HADTS's EIS, GIS, and HANS components. Currently, the system executes on an IBM-compatible 486 microcomputer with 8MB of RAM, a color graphics display, and a printer compatible with the microcomputer. It runs the SAS information delivery system and the ATLAS/GIS geographic information system through the OS/2 operating system. This configuration was selected because it offered a more consistent, less time-consuming, less costly, and more flexible development and implementation environment than the available alternatives.

By double clicking the HADTS icon on the OS/2 desktop, the user accesses a display with a welcome message, instructions, and a push-button link to the EIS. The EIS acts as a front-end to HADTS's database management system (DBMS), GIS, and HANS (Dadam and Linnemann, 1989; Targowski, 1990; and Wang and Walker, 1989). Once in the EIS, the user with the correct password can interactively identify from screen icons in sequence the installation's Major Army Command (MACOM), specific installation (fort), and the current year. These operations automatically subset the HADTS database, provide the data needed for further processing, and access the HADTS processing display. From this display, the user can select the type of processing desired—GIS (maps of the HMA) or HANS (inputs and reports).

Like many geographic information systems, HADTS's GIS organizes the collected spatial and attribute data (in vector format), captures the data, and stores the key offpost variables as a dBASE IV-based, DBF-formatted, relational database (Bruno 1992, Fischer and Nijkamp 1993, Franklin 1992, Grupe, 1992a and 1992b and Huxhold, 1991). HADTS's GIS then structures the HMA maps, locates available rental housing on the HMA maps, and simulates socio-economic variables and housing characteristics within the HMAs. The system also enables the housing manager to interactively modify the HMA, display tabular statistical reports that summarize housing characteristics in the HMA, and print hard copies of the HMA maps and summary statistics.

By using the DBMS, the user can extract HMA market conditions from the GIS and installation housing characteristics from Army information systems, display the data, modify the displayed data, and store the SHMA-relevant information. The HANS component then utilizes the DBMS-generated onpost and offpost data to automatically forecast market conditions and Army housing supplies from the upgraded econometric model, perform upgraded deficit reduction heuristics, and generate detailed reports of the results automatically without human (manual) intervention.

As indicated by the top feedback loop in Figure 3, offpost and onpost data, reports, and maps created during HADTS's analyses and evaluations can be captured and stored as inputs for future processing. These captured inputs are stored as additional or revised fields and records, thereby updating the data base dynamically. The user executes the functions with mouse-controlled point-and-click operations on attractive visual displays that make the computer processing virtually invisible (transparent) to the user.

Outputs

Processing automatically generates visual displays of the outputs desired by housing managers (Turban 1993). Outputs include HMA maps and associated deficit forecasts and reports. The maps define the boundaries of the HMA, give the road and street patterns, identify important landmarks, locate the military installation within the HMA, and highlight the locations of rental properties on the HMA roads and streets. Deficit forecasts project the corresponding market conditions and their effects on Army housing deficits/surpluses. The results are displayed as a series of summary and detailed housing reports. A summary report gives the final military deficit by grade group and bedroom count for the selected personnel category. Detail reports give summaries of the explanatory computations that justify the summary report. These intermediate descriptions list the HMA market-clearing rents and rental quantities by bedroom count and deficit computations by bedroom count and grade. Deficit computation reports include the offpost rentals that will go to Army personnel, Army housing requirements, available onpost housing, net deficits before reassignments, net deficits after reassignments, and the distribution of reassignments.

As indicated by the bottom feedback loop in Figure 3, the user can utilize the outputs to guide further HADTS processing before exiting the system (Sengupta and Abdel-Hamid, 1993 and Watson, Rainer, and Houdeshel, 1992). Typically, the feedback will involve sensitivity analyses in which the user modifies the HMA boundaries and observes the effects on market conditions or the user adjusts onpost variables and observes the effects on housing deficits.

Current Status of the Project

To ensure that the information system accurately replicated the inputs, HADTS's data conversion rules were tested against historical data for existing Army installations. In the testing, housing statistics displayed from the system were compared with the corresponding actual values. According to the results, HADTS reproduced the actual data exactly.

HADTS's econometric model was tested against Census data from the counties surrounding existing Army installations. In the testing, projected socio-economic variables from the quantity block were compared with the corresponding actual Census values. According to the results, the estimated equations predicted between 81.52% to 95.84% of the variance in the supply (quantity) data and between 42.77% to 80.92% of the variance in the rent data. Root mean squared (RMS) error percentages ranged between 0% to 14.5572%, with most values less than 5%, from the bedroom-count supply and rent equations. Also, projected variables from the market share block were compared with the corresponding actual Army records. According to the results, the estimated equations predicted between 0.08% to 99.96% of the variance in the market share data. Root mean squared (RMS) errors ranged from .00003 to .0334 for all market share equations.

Hypothetical, but realistic, data on housing requirements, onpost (Army) assets, and private assets were used to test the final set of upgraded deficit reduction heuristics. In the testing, model-computed surpluses and deficits were compared to the values expected at each stage of the offsetting process. This testing revealed that the heuristic programming model always generated the correct surpluses and deficits at all offsetting stages.

Based on the test results, the Department of the Army decided to implement HADTS. The system has been in use for over a year. Results from the implementation indicate that the decision technology system will have significant economic and management benefits, offer important lessons, and present key challenges for Army housing management.

Successes and Failures

HADTS simplifies and automates the SHMA process, reduces training requirements to a minimum, decreases the volume of documentation, and increases computer processing efficiency. These substantial improvements have saved, and will continue to save, the Army approximately $5,860,000 per year in SHMA implementation, data management, and lease location costs and $1,024,200,000 in budgeted construction expenses. The Army spent about $250,000 to develop and implement the HADTS system that provides these economic benefits. Such economic gains are quite timely in light of federal budget restrictions and the Army's current direction of large scale force reductions and base closures.

The HADTS system also provides management benefits. In the original SHMA process and in the manual search for lease locations, the nearly exclusive reliance on tedious manual procedures often resulted in inaccurate, incomplete, and redundant data collection. HADTS provides: (a) quicker analyses of the rental housing market and its impact on Army housing, (b) operationally and computationally error-free SHMA and lease-location processes, (c) more timely policy analyses and evaluations, (d) rapid sensitivity analyses of HMA boundary, market condition, and policy changes, (e) efficient flagging of data and information deficiencies, and (f) more effective evaluation of field-generated housing requests. These enhanced capabilities will enable Army officials to more efficiently and effectively manage the $55 billion in housing assets under their control.

The project identified data sharing, model management, and mapping limitations that present profound challenges to Army housing management. At the present time, there is limited data available

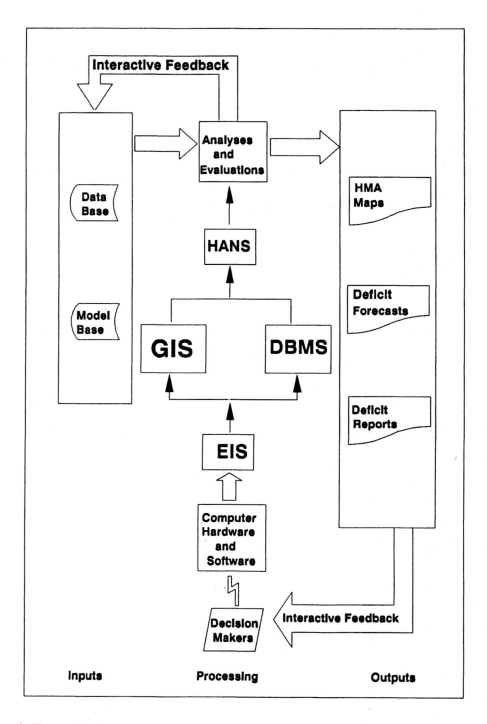

Figure 3: HADTS Architecture

to estimate the equations in the market share segment of the econometric model. These data limitations precluded a meticulous application of theoretical market share housing models and resulted in deficit forecasting anomalies for some Army installations. Needed data exist in other military information systems, and computer programs have been written and embedded within HADTS to perform the database updating when the appropriate government agencies work out technical data sharing arrangements.

As new data becomes available, variables may be added or deleted from, and parameters may change in, the original formulations (Billman and Courtney, 1993; Cook, 1993; and West and Courtney, 1993). The typical HADTS user will not have the technical expertise to perform the consequent econometric analyses needed to update the system without considerable assistance. Senior Army officials have commissioned another project that will embellish HADTS to perform the updating tasks automatically without human (manual) intervention.

Maps are displayed and the corresponding offpost housing data are generated through ATLAS/GIS, while the offpost data are utilized within SAS to create deficit reports. Using two different software tools (SAS and ATLAS/GIS) reduces computer processing efficiency and increases system maintenance requirements. These difficulties can be alleviated by replacing the ATLAS/GIS tool with SAS/GIS when it becomes available.

Epilogue and Lessons Learned

Lessons were learned (and are still being learned) from HADTS implementation and development. Improved accuracy in housing deficit projections is important to the Army and society. Underestimating deficits can leave Army personnel inadequately housed, lower soldier morale and family well-being, and jeopardize military preparedness. Unnecessary housing construction can waste scarce natural resources and, in the process, alienate local residents, environmentalists, and other interest groups. Reducing housing deficits can help the Department of the Army avoid these undesirable consequences.

Since the original spreadsheet model had a limited quantity, and no market share component, the housing manager was left with an incomplete understanding of the data requirements needed for the SHMA process. As a result, managers often collected and captured irrelevant and redundant data. The upgraded econometric model identifies all offpost and onpost data relevant to the housing forecast process, and the HADTS system provides a mechanism that facilitates data entry while reducing errors and providing accurate, reliable, and consistent data.

Partially because of government auditors' concerns, there has been significant movement within the armed services to standardize the processes of requesting and locating rental housing. Top-level policy makers realize that all the services use similar processes, and HADTS's success may convince them that the processes can be substantially enhanced with decision technology support. Consequently, the Army's HADTS-supported SHMA and lease location processes can be offered as the standards for all the armed services.

Questions for Discussion

1. Why did the Army develop HADTS in an iterative manner, using the ADS rather than the traditional system development life cycle approach? Be specific about the user, organization, and

other technical factors that lead to this strategy choice.

2. What decision support principles have been applied in the development and implementation of HADTS? Be specific about the dialog, model, and data management characteristics of the system.

3. Why is the Army's system refered to as a decision technology, rather than decision support, system? Be specific about the phases of decision making being supported and how HADTS delivers the required support.

4. What future internal information technology management challenges will be created by the deployment of HADTS? Be specific about the effect of the system on organizational culture, the span of management control, and organizational structure.

5. Will there be any political challenges for the Army and other armed services created by the deployment of HADTS? Be specific about funding, interservice rivalry, and auditing requirements.

References

Adelman, L. (1992). *Evaluating Decision Support and Expert Systems*. New York: Wiley.

Benbasat, I., & Nault, B. R. (1990). An evaluation of empirical research in managerial support systems. *Decision Support Systems, 6*(1), 203-226.

Billman, B., & Courtney, J. F. (1993). Automated discovery in managerial problem formulation: Formation of causal hypotheses for cognitive mapping. *Decision Sciences, 24*(1), 23-41.

Blackley, P., & Ondrich, J. (1988). A limiting joint-choice model for discrete and continuous housing characteristics. *The Review of Economics and Statistics, 70*(2), 266-274.

Bruno, L. (1992). GIS maps out ways to access data in RDBMSes. *Open Systems Today, 12*(11), 50-54.

Carruthers, D. T. (1989). Housing market models and the regional housing system. *Urban Studies, 26*(3), 214-222.

Cook, G. J. (1993). An empirical investigation of information search strategies with implications for decision support systems. *Decision Sciences, 24*(3), 683-697.

Dadam, P., & Linnemann, G. (1989). Advanced information management (AIM): Advanced database technology for integrated applications. *IBM Systems Journal, 28*(4), 661-681.

Fischer, M. M., & Nijkamp, P., Editors. (1993). *Geographic Information Systems, Spatial Modeling, and Policy Evaluation*. New York: Springer-Verlag.

Forgionne, G. A. (1991a). Decision technology systems: A step toward complete decision support. *Journal of Information Systems Management, 8*(4), 34-43.

Forgionne, G. A. (1991b). HANS: A decision support system for military housing managers. *Interfaces, 21*(6), 37-51.

Forgionne, G. A. (1992). Projecting military housing needs with a decision support system. *Systems Research, 9*(2), 65-84.

Franklin, C. (1992). An introduction to geographic information systems: Linking maps to databases. *Database, 15*(4), 12-15.

Goodman, A. C. (1988). An econometric model of housing price, permanent income, tenure choice, and housing demand. *Journal of Urban Economics, 23*(5), 327-353.

Grupe, F. H. (1992a). A GIS For county planning: Optimizing the use of government data. *Information Systems Management, 9*(2), 38-44.

Grupe, F. H. (1992b). Can a geographic information system give your business its competitive edge? *Information Strategy, 8*(3), 41-48.

Huxhold, W. E. (1991). *An Introduction to Urban Geographic Information Systems*. Oxford: Oxford University Press.

Kaplan, E. H., & Berman, O. (1988). OR hits the heights: Relocation planning at the Orient Heights housing projects. *Interfaces,* 18(6), 14-22.

Sengupta, K., & Abdel-Hamid, T. K. (1993). Alternative conceptions of feedback in dynamic decision environments: An empirical investigation. *Management Science*, 39(4), 411-428.

Silver, M. (1991). Decisional Guidance for Computer-Based Decision Support. *MIS Quarterly*, 18(3), 105-122.

Targowski, A. (1990). *The Architecture and Planning of Enterprise-Wide Information Management Systems.* Harrisburg: Idea Group Publishing.

Turban, E. (1993). *Decision Support and Expert Systems: Management Support Systems,* 3rd Edition. New York: Macmillan Publishing Company.

Turnbull, G. K. (1988). Market structure, location rents, and the land development process. *Journal of Urban Economics,* 23(2), 261-277.

Turnbull, G. K. (1989). Household behavior in a monocentric urban area with a public sector. *Journal of Urban Economics*, 25(6), 103-115.

Wang, M., & Walker, H. (1989). Creation of an intelligent process planning system within the relational DBMS software environment. *Computers in Industry,* 13(3), 215-228.

Watson, H. J., Rainer, R. K., & Houdeshel, G., Editors. (1992). *Executive Information Systems: Emergence, Development, Impact.* New York: Wiley.

West, L. A., & Courtney, J. F. (1993). The information problems in organizations: A research model for the value of information and information systems. *Decision Sciences,* 24(2), 229-251.

Chapter 4

The Training Challenge:
Installing a POS for Improved Reporting and Customer Satisfaction

Janette Moody
The Citadel

David Jordan
CompuTech Consulting

Executive Summary

This case chronicles the problems that can arise in outsourcing agreements due to factors such as poorly defined user requirements, passive resistance from technical support personnel, and lack of contract specificity and documentation detailing who performs what. It illustrates how delays up front will impact the final end–user, i.e., the organization's customers. Eventually, in this case, all personnel became familiar with the new system and it became an asset to the organization. The issues noted in this case are applicable to the implementation of technology by any organization handling both retail and service activities.

Background

University Golden (UG) enjoys a prestigious 175–year history that is reflected in its distinctive architecture, reminiscent of European villas on the Rhine. Located on 125 rolling acres overlooking the Oyster River, University Golden has 2,000 full–time residential undergraduate students and over 4,000 commuter graduate students who represent members of the surrounding professional community. Over the years, University Golden's services to students, faculty, employees, and the numerous tourists who visit to view its museum and architecture, have grown beyond the traditional text book and gift store features to include dining facilities, catering and canteen services, barber shop, laundry, tailoring and infirmary services, plus athletic and special event ticket sales. Each of these functions

(all names have been changed but the details and events are based on actual experiences selected to highlight relevant issues)

utilized an independent sales system with their respective input and reporting requirements. Some utilized bar coding for inventory control and reporting (text book and gift sales) while others were strictly cash transactions (barber shop, dining facility and canteen services). Physically dispersed over the campus, the employees handling sales and inventories in these various areas followed diverse operating procedures ranging from the use of relatively advanced electronic cash registers to simple one–step cash drawers. Although the Book Store used barcoding for pricing and collection of sales data, it did not have the ability to maintain a perpetual inventory. As a result, the organization's auditors had expressed concern over the tracking and reporting of stock losses. In addition, increased sales caused the Gift Shop to outgrow its present recording system and expand its reporting requirements. Both the Book Store and the Gift Store manager, who operated independent entities but reported to the same vice president (VP) of finance, agreed that it was time to investigate a new and improved system.

Setting The Stage

In order to provide better inventory control and reporting features, plus improve service to its customers, UG decided to establish a Point of Sale (POS) system that, in addition to accepting cash and credit cards, would utilize photo identification (ID) cards to authorize charges on personal accounts at these diverse facilities. Not only would this decision involve handling the technical details of installing new hardware and software, it would also necessitate the re–training of all sales personnel as well as the customers. No longer could a customer drop by the tailor shop to have alterations handled on a signature and a smile – now the proper use of a scanned ID card would be required.

Once the decision was made to install a POS system, the next step was to find a suitable vendor at an acceptable price. A Request for Proposals (RFP) that laid out general, overall system requirements and guidelines for bidding was sent to seven vendors on January 26, 1994, with a pre-proposal conference set for March 11, 1994. The intent was to obtain an off–the–shelf package that would allow for a turn–key operation rather than one that was customized, so that the system could be up and running as soon as possible. The RFP set forth the following conditions:

RFP – GENERAL
The University desires to solicit proposals to acquire a state–of–the–art bookstore automation system. The system must contain specialized, comprehensive inventory management facilities with specialized applications for each of the following: Textbooks, General Books, Point–of–Sale, and General Merchandise. As such, it must be able to handle all phases of inventory management: ordering, receiving, invoicing, returns, special orders, and textbook buyback. It must also be capable of maintaining perpetual inventories at two stores, the bookstore and the gift shop, and interface with the organization's present financial records system.

The University operates a book store and a gift shop which operate separately of each other and are also physically separated on the campus. The book store is responsible for the sale of text books, specialized clothing, computers, and other student related items. The gift shop is responsible for sale of gift and sundry items, barber shop, vending operations and snack bar. The vending operations and snack bar are not to be considered in the scope of work for this proposal. Additionally, cash registers are located in the Tailor Shop, Laundry, and Athletic Department which must be interfaced into the system.

The book store carries approximately 1,500 text books, 500 specialty clothing items, and 200 miscellaneous items for a total of 2,200 line items in inventory. Normal annual inventory runs approximately US$1.8 million and turns 2.5 times a year. Annual sales of all items is approximately US$2.6 million. The gift shop carries approximately 4,700 items of inventory. Normal annual inventory runs approximately US$234,000 and turns 3.5 times a year. Annual sales of all items is approximately US$1.7 million.

The book store and the gift shop presently interface with the university's financial records by ASCII file transfer. These file transfers are made on demand. The system processes transactions by batch in the evenings. The desire is to continue such processing in the future.

ACCOUNTING CAPABILITIES
The system proposed must be a fully integrated system, to include general ledger, accounts receivable, accounts payable and a purchase order system. For example, receiving information keyed in must be available for use in accounts payable, with appropriate controls and audit trails.

POINT–OF–SALE SUPPORT CAPABILITIES
Capabilities should include automatic preparation of price–look–up files and credit authorization files, and the capability of transmitting these files to a point–of–sale (POS) system. The system must be capable of accepting complete transaction files from the POS systems, and allow the user to audit POS activity, automatically post to the proper general ledger account, and post sales activity occurring at the POS to the account receivable files. It must be capable of processing bar coded marked merchandise. The facilities for price–look–up, complete transaction logging, and in–house credit authorization must be provided.

COMPUTER HARDWARE
The system must be modular, allowing for installation and implementation in a step–wise fashion. The system must be capable of interfacing with the organization's VAX mainframe. The back–office software must run on a true multi–user, multi–tasking computer system. The computer hardware must have multiple specialized processors handling the various tasks such as workstation input/output (I/O), Disk I/O, etc. Multiple terminals and printers, including price–tag (bar code) printers must be supported. Adequate facilities for communications and backup must be available.

REPORTS
A full range of reports should be provided for all segments of the system. Reports should be easy to read and should allow for printing on a continuous schedule basis or on a selected basis. String report printing (ability to press one key to generate a series of reports) capabilities are desired.

TRAINING
Offeror must provide all training necessary. Training should be scheduled to be conducted on the organization's premises to the maximum extent possible.

INSTALLATION
The offeror shall be responsible for all installation of hardware and software. The organization will provide adequate electric connections and access to the facilities. The offeror shall inspect the current wiring to determine the wiring and connections which may be saved with the new installation. Installation is to be accomplished in a manner to minimize disruption to the operation of the Book Store and Gift Shop, beginning with the Book Store in the fall of 1994 with the Gift Shop following in January 1995.

Four vendors responded with proposals. A five person committee, made up of the Book Store manager, the Gift Shop manager, the Budget Director, a representative from the Computer Technology Department (CTD), and a representative from Athletic Activities, voted on the four proposals. The two top contenders were MoreBooks Corporation and TotalText Corporation. MoreBooks had supplied the system for some neighboring universities, and as such, was more familiar to the book store and gift shop managers. Its proposal was based on using NCR equipment which could not easily tie into the organization's present IBM platform and would require the use of modems and phone lines. TotalText Corporation, on the other hand, used an IBM platform and would be fully compatible with the current system without the use of phone lines. The vote was split with the CTD representative voting for the compatible system and the others voting for the system that was most familiar to the store managers and also less expensive. The decision to go with the non–compatible system set the tone for later interactions with the CTD, which decided to step back from the project, leaving it to the rest of the committee, none of whom had any technical background, to handle the bulk of the implementation of the new system.

Project Description

In May 1994, the contract was officially awarded to MoreBooks Corporation. This publicly–held company was started by brothers who entered the industry as retail bookstore entrepreneurs and later expanded into the computerization of textbook management systems for college bookstores. Their familiarity with college bookstore management led them into the development of a point–of–sale package that includes an extensive accounting module with features such as the ability to process special orders, transact rentals, print/validate customer checks at the POS location, and interface with major credit and debit card systems. Some of the on–line register functions include: barcode scanning, price look–up and search features using keywords, multiple payment methods, cash drawer balancing, and exception reporting. In addition, the system maintains inventory on a First In–First Out (FIFO) method and provides immediate quantity on–hand adjustment at the point of sale.

The system selected by UG would use two processors. The Host Processor would be physically housed in the Gift Shop and the POS Controller would be in the Book Store (see Appendix A for the hardware layout). The cost of the hardware totaled US$109,346, the software totaled US$28,670, and system training added another US$12,600, for a total system cost of $150, 616 (see Appendix B for details). The physical layout of the campus is found in Appendix C.

Training was to be provided in three phases. Phase I would take the book store and gift shop managers to the headquarters of MoreBooks for 4 days of intensive instruction. Phase II would be five days of on–site training to input current inventory details with new hardware and software in place. It would involve all hardware setup, testing, and employee familiarization with the system. Inventory and vendor master records would have to be created and related to cost information. POS function keys would have to be defined and recorded for each register. Barcode ticketing programs would be set–up and certified by each store manager. There would need to be a physical inventory freeze with data entry and update before any on–line POS processing could begin.

Phase III would take the POS live, with full credit card settlement, inventory ordering, receiving, and returning, textbook buyback processing, textbook electronic ordering, and financial reporting systems operating. At this time, MoreBooks would finalize training for specific job functions, including those of laundry, tailor shop, barber shop, and food services personnel.

During the summer of 1994, the Book Store manager (Todd) and the Gift Shop manager (Vernon) flew across the country to MoreBooks headquarters for training. Their first impression of the offsite training was positive. A training lab was set up with equipment similar to that ordered for

UG's campus. The trainers used a sample company which seemed to help communicate the course. But, by the middle of the first day, Vernon and Todd discovered that some of the training was above their heads. They felt that MoreBooks expected them to know more about perpetual accounting systems than they did. To add to the difficulty, the training and general operational manuals were written from the point of a knowledgeable systems administrator, not an end–user. Todd and Vernon hoped that the on–site training would be easier to understand since it would be in their home environment using their own data.

As the installation date approached, it was apparent that a POS Implementation Committee was needed and the VP of Finance delegated the function to Ernie, Director of Financial Services, an even–tempered Certified Public Accountant who would be thorough in his attention to details yet able to accommodate the diverse interests and personalities on the committee. Representatives on the committee were:

POS IMPLEMENTATION COMMITTEE

Roger	.......Computer Technology Department	Todd	.........Book Store
Vernon	......Gift Shop	Bruce	........Procurement Director
Darlene	.....Laundry	Geraldine	...Tailor Shop
Sam	...........Accounting Manager	Brenda	.......Food Services
Hank	..........Treasurer	Woody	.......Athletic Ticket Sales

The first meeting was set for August 9, 1994, with an agenda to:

AGENDA
A. discuss purpose of the committee
B. discuss critical steps that would have to be taken and approximate completion time
C. give out assignments
D. set time for next meeting

The August 9th meeting got off to a good start with various items determined:

1. It was decided, and confirmed with the vendor, to have Phase II training take place the week of October 17th. Phase II would be when the hardware was delivered and basic terminal training held for the employees. The training would cover 5 days, with the inventory loading and setting of register keys. Several items needed to be resolved before that time and were assigned to the concerned parties:
   a. Vernon wanted to have a separate database for the Gift Shop so that Book Store personnel could not read the credit card numbers for his customers and needed to investigate the feasibility of doing this.
   b. Todd was to obtain the phone line needed for data transfer between the Book Store and the Gift Shop.
   c. Roger was to schedule and determine the format of the data upload and download.
   d. All persons who would be using the POS registers were to layout the proposed register keyboard setups and bring it to the next meeting so all could see what each other would be doing.
2. An physical inventory was scheduled by the Book Store (which had no perpetual inventory) prior to the new system coming on line. The Gift Shop would use its current perpetual inventory records.
3. Phase III (final training and implementation) was set for four days beginning November 28, under the vendor's supervision.

The committee met again on August 29, 1994. A great deal of time was spent discussing

Vernon's desire to have a separate database for Gift Store customers. The original plan was to have a single database for the Gift Shop and Book Store. Vernon said he was concerned about the security of credit card numbers which he wanted to keep in his database so he could confirm charge numbers when customers placed orders over the phone. He was not happy that other personnel using the system might be able to see these numbers. The others said they had no desire to see the credit card numbers and felt that multiple databases would just complicate matters and be more cumbersome. Roger agreed to discuss with the vendor the possibility of data field security to see if those fields could be protected from access by others.

In addition, the committee became aware of the fact that the cable requirements between the cash registers and the host computer were not clear. The committee wanted to have system documentation in hand to be able to review it during the planning stages. MoreBooks had said they would bring it at the time of implementation. Bruce said he would investigate all these items with the vendor before the next meeting.

MoreBooks still had not sent the chart detailing the cable requirements by the time the Implementation Committee met on September 22nd. The committee assumed that only the connection to one of the dining facilities would require new hookups which could be solved by getting additional telephone lines. They based this assumption on MoreBooks' proposal which read:

VI. ELECTRICAL AND DATA WIRING
6.1 Electrical Wiring – The existing and/or designed wiring (Gift Shop) meets all anticipated needs and requirements for system installation. No additional electrical facilities will be required for the processors, workstations, printers, POS terminals, or other peripherals.

6.2 Data Cabling –The data cabling serving existing cash registers at the Book Store, Laundry, and Tailor Shop meets requirements. The data cabling as designed for the Gift Shop and corresponding service to the Barber Shop meets anticipated requirements.

The POS equipment was scheduled to arrive on Oct. 11th and to be set up by a MoreBooks representative in anticipation of the implementation.

On Oct. 3rd, a fax was received from MoreBooks providing a time line schedule (see Appendix D) and detailing the cable requirements. Ernie immediately sent it over to the Computer Technology Department with a cover letter stating:

"We have obtained the data line requirements from the POS system vendor. The attached document notes the cabling and connection requirements that are needed for the system. The POS committee does not have the expertise to determine if the lines and connections are available. We believe that many of the requirements can be met by wires and cables that are currently installed, but we do not know what else needs to be done.

I request that you 1) indicate on the forms what currently is in place, and 2) indicate what items need to be done and how much they are estimated to cost. If you have any immediate questions, you should contact Bruce and he can get you in contact with the vendor. A representative will be on campus the week of the 11th. We need information as soon as possible because the system is due to go 'live' during November. We will receive formal training on the system on Oct. 17th and need to have as much done as possible by that time. I apologize for the short time frame on this but we have been asking the vendor for the cable requirements and they were just faxed in today."

The committee met on Oct. 3rd and some concerns were expressed regarding the ability of the system to function in the Tailor shop and Laundry given the diversity of transaction codes needed (type of clothing, color, action to take, special conditions, etc.). The vendor had assured Bruce that they had set up another customer exactly the way UG required and had encountered no problems. In addition, it was discovered that under the new system, the managers could no longer assign product codes because the system automatically assigned them. The stores needed to create special codes because students on athletic scholarships are prohibited from purchasing certain items with scholarship funds. Special codes would flag the clerk that these items should not be charged by the student against a scholarship account. If the codes could not be assigned, more training of the staff would be required to know what items should be blocked.

October 11th arrived and with it, the vendor's technician who announced that the wiring was not adequate to complete the system. E–mail messages began flying as Golden's electricians and CTD reps each thought the other should be handling the problem. One message said:

"This is to keep you abreast of the what is happening with the lines. The vendor rep has found that several lines need to be run to connect the various machines together. First priority is to run lines in the book store to connect the host computer in Todd's office to the receiving area. Second priority is to run a line through the conduit in the Gift Shop to its receiving area. Third priority (and toughest job) is to run a line from the computer in the Gift Shop to the Snack Bar. This will require boring through 18 inches of concrete and was not anticipated when the Snack Bar was renovated. Work orders have been pulled and we will keep track of the costs. We will have to sort out who pays for what when Bruce gets back. Connectors have to be attached to the wires. I am asking Roger to coordinate this between the electricians and the Computer Technology staff."

By Oct. 13, the frustration of having the clock ticking and no training getting started is reflected in the next message from Ernie:

" It appears that no one has the capability/time to put connectors on to the wires being pulled for the POS system. I understand that there are 90+ connectors to add. It may be that the vendor is responsible and we can assess the costs to him but that will require further analysis of the RFP. The vendor rep says he cannot put on all those connectors. Since I cannot get help to get the connectors done from working with the workers, I am now coming to the heads of the activities that should do the work. Are we going to let a $150,000 system, impacting many areas of the campus, not come up because of a question of whether the connector should be done by the contractor? The electrician says it is beyond his capability and he is pulling wires. CT Dept. tells me if it is the vendor's responsibility, then he should do it. Could CT Dept. and Physical Plant supervisors get together and give me a suggestion of what to do? (Meanwhile nothing is happening with getting connectors attached!)'

At the end of the week, the vendor reps left campus with very little in the way of training being accomplished and the discovery of new glitches in the system. The following message from the POS Implementation chairman sums up where the project stood at this point:

"The POS system people are leaving today and there are still a number of items we need from the vendor. Some of these things may be add–ons to the purchase order, some may be items that Bruce needs to negotiate with the vendor because we anticipate that they were part of the contract. We need:

1) an unlimited site license for software that will enable us to use our PCs and monitors in place of additional monitors. Cost should be around $800 and will keep Todd and Vernon from having to have two monitors on their desks. THIS IS CLEARLY A NEW, UNCONTESTED REQUEST.

2) programming to enable us to upload and download with the format and coding we need. Roger believes that the modifications and programming we want are part of the specs of the RFP. MoreBooks says what we want is outside of the RFP. THIS IS HIGHLY CONTESTED AS TO WHO SHOULD PAY...BUT IT IS EXTREMELY NECESSARY AND THE COST SHOULD NOT BE HIGH.

3) five days for 2 trainers to finalize hookup/installation and train. We got very little training done this week because we did not have wires run, connections made, phone lines available, etc. We used their folks to do a little training but a lot of their time was spent in getting hardware hooked up. We want them for this during Nov. 28–Dec. 2. THIS IS HIGHLY NECESSARY AND THIS NEEDS TO BE NEGOTIATED BECAUSE WHAT THEY TOLD US IN THE RFP MADE US THINK THAT THERE WAS LITTLE THAT NEEDED TO BE DONE. PLUS WE HAD TROUBLE GETTING THE WIRING REQUIREMENTS FROM THEM ON A TIMELY BASIS."

Other details that needed attention came to light shortly thereafter. MoreBooks said that backups had to be made each night and the system initialized for the next day's activities. Since the host was located in the Book Store, that meant that Todd had to come in every day, including weekends, to back–up the system. The managers thought they could get by with not backing up the system on the weekends since little activity took place then, although it might be a different story for the snack bar. If necessary, cash register tapes could be used to re–input the data. This item was to be discussed with the vendor. Due to the chaos that had surrounded the first on–site attempt at training, it was decided to try to schedule Phase III as soon as possible after Phase II, preferably Dec. 5–8.

During a routine posting transaction, the Book Store manager discovered that the Book Store and Gift Shop could sell the exact same item with the same description on file but at a different price. One store could see the other's cost data but not retail prices, although MoreBooks said this could not be possible.

On October 25, MoreBooks sent a three–page letter detailing items that needed to be un–installed, connectors attached, and re–installed. They estimated that all items could be accomplished in three days by two on–site vendor reps if cabling were installed where needed, phone lines were live where required, electrical requirements met, the stores closed, and Golden's personnel de–installed, disconnected, and removed existing register systems. That would leave two days in the week to monitor routine questions and problems that might arise while all registers were on–line. At the same time, the download/upload programs and procedures could be checked. He suggested that they schedule all of this for the week of November 27–December 8.

The MoreBooks manager pointed out in his letter that on his rep's last visit to Golden's site, he found that cables had not been pulled, labeled, or fitted with connectors, that registers with existing cables were not disconnected and crimped with the proper connectors, and that proper electrical environments were not met because existing systems were still running. He noted that Golden's employees would still need additional training since approximately 1600 procedures and programs would have to be learned. On a more positive note, he added that the request by the Gift Shop manager to have some customer accounts "blocked" as to the products they could purchase would be a feature applicable to other MoreBooks customers and therefore they would make it a standard feature in the next release of their software.

After reading MoreBooks's list of hardware items that still needed attention and considering the peak buying season impacting the stores, Golden decided to delay Phase II training until February, with Phase III training to begin immediately thereafter.

By December 14, the account representative for MoreBooks proposed a new look at getting this project finished and providing training. His letter stated:

"...on the topic of training, let me preface by saying that to bid training is possibly the toughest task in the whole process. Given that all the installation functions go according to plan, the statement of training provided in a proposal is any vendor's best effort at stating the necessary level of training to attain adequate knowledge of the system's operations. Obviously, we can only suggest that a certain amount of training is going to be adequate and that amount is necessarily based on certain assumptions.

The estimated training needed to complete preparation of staff for total system operation is 10 additional training days with two MoreBooks trainers on–site. This can be accomplished during the period of Feb. 13–24, 1995 which is currently reserved for this purpose by our staff. Please note the requirements listed concerning the removal of existing equipment and the necessity of the stores' activity being halted to effect changeover.

Because of the problems encountered during the installation phase, (weather, cable and phone line placement, and general misunderstanding) and to ensure that Golden considers that it has received fair value for its investment and that store personnel are prepared to use the system, MoreBooks proposes the following:

a) MoreBooks will provide six trainer days ($4,800) at no additional costs. These six days are offered to offset any misunderstanding of installation requirements and underestimation of training needs.

b) MoreBooks will provide the other ten trainer days at a cost of $8,000 (or $4,500 plus direct travel expenses) and will offer book transaction credits to offset this cost. The need for these ten trainer days is a product of
    1) the addition of other users (food services)
    2) the delays encountered during the last training session
    3) anticipated increase in training needed by staff on textbook management
    4) some refreshing required due to the time spread between Phase I and
       now?"

On January 11, 1995 Golden met to lay out responsibilities to be ready for MoreBooks's visit. It was decided that if any problems came up during training that involved MoreBooks, those encountering the problems should call Todd, who was administering the contract, or Bruce, the procurement director. Only those two people should be dealing with MoreBooks on these issues. MoreBooks was obviously also taking a cautious approach to this next phase as they wrote a letter asking that Golden give them in writing a response to the October 25th letter, paragraph by paragraph, indicating which steps were to be accomplished by MoreBooks. The goal was to have a complete understanding of : 1) what is to be done, 2) who is to do it, 3) when it is to be done, and 4) who is to say it has been done. The goal was to avoid any finger pointing or ill feelings at any cost by having a well–thought out plan detailing the different locations and people involved.

As it got closer to training time, Golden was having second thoughts about shutting down all the activities completely. The Laundry and Tailor shop could not be closed for 3 days but would have to stay open to respond to customer demands. It was decided that the Laundry and Tailor Shop would remain open, collect the charge data manually and enter it after the system was live. They would shut down for the actual training which should take only a few hours.

The February training took place as planned and the new system was brought on line. In going live, several problems were encountered that still had to be addressed byMoreBooks. The Gift Shop's barcode printer was not operating properly. One of the registers was rejecting data related to the Special Order feature in customer files. The Laundry's register was not fully programmed. In addition, some of the ID Card Readers malfunctioned. The employees felt that they would need more training because the problems that came up detracted from the training time. Other problems included having to update two systems separately for POS customer data now that the Gift Shop had succeeded in getting a database separate from the Book Store.

The real test of the system came in the middle of March when the largest crowd of customers arrived for a special weekend. This test revealed that Purchase Orders were more cumbersome to produce under the new system. The system required some staff input after working hours. The "file, save, restore" procedure was time consuming and could only be done when no one was on the system and all the registers were shut down. It was hoped that this could be accomplished by the managers via modem from home. If not, they would have to have complete cross–training so that they could alternate and have one come in on the weekend to do both systems. The Laundry and Tailor Shop were getting duplicate receipts for charge transactions and the printer was too slow. Each operation had a different preference for the printer: the retail stores wanted it not to print until the transaction was complete, the snack bar liked having it print a line each time an item was keyed, and the laundry also wanted each line to print as the items were entered.

The laundry system continued to have problems because the functions handled there were so different from a retail operation. The check–in procedures were greatly slowed down due to the new system. Using a computer screen instead of a cash register was frustrating to the staff which had to look for items such as "shirt," then "blue," etc. It was recommended that they try to use a fast food type keyboard that would have a key to press for each of the options.

The POS Implementation committee met again on June 7, 1995. It had been six weeks since Golden had asked MoreBooks to review the procedures in the laundry and there was still no answer. The Gift Shop was having problems costing out the inventory for items purchased prior to the POS system. The general mood at this meeting was one of dissatisfaction with MoreBooks' responsiveness to questions as well as their accuracy when they did respond. The committee developed a list to be sent to MoreBooks of their specific training requirements for a tentative training date of July 17, 1995. These needs were detailed by functional area as follows:

A. **Gift Shop**:
1. Accounting Module – setup chart of accounts to acquire information needed by staff personnel.
2. Passwords and Register Security – functions that can only be accomplished by a supervisor.
3. Purging – invoices and special orders
4. Customer Service Processing – special orders, finalizing the sales process and purging to purchase orders
5. Customer Files – how to setup from electronic download without customer service assistance

B. **Book Store:**
1. Complete overview of the entire system but concentrate on electronic ordering, textbook returns and receiving.

2. Instruction on use of report writer (English statement), general review of available reports and purchase order review.

C. **Laundry:**

1. Key In – overview and suggestions for faster process.

2. Cost sales – review of present process and suggestions on improving the process.

D. **Snack Bar:**

1. Report Writer – overview and instructions on how to use.

2. New Item Input – overview and instructions for entering new items.

As of July 12, Golden had not received a reply regarding the requested additional training. In the meantime, more problems were experienced. A lightening strike on the Laundry's modem also brought down the Book Store. Once the Laundry terminal was disconnected, the Book Store was able to get back on line. The need for backup hardware was now apparent, as well as the need for a set of procedures to follow for routine backups and emergency situations. For example, it had been set up that if one system were down, the Book Store and Gift Shop could switch some cables and work off the other's system with no interruptions for either location. Somehow the instructions regarding which cables to dis–connect and re–connect were lost and no one could remember how to make the switch. Without the computer technology department's support of the system, Golden had to wait until MoreBooks could come back to provide additional training to help in these areas. The summer progressed with no resolution of these nagging problems.

By September 28, 1995 MoreBooks had responded with a letter addressing the additional training needs and costs. The new training was set for October 23. To get ready for this visit, Golden installed extra lines between the Laundry and Book Store and the Computer Technology Department attached the required connectors. Training was set for 5 days with 2 trainers on site. Each location was to get at least one–half day of intensive training, with everyone getting another half day of training in writing reports. The Implementation Committee met on October 17 to review items that needed to be covered when MoreBooks was on campus:

1. Snack Bar: when swiping an ID card, if the card holder's name does not appear on the screen as it should, a second swiping will charge the next person in the alphabet, not the cardholder. The register person must totally exit the transaction and re–start it in order to prevent charging the wrong person. This slows down the check–out process considerably.

2. The Book Store experienced problems all summer in that if the system would not come up, they would have to disconnect the Laundry, re–start the system, then re–connect the Laundry. This was a severe and inconvenient problem. Unfortunately, the Laundry seemed to go down for no reason at all, even though two lines were running between it and the Book Store to ensure that it was not a line problem. The Tailor Shop, physically in the same building as the Laundry, was not experiencing these problems.

3. The Book Store and Gift Shop were supposed to be cross–connected so if one location went down, it could continue to function off the system via the other location. This feature was available when the system was first set–up but seemed to have disappeared. In addition, the Book Store had to do the "file/save/restore" function in conjunction with the Gift Shop, which took a considerable amount of time. MoreBooks had indicated that these functions could be done separately by the two

locations, but Golden had not been able to accomplish it.
4. The Gift Shop needed more ports. When all registers were operating and the Dining Service on line, the system bogged down. The memory size of the POS controller located in the Gift Shop was not large enough for all the transactions being handled, which caused system crashes and required the frequent purging of records to provide enough space.

The committee agreed that they were pushing what had originally been envisioned as a book store system to become a campus–wide system that was more complex than they or the vendor had envisioned. They believed the system could work but were greatly in need of training to make sure they were using it to its fullest capability.

Current Status Of The Project

The October training was thorough and specific and as a result, procedures were improved and the efficiency of the various operations was enhanced over their pre–POS levels. Customers were served promptly and reporting requirements were met on a timely basis. From time to time some minor problems erupted and there was some concern about how much longer Golden could call MoreBooks for free software support. It was decided to form an internal e–mail group so that when problems arose, they could consult the group first to see who might have experienced the same problem and be able to offer a likely solution. Consulting the e–mail group would also let them know if someone was currently talking with MoreBooks about a problem so that MoreBooks would not be taking multiple calls on the same problem.

Successes And Failures

Various failures occurred early in the project. For example, the vendor failed to accurately assess Golden's user requirements and test existing cables and connectors which led to numerous delays in the project. Golden failed to adequately bind the vendor with a contract that specified procedures for handling contract disputes. Finally, the project did not have a strong internal champion who could spearhead the project from inception to completion. A defacto committee had to be formed after the contract was awarded to actually follow–up on all the details.

However, ultimately the system was considered an overall success in that diverse functional areas were able to adapt the software to both retail and service activities. As a result of the struggle with the new system, employees gained increased confidence in their ability to learn new functions and creatively handle problems as they arose, independent of the CTD. The newly created e–mail users group provided a cross–departmental support structure that greatly enhanced communications among the functional areas. Finally, Golden and MoreBooks were able to negotiate contractual miscommunications without resorting to costly litigation, an all too prevalent result of many outsourcing arrangements.

Epilogue And Lessons Learned

There were several lessons learned from this experience, all of which will assist Golden in the development and implementation of their next major information system and provide direction to others considering similar projects. These lessons are summarized as follows:

First, recognize that the vendor will have to be thoroughly educated about your needs and may not know what questions to ask to gain that knowledge. Have current job descriptions and procedures documented for the functional areas to be affected by the new system and provide these to the vendor. Once the overall scope of the project has been determined in general terms, detail the functions and responsibilities of the various parties necessary to accomplish the project. Document these activities as they occur and plan for the inevitable delays that will occur. Remember that once the contract is signed, freedom for negotiations is greatly reduced.

Specify clearly identifiable milestones, how they will be measured and by whom, to avoid miscommunications. Make sure that termination clauses provide the necessary recourse in the event of irresolvable disputes. Finally, if possible, install the system in phases and have fall–back procedures in place in the event that environmental factors impact the system.

Questions for Discussion

1. When outsourcing the development and implementation of an information system, what steps if any, of the Systems Development Life Cycle (SDLC) should be followed?

2. What factors are relevant to an organization's decision to outsource the development of an information system?

3. What steps could the vendor have taken to ensure that all training needs would be met?

4. What steps could the organization have taken to insure that its training needs were met?

5. Discuss the pro's and con's of off–site training for a new information system.

References

Turban, E., McLean, E. & Wetherbe, J. (1996). *Information Technology for Management: Improving Quality and Productivity* . New York: John Wiley & Son, Inc.

Gupta, U. (1996). *Management Information Systems: A Managerial Perspective.* Minneapolis/St. Paul: West Publishing Company.

Appendix A

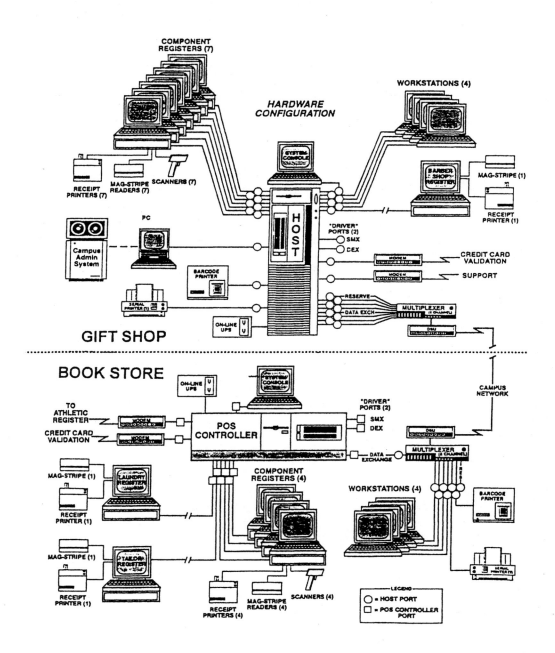

Appendix B

9.0 General - The flexibility of this system allows for different approaches to configuring system hardware. Given the multiple locations of POS terminals and user workstations on the Golden campus and the need to insure continuing operation, MoreBooks presents two (2) alternative configurations for consideration. The functions of the system do not change between the two configurations.[**Only Configuration A, selected by Golden, is detailed here.**]

9.1 Configuration A - This configuration is the recommended system configuration. It provides more than adequate capacities of storage and user interfaces with a two (2) processor architecture. It is suggested that the Host Processor be physically placed at the Gift Shop and the POS Controller be physically placed at the Book Store. [**See Appendix A for a representation of this system configuration.**]

As stated above, this configuration provides the entire range of POS functions with normal system administrative functions performed by store operations personnel. This configuration is the normal installation at our customer premises.

PRICES FOR CONFIGURATION A

HOST PROCESSOR:
INTEL 486DX2 66mhz with 256kb Cache Memory, 32mb SIMMs Memory, 3.5" 1.44mb Flex Drive, 520mb IDE Fixed Disk Drive, 150/250MB Cartridge Tape Drive, 14" VGA Monochrome Monitor, 101-key Workstation Keyboard, 2 internal Communication Ports, 24 external serial Communication Ports, Operating System (22 user), Communications Software, Uninterruptable Power Supply, Manuals. $ 19,405.00

POS PROCESSOR:
INTEL 486DX2 66mhz with 256kb Cache Memory, 16mb SIMMs Memory, 3.5" 1.44mb Flex Disk, 120mb IDE Fixed Disk Drive, 150/250mb CartridgeTape Drive, 14" VGA Monochrome Monitor, 101-key Workstation Keyboard, 2 internal Communication Ports, 16 external serial Communication Ports, Operating System (16 user), Communications Software, Uninterruptible Power Supply, Manuals. $ 14,100.00

PERIPHERAL DEVICES:

11 - Component POS TERMINAL including: Dual-Port CRT, Printer, Cash Drawer, Scanner, Card Decoder, Magstripe Reader, ($4,290.00 ea.)	$ 47,190.00
4 - Component POS TERMINAL including: Dual-Port CRT, Receipt Printer, Card Decoder and Dual-Track Magnetic Stripe Reader. ($2,295.00 ea.)	$ 9,180.00
8 - ASCII Terminal	$ 4,960.00
2 - 9-pin Dot-Matrix Printer	$ 1,640.00
2 - Bar Code Printer	$ 4,990.00
3 - 2400 baud Modems	$ 1,347.00
2 - Statistical Multiplexor	$ 3,198.00
2 - Digital Service Unit	$ 1,598.00
2 - 9600 baud Modem	$ 1,738.00
System Hardware Subtotal	$109,346.00

1 - POS Application Software including:
 Text Management, General Merchandise Management, Point-of-Sale Processing,
   Accounting and On-line Data Exchange, Mainframe Transfer $ 28,670.00
1 - System Training $ 12,600.00
              Total System Cost $150,616.00

Annual Maintenance:

Year -	1	2	3	4	5
System Hardware	1050.50	1910.00	1910.00	2578.00	2578.00
System Software	3190.00	3190.00	3190.00	3190.00	3190.00
Total Maintenance	4240.50	5100.00	5100.00	5768.00	5768.00

Appendix C

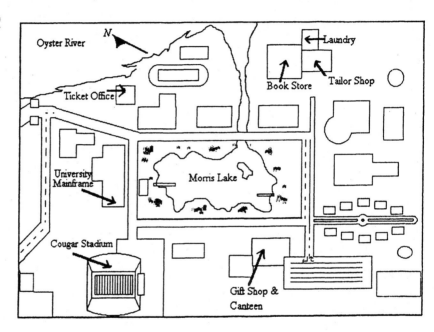

Appendix D

Installation and Training Schedule
October

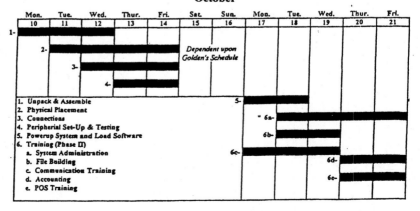

Chapter 5

Changing The Old Order:
Sequencing Organizational and Information Technology Change to Achieve Successful Organizational Transformation

Chris Sauer[1]
The University of New South Wales

Executive Summary

This chapter describes the transformation of the motor vehicle registration and driver licensing business of the Roads and Traffic Authority of the Australian state of New South Wales. At the heart of this transformation which took place between 1989 and 1992 is a system called DRIVES. The project was innovative in the technology platform it devised and in the CASE technology it used to build the application. The new system has paid for itself at the same time as transforming the Roads and Traffic Authority's way of doing the business. In addition it has generated new strategic opportunities.

The iterating sequence of steps, or looped path, by which the Roads and Traffic Authority achieved its organizational transformation is compared with the more traditional top-down path. The looped path helps prepare the organization for the information technology change, makes risk more manageable by reducing the dependence between steps in the path, and leads to strategic benefits after the organizational changes have been mastered. Thus, we say that the particular order in which change was undertaken led to the new organizational order.

Background

The state of New South Wales (NSW) is situated in the south-east of Australia. It is an area 15% larger than Texas with a population of six million. The state capital is Sydney which is the same size as Los Angeles with a population of 3.7 million. For most of the 1980s the government of New South Wales administered roads and their use through two separate departments. The Department of Main

Roads planned, built and maintained roads. It was a major spending department with a billion dollar budget. The Department of Motor Transport registered and licensed the vehicles and drivers who used the roads. It collected revenues for the state Treasury amounting to approximately the figure spent by the Department of Main Roads. Although running very different types of business, the two departments were both old-fashioned in their conduct of business. The Department of Main Roads was strongly influenced by its established engineering culture rather than business values. The Department of Motor Transport was viewed as a bureaucratic backwater from which bright managers sought to escape. Staff described its business practices as "Dickensian."

As the 1980s progressed, the climate in government and public administration began to change. Governments reduced the scope of their activities and increasingly imposed commercial values and practices on their major service providing departments.

In 1988, the government decided to merge the Department of Main Roads, the Department of Motor Transport, and the much smaller NSW Traffic Authority which was responsible for road safety. In January 1989, the Roads and Traffic Authority (RTA) came into existence as a super department of almost 12,000 employees and a budget in excess of $A1 billion. The head of the Department of Main Roads, Bernard Fisk, was appointed Chief Executive of the RTA.

Setting the Stage

Our concern in this chapter is confined to the vehicle registration and driver licensing part of the RTA's business. Initially, the RTA had no choice but to continue to operate the Department of Motor Transport's existing business processes. These separated the delivery of licenses and registration from back office administrative processing. Delivery was through the RTA's 138 motor registries which are locally situated shopfronts at which members of the public pay their fees and obtain their licenses and registration documents. Registries perform a wide variety of tasks related to registration and licensing. They also administer driver's tests.

Each registry has its own manager who is responsible through line management to a regional director. In 1989, at the time of the merger, a typical registry had 12 to 15 staff each of whom carried out highly specialized tasks. For customers this specialization resulted in a frustrating lack of customer service. They were required to join one queue to submit their application and renewal forms and then another to pay. If there were difficulties with their paperwork they might have to join other queues as well. After all that, there was a strong possibility that the registry would be unable to resolve the problem and so would have to refer them to the central administrative processing unit at Rosebery in inner Sydney which dealt with problems and handled all the data collection forms and computer processing.

In the old business process, customer records would take around 10 days to be updated and customers could sometimes wait weeks for new registration documents to reach them in the post. For the police, it was hard to enforce registration and licensing law because offenders could claim that their missing documentation was "in the mail." There were insufficient controls to detect corrupt practice in the registries. An inquiry by the New South Wales Independent Commission Against Corruption found "endemic corruption in a number of motor registries in the Sydney metropolitan area". Some driving examiners were systematically accepting bribes from driving schools to pass students and certain registry staff were falsifying or selling license and registration information.

The central computer system operated by the staff at the Rosebery unit consisted of two IBM 4381 mainframes. The application software was 14 years old and prone to intermittent failure. Much of it was written in undocumented Assembler and had been so heavily amended to cope with legislative and administrative changes that the programmers were doubtful they could continue to change it without making it more error prone.

The CEO was acutely aware of his legacy: "Something had to be done. Any query was a matter of using a group of specialist programmers, it would take a long time, and there was always the danger that the system would fall over in seeking to extract that information. The Minister wanted better information on which to base policy and I wanted better service to motor registry customers."

The task of determining what should be done was assigned to the RTA's General Manager of Information Services, Geoff Deacon, who had joined the Department of Main Roads in 1987 as Head of Information Technology (IT). His work in trying to bring order to the Department of Main Roads' different systems and technologies was to prove important for the new project in that he came to recognize the potential of an open systems platform, "I . . . started to get a feeling that Unix was to be the way of the future. We wanted to move towards a single integrated network and open systems were definitely the way to go. We figured an open system approach would ensure that new technology could be implemented with minimal disruption as it became available." His technology choice was a Fujitsu mainframe running the UTS/M version of Unix. This was unconventional in that the accepted Unix configuration involved multiple minicomputers.

Deacon was faced with the choice of an application rewrite or implementing a new system. Rewriting was nearly impossible because the system was so poorly documented. He therefore proposed a new system under the name DRIVES (DRIver and VEhicle System).

The RTA's chief executive did not wait for DRIVES to be implemented to start a program of organizational change. He was conscious of the new mood in government to improve public perceptions of government services. He therefore moved quickly to position the RTA strategically as a more customer responsive body.

Fisk's first change was to structure the RTA into regions both for its road development responsibilities and its registration and licensing business. The new structure transferred accountability and authority from Head Office to the field and reduced levels of management. In the process, Fisk refilled managerial positions to ensure that his strategy would be in the hands of staff who were up to the challenge.

The RTA then set about changes that would be evident to the public. It transformed the registries from a highly differentiated workplace with many grades of staff to a multi-skilled workplace with just two grades of customer service officer, and a supervisor and a manager. Intense specialization was replaced by a more customer oriented flexibility. While the registries had to continue to use the old business systems, this new flexibility made it possible for managers to make some immediate improvements in customer service.

Project/Case Description

The DRIVES project had two main objectives. The first was to replace the old application technology with a robust, modern system which would eliminate the risk of an irrecoverable failure. The second was to remove the need for the central processing unit, thereby saving $A20 million per year in staff costs and at the same time providing a swifter service to registry customers. Other benefits included enhanced accuracy and timeliness of records, improved security of data, flexibility of access to data, potential to expand, rapid communications and better management information. In providing for flexibility and the ability to grow and develop as the business and the technology changed, the RTA was preparing itself for the future.

In late 1989, the RTA approved a budget of $A28.6 million for building a new licensing and registration system. The CEO signaled his desire for a quick implementation by renaming the project DRIVES '90: "I deliberately set an unrealistic timeframe, I had to keep the pressure on Geoff [Deacon] to perform because I was scared of the existing system falling over."

The RTA decided to build DRIVES itself because Deacon was unable to find an adequate package solution. Success required that the RTA be able to manage technology, application, and organizational challenges. Technology challenges included developing the technology platform; adopting the unproven pairing of Unix on a Fujitsu mainframe; and learning to use a Computer-Aided Software Engineering (CASE) tool which itself had to be converted from IBM's MVS operating system to suit the RTA's environment. Application challenges included the size and complexity of the application, changes to the data model, and the difficulties involved in converting records because of the poor quality of the data. The main organizational challenge was the management of change in the motor registries. One task was to change registry staff attitudes - "We were trying to change a group whose whole focus was to get the money off the customer, stamp something and then put the paperwork in the background for somebody else to fix, into a culture where we said you have the power and the responsibility to do it at the front counter with this complicated system." Registry change was also complicated by a continuing industrial dispute between the RTA and a union which was trying to avoid losing its position to a competitor.

Deacon managed the technical, application, and organizational challenges in a number of ways. His innovations included establishment of a Change Management Team. In the course of the project, this team undertook a refurbishment of the registry offices and trained 1,500 customer service officers.

Deacon was particularly helped by the support he received from his CEO. Fisk's support for resourcing the project meant that Deacon could quickly build up the project organization with good quality contract staff and technical specialists employed by suppliers. This meant that technology challenges could be tackled by technically proficient staff. When delays occurred, Fisk accepted them but continued to push for system delivery. When the project ran into any difficulty he made resources available to help solve it. When the budget was exceeded, his view was, "If I can't find a spare five to ten million dollars, there is something wrong." His evident commitment convinced both Fujitsu and Texas Instruments that it was worth putting in extra effort to solve technical problems. According to Fujitsu Australia's Managing Director, his company was happy to continue to make special efforts because it was confident of Fisk's commitment to the project: "The management team from Bernard Fisk down were absolutely convinced that they had made the right strategic decision and they knew the benefits they were going to get."

Support from the top extended even further in the case of the industrial dispute. When the union launched a campaign of public criticisms in the press, not only did the CEO appear on a local radio program and Deacon invite journalists to a briefing, but also the RTA's minister, Wal Murray, made strong statements of support in parliament. In the face of such a solid reaction from the RTA, the criticism quickly died away.

Current Status of the Project

In September 1991, the Licensing component of DRIVES was implemented in the registries. Ninety staff at the central administrative processing unit left the RTA in accordance with the terms of an earlier agreement resulting in immediate staff savings. In June 1992, the Registration component was implemented, and the remaining 400 employees left under the same terms thus yielding the full, expected staff savings of $A20 million per year.

Both phases of implementation experienced teething problems. The registries experienced a number of start up problems with the Licensing data which caused delays at the counters with a build-up of queues in the registries but which were overcome in time. Registration which is a high volume transaction initially struggled to achieve a satisfactory processing throughput. Response times at the registries averaged 6 to 10 seconds. For a period, customers were openly dissatisfied at the long queues they faced. The combined efforts of the DRIVES Systems team, assisted by Fujitsu specialists gradually brought performance up so that response times were close to target by December 1992. Once Fujitsu delivered its multi-processor Unix in January 1993, response times fell to around two seconds, the target envisaged in 1989.

Since 1993, the RTA has been able to further develop the applications and to maintain them without significant difficulty. New versions of the software have been installed smoothly without adverse effects on business processing.

Successes and Failures

DRIVES has been a major success. The RTA has met its two objectives of replacing the old system and achieving productivity gains leading to $A18 million cost savings[2] and an estimated $A5 million revenue increase annually. In the process the RTA has transformed the way it does registration and licensing business, giving it organizational, business, and technological benefits. At the same time, it has created new strategic opportunities. DRIVES has resulted in improved service in the motor registries which are now able to complete customer transactions at a single counter position and solve problems on the spot. Surveys conducted by an independent research company have shown that customers appreciate the changes in terms of reduced waiting times, better service, fewer queues and improved registry appearance.

DRIVES has also speeded up essential registry activities such as banking. Before, a separate cashier handled the registry's takings and did a manual daily balance. Now, DRIVES automatically balances each officer's cash drawer. What used to take two clerks up to an hour to complete at the end of each day is done in 15 minutes.

DRIVES has also helped the RTA combat corrupt practices both by limiting opportunities and exposing misconduct. DRIVES contains a high level of auditability and is protected through a combination of passwords and access levels. The RTA is able to detect and investigate unusual patterns of usage. RTA employees found to have engaged in corrupt practices have been swiftly dismissed and prosecuted on the basis of DRIVES information.

With the safety of corporate information assured, the RTA has been able to evaluate opportunities such as installing DRIVES terminals in car-dealer offices and at motor auctions. This move would allow cars to be registered at their point of sale while administrative savings would be made by both the RTA and the dealers. The range of other opportunities includes outsourcing the entire licensing and registration operation, using information available through DRIVES to lower the state's $A70 million fine default bill, and introducing phone-in license and registration renewals or do-it-yourself booths at large shopping centers.

DRIVES has improved the identification of stolen and unregistered vehicles, and assists police with driving and vehicle offenses. In the future, DRIVES could be used to get unregistered vehicles off the road more quickly through electronically exchanging information with external stakeholders such as the Police and the Traffic Infringement Processing Bureau.

Safe-T-Cam is an example of a truly innovative project enabled by DRIVES. It is a system for electronically collecting data on heavy vehicles. As trucks or semi-trailers pull up to weighing stations on the highways of NSW, their image is captured and their number-plates read. This information is transmitted to DRIVES which returns an alert if a vehicle is over-weight or unregistered. Problem vehicles are called into the station and the others are waved on. Safe-T-Cam sites on major highways permit automatic checks on long distance speeding. Safe-T-Cam is able to access DRIVES to obtain up to date owner information. The State saves money through a reduced accident bill while the road transport industry benefits from the decrease in driver delays at the weighing stations.

Various technological benefits have also emerged. As well as permitting easy upgrade and enhancement, the open systems platform has allowed the RTA to explore mid-range alternatives to its mainframe technology without having to rewrite its systems. It is thus able to keep up to date and to explore newer technologies such as client/server without incurring major overheads.

Against such a substantial success, the project's downside pales into insignificance. Budget and schedule overruns were financially significant, but they did not prevent the project from giving a net positive return on investment within two years. From the organizational perspective such budget and schedule problems were negligible. The CEO did not expect the project to come in on time, rather he used the schedule to maintain the pressure to achieve implementation at the earliest possible moment. The strategic importance of the new system was such that he was prepared to fund the budget overrun. The system performance problems were essentially just teething problems. They had a short term effect on customer satisfaction but the improvements to registry service have in the longer term far outweighed initial dissatisfaction.

Epilogue and Lessons Learned

Popular writers on organizations and management have made much of IT's potential to transform organizations. The DRIVES experience shows that organizational transformation is not the outcome of a technology project alone. DRIVES' contribution to the transformation of the RTA was one part of a larger program of corporate renewal. A successful technology project on its own would have yielded benefits by removing the threat of the old system failing catastrophically, but the RTA was able to transform the way it did business because of the interaction between the technology and the other organizational change that took place. It is important therefore (1) to recognize that technology is most effective when it is complemented by other organizational change, and (2) to understand IT management in this wider corporate context.

In the past, those IT professionals who have recognized the importance of the interrelationship between technology and organization have recommended that IT systems should *fit their organizational context* (Ein-Dor & Segev, 1981; Keen, 1981). Unfortunately, this has been interpreted to mean that systems should be developed and implemented for the existing state of the organization rather than that IT and the organization should be managed in a mutually complementary fashion.

More recently, proponents of IT-based organizational transformation have tried to locate IT developments in the context of a configuration of organizational elements which includes strategy,

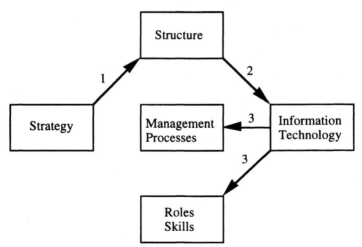

Figure 1: The top-down path to IT-based organizational transformation

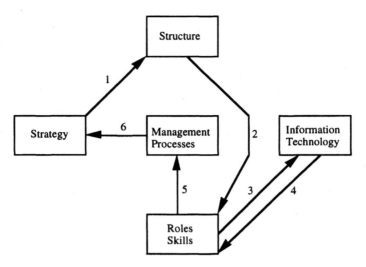

Figure 2: The RTA's looped path to organizational transformation

structure, management processes, and individuals' roles and skills (Walton, 1989; Scott Morton, 1991; Henderson & Venkatraman, 1992). On this view, technology is one component among several, *all of which must fit each other* for substantial performance benefits to be achieved. The conventional view of how to achieve this is to tackle the organizational change sequentially taking a top-down path. This path (Figure 1) proceeds from strategy to structure, then to technology and on to management processes, and roles and skills (Scott Morton, 1988, 1991; Yetton, Johnston & Craig, 1994; Yetton, Craig & Johnston, 1995). In starting from strategy and proceeding downwards, this order of change is rationally appealing. However, it is also limiting in that it can encourage a view of technology as exclusively driven by a strategic vision which foresees the technology's full potential. It can also encourage the technologist's view of the technology project as a project-in-isolation (Abdel-Hamid, 1993), because strategy and structure are taken as givens, decided by business managers in advance of technology investment, while roles, skills and management processes are finer detail which technologists expect lower level managers to change to fit the technology.

Recent research has demonstrated that successful transformations can and do occur when rather different paths of change are followed. In some cases the technology leads the rest of the organization while in others it lags behind (Ciborra, 1991; Yetton et al., 1994, 1995; Burn, 1994). One of the advantages of recognizing the value of different paths is that management of IT is seen less in isolation and more as part of the management of the whole organization. The DRIVES case demonstrates a different path and explains how it contributed to the RTA's success.

Figure 2 illustrates the path taken by the RTA. It goes from the strategy of developing quality of service to customers, to structuring geographically to achieve greater customer focus, to introducing restructuring and multi-skilling in the registries, to implementing DRIVES, to acquiring and mastering the skills to work with DRIVES, to improved management control in the registries, to the exploration of new strategic opportunities. It differs from the top-down path in including two loops. The small loop depicts change to roles and skills in the registries both before and after DRIVES was implemented. The larger loop starts with strategy and revisits strategy after all the other major changes have been completed.

We can identify several lessons from the RTA's looped path to organizational transformation. First, by introducing multi-skilling and de-layering at the registries in advance of the implementation of DRIVES, the RTA reduced the organizational change subsequently needed to work effectively with the new system. Once these changes had been made in the registries, DRIVES made more sense as a work technology than the old system. Thus the sequence of organizational change eased the path for DRIVES so that on implementation, customer service staff could concentrate on learning to use DRIVES. Had the RTA waited for DRIVES to be implemented to make its organizational changes in the registries the implementation which was taxing enough might have easily become intolerable for the staff because too great a burden of new learning would have been placed upon them.

Second, the initial steps through strategy, structure and roles and skills were worthwhile in themselves. They generated benefits for the RTA independently of the new system. This both helped sustain the momentum of transformation and made it easier to manage because each step was not dependent on others yet to be taken.

Third, new strategic opportunities arose at the end of the RTA's path of change not because they had been identified in a detailed strategic vision years earlier, although DRIVES had been designed as a platform for the future, but more because as the RTA developed the technology and learnt its characteristics and possibilities it was able to recognize and subsequently explore new opportunities. Thus, effective implementation of both technological and organizational change can create a platform for the emergence of opportunities. But these are discovered through familiarity with the new organizational way of working rather than by inspired acts of creativity at the time of conception of either strategy or technology.

Organizational transformation is a risky business as the proponents of business process reengineering have always made clear (Davenport, 1993; Hammer & Champy, 1993). Risk is at its most extreme if the path of change is sequenced such that none of the benefits of transformation are reaped until every step of the path has been successfully completed. Risk is more easily managed if it can be confined to individual steps (Yetton et al., 1995).

The RTA's path helped it manage the risks it faced. The substantial benefits in multi-skilling and restructuring the registries meant that risk was reduced because these steps were not dependent on the success of DRIVES. Risks associated with the technology step were managed in part through the CEO's active support for the project. That support was a natural consequence of DRIVES' being an integral part of the RTA's strategy of improving quality of service. Had the strategic benefits of DRIVES been purely emergent, that is, had strategy only appeared last in the path in Figure 2, then it is likely that the risks of such an innovative project would have been harder to manage.

The RTA case demonstrates the importance of the order in which organizations undertake change to change the old organizational order. It shows advantages to sequences of change which vary from the top-down path. In particular, sequences which yield pay-offs independent of the technology and which permit important learning to take place prior to implementation reduce the burden of learning and risk associated with implementation.

Questions for Discussion

1. What was DRIVES' strategic importance to the RTA in 1989?

2. What is the value of changing structure, roles and skills before technology?

3. Why were so many benefits emergent rather than planned?

4. How did the order in which the RTA undertook change help it to manage its risks?

5. Is the RTA's experience transferable to the private sector?

Endnotes
[1] The author is grateful to Wendy Jones for her part in researching and writing up the case on which this chapter is based.

[2] While DRIVES savings are $A20 million per annum, $A2 million is usually subtracted as the cost of maintaining the system.

References

Abdel-Hamid, T.K. (1993). A multi-project perspective on single-project dynamics. *Journal of Systems and Software,* 22, pp. 151-165.

Burn, C.J. (1994). A "R"evolutionary stage growth model of information systems planning. In J.I. DeGross, Huff, S.L. & Munro, M.C. (Eds.), *Proceedings of the 15th Annual International Conference on Information Systems* (pp. 395-406). Vancouver, BC.

Ciborra, C.U. (1991). From thinking to tinkering: The grassroots of strategic information systems. In J.I. DeGross, Benbasat, I., DeSanctis, G. & Beath, C.M. (Eds.), *Proceedings of the Twelfth International Conference on Information Systems* (pp. 283-291). New York.

Davenport, T.H. (1993). *Process innovation: Reengineering work through information technology.* Boston, Mass: Harvard Business School Press.

Ein-Dor, P., & Segev, E. (1981). *A paradigm for management information systems.* New York: Praeger.

Hammer, M., & Champy, J. (1993). *Reengineering the corporation: A manifesto for business revolution.* New York: Harper Collins.

Henderson, J.C. & Venkatraman, N. (1992). Strategic alignment: A model for organizational transformation through information technology. In T. Kochan, & Useem, M. (Eds.), *Transforming organizations,* (pp.97-117). New York: Oxford University Press.

Keen, P.G.W. (1981). Information systems and organizational change. *Communications of the ACM,* 24 (1), pp. 24-33.

Scott Morton, M. (1988). Strategy formulation methodologies and IT. In M.J. Earl (Ed.), *Information management: The strategic dimension.* (pp. 54-67) Oxford: Clarendon Press.

Scott Morton, M. (1991) (Ed.). *The corporation of the 1990s: Information technology and organizational transformation.* Oxford: Oxford University Press.

Walton, R.E. (1989). *Up and running: Integrating information technology and the organization.* Boston, Mass: Harvard Business School Press.

Yetton, P.W., Johnston, K.D. & Craig, J.F. (1994). Computer-aided architects: a case study of IT and strategic change. *Sloan Management Review,* 35 (4), pp. 57-67.

Yetton, P.W., Craig, J.F. & Johnston, K. (1995). Fit, simplicity and risk: Multiple paths to strategic IT change, In J.I. DeGross, Ariav, G., Beath, C., Hoyer, R. & Kemerer, C. (Eds.), *Proceedings of the Sixteenth International Conference on Information Systems.* (pp. 1-11). Amsterdam, Netherlands.

Chapter 6

Costs and Benefits of Software Engineering in Product Development Environments

Sorel Reisman
California State University, Fullerton

Executive Summary

A computer-based cost benefit (CBFM) forecasting model was developed to investigate possible long term effects of improved productivity that might be realized from the use of modern software engineering tools. The model was implemented in the development environment of Company X, a multinational corporation that manufactures embedded processor based control system products. The primary purpose of the model was to generate comparative data to answer "what if" questions posed by senior corporate management attempting to understand possible overall effects of introducing the new software development methodologies. The model provided comparative data regarding programmer labor costs, probably this company's most visible yet least understood line item in their monthly status reports. For Company X, the assumptions that were used to develop the CBFM were tailored to senior management's own priorities. Hence the model produced comparative summaries that ultimately allowed Company X to make the decision to begin implementing new software engineering strategies for product development.

Background

Information technology plays an important role in the survival of an organization (Drucker, 1988). Coupled with the plummeting costs of computer hardware, it becomes a vital source for deriving efficient and cost effective solutions to many of today's business problems. A well managed information system enhances a firm's ability to compete favorably and it minimizes the assumptions and guesswork in decision making that could lead to unsatisfactory performance.

In many companies information technology also shapes the process of product development (Abdel-Hamid, 1990). Organizations that are able to adapt new information technologies into their development process have often seen increased productivity and improvements in product quality. Many companies have investigated the utility of such information based processes as CASE (Computer Assisted Software Engineering) methodologies, hoping to realize faster product development cycles, shorter production schedules, higher quality products, and lower overheads.

The cost of software development systems, like any information systems, stems directly from the cost of the resources required to provide and support the functions of the systems. The adoption of software development methodologies can be a serious strategic change. Therefore, "before management can support [software engineering] tool implementation, it must have a realistic understanding of the costs and benefits of the tools (Smith & Oman, 1990). Cost benefit analyses usually weigh the relationships between the costs and values of a system (Ein Dor & Jones, 1985). Like any capital investment, the benefits must exceed the costs to justify the expense.

The economics of software engineering has often focused on software cost estimation, essentially a consideration of the costs related to single development projects. For example, software cost estimation techniques and models have tended to link software development costs to a project's size, its functional complexity, manpower requirements, and ultimately to the duration of the software development. Examples include SLIM (Putnam, 1980), COCOMO (Boehm, 1981), Function Point Analysis (Dreger, 1989), ESTIMACS, and Price S (Kemerer, 1987).

Because the successful implementation of software development tools requires a critical shift in senior management philosophy, it is essential to be able to justify the upheaval likely to result from these shifts. Within corporate environments such a justification is usually based on economic issues and related benefits, i.e., a sound business case. The economics of justifying these new methodologies to senior management requires a more global view of their costs and benefits than is typically found in the more detailed techniques mentioned above. That view must cut across projects, and focus on the effects of the methodologies on the totality of the development environment. In fact, as software engineering products (e.g., CASE tools) evolve into more integrated systems, they should begin more and more to address the needs of all phases of the system development life cycle.

For companies that may consider software engineering as a process that can improve the development of their own marketable products, a commitment to it should require the cooperative involvement from such diverse areas of the organization as sales, marketing, and customer service. For companies that instead consider that the methodologies may benefit their own internal systems development, the effect on the companies' own internal end user community can be substantial. In either event, the decision to employ these methodologies requires unified agreement within the infrastructure of the organization to support the new practices. (See for example, Cash, 1986; Gibson & Huges, 1994; McClure, 1989; McCleod, 1994; Statland, 1986.)

Setting The Stage

Often, because of time limitations, newness of technology, or simply because of a lack of industry knowledge and/or experience, senior management will base strategic decisions on global factors that relate only indirectly to the issue being considered. Consequently, in preparing the justifying business case for implementing new systems, it is important that accurate, appropriate, but most of all relevant factors be presented to senior management. Because relevant factors are primarily concerned with costs and revenues, a justification that can be quantified in that perspective will likely be better received by senior management. While it can be argued that implementing new software engineering methodologies will result in improved product quality (McGrath et al., 1992; Taylor, 1992), it may be very difficult to convince senior management of the appropriateness of those arguments to their own career objectives within the corporate environment.

Nonetheless, arguments based on reduced costs resulting directly from improved developer productivity are more easily understood if the reduced costs are associated with improved productivity. And because the single largest cost factor in most development environments is labor, schemes to reduce that cost without negatively impacting on product quality and schedules will certainly receive significant management attention.

Such was the case with Company X, a U.S. based subsidiary of a European multinational corporation that develops and markets high technology, embedded microprocessor based process control products which are distributed throughout the world. The company, which has been in business for more almost 25 years, is obligated to maintain and update the software that is resident in those products for years after they are first shipped. In addition to software maintenance, the company's 100 software engineers continue to develop new products, but without using modern software development tools. In fact, by 1994 almost 40% of all software developers were assigned full time to maintaining existing products while only 60% were developing new ones.

For the previous five years Company X experienced a constant shift of resources into software maintenance, generally an activity that tended to produce almost no incremental revenue. In order to sustain a consistently growing revenue stream, Company X's strategic plan called for the introduction of new products over a five year period. Resource forecasts for the development of those products indicated that unless significant changes were made in the way that products were developed, the total number of software engineers that would be required to work on new products, and maintain old and new ones would become untenable. Clearly a change was required.

The planning division of Company X decided to investigate the utility of modern integrated software engineering methodologies and tools as a solution to this problem. To accomplish this, they developed a cost benefit forecasting model (CBFM) to allow them to explore, project, and compare the costs and effects of introducing such software engineering tools, tailored to their own development environment, focusing on senior management's particular concerns. The specific objective was to determine whether or not acquiring and implementing new software engineering tools could result in reduced long term development and maintenance costs. Except by implication, the quality of developed products was not addressed in the model. The model was used to analyze alternative scenarios to consider the consequences of Company X's decision to invest in software engineering methodologies as well as CASE products. The CBFM did eventually provide the basis for this company's commitment to new software development tools and practices.

In planning the design of the CBFM, an analysis of Company X's historical product development plans revealed that the cost element that most greatly affected their development budgets was software engineer (developer) headcount. This finding was consistent across all the company's development projects in all its development centers, irrespective of the kinds of products developed as well as the countries in which the centers were located. Consequently, it was decided that since this "variable" was one that was most easily controlled in terms of the company's own recruiting/layoff policies, it would also be a major variable in the cost benefit forecasting considerations.

An examination of the mix of employee titles, seniority, and job responsibilities across Company X's development projects revealed relative uniformity that, for the sake of forecasting, allowed all software engineers to be classified into two categories, those who participated in the development of new code and those who participated in the maintenance of existing code. It was felt that the "sensitivity level" of analyses needed to make the kinds of decisions that were required, precluded the need to differentiate among job categories in greater detail. As a result, developer headcount became the dependent variable upon which other variables were based. These included salary, overhead, training, and workstation (hardware and software) costs.

In keeping with Company X's need for a global view of cost estimating for software engineering justification, the development environment was considered to consist of any number of projects, all of which would eventually utilize the new methodologies and tools. In other words, the CBFM was considered to be a company wide consolidation of single project cost benefit estimates.

Case Description

The cost benefit model that was developed was used to compare and contrast two scenarios over a user definable forecast period. The first was the "no change" scenario. No change implied that current practices would continue and that no drastic changes in the development environment would occur. The second scenario was the "if change" situation. In the context of the model this meant that software engineering products would be introduced into the organization in the first year and would result in a need for additional expenditures; there would also be immediate and long term effects derived from the use of the tools. The extra expenditures would be used for new or additional hardware and software as well as to provide more and ongoing training. Implied benefits that would result from the use of the new tools were considered to be related to improved efficiency of new code development, improved quality of software, and a subsequent improvement in the efficiency of software maintenance.

The CBFM that was developed was independent of any particular software engineering products or processes. Its design was based upon Company X management's appreciation of the overall benefits and conditions that could prevail within their software development environment if software engineering tools were introduced into the organization.

Status of the Case

The appendix in this chapter details the characteristics, parameters, and equations that were defined and utilized in the implementation of the Cost Benefit Forecasting Model. Based on these, the CBFM was implemented and used i) to analyze the software development environment for Company X, and ii) to justify the company's strategic decision to adopt software engineering products and methodologies.

Table 1 summarizes the current status (Known Values) of Company X. Table 2 lists the Assumed Values necessary to use the CBFM to model Company X.

Current year:	$n = 1995$
Total development personnel headcount:	$HT_0 = 100$
Average per capita cost for development staff:	$C_0 = \$.11M$
Ratio of maintenance/total headcount:	$M = .4$

Table 1: Current Status of Company X

Annual Average Headcount Growth:	$R = 5\%$ Annual
Average Inflation Rate:	$I = 4\%$ Annual
Average Change in Maintenance/Total Headcount:	$S = +2\%$

Table 2: Assumed Changes During Forecast Period

YEAR	NON MAINT H.C. (HD$_n$)	MAINT H.C. (HMn)	TOTAL H.C. (HT$_n$)	LABOR COST (M$) (C$_n$)	TOTAL LABOR (M$) (CT$_n$)
1995	60	40	100	0.11	11.00
1996	61	44	105	0.11	12.01
1997	62	49	110	0.12	13.12
1998	63	53	116	0.12	14.32
1999	63	58	122	0.13	15.64
			GRAND TOTAL:		$66.09

Table 3: Five Year "No Change" Forecast

"No Change" Forecast

Using the "no change" formulas shown in Figure 2, the effects of the data shown in Tables 1 and 2 were forecast. Table 3 contains that forecast and illustrates that after five years Company X will have spent more than $66 million on development personnel. By 1999 there will be 22 additional software engineers of which 18 will be assigned to software maintenance! This increase can be expected to result from the assignment of more programmers to support new, poorly designed code developed from 1995-1999.

"If Change" Forecast

To compare and contrast the effects of introducing new methodologies into Company X, it was necessary to presume some of the likely benefits that the company would realize. For the sake of this analysis it was assumed that as a result of the new practices, the proportion of programmers working on maintenance projects would decrease at a rate of 2% over five years (S= 2%).

Over the five year period Company X must continue to develop new products in order to remain competitive or even to avoid being shut down! To do this, the company would have to hire new programmers, all of whom will use the new tools and methodologies. As their proficiency with the new tools grows, so will their coding efficiency. This efficiency would begin to level off in the third or fourth year.

As newly developed products are released into the marketplace, those new products would constitute a growing percentage of products requiring maintenance. However, because of the improved quality of those products, programmers responsible for their maintenance should be able to perform with increasing efficiency. Table 4 illustrates one set of hypothetical efficiency trends that might be expected.

As described above, improvements in efficiency come about as a consequence of additional expenditures in hardware, software, and a continuing training program. Table 5 contains a set of values that would be associated with these items.

Based on the efficiency improvement factors and the additional costs inherent in introducing new software engineering practices, CBFM recalculated the additional costs to be realized over the forecast period. Table 6 indicates that after five years Company X will have spent an additional $3.71 million to implement new software engineering products and methodologies.

However, the efficiencies of the new practices provide significant benefits in terms of headcount cost savings that will result from the efficiencies assumed in Table 4. Table 7 illustrates the effects of those efficiencies. A comparison of this table with the "no change" forecast shown in Table 3 reveals

YEAR	NEW CODE EFFICIENCY(%) (QNn)	MAINTENANCE EFFICIENCY(%) (QMn)
1995	0	0
1996	10	8
1997	20	16
1998	25	25
1999	30	30

Table 4: Efficiency Improvement Rates

1. New Hardware And Software

New Hardware Cost per capita:	CH = \$7,500
New Software Cost per capita:	CS = \$4,000
Initial Equipment Replacement Rate:	E_0 = E_1 = 50%
Annual Equipment Upgrade Rate:	E_n = 15% (n = 2,3,4)
Depreciation Schedule:	D_0 = 12.5; D1 = 25
	D_2 = 25; D_3 = 25; D_4 = 12.5%

2. Training

Weekly Training Cost:	WTC = \$2,200
Initial Training Period:	NT = 2.5 weeks
Steady State Training Period:	ST = 1.5 weeks
Headcount after Attrition:	B = 90%

Table 5: Associated Cost Factors

YEAR	EQUIPMENT COST (M\$)	TRAINING COST (M\$)	TOTAL COST (M\$)
1995	0.42	0.55	0.97
1996	0.50	0.34	0.85
1997	0.26	0.32	0.59
1998	0.32	0.34	0.66
1999	0.30	0.35	0.64
TOTAL	\$1.80	\$1.90	\$3.71

Table 6: Costs of New Methodologies

that there is approximately \$12 million saving in personnel reduction and costs due to the new efficiencies (\$66.09 million versus \$54.27 million). Furthermore, as Table 8 illustrates, in the fifth year a larger percentage of all developers will be assigned to non-maintenance programming tasks.

Table 9 illustrates the total budgetary comparison of the "no change" versus "if change" scenarios. An examination of the data reveals that over the five year period Company X would realize a savings of more than \$8 million dollars. However, it is likely that during the first two years, when large capital outlays are more obvious than gains in productivity, that senior management may view

YEAR	NON MAINT H.C. (HDn)	MAINT H.C (HMn)	TOTAL H.C. (HTn)	TOTAL (M$) (CTn)
1995	60	40	100	11.00
1996	59	37	96	10.98
1997	56	33	89	10.59
1998	57	30	87	10.76
1999	58	27	85	10.94
			TOTAL:	$54.27

Table 7: Five Year "If Change" Forecast

YEAR	HEADCOUNT REDUCTION	NO CHANGE MAINT RATIO	IF CHANGE MAINT RATIO
1995	0	.40	.40
1996	9	.42	.36
1997	21	.45	.37
1998	29	.46	.34
1999	37	.48	.32

Table 8: Headcount Comparison

YEAR	NO CHANGE HEADCOUNT TOTAL (M$)	IF CHANGE HEADCOUNT TOTAL (M$)	OTHER TOTAL (M$)	ANNUAL TOTAL (M$)	TOTAL SAVINGS (M$)
1995	11.00	11.00	0.97	11.97	(0.97)
1996	12.01	10.98	0.85	11.83	0.18
1997	13.12	10.59	0.59	11.18	1.94
1998	14.32	10.76	0.66	11.42	2.90
1999	15.64	10.94	0.64	11.58	4.06
TOTAL:	66.09	54.27	3.71	57.98	8.11

Table 9: Overall Budget Comparison

the introduction of the new practices at best, with suspicion, and at worst, with outright hostility. However, if the storm can be weathered for those two years, dramatic improvements start to be realized at the end of the third year.

Successes and Failures

CBFM, which is essentially a Decision Support System (DSS) was designed to permit Company X analysts to quantify categorized, anecdotal benefits of software engineering practices and products, particularly CASE tools. The value of the model lay in the ease with which the effect of "programmer productivity" on the company's software engineering labor force could be examined. Users of the model did not require a substantial detailed database, but instead could intuitively incorporate their own knowledge base into assumptions necessary to use the model. CBFM required the analysts to quantify such issues in terms of a straightforward, multi-year software developer productivity profile from which they could quickly determine the effects of their assumptions. Furthermore, the level at which the model analyzed data and reported its results was oriented specifically to the interests and concerns of senior corporate management in Company X.

One of the major limitations of CBFM was that it only focused on costs associated with specific activities within specific phases of the traditional system development life cycle that involved software engineers. The model did not address issues and the related costs that might be associated with integrating software engineering methodologies across all dimensions of the corporate structure.

In fact, until we are better able to articulate what those issues are, it will be extremely difficult to understand the cost implications of corporate-wide adoption of software engineering practices. Orlikowski (1993) conducted a study of two corporations in order to address this problem and developed a theoretical framework that reflects the corporate complexities involved in this problem. Huff (1992) developed a budget framework which emphasizes the entire life cycle costs for CASE adoption. However, even ignoring the fact that this is a work in development, using the framework requires the selection of particular environmental-specific cost drivers.

CBFM was really concerned with a subset of such cost drivers— those related to costs and benefits of acquiring and using software engineering products rather than fully integrated systems and practices. In any case, until and unless fully integrated software engineering products become standard, practical, and cost effective, there is probably no real value in attempting to develop a computerized cost benefit model that considers "soft" costs that may perhaps one day, in some utopian environment be relevant to software development.

In its current form, one could argue that CBFM lacks precision. For example, the model does not distinguish among different levels of programmer. If it did, it might be argued that the introduction of modern software engineering tools may effect the productivity of experienced, senior programmers differently than that of inexperienced, junior programmers. Modification of this model to include more than one level of programmer would not be difficult. However, requiring an analyst to provide such a model with a different multi year productivity profile for each programmer level might prove to be a terribly onerous chore with questionable, if not diminishing returns for the effort.

Another dimension of precision not inherent in the design of this CBFM is consideration of analyses on a project by project basis. For example, as described in this chapter, the CBFM for Company X was used to compare overall effects of development resources under the "if change" and "no change" scenarios. More precise results might have been be forthcoming if, for example, equivalent analyses had been performed on a project by project basis, then consolidated into a corporate aggregate.

A similar argument might be made regarding the fact the CBFM used the same assumptions across all Company X development centers. It did not consider that there might be individual differences from center to center based on such factors as geographical, cultural, local economic, or even historical differences.

Finally, it might be argued that the model's lack of facilities to enable analysts to explicitly quantify those intuitive issues discussed earlier in this chapter were a drawback to its utility. For example, the model did not explicitly address the difficult learning curves associated with the introduction of new software development tools. It did not specifically address realities of vendor products that include poor product support, inadequate documentation, buggy products, ever-changing standards, etc. Certainly, if the model had contained such quantifiable measures within a useful analytical paradigm, it would have been able to assist analysts in focusing on issues that lie at the heart of many of the controversies that have surrounded software engineering.

Despite the absence of these or other related factors, from a practical standpoint it remains to be seen whether or not the inclusion of such items would have produced substantially different results from the current model. And herein lies another drawback to this CBFM, either in its current form or as it might be extended. Any model requires validation through the use of real data from real environments. At the present time, considering the lack of uniformity of software engineering practices within the software development community, the kinds of data required to validate this model are simply unavailable. Despite the widespread accessibility of products such as CASE tools, many companies are unwilling to divulge the proprietary competitive advantage that their software development methodologies have provided them. Could it be that they are unwilling to confess to the difficulties and failures they have experienced?

Epilogue and Lessons Learned

The cost benefit forecasting methods described in this chapter were developed to investigate possible long term effects of improved productivity that might be realized from the use of modern software engineering tools. A computer based forecasting model was designed based upon the development environment of Company X, a multinational corporation that manufactures embedded processor-based control system products. The primary purpose of the model was to generate comparative data to answer "what if" questions posed by senior corporate management attempting to understand possible overall effects of introducing the new methodologies. The strengths of this particular analytical approach are reflected in the fact that the model provided comparative data regarding programmer labor costs, probably this company's most visible yet least understood line item in their monthly status reports. For Company X, the assumptions that were used to develop the CBFM were tailored to senior management's own priorities, hence the model produced comparative summaries that allowed Company X to make the decision to begin implementing new strategies for product development.

Improving productivity through automation is an excellent method of cost control. Automation, a proven, cost effective approach in many production and manufacturing environments can be extended to support software production (Levy, 1987). Until recently, system developers have been so caught up in automating users' systems that they have completely overlooked their own (Case, 1986). In addition, some practitioners have perceived systems development as an art that cannot be crafted by machines. However, as economic factors begin to impose on the development process, there becomes an increasing need to automate labor-intensive activities and processes.

New products and methodologies extend software development through automation. Like most automated systems, these systems provide tremendous potential to reduce the costs of labor by increasing development productivity while at the same time enhancing product reliability. The fundamental concept is to support the various phases of the system development life cycle with an integrated set of labor saving tools.

But do these new techniques really work? It is too early to come to a firm conclusion one way or the other. The adoption of the new systems does not always assure success. Some testimonies that report a positive impact of CASE products have been quite encouraging (McClure, 1989) while other reports have been mixed (Taft, 1989). There are similar debates regarding Rapid Application Development (Gordon & Bieman, 1995) as well as other software development related matters (Andriole, 1995). One of the reasons for this may be attributed to the current nature of the products. But as the technology evolves, product shortcomings that include inadequate functionality or integration will be resolved.

Another and perhaps more serious problem may be management related. In some instances there may be a misunderstanding about what certain software engineering products can or cannot accomplish. For example, corporate management may view CASE tools as the ultimate software development solution while neglecting to correct deficiencies in project management practices. Reasons for failure may also be due to a lack of training or to poor enforcement of existing development methodologies and standards.

Product such as CASE tools should not be promoted on the basis of the merits of their technology. Instead, they should be considered as an investment that has the potential to address the problem of the rising costs of software production and maintenance. Toward this end, the implementation of new software engineering methodologies must offer a company economic justification. In the absence of mechanisms to project the costs and benefits of these technologies, it is difficult to demonstrate such justification. Until there is broad, cross industry experience upon which deterministic decisions can be made, the cost benefit forecasting models such as those used for Company X are tools that can be used to narrow the options.

Questions for Discussion

1. What are some of the pros and cons a company can expect from adopting formal software engineering methods?

2. If a software development organization does not adopt software engineering methods, what kinds of changes can it expect to see over the next few years?

3. What, if anything, is unique about using cost-benefit analyses to determine whether or not to adopt software engineering methods?

4. Are there cost-benefit methodologies that can be mechanistically applied to any organization to ascertain accurately the costs and resultant benefits of adopting software engineering methods?

5. In this case, what were the main cost drivers chosen by Company X, and why?

Appendix

The Case Cost Benefit Model

This section describes the characteristics and parameters that were developed to forecast and analyze alternative scenarios for Company X. The model and its description are relevant to any organization that is in need of making similar decisions, provided that the organization accepts the assumptions made by Company X.

The model is based upon a five year period ($n = 0, 1, 2, 3, 4$) for which comparative headcount and related costs are forecasted. Known values for the initial baseline condition must be set. As in the case of Company X, these values can be determined from an operating or strategic plan. A second set of "assumed" values is required to forecast the effect of natural changes that might take place during the forecast period, whether or not new software engineering methodologies are introduced. Figure 1 lists the required parameters.

1. Known Values

Total Development Personnel Headcount:	HT_0
Average per Capita Cost for Development Staff ($):	C_0
Ratio of Maintenance/Total Headcount:	M

2. Assumed Values

Annual Average Headcount Growth (%):	R
Annual Average Inflation Rate (%):	I
Annual Average Change in the Ratio of Maintenance/Total Headcount (%):	S

Figure 1: Initial Forecast Values

Initial Maintenance Headcount:	$HM_0 = M \cdot HT_0$
Total Headcount in Year n:	$HT_n = HT_0 \cdot (1 + R)^n$
Maintenance Headcount in Year n:	$HM_n = HM_0 \cdot (1 + S)^n$
Non Maintenance Headcount in Year n:	$HD_n = HTn - HM_n$
Per capita Labor Cost in Year n ($):	$C_n = C_0 \cdot (1 + I)^n$
Total Labor Cost in Year n ($):	$CT_n = HT_n \cdot C_n$
Maintenance Cost in Year n ($):	$CM_n = HM_n \cdot C_n$
Non Maintenance Cost in Year n ($):	$CD_n = CT_n - CM_n$

Figure 2: Resource Forecasting Relationships

The model assumes that the initial and ongoing average per capita developer cost (C_0) is the fully burdened cost. That is, it includes salary, benefits, overhead, etc.

Organizations that investigate the use of new, software engineering tools are often concerned with the ever-increasing problem of maintaining older or poorly designed code. As these systems age, the need for maintenance developers to upgrade or fix bugs can become overwhelming. Setting a positive value for the variable S (in Figure 1) will reflect that situation.

The "No Change" Condition

For the "no change" situation, the variables shown in Figure 1 can be used in the formulae shown in Figure 2 to calculate the total annual headcount and labor costs as well as the ratio of headcount allocated to maintenance versus the headcount allocated to the development of new code.

These relationships permit the following items to be forecast:

• Annual headcount and cost of maintenance developers.
• Annual headcount and cost of new code (non maintenance) developers.
• Total annual headcount and cost.
• Total headcount expenditure over the forecast period.

The "If Change" Condition

In order to examine the "if change" condition it is necessary to consider the benefits that software engineering methodologies can provide as well as the additional cost factors necessary to bring about those benefits.

The Benefits of Software Engineering

Productivity gains that should be realized from the application of new methodologies suggest that their use will alter the ratio of maintenance to new-code developer headcount. It should also improve the *productivity* of all developers. These effects can be shown in two ways.

First, there may be the opportunity to reduce the number of developers assigned to software maintenance. Within the model such a change can be explored by setting the variable S to a negative value. This variable is the annual average change of the ratio of maintenance headcount to total headcount; a positive value reflects growth and a negative value indicates shrinkage.

Secondly, there should be an improvement in the productivity of all developers whether they are developing new code or whether they are involved in maintaining newly developed and easier-to-maintain code that will eventually enter the maintenance phase of the system development life cycle.

The model reflects both of these possibilities through the definition of productivity improvement variables, QN_n and QM_n. These variables may be used to define the yearly efficiency improvement pattern or trend of both new code development and code maintenance. For each of the forecast years, the following may be set;

New Code Efficiency Improvement (%): $QN_0, QN_1,... QN_4$
Maintenance Efficiency Improvement (%): $QM_0, QM_1,... QM_4$

On an annual basis, the effect of these variables would be to reduce the total number of maintenance and new code developers, each by the percentage indicated by QN_n or QMn.

The Costs of The New Practices

There are two major costs that the implementation of new tools introduces. These are i) the cost of new equipment (hardware and software), and ii) the cost to train and retrain all development personnel.

Hardware and Software Costs. The decision to implement new tools is likely to result in a number of additional expenses that would otherwise not need to be borne. One of the more significant costs is for the purchase of new workstation equipment that can effectively capitalize on the functions available in modern software engineering tools. There will also be the cost of the new software itself.

In a development environment it is simply not realistic to insist that all developers or all ongoing projects convert immediately to the new systems. So, while conversion must be an evolutionary process, the implementation of new systems also requires a considerable and immediate commitment by management. The forecasting model reflects the need for that commitment by assuming that there will be substantial hardware and software acquisition in the first two years. Thereafter, a proportionally smaller expense relating to such factors as hardware/software upgrade or maintenance will be required annually.

Equipment costs are determined by setting the following values:
- New Hardware Cost per capita ($): CH
- New Software Cost per capita ($): CS
- Initial Equipment Replacement Rate (%): E_0, E_1
- Subsequent) Annual Equipment Upgrade Rate (%): E_n (n = 2, 3, 4)
- Annual Hardware Depreciation Schedule (%): $D_0, D_1, ... D_4$

A logical constraint on the sum of the replacement rates (E_n) and the total depreciation (D_n) over the forecast period is that each sum must be less than or equal to 100%. Depreciation rates should be determined on the basis of the organization's financial policies.

Using these constants, CE_n, the annual expenditure for equipment (software, hardware, and maintenance) can be calculated for all development headcount (HT_n) as:

$$CE_n = HT_n \cdot E_n \cdot (CS + CH \cdot D_n)$$

The total equipment cost, TCE, over the forecast period is:

$$TCE = CE_0 + CE_1 + CE_2 + CE_3 + CE_4$$

Training Costs. Another cost that will be incurred when new software development tools and methodologies are introduced into an organization is for the retraining of existing personnel. The model assumes that initially, all currently employed developers will require a significant amount of new training (NT), the costs of which must be borne by the organization. CBFM assumes that in the first year there will be an extensive training program for all developers. Thereafter, all previously trained employees will continue to require annual training, but to a lesser degree (ST).

The model also considers that of the total pool of developers there will be an annual attrition rate. Given the realities of the employment marketplace for experienced software engineers it must be assumed that there will be a steady annual influx of less experienced developers. These replacement personnel, as well as other newly hired developers will require a greater amount of training in their first year than they will in subsequent years.

In order to calculate the costs associated with these training requirements, the following values are required:

- Present Value of Weekly Training Cost ($): WTC
- Initial Training Period (weeks): NT
- Steady State Training Period (weeks): ST
- Remaining Headcount after Attrition (%): B

Annual training costs can be calculated as the cost to train all new employees plus the cost to train the replacement employees; additional costs must be borne to train, but to a lesser degree, all previously hired employees. If HT_n is the headcount total for year n, then the annual training cost (ATCn) can be shown to be:

In the first year:

$$ATC_0 = WTC \cdot NT \cdot HT_0$$

In subsequent years (i.e. n > 0):

$$ATC_n = WTC \bullet [\, NT \bullet (HT_n - HT_{n-1}) + ST \bullet B \bullet HT_{n-1}\,]$$

Total Costs

The consequence of undertaking the use of new software engineering tools will be an ongoing training program as well as the continued acquisition of new hardware and software. The annual total cost (TAC) associated with these new and additional expenditures is:

$$TAC_n = ATC_n + CE_n$$

Because software engineering methodologies are intended to provide long term benefits to an organization, it is unrealistic to expect immediate cost savings in the early years of the program. In fact, because of the extra expenditure required, it is more likely that in the early years the "if change" scenario will cost more than the "no change" scenario. Because of this it is more useful to examine and compare the total expenditure over the five year period.

References

Abdel-Hamid, T.K. (1990). Investigating the cost/schedule trade-off in software development. *IEEE Software*, 7 (1), 97-105.

Andriole, S. J. (1995). Debatable development: what should we believe? *IEEE Software*, 12 (40), 13-18.

Boehm, B.W. (1981). *Software Engineering Economics*. Prentice-Hall: Englewood Cliffs, New Jersey.

Case, A. F., Jr. (1986). *Information Systems Development: Principles of Computer-Aided Software Engineering*. Prentice-Hall, Englewood Cliffs, New Jersey.

Cash, J. I, Eccles, R. G., Nohria, N., and Nolan, R. L. (1994). *Building the Information-Age Organization: Structure, Control, and Information Technologies*. Richard D. Irwin, Inc., Boston.

Dreger, J. B. (1989). *Function Point Analysis*. Prentice-Hall, Englewood Cliffs, New Jersey.

Drucker, P. F. (1988). The coming of the new organization. *Harvard Business Review*, January-February 1988, 45-53.

Ein-Dor, P. and Jones, C. R. (1985). *Information Systems Management: Analytical Tools and Techniques*. Elsevier, New York.

Gibson, L. G. and Huges, C, T. (1994). *Systems Analysis and Design: A Comprehensive Methodology with CASE*. Boyd & Fraser, Danver Massachusetts.

Gordon, V. S., and Bieman, J. M. (1995). Rapid prototyping: lessons learned. *IEEE Software*, 12(1), 85-94.

Huff, C. C. (1992) Elements of a Realistic CASE Tool Adoption Budget. *Communications of the ACM*. April, 45-54.

Kemerer, C. F. (1987). An empirical validation of software cost estimation models. *Communications of the ACM*. May, 416-429.

Levy, L. S. (1987). *Taming the Tiger: Software Engineering and Software Economics*. Springer-Verlag, New York.

McClure, C. (1989). *CASE is Software Automation*. Prentice-Hall, Englewood Cliffs, New Jersey.

McLeod, R. (1994). *Systems Analysis an Design - An Organizational Approach*. The Dryden Press, Orlando.

McGrath, M. E., Anthony, M. T., & Shapiro, A. R. (1992). *Product Development*, Butterworth-Heinemann, Stoneham, MA.

Orlikowski, W. J. (1993). CASE Tools as Organizational Change: Investigating Incremental and Radical Changes in Systems Development. *MIS Quarterly*, 17(3),

Putnam, L. H. (1980). *Tutorial, Software Cost Estimating and Life-Cycle Control: Getting the Software Numbers*, IEEE Computer Society, New York.

Smith, D. B. and Oman, P. W. (1990). Software In context. *IEEE Software,* 7(3),15-19.

Statland, N. (1986). *Controlling Software Development,* John Wiley & Sons, New York.

Taft, D. K. (1989). Four agencies using case tools get mixed results. *Government Computer News,* May 29, 37-38.

Taylor, D. A. (1992). *Object-oriented information systems planning and implementation,* John Wiley & Sons, New York.

Chapter 7

Implementing a Wide-Area Network at a Naval Air Station: A Stakeholder Analysis[1]

Susan Page Hocevar
Naval Postgraduate School

Barry A. Frew
Naval Postgraduate School

LCDR Virginia Callaghan Bayer
United States Navy

Executive Summary

The Naval Air Systems Team is an organization wishing to capitalize on the benefits derived from connecting geographic stakeholders using wide–area network technologies. The introduction of common email, file transfer, and directory services among these organizations is envisioned as a significant enabler to improve the quality of their aggregate product. At the same time this organization has decided to transform itself from a traditional functionally hierarchic organization to a competency based organization. The new model introduces a modified matrix organization consisting of integrated program teams at twenty–two geographically separate sites in the United States. This case study illustrates the use of a non–traditional approach to determine the requirements for the Naval Air Systems Team Wide–Area Network (NAVWAN). It is considered to be non–traditional because the case data enable the use of Stakeholder Analysis and SWOT (strengths, weaknesses, opportunities, threats) assessments to determine the requirements instead of asking functional proponents about function and data requirements. This is an action planning case. The case objective is to apply these methodologies and an understanding of organizational change to developing an action plan recommendation for implementation of a wide–area network.

Background

The Naval Air Systems Team (NAST) is the component of the United States Department of Defense that is responsible for delivering aircraft and related systems to be operated, based, and supported at sea. To that end, this organization employs 42,000 civilians and 4,500 military personnel[2] at commands and bases throughout the country. Examples of products provided by this organization include air anti–submarine warfare mission systems; aircraft and related systems for aircraft carriers; maritime and air launched and strike weapons systems; and training in the operation and maintenance of these systems.

In April 1992, NAST, then headed by Vice Admiral (VADM) William C. Bowes, initiated a significant organizational restructuring as part of a large–scale change effort to enhance organizational effectiveness. The structure changed from that of a traditional functional hierarchy to a Competency Aligned Organization (CAO) which is a modified matrix organization that established dedicated Integrated Program Teams located at twenty–two different sites across the country. These teams are comprised of personnel from relevant functional competencies and coordinate activities that often span multiple command locations. A wide–area network (WAN) was identified as a critical infrastructure requirement for the success of these teams.

VADM Bowes became the champion for the implementation of a Naval Air System Team Wide–Area Network (NAVWAN) system. He viewed this infrastructure upgrade as critical to the success of the Competency Aligned Organization. He established a Demonstration–Validation team to perform the systems analysis, design, and implementation of the NAVWAN. This team identified several prototype implementation sites to be used to both validate the functionality of the NAVWAN and provide data to support a full system implementation.

As part of this effort, the Validation Team sponsored a research effort to conduct a stakeholder analysis at one of the prototype implementation sites. This analysis was designed as an alternative to the traditional design phase for a new information system implementation. The Department of the Navy has traditionally used a waterfall method to design and implement new information system technologies. This method begins with a requirements analysis and is followed by design, coding, testing, and maintenance. The focus of the case study presented in this chapter is on the requirements analysis phase. In the requirements analysis phase, the traditional waterfall method would focus on identifying specific types of data the system would need to be able to manipulate and on the business functions being performed.

The data gathered and presented in this case are intended to provide an alternative methodology for requirements analysis and implementation planning. These data were derived from interviews with representatives of each of the critical stakeholders at this implementation site. This case changes the traditional requirements analysis focus from that of data and function for the waterfall method to that of broader stakeholder issues in the application being developed.

This is an action planning case. The data presented provide information that can be used to develop a set of recommendations to be presented to the Validation Team and ultimately to VADM Bowes regarding the NAVWAN, including: planning strategies; user requirements; implementation strategies and schedules; resource allocation; training strategies and schedules; and maintenance strategies. The task of the reader, at the close of this case, will be to generate the recommendations supported by this stakeholder analysis.

Setting the Stage: NAVWAN Prototype Implementation Site

The Miramar Naval Air Station (NAS) is located in Southern California just north of the city of San Diego. The Naval Air Station chain of command is similar to other air stations and includes a Commanding Officer, Executive Officer, Supply Officer, Aviation Intermediate Maintenance Officer, Administrative Officer, Security Officer, and a Staff Civil Engineer. At this base, there are also several tenant activities. Tenant activities have their own chain of command, but they are located at the NAS and they rely on the NAS to provide infrastructure support including supply, facilities maintenance, and administrative services. NAS Miramar and the tenant activities who are participating in the Naval Air Systems Team (NAST) are potential users of the NAVWAN. (An Organization Chart is presented in the Appendix .)

Stakeholders

A stakeholder is defined as an individual or group who can affect or is affected by the achievement of a given mission, objective, or change strategy (Freeman, 1984; Roberts & King, 1989). From the perspective of site–level implementation, NAST and the NAVWAN Demonstration–Validation Team represent external stakeholders. Internal stakeholders include the departments within NAS Miramar and the tenant activities. Each stakeholder and the general mission of their organization is presented below. While the Department of the Navy uses "alphabet soup" acronyms, a translated title for each of these stakeholders is presented in quotes and these will be used in the presentation of data in the case. The official organization title and acronym are also included:

(a) *Validation Team.* The NAVWAN Demonstration–Validation Team was established by VADM Bowes. This team is led by the Program Manager responsible for the NAVWAN implementation at Headquarters, Naval Air Systems Command [NAVAIRSYSCOM].

(b) *The Maintenance Office* is responsible for all aspects of naval aviation maintenance and administration programs [Naval Aviation Maintenance Office: NAMO]

(c) *The Maintenance Depot* provides intermediate level aviation maintenance support for Pacific Fleet aviation activities. Intermediate level maintenance reflects a more complex maintenance action that is beyond the capability of squadron and station organizations. [Naval Aviation Depot, NAS North Island: NADEP]

(d) *Pacific Region Aviation Command* promulgates policy and asset management direction to all Pacific Fleet aviation activities. [Commander, Naval Air Force, U.S. Pacific Fleet: CNAP]

(e) The *SUPPLY Department* is responsible for all logistic and supply support required by the squadrons and tenant activities of NAS Miramar.

(f) The *Intermediate Maintenance Department* is responsible for all intermediate maintenance services required by the squadrons at NAS Miramar. [Aviation Intermediate Maintenance Department, NAS Miramar: AIMD]

(g) The*ADMIN Department* is responsible for all postal and administrative services required by personnel of NAS Miramar and its tenant activities.

(h) The*Civil Engineering Department* is responsible for all facilities maintenance, construction, hazardous waste management, and environmental conservation required by NAS Miramar and its tenant activities.

(i) *Personnel* is the activity responsible for all personnel and disbursing functions for NAS Miramar and tenant activity personnel. [Personnel Support Activity Detachment, NAS Miramar: PSD]

(j) *Aviation Wing* are two aviation type wings that are responsible for administration of all operational, maintenance, and administrative support for the squadrons located at NAS Miramar. There is one stakeholder representative for both commands. [Commander Fighter Wing Pacific: COMFITWING; and Airborne Early Warning Wing Pacific: COMAEWWING]

(k) The*Engineering Support Facility* is the activity responsible for providing technical support and maintenance training to organizational activities throughout the Pacific Fleet. [Naval Aviation Engineering Support Unit: NAESU]

(l) The *Information Systems Department* is responsible for providing information technology support to NAS Miramar and tenant activities. [Information Systems Support Office, NAS Miramar: ISSO]

Status Quo

All NAS Miramar offices are currently connected to an Ethernet local area network (LAN). Each stakeholder has implemented LANs in an autonomous way and the systems used at stakeholder activities are not well integrated. These stakeholders have diverse missions and responsibilities. The NAVWAN is intended to be a conduit for communication at the local, metropolitan, and global levels. This improved communication will better support the information requirements of the Competency Aligned Organization. Also important is the improved integrated communication capabilities offered to the larger Navy organization.

Although their missions differ, many of the above listed stakeholders in the NAVWAN have similar information technology requirements. Because of the NAVWAN open systems architecture, stakeholders do not expect it to significantly constrain their mission accomplishment. In fact, all the stakeholders anticipated significant benefits from interconnectivity with an array of Department of Defense, federal, academic, and civilian organizations.

The technologies needed to support the NAVWAN are available. The only technology oriented concerns, therefore, are whether the correct combination of technologies can be determined, acquired, implemented and maintained within this culture and resource environment.

Project/Case Description

For purposes of gathering the data for this case, representatives of each of the stakeholder groups were individually interviewed in regard to the NAVWAN implementation.[3] Analyzing the stakeholders' perceptions regarding NAVWAN provides information valuable to the identification of requirements, the implementation design process, as well as predictions of the ultimate effectiveness of NAVWAN. The information outlined below highlights themes that emerged from the stakeholder interviews regarding NAVWAN implementation.

Overall, the stakeholders see benefits to NAVWAN that would initially include: broader more integrated electronic mail, file transfer, and directory services. Because of these benefits, the stakeholders are strongly motivated to employ the NAVWAN. They anticipate it will significantly increase user productivity over the long run. However, there are also barriers to the implementation of the NAVWAN at the prototype site. Stakeholders identified potential barriers and, in some cases, offered solutions. Knowledge of the benefits, barriers and recommendations identified by stakeholders at this site offers the Validation Team important information as they proceed with planning full system implementation.

Stakeholder Functional Requirements

Many of the stakeholder information technology functional requirements are common to all the stakeholders. Office automation, including word processing and file transfer, is required by all stakeholders. Each stakeholder currently has word processing capability; however, the variety of vendors and versions supporting this capability pose a challenge for documentation management among the activities. Communication tools, such as message traffic management, bulletin boards, database management, and electronic mail applications, are other common requirements for all stakeholders.

Several stakeholders require access to a database management system (DBMS). This access must include a structured query capability for ad hoc queries. Several stakeholders require decision support tools including spreadsheets and graphic presentation. A few stakeholders require access to three dimensional graphics and access to technical CAD/CAM drawings. A few stakeholders require additional bandwidth in support of televideo conferencing. Some of these requirements are currently not being met and others are being supported by multiple LANs, electronic mail packages, modem connections, postal service, and voice mail.

Stakeholder Knowledge of Planned Capabilities of NAVWAN

At the time the interviews were conducted, nine of the twelve stakeholders had a clear understanding of the initial capabilities of the NAVWAN . Three stakeholder groups had direct representation on the Validation Team led by the NAVWAN program manager: Maintenance Office, Maintenance Depot, and Pacific Region Aviation Command. In addition, five of the remaining stakeholder groups had attended an orientation brief presented by the Validation Team. This briefing provided extensive information about the capabilities of the NAVWAN and the impending implementation at NAS Miramar.

The three stakeholders least familiar with NAVWAN were the Civil Engineering Department, Personnel, and the Engineering Support Facility. These groups were aware of the NAVWAN implementation plan but were not familiar with its specific capabilities. As information technology managers, these stakeholders had a clear understanding of wide–area connectivity, but they were not certain of the exact functionality the NAVWAN will provide.

Stakeholder Perceptions of NAVWAN Benefits

"Increased communication is the single most important thing to come out of the NAVWAN implementation. Next would be potential cost cutting from reduced phone use, and third is the potential Internet access." This quote from one stakeholder representative summarizes the most common response regarding potential NAVWAN benefits. Other stakeholders offered different ways in which increased communication through the WAN would offer benefits. The Engineering Support Facility representative stated the NAVWAN would "improve coordination with the headquarters and the customers at the squadron level." Several stakeholders explained the value in terms of quicker response time: "It will mean less delay in communication, quicker responses and approvals of work." The Pacific Region Aviation Command added,

"Communicating with all the wings at one time, vice sending individual correspondence or phoning them, will increase the speed, and there will be more communication. I believe this will help to prevent problems that occur when people are not informed."

Access to data was another benefit with multiple dimensions supported by several of the stakeholders. First, access to common databases will provide real–time information and reduce errors. According to the Engineering Support Facility representative, this should mean "less finger pointing and improved accountability of the information." The Maintenance Depot representative supported the benefit of improved integrity of data in the databases for logistics and aviation maintenance purposes. A related benefit, according to the Engineering Support Facility, would be improved, real–time technical advice that can contribute to such activities as the Integrated Logistics System Maintenance Training conferences, program management reviews, or investigations.

Cost cutting benefits were supported by several stakeholders who acknowledged savings due to decreased phone use, decreased travel requirements, and the potential for consolidation of support staffs. Regarding the latter, the Maintenance Depot representative commented, "Hopefully the NAVWAN will right–size the systems support staffs by consolidating everyone. There's too much duplication of effort by all the Automated Information System (AIS) staffs." Specifically cited were five information system staffs supporting organizations all closely located. This consolidation was seen as having an additional benefit, "The Navy needs economies of scale in purchasing hardware and software that we can't achieve unless we consolidate."

Elimination of paperwork, and progress toward a paperless Navy were benefits cited by the Personnel Activity representative: "We need to get rid of all the file cabinets." The Personnel Activity's goal is for all personnel records to be computerized and to electronically transfer records between commands. From their perspective, "The number one job of [Personnel] is to provide customer support. With WAN capability we will be able to improve customer service by responding more quickly."

The Intermediate Maintenance Department supported the value of NAVWAN to increased flexibility and responsiveness. He also plans to use NAVWAN to edit and endorse administrative paperwork. He identified an additional benefit by commenting, "It will solve the message traffic problems [on the Defense Message System (DMS)]; we'll be able to stop faxing people messages to make sure they got the stuff sent on DMS." While the Civil Engineer agreed NAVWAN would be an improvement over DMS, he added that the NAVWAN cannot replace DMS because it is not a secure network.

The assessment of the benefits of the NAVWAN from the perspective of the Validation Team emphasized "tangible cost reduction through circuit consolidation, reduced maintenance and support efforts, and improved configuration management." He also stated that "buying more capacity at a better price through economies of scale" would also reduce costs for all the NAVWAN users.

Stakeholder Perceptions of Barriers to Implementation

None of the stakeholders believed the implementation of the NAVWAN would significantly constrain the accomplishment of their functional requirements. Many stakeholders stated that most of their functional requirements are already met by other systems. As a result of the existing systems, the Aviation Wing representative explained that "point to point communication will help a lot, but you will have some duplication of effort until everyone is connected to the NAVWAN." Others felt the duplication may be more than transitional. Specifically, five stakeholder groups did not think elimination of these other systems would occur too easily because users are more familiar with the current system, and they believe existing systems are sufficient. These groups were the Information Systems Department, Maintenance Depot, Maintenance Office, ADMIN Department, and SUPPLY Department.

The issue of network security was raised by three stakeholders: Information Systems Department, ADMIN Department and the Aviation Wings. Each expressed concern that the potential for abuse and security risks would constrain the achievement of functional requirements using NAVWAN. They pointed out people could not use it for anything that is classified or of a sensitive nature. This would include a significant amount of message traffic. "People will still send messages [using DMS] for the important stuff, because that's the standard way of covering your six." ADMIN expressed a similar concern: "The need to protect sensitive information, such as investigations and HIV positive personnel management issues, still exists." The Maintenance Depot representative explored the security topic a bit further. "We are evaluating firewalls and filters, not necessarily to keep people from going out, but to keep other people from coming in."

While most stakeholder representatives stated NAVWAN use will increase productivity, they also expressed a concern that abuse of the system could be a productivity drain. "The temptation to surf all day on the Internet may be too great for some people."

Another concern about abuse of the NAVWAN was voiced by ADMIN who cautioned that people may use the NAVWAN to circumvent the chain of command. Implementing NAVWAN raises "power issues... not just communication issues." By implementing the NAVWAN, "the chain of command loses some power over their subordinates." The Intermediate Maintenance Department representative supported ADMIN stating, "they [senior officers in the chain of command] don't want you talking to anyone outside the chain of command."

A Validation Team representative confirmed the potential challenge that increased communication capability poses to the chain of command. "E-mail is a democratizing agent in the organization." If an airman wants to send the commanding officer E-mail, he can do so without asking his supervisor or division officer. In addition, the effective utilization of the NAVWAN may not be fully supported by commanding officers (COs) and executive officers (XOs) because "the CO and XO want to see it and touch it or edit it before you send anything...This slows down the process and defeats the purpose."

A different source of resistance to implementation was voiced by the Aviation Wing representative who had experienced a problem with the earlier implementation of the Local Area Network (LAN)

People really resisted the network at the start because they are not computer literate and they didn't want to change . . . they felt it would make their job harder, but they get over it once they understand... Many of the potential users still have computer phobia and feel the network is too hard, but then they realize that they have the power to reach out, touch a button, and go across the world.

Nearly every stakeholder agreed money is the single biggest barrier to the NAVWAN implementation. "We just don't have the money we need to support the LAN, let alone the NAVWAN" was the initial reaction of the Aviation Wing representative. Money also limits the technical capabilities of the type wings. This concern was reinforced by the Personnel Activity representative who stated their biggest barrier is "definitely money for the hardware, software, and training."

A Validation Team representative disagrees the greatest barrier is money. He says "it is not so much money itself, but the ability to direct the money; especially where personnel are concerned." From his perspective as the program manager, the development effort is heavily dependent on civil service personnel. He gets frustrated because "we can't hire and fire people as we would like, and we don't have the right mix of people. Eighty percent of the IT people are not involved and the twenty percent who are, don't have the time to dedicate to it."

The problem of dedicating time and manpower was confirmed by several stakeholder representatives. In the Information Systems Department, there are only four people and they are always putting out fires in other places. "We simply don't have the time or people to conduct the necessary training and perform the network administration, maintenance, and support." The Maintenance Depot representative agrees there are limited technical personnel and sufficient manpower resources dedicated to the NAVWAN project. The representative from the Pacific Region Aviation Command adds that because there are so few people, "the barrier to implementation becomes the schedule and workload priorities of the implementation team...There are conflicting priorities for the people working on it, and they have difficulty knowing where the resources are going to go."

A related constraint identified by several stakeholders is the inadequacy of resources. For example, the LAN at the Engineering Support Facility has limited size and capacity, with only five terminals. This limits their ability to communicate with all the regional offices as well as with technical representatives when they are traveling. The Maintenance Office representative expressed a concern regarding a different resource constraint. His concern is that the Validation Team responsible for implementing the NAVWAN does not have direct authority over people within the different stakeholder groups involved in the implementation. Because there are so many commands working together on this project, each with their own primary tasks, schedules, and resource priorities, NAVWAN may not get the attention it needs on critical issues of infrastructure coordination. He cited personal experience with this problem:

I have personally hooked up sites ahead of schedule because I needed them to be online and the infrastructure coordination problems could not be resolved. We had to do a lot of negotiating to get the support we need because the key people don't always work for us.

The representatives from both the Maintenance Depot and the Intermediate Maintenance Department concur. According to the former, "The rice bowls are difficult to overcome. People don't want to admit it, but they want to preserve their islands of communication." He believes people want to "put their own bridges into the NAVWAN, but they want to perpetuate isolated applications."

The Validation Team is also concerned about the political constraints against standardization.

Hopefully we will migrate to one standard because we now have 22 commands doing different things. Each program or project has their own network; each activity has a stovepipe. They are integrated vertically but not horizontally. Just because we have the infrastructure now doesn't mean they will be horizontally integrated. The infrastructure is not sufficient to solve the interoperability problems.

The Validation Team has not been able to overcome these interoperability problems at all the sites. Because they want to take advantage of the existing architecture, they cannot standardize everything to one system. They continue to have problems migrating the existing systems at the 22 NAVAIR activities to the four protocols selected for NAVWAN implementation. "It is technically feasible, but there may be some performance issues that we'll need to measure and correct" is the summary of the Validation Team leader.

Recommendations for NAVWAN Implementation

The data presented above provide the reader information for developing recommendations regarding NAVWAN implementation. The reader's responsibility is to act in the role of the case researcher, review and analyze the data, and prepare a set of recommendations with appropriate justification. The primary audience for these recommendations is the NAVWAN Program Manager and the Demonstration/ValidationTeam. They, in turn, will forward the recommendations to VADM Bowes and the Naval Air Systems Team.

It is predicted that an organization that deliberately manages its relationships with critical stakeholders will be more effective in mission accomplishment (Freeman, 1984; Roberts & King, 1989). In the case of any significant new technology implementation (the NAVWAN in this instance), failure to successfully manage stakeholder relationships can cause significant resistance to the planned change and thus cause an organization to fail to achieve its implementation goals.

The data presented on stakeholder perceptions of the advantages and potential barriers to implementation of the NAVWAN can be used to inform action planning. Analysis of the data can utilize strategic planning techniques such as the SWOT methodology that identifies strengths, weaknesses, opportunities and threats related to the planned implementation. Clearly, any change effort must examine both the benefits and barriers; and the success of the change effort will be influenced by the extent to which benefits are maximized and barriers are minimized. Research on organizational change has identified several categories of resistance to change. These sources of resistance can be either at the individual or the organizational level (Carrell, Jennings & Heavrin, 1997). Individual sources of resistance include: fear of the unknown; threatened loss of self–interest; mistrust of change advocates; different perceptions of the value of the change initiative; preference for the status quo; concern regarding skill capabilities required to be successful. Organizational sources of resistance can include: structural inertia; bureaucratic inertia; organizational culture and norms; threatened power; threatened expertise; resource allocation.

The tasks and questions listed below apply the principles of stakeholder management by focusing attention on specific stakeholder interests and concerns regarding NAVWAN design and implementation. Additional information on stakeholder management can be found in the references listed at the end of this chapter.

Stakeholder Analysis Tasks

1. Identify and map the critical stakeholders.
2. Conduct a stakeholder audit by assessing the stakeholders' interests and concerns regarding the implementation of the NAVWAN.
   a. Summarize the benefits reported for NAVWAN.
   b. Summarize the concerns or impediments to implementation.
      i.   Identify the individual–level sources of resistance.
      ii. Identify the organizational–level sources of resistance.
3. Identify ways in which each stakeholder is likely to support or resist the planned implementation

and the extent to which they influence implementation success.
4. Use the results of the audit to develop implementation strategies that capitalize on stakeholders' interests and address or resolve their concerns. One option here is to use the SWOT analysis technique to formulate specific action recommendations.
   a. Identify strategies that capitalize on Strengths and Opportunities.
   b. Identify strategies that resolve or minimize the risk of Weaknesses and Threats (sources of resistance).

Questions for Discussion

1. How does stakeholder analysis compare with the traditional approach to Information Technology design and implementation planning? What are the advantages and limitations of stakeholder analysis?

2. What is the likelihood that stakeholders will support or resist the planned implementation? How do stakeholder analysis and SWOT diagnosis inform this question?

3. What are the sources of resistance (individual and organizational) that must be managed in this case?

4. What action steps can be taken to optimize the successful implementation of the NAVWAN given stakeholder interests and concerns?

5. How is the risk position of the project impacted by the availability of SWOT and Stakeholder analysis data? Risk should be considered with respect to functionality and with respect to end-user acceptance and use.

Appendix

Stakeholder Organization Chart

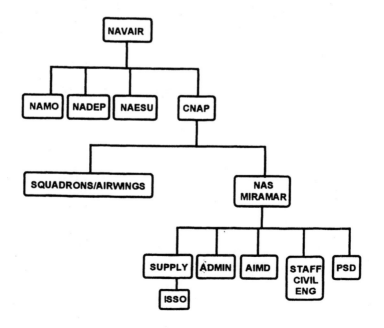

Endnotes

[1] This case is based on Bayer, V.C. (1995) *Analysis of Naval Air Systems Command Wide–Area Network Prototype Implementation.* Masters Thesis. Naval Postgraduate School, Monterey, CA.

[2] Data from Fiscal Year 1994 report of NAST.

[3] The responses are only attributable to the representative and may not reflect the opinions of the chain of command. Any mention of the stakeholder command should be attributed only to the stakeholder representative and **not the organization.**

References

Carrell, M.R., Jennings, D.F. & Heavrin, C. (1997). *Fundamentals of organizational behavior.* Upper Saddle, NJ: Prentice Hall.

Freeman, R.E. (1984). Strategic management: A stakeholder approach. Boston: Pitman Publishing.

Freeman, R.E. & Gilbert, D.R. (1987). Managing stakeholder relationships. In S.P Sethi & C.M Falbe (Eds.), *Business and society: Dimensions of conflict and cooperation* (pp. 397–423). Lexington, MA: Lexington Books.

Roberts, N.C. & King, P.J. (1989). The stakeholder audit goes public. *Organizational Dynamics,* Winter, 63–79.

Chapter 8

Using Information Technology To Enhance Industry Effectiveness: The Case Of The Textile Industry

Ram L. Kumar
University of North Carolina at Charlotte

Connie W. Crook
University of North Carolina at Charlotte

Executive Summary

This case examines the impact of information technology adoption within the textile industry. The textile industry provides a rich environment for the study of technology adoption since it is comprised of a wide variety of different industries ranging from small firms to large multinational corporations. Firms also vary in technological sophistication. While each firm in the textile industry may benefit from an organized approach to technology adoption, most firms make individual decisions to adopt.

Recognizing the need to provide an organized forum for the industry, a major association in the textile industry formed a technology board to review new innovations and technologies. The need for electronic exchange of information was examined and made a priority for the board. The technology board was confronted with the problem of how to serve the members in the organization equitably without regard to company size, technological sophistication, or position in the supply chain.

The textile industry can be classified into retailers, product manufacturers, and fabric, fiber, and yarn manufacturers. According to the technology board, the electronic link between manufacturers and retailers is somewhat formalized; however, much work must be done to facilitate linkages between the suppliers and manufacturers. This is not surprising due to the lack of size and sophistication of some suppliers within the industry.

Background

Information technology (IT) has often been useful in providing competitive advantage for individual organizations. However, with the advent of interorganizational systems (IOS) that electronically link a number of individual trading partners, the role of information technology must be reexamined. Several studies have examined electronic data interchange (EDI) and interorganizational systems from a variety of perspectives. Factors that influence EDI adoption include senior management support (Grover, 1993), sophistication of technology, financial benefits (Iacovou, Benbasat, and Dexter, 1995), power (Hart and Saunders, 1996), and competitive advantage (Sokol, 1989; Venkatraman and Zaheer, 1990). While most studies have examined EDI using firm-level perspectives, there is growing awareness that issues such as power and politics between trading partners need to be examined (Hart and Saunders, 1996).

Firms do not diffuse EDI without trading partner considerations. Each partner in the IOS has separate management, standards, technology, and ways of conducting business. Hart and Saunders (1996) studied EDI adoption use from the standpoint of IOS relationships. They identify several power and trust related factors that impact electronic relationships between organizations.

It is important for all firms involved in a partnership to exploit and benefit from the use of this technology. Organizations such as industry associations or other groups of trading partners play a useful role in managing information technology. The textile industry provided an exciting setting for the study of interorganizational systems and their roles in enhancing industry effectiveness.

The Textile Industry

In 1994, the textile industry could be broadly classified into retailers, product manufacturers (apparel, home furnishings, and industrial), and fabric, fiber, and yarn manufacturers. The structure of the industry and the supply chain is depicted in Figure 1. In the textile industry, fiber is supplied to yarn manufacturers (woven and knit) who in turn supply fabric manufacturers. Fabric is used by product manufacturers to make products such as home furnishing, apparel and industrial products.

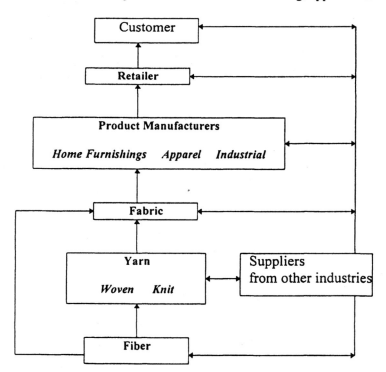

Figure 1: Supply Chain Components and Structure of the Textile Industry

These products are distributed to the customer through retailers. All organizations in the textile industry could also trade with organizations from other industries.

Dr. Tom Malone, President of Millikan & Company, has stated that the US textile industry was represented by 26, 000 companies, employing approximately 1.8 million persons or 18 percent of the entire U.S. workforce (Hall and Walsh, 1993). The U.S. textile industry contributed 23 percent of non-durable goods and furnishing of the U.S. GNP in the same year.

The textile industry consisted of a wide variety of different enterprises ranging from small "mom and pop" shops to large multinational corporations. The supply chain was heterogeneous in terms of company size and technological sophistication. Variations in the use of technology as well as technological skills were apparent. Members of the industry indicated that large organizations perceived the role of information technology to be significantly different from the role seen by small manufacturers. Often, larger organizations dictated that smaller organizations invest in information technology in order to maintain the supplier-customer relationship. It was not clear that smaller organizations derive the same benefits from these investments as large organizations did.

Issues in the United States Textile Industry

Jane Lynch[1] was the chief executive of a major association in the textile industry in 1996. According to Jane, " the U.S. textile industry is healthy at this time." Industry publications such as *Textile World* stated that demand was increasing in a number of product categories such as textile mill shipments, fiber consumption, carpet shipments, and retail apparel sales (Reichard, 1995). However, the number of textile imports into the United States seemed to be increasing rapidly and projected market share of the U.S. textile industry in relation to the market penetration of the international textile industry was expected to taper off (Reichard, 1995).

Foreign competition was a major threat to the U.S. textile industry. Increased foreign competition as well as higher input costs had put pressure on profit margins. Consolidation and globalization were two additional issues that needed to be addressed by the companies in the US textile industry (Wood, 1993). Mergers and acquisitions had reduced the number of textile companies in the past years as foreign investors increased their shares of the U.S. textile market. Consolidations in apparel firms as well as home furnishings companies had lead to larger, more vertical firms.

Globalization in sourcing as well as in marketing was occurring in the industry. Sourcing refers to the use of other companies to perform some duties related to the production of the textiles. Many firms went outside the U.S. to employ personnel to cut and sew the fabric, while finishing was done in the U.S. A large number of manufacturers were concerned about NAFTA because retailers may choose to source from low labor cost countries such as Mexico. Although the U.S. textile industry as a whole supported this treaty, several factions of the industry were concerned about the effects of these policies on current textile production levels. Some manufacturers believed that quick response to customer requirements may be a way for local manufacturers to derive a competitive advantage to offset higher labor costs. Jane and her colleagues from the textile association felt that although the issues of imports, consolidation, and globalization needed to be aggressively addressed by the industry, many companies were optimistic about their future (Wood, 1993).

Information Technology in the Textile Industry

Increasing demands for product flexibility and quality improvement as well as requirements for shorter delivery times and smaller lot sizes fueled the rapid introduction of information technology into the textile industry. Such concepts as Quick Response (QR), Just-In-Time (JIT), Computer Integrated Manufacturing (CIM), Electronic Data Interchange (EDI), and Zero Defects required the adoption of information technology. A survey conducted jointly by Textile World and Deloitte & Touche (Hooper, Hess, and Wielar, 1994) reported that the most popular automated applications in the textile industry were as follows:

• Order entry
• General ledger and financial reporting
• Accounts receivable
• Accounts payable
• Raw materials inventory
• Work-in-process and production reporting
• Purchase order processing
• Cost accounting, and
• Labor reporting/incentive payroll

The same survey listed applications that needed enhancement: production scheduling, cost accounting, plant loading, sales forecasting, order entry, sales analysis, materials requirement planning, and quality control. The media stated that "textile companies are spending more money on information systems (IS), but are increasingly dissatisfied with the cost-effectiveness of their system development efforts" (Hopper et al., 1994: 79). Some dissatisfaction was apparent from the fact that fewer textile companies realized benefits from implementing information systems. There was a significant decrease in the average number of companies recognizing the top four IT-related benefits (improved customer satisfaction, reduced inventory, reduced lead times, and reduced indirect labor). However, a significantly greater percentage of large companies (sales exceeding $200 million) recognized some benefits from implementing information systems than did small companies. The industry as a whole was relatively conservative in terms of MIS (Management Information Systems) spending. For example, only 35 percent of companies had MIS budgets higher than 1 percent of sales between 1988 and 1993. However, 60 percent of large companies had MIS budgets in excess of 1 percent of sales. In the Deloitte & Touche survey, 67 percent of the large companies reported increases in information system budgets, while only 38 percent of the small companies showed an increase (Hooper et al., 1994). That larger companies were spending a greater percentage of sales on Information Technology was an indication that they perceived or anticipated greater benefits from using information systems.

The electronic transfer of information to facilitate commercial gain, commonly referred to as electronic commerce, was used extensively in the textile industry, particularly between apparel manufacturers and retailers. The main objective of electronic commerce in the textile industry was to provide quick response capabilities.

Retail demand for soft goods is extremely sensitive to fashion trends and often highly volatile. The objective of quick response was to enable the soft goods product manufacturers and retailers to be sensitive to customer needs. Manufacturers should be capable of making just-in-time shipments that are sensitive to customer demand. This response can be achieved through a combination of EDI and CIM. Larger companies readily adopted this technology and perceived or anticipated benefits from implementing information systems. Smaller companies lagged behind, with less than half receiving customer orders via EDI.

Role of Industry Associations

In 1994, the textile industry had a large number of professional associations. Examples include the American Apparel Manufacturers Association, the American Association of Textile Chemists and

Colorists, the American Fiber Manufacturers Association, the National Hosiery Manufacturers, and the National Knitwear Sportswear Association. These associations recognized the importance of information systems in keeping the domestic market healthy. The apparel industry looked to information systems for methods of expanding marketing opportunities for US textile and apparel manufacturers and their suppliers. For example, the Associate Members Council of the American Apparel Manufacturers Association and Clemson Apparel Research in cooperation with Bobbin Blenhiem, Inc. developed an electronic catalogue to aid apparel makers in obtaining information about the product and services offered by suppliers. Two associations, the American Apparel Contractors Association and the Southeast Apparel Manufacturers and Suppliers, teamed with the Clemson Apparel Research to develop an electronic sourcing system to allow retailer, apparel manufacturers, and other buyers to determine if a potential contractor had the capability to provide production (Morrissey, 1994). The need to implement specific information technologies such as EDI received some association support across the domestic textile industry. Several associations recognized the importance of EDI across the entire supply chain. Initiatives from the National Textile Center (NTC), a consortium of universities, resulted in a project to investigate the use of EDI in the industry.

Setting the Stage

A board meeting of the textile association and its sponsoring companies had just concluded. The use of technology in the industry had been a major topic of discussion. Jane was thinking about the discussion and reading the minutes of the meeting. The following excerpt highlighted some major issues:

The general consensus was that there are systems already in place but much improvement is needed. One of the biggest challenges is understanding that communications means more than just electronic data interchange. Communications means sharing more information among the three partners (supplier-manufacturer-customer) in the pipeline. It is perceived that the linkage

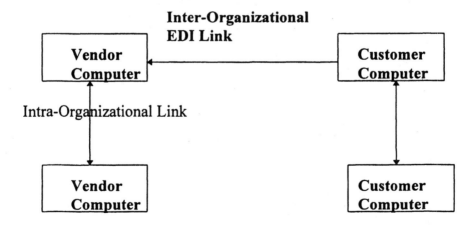

Figure 2: EDI Links Between (inter-organizational) and within (intra-organizational) Organizations

between suppliers and manufacturers is not as good or as formalized as between manufacturers and retailers. Because of this lack of flow of information all the way from the retailer to the raw materials producer, there are excess costs in the pipeline that could be reduced for all three parties.

It seemed to Jane that the industry association could play a major role in facilitating effective use of information technology. However, she felt that some of the association's membership may benefit more than others. The association's mission was to serve all the members without regard to company size, technological sophistication, or position in the supply chain.

Project Description

Overview of the Project

EDI is a generic term for movement of paper-based instruments through electronic telecommunications channels. The movement can be either on the inter-company level, transfer between two separate companies, or on an intra-company level involving users within existing company boundaries as depicted in Figure 2.

Businesses adopt this technology in order to improve productivity, enhance relationships with customers and suppliers, reduce inventory and inventory carrying costs, improve cash flows and reduce data entry and personnel costs (Scala and McGrath, 1993).

Important requirements for successful EDI implementation have included management of technical connectivity, application integration, organizational issues including a skilled work force, trading partner support, and leveraging investment in the technology. Although there were several examples of successful EDI implementation in the textile industry, there were a number of problems as well. Some of these problems had their origins in the heterogeneity of size, structure, skill levels, and management style in the industry. Others were the result of organizational change. These problems could be classified into the categories of technical, economic, and organizational.

Technical Concerns

EDI requires integration of hardware platforms, software, and telecommunication links with trading partners. Hardware platforms ranged from personal computers to mainframes depending on the size of the organization and the volume and history of its information system activities. Several vendors (such as Sterling and Promenos) provide EDI software for a variety of hardware platforms. Value-added telecommunication networks, available from a variety of vendors such as GE and AT&T, were also used.

For some organizations who already had a large number and variety of IT applications, EDI technology was not fundamentally new. Existing information systems personnel were adept at implementing the technology in organizations. In some large organizations, users of EDI technology in departments such as purchasing, shipping, and accounts were thoroughly familiar with information technology as they functioned in organizational cultures that emphasized the use of technology.

In others, especially small "mom and pop" shops, the comfort level with information technology was relatively low. These organizations did not understand the technology and viewed it as something that they were forced to use because of the bargaining power of their customers. For example, one small organization installed three personal computers, each with different EDI software. One machine was used for each of its three major trading partners despite the considerable overlap among customer requirements. It would have been more cost-effective to use a single hardware platform and standardized EDI transactions with appropriate EDI mapping software. The lack of education and understanding of EDI standards contributed to the situation. Often, the source of technical problems was the absence of skilled information technology personnel who could evaluate the IT needs of an organization relative to customer requirements and deal confidently with vendors.

Economic and Organizational Concerns

Investment in EDI-related equipment ranged from a few thousand dollars to hundreds of thousands of dollars, depending on the size of the organization and volume of electronic activity with trading partners. Investment in EDI was usually associated with changes in work practices. For instance, some sophisticated retailers allowed their suppliers to obtain information on sales of different products and adjust their order quantities to cater to customer demand. This concept is referred to as vendor stock replenishment (VSR). This was beneficial for retailers as they received supplies that are synchronized with demand and resulting in reduced inventory holding and stockout costs. However, the suppliers sometimes encountered costs of holding excess inventory and experienced production planning difficulties because of changes in product mix. Production planning problems included the high cost of making machine set-up changes, costs of training for a flexible labor force, and costs of machine idle time.

For EDI to result in tangible business benefits it was important to integrate electronic transactions with business processes. This often required reengineering. For example, a company receiving purchase orders electronically could either process the orders manually or electronically. To process the purchase orders manually required the completion of a paper form to update the order database, keying of the order into the electronic database, production of bills, and distribution of the order through the mail. Electronic processing included automatic updating of an order database and generation of material requirements, purchase orders, and production plans. Benefits of such integrated electronic order processing included reduced paperwork, reduced labor costs (elimination of rekeying documents), faster communication among departments, shorter lead times for purchase order and production plan preparation, and relative ease of modification of those plans. Larger companies in the textile industry had integrated systems (with varying degrees of integration) for order processing; however, smaller companies lacked the know-how and infrastructure to do this kind of processing. In addition, larger companies with huge volumes of electronic transactions could more easily justify investments in hardware, software, and people required for electronically-integrated applications than smaller companies.

EDI was often associated with terms such as just-in time (JIT), quick response, and cycle time reduction, and could provide business benefits such as reduced inventory carrying costs. Jane and several others believed that although a number of companies enjoyed significant benefits, these benefits were not necessarily equally distributed among trading partners. As stated previously, JIT delivery of products to the retailer by suppliers reduced inventory holding and stock-out costs for the retailer. However, others in the pipeline were sometimes forced to hold excess inventory.

Often, the cost of EDI implementation was substantially more than the investment in hardware, software, and training. There was a significant cost associated with reengineering business processes and work practices to derive benefits from electronic transactions. Organizations in the textile industry differed considerably in their view of EDI. Some disgruntled manufacturers in the textile industry viewed EDI as a significant cost and expected their trading partners to compensate them for it. Others viewed EDI as a cost of doing business and were willing to absorb the cost. Some organizations believed EDI was justified because of cost savings as well as strategic benefits such as reduced data entry costs, office supply costs, cost of financing accounts receivable, and personnel costs. Implementation of EDI-based systems involved significant changes in terms of work practices. Employees had to adjust to electronic transactions instead of manual ones. People were not always comfortable with using a screen instead of a piece of paper.

In large organizations, legal and audit departments usually took extended time to adjust to the absence of paper documents for contracts and auditing. Some cross-training of employees was required for successful implementation of EDI. Particularly, employees in accounting, materials management, shipping, marketing and MIS needed to be trained. In addition, EDI increased the degree of customer contact for some employees. MIS personnel needed to accompany marketing personnel on customer visits in order to discuss EDI capabilities. For some employees, especially some technically-oriented MIS personnel, this represented a major change in the nature of their work.

In most small organizations, use of EDI represented a new method of work. Employees had to learn to operate computers for electronic transactions. This was often an extremely difficult task for small organizations. In some cases, large organizations employed intermediaries in order to ensure that they processed electronic transactions even with their smallest, relatively unsophisticated trading partner. Electronic transactions sent by a large organization to an intermediary (often referred to as a clearinghouse or hub) were converted to fax messages to be retransmitted by the intermediaries to less sophisticated trading partners. A similar procedure was used to convert faxes to EDI transactions. The larger organizations benefited from being able to use standardized EDI transactions for all trading partners. For small organizations, the use of EDI as a "glorified fax" was not the best use of technology, but it represented a migration path toward more sophisticated use of technology.

Senior management support was an important factor in influencing the extent of EDI use. Organizations whose senior executives perceived EDI as "just another MIS application" were less sophisticated in their use of EDI when compared with organizations who realized that EDI was a means to derive business benefits such as increased customer satisfaction and decreased operating costs.

Current Status

Jane and several others recognized that use of technology to identify cost reductions, increase revenue, develop awareness of competitive and market conditions, increase switching costs, and provide better customer service was essential to the viability of the textile industry. As exhibited by the following quote, IT management is fundamental to developing and sustaining a competitive advantage for the domestic textile industry:

> Competition in the textile industry is fierce, and is becoming more global in nature. To succeed, companies will have to change the way they use information-related technologies. While most companies are maintaining the status quo, perceptions about the benefits of information-related technology are changing. Whether or not that change is too slow to help most textile companies become more competitive remains to be seen (Sprinkle, Hooper and Hess, 1993: 65).

Some industries had been restructured because of the introduction of technology. For instance, in the financial industry the use of electronic commerce allowed small savings and loan institutions to offer services such as insurance and discount brokerage services which were not previously available to companies of their size. In addition, retailers such as Sears had been allowed to enter the brokerage market, providing stocks and securities trading in their stores. For the financial customer, the distinction among brokerage houses, insurance agencies, and savings institutions was blurred. Structural changes in one element of the industry generated fundamental changes in the entire financial industry, allowing industry boundaries to change to accommodate new relationships and dissolve organizational boundaries.

Diffusion of EDI technology into the domestic textile industry was slow. The desire to establish EDI as a method to support "strategic partnerships," develop service distinction, and produce savings through the efficient use of information and improved information procedures was undertaken only at the firm level. Companies that had not adopted EDI found little incentives to procure the technology. Many times, pressure from large companies to adopt EDI or lose the business opportunities forced companies to adopt the technology. Benefits to smaller companies appeared to be less than for large companies. However, some manufacturers believe that quick response was a way for local manufacturers to derive a competitive advantage. Indications are that technology adoption in the textile industry would strengthen the industry as a whole (Sprinkle et al., 1993). The Deloitte and Touche survey reported that the textile industry "is better preparing itself to incorporate information systems in its competitive battles. ....Several areas are hindering the industry's full recognition of the benefits of its efforts." (Hopper et al., 1994:80). The industry association is still trying to address some of the areas that hinder industry-wide adoption of information technology.

Successes and Failures

The events described in this case illustrate several successes and failures relating to the management of information technology. First, there was industry-wide recognition of the importance of information technology for the sustained performance of the textile industry. This resulted in the industry association realizing that it had an important role to play in promoting the use of different types of information technologies (such as electronic bulletin boards, EDI, and others) among its

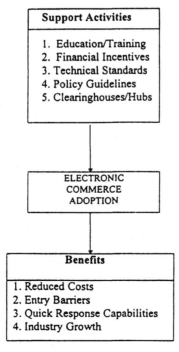

Figure 3: Supporting Technology Adoption

members. Associations in the textile industry have encouraged collaborative IT-related projects with universities and research institutes as discussed earlier. Second, several companies as well as the industry association realized that effective implementation of EDI involved important managerial issues in addition to technical issues. Employee training, trading partner support, senior management support are important factors in effective adoption and use of EDI. Third, some companies are extremely sophisticated users of EDI and derive significant benefits such as reduced inventory, reduced personnel costs, reduced supply costs, and better customer service.

The case also illustrates that several open issues or failures in EDI adoption need to be addressed. While EDI is used successfully by some companies, the benefits are not equally distributed among members of the supply chain. Differential benefits could be due to company size, lack of technical sophistication, and the lack of awareness of the costs and benefits of EDI among management. The process of inducing trading partners to adopt EDI needs to be examined further. More powerful trading partners should strongly consider providing education, incentives, and resolving conflicts among members of the supply chain. There seems to be a perception among many organizations that EDI is merely transfer of electronic messages. However, real benefits are often the result of integrating EDI with other business computer applications such as order processing, purchasing, and payment processing.

Epilogue and Lessons Learned

On the one hand, industry associations and other key players in the textile industry recognized the importance of Information Technology for sustained competitiveness in the textile industry. On the other hand, as evidenced by media comments, the industry needed to ensure that IT-related benefits accrue to all trading partners and address issues relating to industry-wide adoption. Figure 3 details some kinds of support activities that Jane felt could be provided by industry associations as well as the potential benefits.

Support activities could include incentives to increase EDI education and training. Many times this was done by the partner that initiated the use of EDI. Although vendors were available for instruction in some cities, many found that the instruction was not sufficient to meet their needs nor convenient for their partners. In addition, cost of the instruction was prohibitive for smaller firms. Adoption of the technology was inhibited by the lack of financial incentives for the firm, technical standards across the industry, and electronic commerce policies for the industry. To "keep the business"with the trading partner, some companies resorted to sending fax or paper copies to intermediaries for rekeying and distribution to the partner. The number of available clearinghouses and hubs for this purpose needed to be reevaluated by the industry.

Benefits of EDI adoption were not always recognized. Many suppliers did not understand that this technology could reduce cost with reduction in staff and paper, introduce entry barriers due to the requirement that all suppliers must communicate electronically, and enable quick response adoption for inventory control and customer satisfaction. These capabilities needed to be recognized by the adopters to encourage US textile industry growth and prosperity. Jane felt that there was industry-wide awareness of the problems faced in adoption of interorganizational systems. She was certain that industry associations could play a major role in ensuring benefits to all its members.

Questions for Discussion

1. What are the major factors that affect the adoption and use of EDI ?

2. Does the use of an interorganizational system such as EDI along with related process changes result in equal benefits for trading partners ? Explain.

3. How can IT help enhance industry competitiveness ?

4. What kinds of incentives or support activities would encourage the use of EDI among trading partners ?

5. What is the role of industry associations and professional organizations in encouraging the use of IT ?

Endnote
[1] Real name has been concealed.

References

Grover, V. (1993). An empirically derived model for the adoption of customer-based interorganizational systems, *Decision Sciences*, 24 (3), 603-640.

Hall, D. M. and Walsh, W. K. (1993, September). The changing face of textile research, *Textile World*, 100.

Hart, D. and Saunders, C. (1996). Power and trust: Critical factors in the adoption and use of EDI. *Organizational Science*

Hooper, C.C., Hess, J.S., Wielar, S.C., (1994, February). Information technology costs are up, satisfaction down, *Textile World*, 79-80.

Iacovou, C. L., Benbasat, I. and Dexter, A. S. (1995). Electronic data interchange and small organizations: Adoption and impact of technology, *MIS Quarterly*, December, 465-485.

Morrissey, J.A (1994, December). Data processing project expands opportunities for textiles and apparel, *Textile World*, 27.

Reichard, R. S. (1995, January). Textiles looking good in 1995, *Textile World*, 66-71.

Scala, S. and McGrath, R., Jr. (1993). Advantages and disadvantages of electronic data interchange: An industry perspective, *Information & Management*, 25, 85-91.

Sokol, P.K. (1989). *EDI: The Competitive Edge*, New York: McGraw-Hill.

Sprinkle, S. D., Hooper, C. C., Hess, J. S. (1993, January). Perceptions are changing with information systems, *Textile World*, 62-65.

Venkatraman, N. and Zaheer, A. (1990). Electronic integration and strategic advantage: A quasi-experimental study in the insurance industry, *Information Systems Research*, 1 (4), 377-393.

Wood, F. (1993, September). Succeeding in textiles in the nineties, *Textile World*, 45-59.

Chapter 9

A Comprehensive Process Improvement Methodology:
Experiences at Caterpillar's Mossville Engine Center (MEC)

David Paper
Utah State University

Steve Dickinson
Caterpillar, Inc.

Executive Summary

Since the beginning of the 1990s, business process reengineering (BPR) has received considerable attention from the management information systems (MIS) community (Caron et. al, 1994; Davenport, 1993). However, dramatic improvements touted by BPR advocates have failed to materialize in many organizations (Hammer and Champy, 1993; Kotter, 1995). Current research has provided limited explanatory power concerning the underlying reasons behind BPR failure. Hence, in–depth research is needed into companies experimenting with BPR.

This case provides a longitudinal view of Caterpillar Inc. Mossville Engine Center experiences with BPR since 1991. It describes how Caterpillar Inc. (Peoria, IL) introduced BPR into one business unit, Mossville Engine Center (MEC), five years ago and saved between US $10 and $20 million. Caterpillar believes that its success with process improvement can be directly tied to adoption and implementation of an enterprise–wide methodology called Business Process Simplification and Improvement (BPS/I). BPS/I provides a systematic methodology for analysis, design, and implementation of reengineering principles. The methodology provides the structure, techniques, and new job roles to effectively implement redesigned business processes. The role of information technology includes facilitation of data transformation, information flow, and communication through each stage of the BPS/I methodology.

The case was co–authored by the Process Improvement Manager. His job was to facilitate, instruct, and oversee BPR initiatives. Information was gathered via in–depth interviews, observation, company documentation, and consultant information. Our hope is to introduce mechanisms and guidelines to help other firms effectively implement and manage BPR initiatives.

Background

Caterpillar MEC manufactures a variety of small–and–medium–sized diesel engines. The engine center employs approximately 5000 people with 1,200 in management positions. Total revenue for Caterpillar Engine Division is approximately US $3.7 billion.

Historically, the management style has been hierarchical with top–down decision making and bottom–up reporting. Line workers are assigned specific tasks and must adhere to specifications provided by project leaders and managers. Managers are provided directives from upper management and are allowed some latitude in how they delegate assignments. Top management creates directives from long–term strategic plans, decides on priorities for major projects, develops the corporate vision, and communicates the vision to employees.

Setting the Stage

Caterpillar Inc. embarked on a long–term strategy to grow its businesses and rethink existing business units and divisions. Over a seven–year period, beginning in 1987, Caterpillar invested US $1.8 billion in a plant modernization program. The modernization effort enabled the company to improve quality, reduce waste, and helped the Engine Division grow its diesel engine business. In 1990, Caterpillar began a corporate–wide effort to reorganize its business. Its goal was to replace its centralized organization with a decentralized business unit organization focused on meeting customer needs and improving the bottom line. Today, Caterpillar has 17 business units.

In 1991, BPS/I was introduced in several Caterpillar businesses. BPS/I utilizes proven correction, simplification, and reengineering techniques to improve both office and factory business processes. Historically, operational processes have always undergone continuous scrutiny. However, office processes had received little attention. Hence, Caterpillar has shifted its focus to improving inefficient and ineffective office processes.

Formerly, small engine production was part of a larger profit center; consequently, its productivity wasn't as closely scrutinized. As an independent business, Small Engine Products now had to turn a profit in a business that has a lot of competitors and tight profit margins. Small Engine Products management believed that business survival dictated an "improve or perish" mentality. Moreover, it appeared that administrative and cultural changes would be needed to prosper in the future. For these reasons, Small Engine Products management turned to BPS/I.

BPS/I training has two facets. First, candidates undergo intensive training concerning every aspect of BPS/I. Second, they are trained in how to effectively train others. The training isn't over until trainees can effectively demonstrate an ability to train others. Once trainees have successfully completed the program and their performance with a real team has been monitored, they go back to their project as instructor/facilitators (I/F); that is, they are responsible for training and facilitating all team members involved in the BPS/I project. Training local managers is advantageous for two reasons. First, developing instructor/facilitators provides in–house expertise. Second, I/F have deep knowledge of the business at Small Engine Products and can thereby guide BPS/I projects in ways that add value to the business.

Case Description

Organizational transformation continues at Caterpillar. The Small Engine Products business and the Medium Engine Products business have combined to form the MEC. MEC is the business being analyzed throughout the remainder of this case.

Case study analysis of Caterpillar MEC began over four years ago (summer of 1992). Since that time, we have synthesized information from over four dozen BPR initiatives into a set of guidelines and strategies for successful BPR. Projects both large and small have been completed in all MEC business processes. Processes such as engineering, new product introduction, concurrent production, process design, orders, customer support, information systems, and logistics have been beneficiaries. Each of these projects is large in scope; that is, they span functional boundaries and management levels.

Over the past four years, contact was maintained via telephone, e–mail, and fax. The next site visit is tentatively scheduled for Spring 1997. Data was gathered by in–depth interviews, extensive observation, company documentation, consultant information, and the personal experiences of the researchers. The breadth and depth of data collected is extensive as one of the authors is also a key champion of Caterpillar BPR initiatives. He is the BPS/I coordinator and contributes over 28 years of inside experience.

Success centers around the ability of an organization to establish and maintain a systematic BPR methodology like Caterpillar's BPS/I. Hence, data was collected concerning the structure of BPS/I, key factors driving the success of the methodology, and issues surrounding implementation. *For confidentiality reasons, detailed financial analysis was not included.*

Overview of the Case

BPS/I is the "roadmap" for reengineering at Caterpillar. It provides a team structure to help BPS/I teams better deal with process problems. It also offers a systematic methodology for developing and

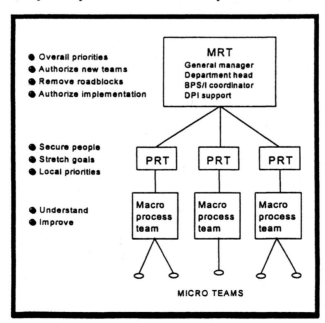

Figure 1: BPS/I Team Structure

implementing process solutions. Following is a detailed discussion of the BPS/I team structure and methodology.

BPS/I Structure. The BPS/I structure consists of a team hierarchy for attacking process problems, as depicted in Figure 1. The hierarchy includes:

- management review team (MRT)
- project review teams (PRT)
- macro process teams
- micro process teams (when deemed necessary)

I/F train and coach process teams. I/F assist and support all levels of the structure by teaching and overseeing the reengineering process. The reengineering coordinator works closely with top management and counsels I/F.

The MRT is the governing body that consists of the General Manager, department heads, BPS/I coordinator, and invited guests depending on the process being considered. The MRT selects and authorizes business processes to be examined that have critical links to Caterpillar business strategies. The "results–oriented" mentality of the company requires that each process meet the twin criteria of potential to reduce costs and provide a high business strategic value. The MRT also guides projects by interacting with the PRT and macro process teams. Senior management buy–in is sought early on because BPS/I projects do not begin until authorized by the MRT. Since the MRT has top management membership, it can also remove political and cultural roadblocks that may hinder the PRT or process team progress.

The PRT consists of mid–to–upper–level managers familiar with the specific process being improved. The PRT sets stretch improvement goals and selects macro process team members. Caterpillar management wants project goals to be stretched to an ever higher level of performance. It also facilitates macro process team activities and communicates the importance of the project to the company. The PRT structure reduces failure as middle managers are forced to work with people on the floor; thereby they gain a better understanding of the process. In addition, it is charged with communicating top management initiatives to the people on the floor. The PRT acts as the communication link between top management and process workers. It is also charged with preparing process teams for final presentations to top management. Process team performance is thereby a direct reflection on the PRT. Quality is improved because everyone in the organization understands the importance of the project and plays an important role in its success.

Macro process teams are cross–functional with six to eight members. Team composition consists of workers who actually perform the process and a supervisor or mid–level manager. Macro process teams recommend detailed process changes. Once the changes are approved, they are the ones who actually do the work. For large processes, a macro process team may form a micro process team to better manage individual issues and details. However, micro teams are only formed out of extreme necessity as coordination problems are greatly intensified with the creation of multiple sub–teams. Process team buy–in is promoted by requiring each team member to sign a BPS/I mission statement for each project. The mission statement serves two purposes. It shifts ownership of the project from management to the team and forces team members to make a commitment. The mission statement includes what they will provide the customer, a time frame for completion, and the level of improvement expected.

Besides process team buy–in, MEC management wants team members to better understand the overall MEC small engine business and adopt a "continuous improvement" mentality. In order to achieve these results, management has attempted to create an environment that encourages teams to challenge status quo processes. Management encourages "out of the box" thinking by involving teams in the decision–making process. MEC experiences with team involvement is that it has dramatically improved team member understanding of the business.

To avoid miscommunication and promote understanding, each level of the BPS/I teamstructure includes at least one member from the level below. The MRT level seats at least one PRT manager (the process owner) as a permanent member. Each PRT level seats at least one macro process team member (the team leaders). Macro process team members lead micro process teams. The BPS/I structure keeps people at all levels informed as it introduces lines of open communication up and down the organization. Managers understand what teams are doing, and teams understand what is important to managers.

The structure sends the message to everyone that it is okay to tinker with existing processes and challenge process paradigms. An environment conducive to involvement is especially important for politically sensitive processes. The people involved in BPS/I need to hear that management supports critical examination of the existing process. Training becomes a key issue because employees in the process may have had little or no previous decision–making experience. Caterpillar had the foresight to commit to training early in the process to help its employees ascend the BPS/I learning curve more quickly.

Caterpillar is committed to BPS/I, however, the structure is only a mechanism to address process reengineering problems. The company has to continue to function during the transition period required by BPS/I. In the meantime, it must satisfy existing customers, stockholders, employees, and other stakeholders. MEC employs a full–time coordinator to act as liaison. Facilitator coordinators work directly with the general manager and department heads. They also facilitate the effort at all levels of the BPS/I hierarchy. In sum, facilitator coordinators are charged with keeping everyone involved in reengineering aligned with the BPS/I methodology. The next section details the steps involved in BPS/I.

BPS/I Process. As depicted in Figure 2, the BPS/I implementation process has five main steps —process selection, process mapping, process improvement, process verification, and process implementation. Each of these steps are discussed in this section.

Process selection. The first step for the MRT is to select critical business processes based on their potential to add value to Caterpillar businesses. A critical responsibility of the MRT, at this step, is to ensure that project guidelines are aligned with business strategies and objectives. The PRT is formed. The PRT secures people for the teams and establishes local priorities based on the MRT plan. Macro process teams are charged with doing the work. After process selection, the processes can then be mapped.

Process mapping. The goal of process mapping is to understand the current process or set of processes and associated problems. Project limitations and the process mission are also established at this step. Process mapping is the most important step as it provides a full view of the process in its entirety, both upstream and downstream along the process path.

Under the periodic guidance of the PRT, macro process teams begin developing a crude map of the process. The map portrays the flow of activities along the process path. Teams use flowcharting to map process flows. Flowcharting is a useful tool as it facilitates understanding and communication. It helps teams identify dangerous loops, redundancies, and incomplete instructions in the process. It also helps teams understand what the process looks like and how changes will alter tasks and activities along the process path. The team can then tweak or radically alter process flows by using the flowchart as a guide. In addition, teams can use flowcharts to facilitate communication with management concerning proposed process changes. The first map is crude by design. Allowing teams to develop the map with their own hands serves two purposes. The team gets more involved in the creative process, and the map acts as a rallying point for team members. Project ownership shifts to the team as they feel like they are in charge. The map allows them to begin identifying redundancies to remove.

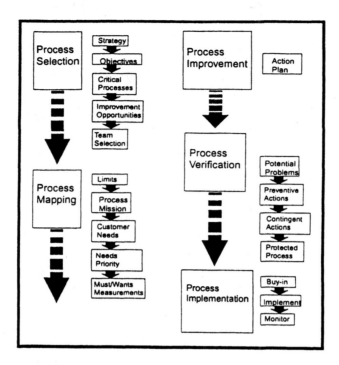

Figure 2: BPS/I Steps

It also acts as a catalyst to begin questioning the accepted process norms. Team members start asking why the process is done in a certain way and why can't it be done in a better way. Related training manuals provide appropriate prompts to the team along the way. Having defined problems associated with the current process, team members are now ready to suggest improvements.

Subsequent drafts of the process map are placed in electronic form with the aid of software flowchart packages such as AllClear. Other tools that are used include pareto analysis (tracks quality), affinity diagrams (for degree of quality), and fishbone diagrams (identify where problem occurs along the process path).

Process improvement. After the team maps the process, process improvement begins. Process improvement involves analysis of existing processes and suggestions for change. Caterpillar believes that process improvement need not be radical. A process can be corrected, simplified or reengineered. Figure 3 depicts the three improvement methods.

At Caterpillar, process improvement usually begins with simplification. Simplification involves streamlining the existing process. If analysis of the process calls for removal of one or more steps, simplification is being used. Smallest in scope is process correction. Correction involves returning the process back to traditional levels of performance. Correction is only used if the current process is performing below traditional levels of expectation. Reengineering involves major (radical) changes to the existing process. Reengineering forces a change in the team's thought processes. They have to rethink the way a job is currently done. Reengineering techniques are often employed in conjunction with simplification. It is not unusual for all three methods to be used on a single process.

The improvement method— process simplification, correction, reengineering — is arrived at during the process improvement step of BPS/I. The team begins process simplification by asking questions about the activities currently being performed: what are the activities, where are they performed, when are they performed, how are they performed, and who performs them. In the next step, the team questions why process activities are done in a certain way. This is a very important question as it breaks status quo thinking. It forces teams to question the logic of a process. In the third step, the team questions the necessity of each process activity. Finally, the team devises alternative ways to perform the process. Reengineering is very similar to simplification except teams are expected to devise alternatives that provide radical rather than incremental improvements.

A common technique to approach process improvement is to break down the process into smaller parts—modular problem solving. Using this technique, teams attempt to find ways to simplify, correct, or reinvent smaller portions of the whole process. They then decide on the implementation priority of each remedy. After priorities are set, the team verifies that each one will work as expected. As simple as this seems, teams are not used to thinking on their own.

Hence, I/F use graphics to facilitate understanding. For instance, teams are shown a graphic depicting a bad condition with many complexities such as a six–foot gorilla. Another graphic shows the problem broken down into manageable components as several monkeys, as depicted in Figure 4. The question is then posed, "Would you rather take on a six–foot gorilla or six, one–foot monkeys?" Caterpillar is also aware of the potential of technology to facilitate process improvement. Teams have e–mail to communicate with each other and management, personal computers to analyze data and document/graph activities, and access to mainframe power to handle larger jobs.

The major deliverable out of the process improvement step is a generation of alternative process flows. Teams are provided tools to help with the analysis, facilitative management for encouragement, and technology to communicate. However, they need a mechanism to stimulate idea generation. Caterpillar has found that the most effective mechanism for idea generation is brainstorming. Brainstorming is used extensively to encourage creative input from team members. Caterpillar has demonstrated its support for brainstorming by developing a set of seven rules as depicted in Figure 5.

Managers act as facilitators of the brainstorming process by allowing team members to voice their opinions and by reserving judgment. Proper management of brainstorming sessions is critical. Hence, a critical component of I/F training is learning how to create an "open" environment for employee ideas, acting as a coach or facilitator rather than a boss, and convincing employees that their ideas or comments will not lead to future reprisals. The next step in the methodology is to determine the ramifications of the suggested process changes.

Process verification. Once the team generates alternative process flows, verification of the choices can begin. In the process verification step, the team determines the impact of each alternative on the company as a whole. The team has made its own decisions and has assumed ownership of the project. At this point, the team is like a race horse. Its members believe that they have the answers and are ready to implement them. The I/F job is to slow down the team and help them assess the value of each alternative generated in the process improvement step. Caterpillar uses potential problem analysis (PPA) to counteract the tendency of teams to jump to conclusions without proper analysis. PPA engages teams to ask questions about the value of each alternative and its impact on other processes. The time allotted to PPA should be at least 1–1.5 hours for each alternative. Table 1 includes a set of possible questions that might be used for PPA.

Team PPA is facilitated by wall posters with questions and places where team members can fill in possible answers to the questions. The main objective of PPA is to identify potential problems associated with an alternative and anticipate the impact of changes required by an alternative on the existing process and other processes along the process path. Deliverables from PPA include a report of potential and anticipated problems associated with the new process. The team completes the PPA analysis keeping in mind what would happen to the existing process, customer satisfaction, and other processes if something went wrong. PPA should help ensure that the alternative chosen by the team

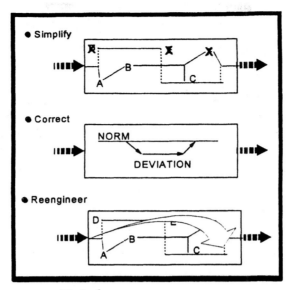

Figure 3: Three Improvement Methods

Figure 4: Divide and Conquer

will have the least negative impact on the organization and other processes along its process path.

Process implementation. The final step of BPS/I is to figure out how to implement the new process. The new process will have a refined process map and a thorough PPA report. The team meets with its PRT to lay out a proposal for presentation to the MRT. The proposal includes a detailed implementation plan, benefits of the new process, and a time table for completion of the project. The PRT acts to facilitate the completion of the proposal and helps the team get ready to present it to the MRT. After all, the PRT has a vested interest in the success of the project as they helped assemble the team.

Brainstorming has Rules

▲ Evaluation or judgment of any idea, either positive or negative, is not allowed by any participant.

▲ Ridicule of any person or his or her idea is prohibited.

▲ Comments or recordings of anything said or implied cannot lead to reprisal.

▲ Everything said is of value and should be treated as such.

▲ Verbalize all your thoughts no matter how ridiculous they may seem to you at the time. Don't let LEFT brain thinking take over.

▲ Listen to other ideas, build on them, or part of them. Use other ideas as triggers for yours.

▲ Avoid questioning an idea unless it is for clarification.

Figure 5: Brainstorming Rules

Technology Concerns

Caterpillar relies on a variety of computer platforms (ie., client/server and mainframe) to transform data into information and facilitate information flow along each step of the BPS/I methodology. Various technology platforms are being considered for future integration. Most team members involved in BPS/I projects use personal computers to facilitate simple data processing and end–user application development. These computers are connected into Caterpillar's telecommunications backbone which also connects to headquarters and the other main business sites.

Data is partially integrated across critical business processes via connections with the mainframe platform. Information is made available on a fairly consistent and timely basis for BPS/I teams along the five critical steps of the methodology. However, information is not available at the fingertips. Reports are processed through the mainframe system and sent to the requesting area by internal and electronic mail. The mail system is efficient, but cannot be compared to a networked personal computer. An important integrating tool is electronic calendaring. As meetings are scheduled, the calendaring system automatically checks everyone's schedule for conflicts. Everyone has access to the schedule via personal computers or dumb terminals in proximity of their work space. Employees have a short time frame to question the schedule. If no one requests a change, schedules are set in stone. The organization's experience with this system has been very favorable. Electronic calendaring has enabled integrated scheduling on an enterprise–wide basis.

MEC utilizes sophisticated technology and equipment at the process level. AutoCAD, Pro/E, and other information system tools are used to facilitate complex diagraming and blueprinting of engines and components. Diagnostic and measurement equipment is used to test parts specifications and tolerance levels. E–mail is used to communicate across the organization. However, the current

PPA Question Set
What is it you are attempting to do?
What could go wrong?
What causes these problems?
How can we prevent problems from occurring?
If problems do occur, how can we minimize them?

Table 1. Question Set for Potential Problem Analysis (PPA).

focus of BPS/I is not on technology integration and information reengineering.

Caterpillar's stance on technology is that of a facilitative tool for employees to perform tasks and activities more efficiently and effectively. Technology does not solve problems; rather it helps people better understand, analyze, and solve problems. The survival of MEC depended on quick solutions to their business problems. Therefore, they had to make an informed choice. Top management decided that process improvements should be made to critical business processes as quickly as possible. Now that MEC is achieving dramatic improvements in many of its critical business processes, they are beginning to look at information reengineering.

Management and Organizational Concerns

Management is concerned with political turmoil and costs associated with BPS/I. However, they have little choice because of the competitive nature of the engine industry. BPS/I is helping to dampen political problems as top management is part of the team and should clear the way for teams to do their jobs. Political resistance remains in "pockets," but a strong commitment from top management has drastically lessened negative effects.

The enterprise–wide nature of BPS/I calls for all constituents in the organization to work together. Proper implementation of BPS/I is equitable and profitable. It is equitable in that all employees count. Their ideas are important and carefully considered by management. Management has a new role ? that of coach and facilitator of work. The initial focus of BPS/I on office processes was a calculated strategy to highlight value–added results for Caterpillar management and better working conditions for employees.

BPS/I anxiety is a concern. Process improvement can significantly change organizational structure and reduce headcount. Employees are very concerned with headcount reduction in that it may mean job reassignment. However, when BPS/I projects identify surplus positions in a process, something must be done. To remedy the situation, MEC tries to redeploy surplus employees to other (sometimes better) jobs within the organization. Nevertheless, employees experience anxiety because they never really know if they will remain in their existing position once BPS/I begins. Therefore, a major strike against reengineering, in the minds of many employees, is the threat against job security.

Current Status of the Case

Since 1991, MEC has been involved with over four dozen BPS/I projects. Since Caterpillar is a results–oriented organization, every project must show potential to add value to the process and generate revenue for the company. Therefore, team members must continually justify their decisions and work toward making the business better serve Caterpillar customers. To date, BPS/I projects have been very successful. Success can be attributed to strong top management commitment to the methodology, employee dedication, organizational buy–in, and meeting or exceeding customer expectations. In addition, BPS/I initiatives are directly linked to corporate strategy and objectives. The MRT selects critical processes that have strategic value to drive the success of the core business.

The biggest impetus driving BPS/I success is organizational survival. Presence in the small engine marketplace is not assured. Hence, MEC management has a large stake in the success of the projects. Granted, some managers are resistant to change. However, continuous communication from top management endorsing BPS/I is going a long way to dampen resistance. Moreover, the reward system has been changed. Team rewards are tied to the accomplishment of the team's mission. Examples of this recognition include:

• Caterpillar apparel
• Restaurant certificate from the MRT (US $30–$50 with spouse)
• Annual performance review will include detailed information on team accomplishments
• MRT recognition and approval
• Corporate–wide visibility

Successes and Failures

Caterpillar invested in BPS/I to get results. To date, its BPS/I efforts have paid off quite well. Figure 6 depicts some of the highlights.

On the average, process cycle times have been decreased by 50%, the number of process steps in a business process have been cut by 45%, and process resources (people) have been reduced by 8% for those projects where manpower was a mission statement goal. In addition, Caterpillar has added three business process cells and completed over a dozen BPS/I projects. Prior to business process cells, groups of employees used to perform a portion of the process. In the cell, the employee now performs the full process. In terms of soft dollars, cross–divisional interactions have increased (teamwork building), employees better understand business processes (better decisions), and employees have gained experience with an effective reengineering methodology (more effective work habits).

In general, introduction of BPS/I at Caterpillar MEC has helped to make process improvement a way of life for employees. Employees are rewarded for process thinking and creativity. Employee involvement in decision making has also become more common. However, with additional involvement comes accountability. Employees are given the freedom to make decisions, but must prove to management the value of those decisions to the organization.

Overall, Caterpillar has been able to reap millions of dollars in benefits from reengineering. However, these benefits did not occur without a cost to the organization. Change is painful, risky, and expensive. Political battles have been waged by managers who don't want to change. Some employees cannot or will not adapt to the changes in job roles required by the methodology. Every project is risky because there are costs associated with changing a process such as new equipment, new technology, training, extra management time for coaching, and dealing with politics. Therefore, reengineering efforts need leadership from the top of the organization because only top management can effectively deal with political obstacles, budget for resources, and change the culture of the organization.

Epilogue and Lessons Learned

The key to BPS/I success at MEC pivots on commitment in seven areas— to meet or exceed customer expectations, a long–term strategic corporate vision, a systematic reengineering methodol-

```
┌─────────────────────────────────────────────┐
│ ┌─────────────────────────────────────────┐ │
│ │  Quantifiable Benefits (average)         │ │
│ │                                          │ │
│ │  ▲ Process cycle time (reduction 50%)    │ │
│ │  ▲ Process steps (reduction 45%)         │ │
│ │  ▲ Process resources (people reduction 8%) │ │
│ │  ▲ Business process cells (three new ones) │ │
│ │                                          │ │
│ │  Nonquantifiable Benefits                │ │
│ │                                          │ │
│ │  ▲ Improvement becoming way-of-life      │ │
│ │  ▲ Employees becoming business people    │ │
│ │  ▲ Multi-million dollar bottom-line impact │ │
│ │  ▲ Accountability/responsibility pushed down │ │
│ │  ▲ Employee involvement in decision making │ │
│ └─────────────────────────────────────────┘ │
└─────────────────────────────────────────────┘
```

Figure 6: Summary of Outcomes

ogy, process classification, training, cultural change, and communication. In addition, the desire to survive as a manufacturer of engines has served as a driving force to succeed.

Since commitment to the customer is a top priority at Caterpillar MEC, most BPS/I projects are established to solve customer problems. For BPS/I to succeed, top management must make a long–term strategic commitment to reengineering. Moreover, they must be able to communicate the corporate reengineering vision to all levels of the organization. BPS/I enables classification of process changes based on the scope of the problem. Classification into three categories guides project teams in their efforts, informs management of the scope of each problem, and determines the magnitude of resource commitments on a project–by–project basis. Classification, analysis, and implementation may be misguided without proper BPR training. Hence, the company invests heavily into training employees about the critical aspects of the methodology. BPS/I helps management create a culture of change. Few people like change, but BPS/I provides a "change–oriented" structure, a guiding methodology, and new job roles which give employees a guiding path to succeed in a changing environment.

From the in–depth case study of Caterpillar's MEC division, we learned several lessons about process reengineering. The lessons are not intended as exhaustive, rather as a guideline to others wrestling with reengineering projects.

Lesson 1: Although success is never guaranteed, adoption and implementation of a systematic reengineering methodology is critical to success.

Lesson 2: Progress should be measured in the short–and–long–term. Since BPS/I projects tend to be large in scope, management may believe that measurable benefits lie *only* in the distant future. Short–term results are good for the long–term survival of the project.

Lesson 3: Process changes should be driven by a focus on the customer, strategic business issues or senior management.

Lesson 4: Senior management should be personally and visibly committed and actively participating in BPS/I projects.

Lesson 5: Reengineering organizational change requires a strategic orientation rather than a tactical or operational one.

For confidentiality reasons, we are not free to discuss how cost savings were obtained or how results from BPS/I projects were tied to profits. Instead, we articulated the use of BPS/I to solve business problems. Caterpillar chose BPS/I because of the systematic way the methodology approaches reengineering. Like most successful organizations, Caterpillar is results–oriented. It doesn't want to change for the sake of changing. It wants to change to make more money, to gain market share, and successfully compete with powerful rivals. Unlike many reengineering methods available on the market, BPS/I offered a system to meet Caterpillar's aggressive goals and strengthen its employees through training and guidance.

The difference between success and failure hinges upon an organization's view of reengineering. Reengineering must be carefully planned, properly financed, and strongly reinforced. Reengineering is not a short–term methodology. It requires long–term commitment of time and resources to enable significant benefits. Hence, reengineering should be considered in the strategic plan of the organization since it must be endorsed and enforced by top management.

Questions for Discussion

1. What makes BPS/I work?

2. How does Caterpillar deal with loss of momentum for BPS/I projects?

3. How is empowerment facilitated at MEC?

4. What role does culture play?

5. Is BPS/I always necessary to solve process problems?

6. What was the key to developing a longitudinal case study with Caterpillar MEC?

References

Caron, J.R., Jarvenpaa, S.L., & Stoddard, D.B. (1994). Business reengineering at CIGNA corporation: Experiences and lessons learned from the first five years. *MIS Quarterly*, September, 233–250.

Davenport, T.H. (1993). *Process inovation: Reengineering work through information technology*. Boston, Massachusetts: Harvard Business Press.

Hammer, M. & Champy, J. (1993). *Reengineering the corporation*. New York, N.Y.: Harper Collins Books.

Kotter, J.P. (1995). Leading change: Why transformation efforts fail. *Harvard Business Review*, March–April, 59–67.

Chapter 10

Systems Requirements and Prototyping

Vincent C. Yen
Wright State University

Executive Summary

This case study is based on a multi-year information systems plan for a marketing firm. Initially, the investigation was enterprise-wide. We describe the critical components of the enterprise system, including the software and hardware architectures. For the application systems, the accounting system and the job scheduling system receive top priority. Since the accounting system was a commercial off-the-shelf product, our focus was on the development of the job scheduling system. We explain the manual job scheduling process and how the automated system might be developed. The justification for adopting Microsoft's Access, SQL server, Exchange, and Project as the development tools is presented. Microsoft Access was used just for the prototyping. Eventually, the job scheduling system will be implemented on the Project software with some rewriting of Visual Basic codes.

To date, a prototype using Access had been developed and demonstrated. It received favorable comments and has been approved for the next development phase. The case study concludes with remarks on the advantages, issues and lessons learned from the project.

Background

The subject of our study is a reputable market research firm that spans more than sixty years. The firm is employee owned. Clients of the firm include well-known names in business and Fortune 500 companies. The firm maintains sales offices in Atlanta, Boston, Cincinnati, Dallas, Detroit, Los Angeles, New York, Philadelphia, and San Francisco. The company had a mission "to help clients measure and monitor customer needed and requirements in order to provide a fact-based foundation for continuous quality improvement efforts focused on enhanced customer satisfaction and retention." Currently, the firm offers a variety of services; including:

1. Assessment of internal and/or external client profile.
2. Analysis of performance goals at managerial and operational levels, products and services, and customer satisfaction.
3. Assistance in design, implementation, and training of program evaluation processes.

All of these services involve data collection and analysis. For data collection, the company offers:

- Telephone and mail surveys
- Personal in-depth interviews and group sessions
- Comment cards in-room, point-of-transaction or with product
- Traditional in-person focus group discussions
- Teleconference focus group discussions
- Benchmarking visits to best in class companies
- Mystery shopper and quality audits of performance
- On-site visits to customer locations to facilitate client/customer team meetings

Usually the data needed by a project requires a combination of the above activities. The design and analysis of data were managed by the statisticians of the company, many of whom hold advanced degrees. The company strives to produce quality services for its clients corresponding to the mission statement.

The Organizational Structure

The organization of the company was straight forward. Units of the organization were setup by functions. The president of the company directly manages: administrative division (human services, accounting, computer operations, etc.), marketing division, consulting/analytical service division (data analysis), research service division (managing project and report production), customer satisfaction division, and the customer research division. A number of departments may exist within each division. For example, the human services department was a branch of the administrative division.

Current Information Systems

The company had a small systems department responsible for maintaining hardware and software operations. It did not have staff to support information systems development. Installed hardware included Windows-based personal computers, Sun workstations, and Macintoshes. Local area networks were installed, and remote connections were available between the sales office and the corporate office. They use four different operating systems: DOS, WINDOWS, UNIX, and Apple's SYSTEM 7.

The various commercial software used were routinely dedicated to a single purpose or function. For example, SAS was used as the statistical analysis system, and ACE was an automated cost estimating system developed by end-users with Foxpro. With the exception of the accounting department (whose systems and its support were out-sourced), all other applications were either purchased or developed by in-house end-users. Because the company did not have a software procurement policy, different word processors, spreadsheet programs, and database software co-exist. For example, Sybase, Foxbase+, Foxpro2, and Paradox were databases used by the company. Due to differences between the files' data format, it was frequently difficult to exchange data between applications. The applications developed by end-users were created to provide a solution to a particular operational problem. For example, end-users have used Foxpro in developing a cost estimating program, a weekly activity report program, and a job order information database. These applications were ad-hoc in nature and generally were both ill-designed and isolated.

The Management Initiatives

The firm's arena of market research had been booming in the last few years. Very often, the company receives more than ten job orders a day. Managing these projects becomes more demanding both in accountability and timing. Recognizing the rapid advancement of information technology and its potential impact to the service industry, the firm decided to investigate opportunities in IT that may improve its competitiveness. Because of limited in-house IT capabilities, in the spring of 1993, the firm issued a request for proposal with the following stated objectives.

1. Improve the efficiency of the project management and financial accounting processes.
2. Improve the data transportability and the applications integration across the diverse platforms and operating systems.
3. Maximize the efficiency of existing data networks.
4. Explore new information technologies for long-term productivity improvements.

In short, the management of the firm was interested in improving its productivity and efficiency through streamlining the existing information system, while selecting an information systems architecture for long-term growth. After a lengthy search process, a consulting company was given the contract. The contractor assembled a team of investigators consisting of a systems analyst, a computer engineer, and a programmer to work with the project. On the company side, a project coordinator was assigned to work with the team. The coordinator was a knowledgeable staff member who was familiar with the company operations and capable of answering many questions. The appointment of a coordinator had benefited the company and the project team immensely. Following the systems development life cycle methodology, the project team's first major task was the requirements analysis.

Defining Requirements

Methodologies

The first phase of systems development was requirement analysis. The team needed to understand how the existing system works. The data and knowledge gained through the analysis will serve as the basis for defining system boundaries, project scope, and the new system features and functions. However, in order to obtain the right kind of information, it must be carefully planned. The team proceeded with several information collection techniques, such as structured interviews, critical success factors (CSF) analysis, joint application development (Wetherbe, 1991), and document reviews.

To facilitate the data/information gathering, the company established a cross-function advisory committee comprised of departmental chiefs, division heads, or their representatives. The team had several meetings with the committee, including a brain storming session about the company's business operations and procedures. These meetings provided the team members with an overall conceptual business model and information of how the existing "system" works.

More detailed information about the existing system was pursued by: (1) interviewing the members of the advisory committee, (2) studying the employee job specification handbook, and (3) reviewing current information systems. During this process, the team collects sample forms, reports, business procedures, information systems documents, etc.

To find out the information requirements at the managerial level, the team conducted a structured survey according to the concepts of business systems planning, critical success factors, and end/means analysis. The survey had about forty-five participants including members of the advisory committee. Participants were given two weeks to respond the questionnaires. The questionnaire consists of questions each with a maximum of five open-ended sub-questions. As a result, a wealth of information was collected. The data set reveals the information systems requirements of the company and serves as the basis for the design of the firm's information system architecture.

Techniques used so far for information gathering or requirements identification may still leave out certain activities/interfaces between functional areas. For this reason, the team conducted two joint application development (JAD) meetings with the members of the cross-function advisory committee. JAD meetings were not only capable of eliciting information of importance to two or more functional areas but also capable of producing the desired new system functions or characteristics (e.g., scheduling/job tracking systems).

Survey Results

The survey participants were very cooperative, they responded to each question whenever they could. The enthusiasm was probably due to the common desire to achieve a higher level of productivity while simplifying the operational process. Upon analysis of the survey, it was clear that the company needed a comprehensive information system, including but not limited to, job tracking, accounting, scheduling, experience database, time keeping, and data networks. The questions based on the CSF concept were given to middle level managers and staff. The following list highlights some salient information systems requirements perceived by the management:

1. Up-to-date information on the progress and the cost of an active project.
2. Accessing schedules of all persons working on a particular project.
3. Consistent estimated results from ACE (automated cost estimating software).
4. Complete information on the client requirements and expectations.
5. Internal communication.

In addition to the survey results, separate findings on accounting, data networks, job tracking, scheduling, experience database, and time keeping were documented, along with an enterprise-wide data flow diagram in the Phase I report. The report points out many information systems worthy for development, including: sales and marketing support, cost estimating, financial accounting, job costing, job order, job tracking, time reporting, job scheduling, and progress reporting. Upon evaluations by the company staff, the firm gave the accounting system the first priority. This was because the company wants to be in full control of the accounting data as opposed to the current out-sourced service that did not permit easy access of required data. In addition, there were many accounting packages which were immediately available, reasonably priced and meeting their needs. After a detailed comparison of features and costs among several major accounting packages, the company purchased the Windows-based Platinum Accounting Systems (compatible with many popular databases like Foxpro and Access). The compatibility feature was important because otherwise, accounting data could not be easily shared with other users of the company.

After the purchase of the accounting system, work on data conversion, the system installation, the system testing, and end-user training took an extended length of time. Since Platinum provided all the services needed by the company, the consulting team did not involve in the implementation of the system. When the new accounting system was successfully completed, in the spring of 1995, the company wants to proceed with the computerized job scheduling system because of its practical and strategic value.

Current Job Scheduling System

The current job scheduling system relies, for the most part, on paper, pencil, telephone or e-mail coordinations, and schedulers' judgment. There were several databases supporting the job scheduling, for example, the job order database, and the experience database. The job order database consists of a client file and a job file. The client file had all pertinent data about the client, while the job file contains records about the job's survey research methods, field survey dates, contract price, etc. Scheduling was entirely manual. Since these databases were not properly designed and normalized they subject to data redundancy and anomaly problems. In this section, we describe the current job scheduling system.

Marketing

The company's account executives (AE) were responsible for the sales or marketing efforts of the company's services. Account executives were expected to contact all prospective clients and provide them with assistance in determining and refining research objectives, designing appropriate research plans, and presenting research results and recommendations. In addition, AEs were responsible for providing a full-range of research expertise and to manage client relationships while meeting specific sales and profitability goals. Normally, after several meetings with his/her client, the AEs have determined critical requirements of the client's potential research project, such as objectives of the project, types of sampling method (e.g., mailing, telephone, interview), sample sizes, tabulation of survey results, statistical analysis, project start date, project ending date, and graphical representation. Requirements of the project were used to generate an estimate of the cost and time for the project. The project's cost and time estimates were then sent to the client for approval. Once the project was sold a unique job number for the project was created by the research services division and this number was also used by the accounting department to keep track of the project payments and costs of company resources.

Estimating Cost and Completion Time

Before the closing of a job AE must provide the client with an estimate of the cost and completion date of the job. A prompt response of the cost and completion date will generally lead to an earlier client decision on the job. These estimates were currently given by the experienced staff and the ACE (automated cost estimating) system. The present ACE system was inadequate in that (1) it only provided estimates for a small subset of tasks, (2) estimates were not within the reasonable range of accuracy, and (3) it did not update automatically when the new project data were entered.

The ACE system demonstrates that the company was aware of the value of the past project experience. Apparently, they hope one day ACE would be capable of generating the estimates for the cost, labor, and time of a project automatically. This was a difficult, if not impossible, task. But, there was no disagreement that the present ACE system could be potentially upgraded to a much useful operational and competitive information system. Consequently, ACE was recommended as one of the high priority projects.

The Experience Database

The database used by the ACE system was called the experience database because it was a database of past projects. The experience database provided historic data for the costs, labor time, duration, and research design of the past projects. Since similar projects share many common characteristics the experience database was valuable for developing standards for them. The development of standards requires the use of statistical techniques. The standard time and cost for each task not only could be used for the price quotes of new projects but also could be used for scheduling new projects. Unfortunately, the experience database was not computerized at this time. The existing automated cost estimating (ACE) program uses a limited number of past case data as the basis of estimation. Thus, the estimates provided by the experience database may be quite inaccurate. This explains why staff must use their judgment to manually make adjustments and modifications for the job schedules.

Senior Account Managers (SAM)

Once a new project was sold, senior account managers (SAMs) assume project management responsibility to oversee all facets of a research study from questionnaire design, cross-tab planning, report compilation to analysis and interpretation of research data. Thus, following the job number creation, SAM will produce an initial project schedule with several critical due dates assigned, e.g. project starting date, project finish date. The critical due dates were referred to as milestones of a project, they also include the field survey start date, and the field survey ending date. This was because the survey was the heart of the project, it carries much information about their products or services in the market place. Clients were eager to see the raw survey results before the sophisticated statistical analysis because the raw results could provide the initial confirmation about the survey objectives.

The completed preliminary job schedule was sent to various departments by e-mail. Departments assign its staff to the job schedule on a task by task basis. In the event that departments cannot scheduled tasks without impacting timely completion of milestones, then the departmental scheduler (normally the head of the department) will have to work out a revised job schedule with a SAM. Obviously, such a job scheduling system was quite labor intensive and chaotic when the number of daily job orders were large.

The Case of the New Scheduling System

The new job scheduling system was considered as a competitive information system by the management. The decision to develop the scheduling system had led to several meetings between the development team and the firm's sponsors. These meetings have produced the following set of objectives for the new scheduling system:

1. Provide for standard job inputs.
2. All schedules should be available online and real time. Changes will be restricted to those that have permission to do so.
3. Automatically adjust the time elements of all related tasks due to changes of task durations, or resource utilization and availability.
4. Monitor costs and resource utilization.
5. Produce job status reports.

6. Provide links with the accounting system.

Before proceeding, it was made clear that the new scheduling system will seek for maximizing the automation of routine scheduling operations, not for optimizing the resource allocation purpose. The reason was that the latter problem did not have easy solutions for large scheduling projects.

An Overview of the System

There were many options capable of achieving the above objectives, for example, reengineering the current system. However, after a number of interviews, it was clear that users would like to preserve the essential scheduling process as described in Section 3. The reason for preserving the current process might be due to the comprehension of the existing system and the unwillingness of taking risks.

Before developing the system the manual process must be clearly defined. Studies of the current process suggest that a structured three-level cooperative model was the underlying system framework. At level one, the top level, for each job proposal the main project scheduler (PD or SAM) will use data from the estimates of ACE, the judgments of AEs and SAMs, clients requests, etc., to determine the major milestones and the associated due dates of the job. The output of this level was the initial job schedule. Then, through e-mail (Microsoft Exchange), the initial job schedule was sent to the respective departments, which was level two. The department managers allocate their resources to the initial job schedule from the department's resource schedule (that was a combined individual staff schedule and time sheets of actual time worked). The output of the second level was either a completed schedule meeting all critical due dates or an incomplete schedule. In the latter case, they were resolved by juggling resources and due dates until all parties will agree. So resolving a scheduling conflict was an iterative process between the department managers and the main project scheduler. It should be pointed out that the conflict was inevitable because the main project scheduler tends to go along with the customer demands in closing a sale. Finally, the level three was the individual staff schedule including the time sheet processing. However, the individual at the third level may not be an internal employee, because he/she could be a contractor responsible for telephone surveys, mall surveys, and mail surveys. The scheduling at the survey centers or at the contractors level did not belong to the scope of this project.

Evaluation of Alternatives

How should the system be developed? The team considered three typical alternatives: (1) developing from scratch using the system development life cycle methodology, (2) purchased package, and (3) prototyping. The first alternative was quickly ruled out because it was not feasible with the given time and budget constraints.

The second alternative calls for an evaluation of all commercial applicable packages. Fortunately, a timely review article (King 1995) had detail information and critique on the following project scheduling packages: CA-SuperProject 3.0 for Windows, Microsoft Project 4.0 for Windows, Project Scheduler 6 for Windows, SureTrack Project Manager for Windows, Texim Project for Windows 2.0, and Time Line for Windows 6.1. The team requested product literature, and obtained copies of the scheduling system (some companies provide a free 30-day evaluation copy, e.g., Microsoft). The packages were evaluated on the basis of cost, ease of use, data compatibility, networking capability, PC Windows/Windows NT environment, and modification flexibility. In the end, Microsoft's Project 4.0 emerges as best meeting the criteria except the flexibility in program modification and the number of simultaneously adjustable resources of the related projects (limited to 80). Incidentally, project 4.0

is modifiable with the Microsoft Visual Basic programming language.

The third alternative "prototyping" (Jenkins and Naumann, 1982) is a well understood and practiced methodology today. It could be used to build a model of the proposed system and using it to test our understanding of the real requirements. The prototyping process is iterative, evolutionary, and with an emphasis of fast delivery. So, prototyping requires some levels of support by the computer aided software engineering (CASE) tools. A minimum set of components in the CASE is a strong fourth generation language, graphical user interface tools for input and report generation, end-user query language, and database facility. Today, there are plenty of low-cost and PC-based software available for prototyping. Examples are Microsoft's Access, Foxpro, and Visual Basic, Borland's dBase for Windows, Borland's Delphi, and Sybase's PowerBuilder, and many others. These software have strong relational database support, semi-object-oriented programming styles, and a rich set of tools for input forms creation and output report generation.

The evaluation of the three alternatives was also based on time, budget, and company's technology architecture grounds. The final development strategy calls for the use of Microsoft's Access as the prototyping tool and Microsoft's Project as the implementation system. This was because Project was not a prototyping tool. By using Access, the analyst and end-users could build a job scheduling system prototype with databases supporting customized input forms and report features. The prototype will be used as a basis to customize the Project for the final target system. Another reason for choosing Access and Project was that they fit in the company's application development architecture. The architecture will be based on Windows NT, SQL Server, and Exchange (a groupware similar to Lotus Notes.) One of the advantages of these software was the built-in OLE (object linking and embedding), OLE automation, ODBC (open database connectivity), and MAPI (massaging application programming interface) tools allowing "seamless" integration between application systems.

The Project Scope

As the detail of the system requirements unfolds, the company management and the team learn that a job scheduling system (JSS) could be extremely complex. For example, a JSS had many interfaces with subsystems/functions ranging from the client and proposal management to the billing and reports production. Updating a schedule change and optimizing the resource utilization were even more difficult. With this understanding, the firm's management decided to take an evolutionary approach by starting development of a small set of core components of the project. The core components were the job order system, the job tracking system, the resource scheduling system, the job costing system, the experience database management system, and the report generation system. Figure 1 depicts these core components and their related sub-systems.

The Data Model

The forms, reports and computer systems documents collected earlier contain valuable information for data modeling. Using the entity-relationship (E/R) approach, the analysis of data results in a conceptual database model (Figure 2). The model will be used to establish the database files. A brief explanation of the E/R diagram follows. An account executive could have many clients. A client could order many market research jobs. A job could be performed or researched in several ways; thus a job may have many sub-jobs (or job versions). Each sub-job must have one study design. Of course, a study/research design may be used by many sub-jobs. A sub-job consists of many tasks and a task could belong to many sub-jobs, thus we have a many-to-many relationship between the sub-job entity and

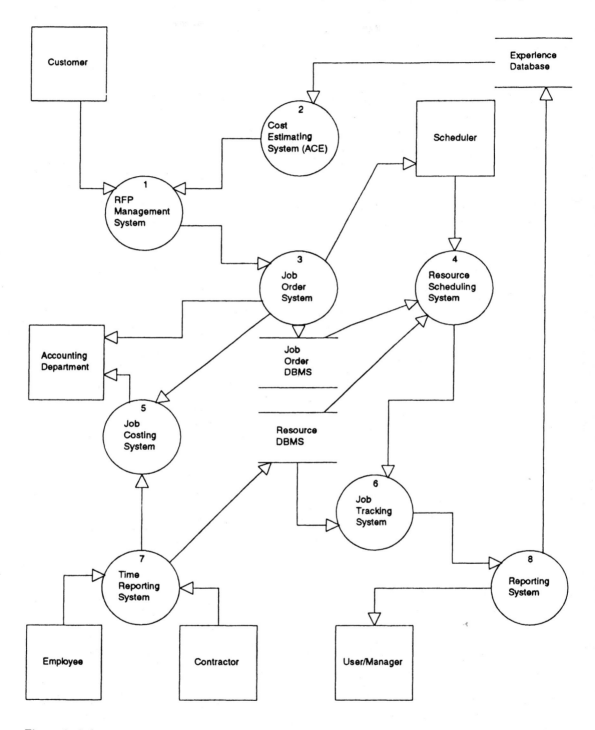

Figure 1: Sub-systems of the Job Scheduling System

the task entity. Hence, we create an intersection entity: task-subjob schedule, containing scheduling data of the tasks of a sub-job. Since tasks have precedence relationships, the set of all task-precedent pairs forms the task-structure entity. One task had many task-structures but a task-structure could only be related to one task. A "task-subjob schedule" could be assigned to many employees and an employee could work on many task-subjob schedules, here was another many-to-many relationship. An entity assignment schedule was created to break up the many-to-many relationship. An employee files many weekly time sheets a year, and of course a time sheet could only belong to one employee. A department had many employees and one of the employees was the head of a department.

Current Status: A Prototype

Based on the structured three-level cooperative model and the data model, the team built a job scheduling system prototype in the fall of 1995. The prototyping began with the input forms of the scheduling system.

Input Screens

For each table of the database, an input screen was built for data maintenance functions. User interface forms were established on the top of the database according to the user operational requirements. Formal approaches to the design of user interface screens should begin with analyzing users, and tasks they perform (Lee, 1993).

Next, the main screen of the job scheduling was created. The main screen acts like a switchboard that provided the navigation path between screens of data and operations. The menu bar of the main screen had the following options:

Job - for the job level operations like: New, Open, Close, Save, Mail to, options, etc.,
View - for displaying the job order related screens like Client, Research Team, and Job
      Master Schedule, ACE, etc.,
Reports - for generating job progress reports, status reports, etc.,
Database - for maintenance of tables of the job scheduling database,
Resource - for resource allocation/assignment at the departmental level, and
Time - for maintenance of time sheets.

Following the three level scheduling system concept, an input form "job master schedule" for each job was created in level one. This form was in the View menu of the main screen described above. The job's master schedule defines tasks that must be performed and the starting and the ending date of the "critical" tasks. The ending dates of the critical tasks were referred to as milestones. The milestone dates were entered by the master scheduler (SAM/AE) with/without consultation with department managers. In the job master schedule screen, the scheduler could invoke the ACE program and show its output in the same screen. Upon completion of the due date assignment, the schedule was then distributed to all departments via e-mail.

In level two, each department manager had access to his/her staff schedule showing the job assignments and its percentage of completion, by each staff and job. The staff schedule was used for tracking job progress, for determining the feasibility of the job master schedule, and for staff task assignments. The department manager could open the staff schedule as a subscreen of the job master schedule. The assignment of staff to tasks was manually done by the department managers with occasional reference of ACE estimates. If the milestones could be supported at this level, the manager

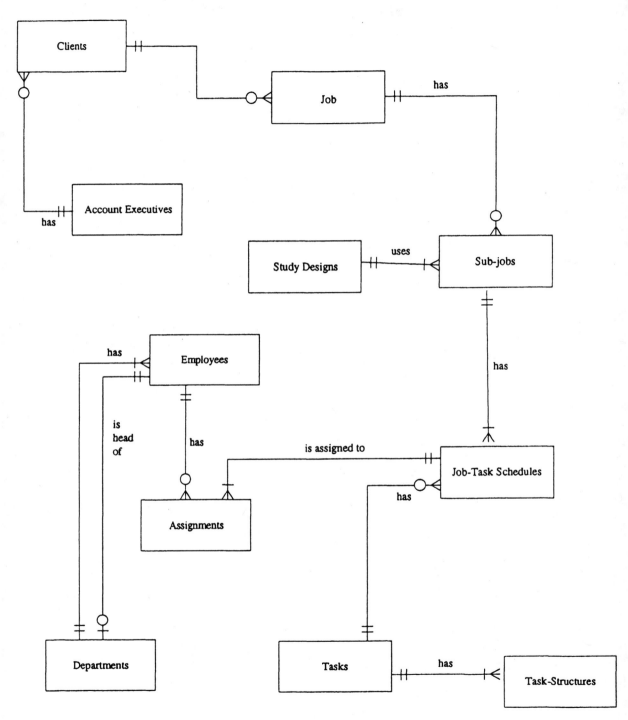

Figure 2: The E/R Diagram for the Job Scheduling System

completes and sends back the initial job schedule to the level 1, and, notifies the staff for the assignments.

In level three, each staff had a time sheet input screen that contains task assignments, scheduled completion dates, and the regular time or overtime entries, etc. Staff executes his/her assignments according to the staff schedule, and enters the amount of time worked, and posts sick and vacation days, etc. to the time sheets. Obviously, the time sheet data were interrelated with the departmental staff schedule.

Since data entered at each level were stored in the Access database end-users could now retrieve the job related information more flexibly and timely. The prototype did not have a "resource leveling" component at this time, but it will have once it was converted to the Microsoft Project.

Output Screens

The output screens were mainly reports for users and managers; some examples were:

1) Client and job profile report. It contains the client and the job contract information.
2) Job progress report. It provided the status of each task and the percentage of completion of a job.
3) Job cost/estimate report. It provided the up-to-date actual job cost data. It could also be used as for estimating the cost of a proposed project.
4) Time report. It was a weekly employee hours worked report for accounting, payroll and staff schedule updates.
5) Job summary report. It was a summery of all job progress and cost status over a specified time by each client.

Successes and Failures

The prototype was demonstrated and scored well, but did not confirm that the entire development process was error-free. The following is some successes and failures observed.

Successes

1. The design of the software and hardware architecture.

2. The objectives of the new scheduling system as stated in section 4 were realized; except that it did not allow for the update of due dates when changes were made.

3. The data model was correctly specified this allows end-users retrieve the information they want more easily.

4. The new system will greatly reduce the effort and time spent in updating the schedule when resource and due dates change.

5. The experience database was established as a by-product of the scheduling system (with some modifications).

Failures

1. The computerized scheduling system did not completely substitute the manual system because (a) it could be inflexible if tasks required were not in the database, (b) it was difficult to reach an agreement when more than two parties have scheduling conflicts (no conference call facility), and (c) above all, impersonal.

2. The scheduling was not user friendly because the prototype did not have a graphical scheduling facility such as the Gantt chart.

3. The response time of *Access* and *Project* was below expectations.

4. The lack of detail process description in the functional analysis had led to the (three months) delay of the prototype development. An example was the precedence relationship between tasks, a critical feature in any scheduling system, but a written master precedence relationship table did not exist.

5. The program (in ACCESS Basic) for the automatic adjustment of time due to changes in due dates and/or resource availability still had bugs. This prevents a lively demonstration of the prototype.

6. The inability of dealing with the "resource leveling" function.

Epilogue and Lessons Learned

The project presented here had well defined objectives. The manual job scheduling system, although developed internally, had been working for many years and was relatively stable. However the manual system was not a sophisticated scheduling system; it was labor intensive and prone to errors. So replacing the current system by a computerized scheduling system, the company could potentially improve operational efficiency and gain a competitive advantage.

In this project, we have created a prototype. Following the development strategy, the next phase was to migrate the database to the Microsoft SQL Server, and to customize the Microsoft Project according to the prototype model. A proficient Visual Basic programmer was indispensable in this phase.

The following were some of the important lessons learned from this project:

1. Defining the project scope. The project had many interfaces with other systems (e.g., accounting system; See Fig. 1). This increased the complexity of the project and the development risk. One way to contain the complexity and the risk would be to start small by limiting the project scope to a few functions and interfaces.

2. Document the process procedure. Although a lot of forms, manuals, reports, and program listings were received, these were bits and pieces about the job scheduling system in question. How these bits and pieces work together to support various functions of a company should be clearly spelled out. The process documentation was important in that (a) it could lead to the early discovery of inadequate procedures, and (b) it could augment comprehensive support for latter stages of system development.

3. Avoid project interruption. The scheduling project should not be interrupted by the accounting system implementation (which took about nine months) because the team must relearn the system and the business when they resume their work. This was particularly true when there were two turnovers in the development team.

4. Select the right technology. Knowing the state and the trend of information technology (hardware and software) is vital in the design of the hardware and software architecture.

Questions for Discussion

1. Why were the experience database and the automated cost estimating system so important to the company?

2. What were the possible applications of the experience database (besides serving as a source of data for estimating the task time and the cost)?

3. What were the reasons for the top management to launch this project?

4. What were the reasons for selecting Microsoft products in this project?

5. Had the company worked out the detailed procedures of the job scheduling system? Explain.

References

King N. H. (1995). On Time and On Budget, *PC Magazine,* (April 11) , 165-199.

Geoff L. (1993). *Object-Oriented GUI Application Development,* PTR-Prentice Hall, Inc.

March, S. T., & Kim, Y-Gm (1992). Information Resource Management: Integrating the Pieces, *DATA-BASE,* (Summer, 1992), 27-37.

Milton, J. A. & Naumann, J. D. (1982). Prototyping: The new paradigm for systems development. *MIS Quarterly* 6 , 29-44.

Bischofberger, W. & Keller, R. (1989). Enhancing the Software Life Cycle by Prototyping. *Structured Programming,* (1989), 1, 47-59.

Wetherbe, J. C. (1991). Executive Information Requirements: Getting It Right. *MIS Quarterly,* March, 51-65.

Chapter 11

Risks and Rewards at Frontier Communications: Improving Customer Service Using Client/Server Technology

Kieran Mathieson
Oakland University

Tim Toland
Frontier Communications, Inc.

Executive Summary

Frontier Communications provides a variety of telecommunications services to business customers around the United States. The telecommunications industry is fiercely competitive, with suppliers constantly seeking to improve their market share. Maintaining good relationships with business customers is very important, since they can easily change from one carrier to another and still receive the same basic communications products. Frontier considers customer service to be one of the firm's most critical functions.

Customers with questions or complaints interact with Frontier's customer service representatives (CSRs). CSRs' tasks vary considerably depending on the situation, but they always strive to give customers an immediate and appropriate response to their inquiries. Achieving this goal requires that CSRs have access to a wide variety of customer information.

Allnet Communications, acquired by Frontier Communications in 1995, had developed a sophisticated mainframe-based system to support its CSRs. Although the system provided most of the data CSRs needed, it was not flexible enough to help them (1) get a complete picture of customers' activities, (2) research a problem and evaluate potential solutions, and (3) identify sales opportunities.

Allnet's management information systems (MIS) group developed a graphical user interface (GUI)-based customer service workstation. Significant effort was devoted to understanding the tasks that CSRs perform, and how an improved information system could increase their effectiveness. The system was also the MIS group's first major GUI, client/server system. This added to the risk of the project, a significant issue given the importance of the system. Allnet reduced the risk of failure by basing the new system on their existing mainframe systems rather than replacing them outright. This protected Allnet's investment in its existing systems and took advantage of their stability, although at the cost of maintaining two separate hardware platforms. The workstation is well-regarded by CSRs, and led to measurable improvements in customer service and sales.

The case shows how a firm can improve a critical business function with new technology. There are two main lessons here. First, an information system can alter the work that its users perform, helping them better achieve organizational objectives. The customer service workstation enabled CSRs to take a more proactive approach to solving customers' problems, giving them the tools to move from being system operators to company representatives. It also helped them sell additional services, a function that CSRs were not performing prior to the introduction of the new system. Second, the case shows that a firm can use new technology to build mission-critical information systems. However, the firm needs to carefully control the risk inherent in such projects. At Allnet, this was done by (1) involving users in the development process, (2) basing the new system on an existing system, rather than replacing the old system entirely, (3) involving an experienced consultant in the project, and (4) using prototyping to test the new system's design before development.

Background

Allnet Communications Services was formed by a merger of Allnet of Chicago and Lexitel Corporation of Birmingham, Michigan. The company aimed to be the preferred long distance carrier for small to medium-sized businesses. Allnet received its license to operate in the long distance telephone market from the Federal Communications Commission in 1981, and began marketing its services in Chicago, St. Louis and Cleveland. Allnet was acquired by Frontier Communications, formerly Rochester Telephone, in 1995. Frontier Communications is the primary provider of local telephone service in several eastern states, and has entered the long distance market by acquiring several smaller long distance carriers. Today, the firm is one of the nation's largest providers of telecommunications services to business customers.

The telecommunications industry is fiercely competitive. Note that:

• Most suppliers offer the same basic services. Product differentiation is somewhat more difficult in the telecommunications industry than in others.
• Customers' switching costs are low, that is, it costs customers little to change from one supplier to another.
• Telecommunications deregulation has opened the market to greater competition from a wide range of suppliers.

Profit margins are slim in such a competitive environment, particularly when serving cost-conscious business customers. Suppliers constantly seek to improve their market share at the expense of their rivals.

Frontier has concentrated on providing telecommunications solutions for its business customers, bringing products to the market before the competition. The firm integrates several products and services, including long distance service, wireless (such as paging and cellular), toll-free service, broadcast FAX, and teleconferencing. By integrating these products, Frontier is able to offer the customer one point of contact for all their telecommunication needs, and more importantly, a single invoice.

Customer service is critical in maintaining good customer relationships. A customer with a question or a complaints wants fast, effective service from staff who are informed not only about Frontier's products, but also about the customer's relationship with the firm. Key to achieving this objective are the customer service representatives (CSRs), who work directly with customers to resolve any problems that occur. CSRs' tasks vary substantially, depending on account circumstances. They must often coordinate with personnel in other departments, such as the Credit and Collections department, to address a customer's concern. Whatever the task, however, the CSRs strive to ensure that customers receive immediate and appropriate resolution of complaints, inquiries or other requests. The objective is to provide complete service within a single telephone call.

Setting the Stage

Achieving service goals requires that CSRs have access to a wide variety of customer information, such as the products they currently purchase, the status of their accounts, information on pending service requests and so on. Allnet developed a sophisticated on-line transaction processing system to support the CSRs. It was a traditional mainframe-based system, communicating with CSRs through character-oriented displays. Although the system gave CSRs access to most of the data they needed, it had two main limitations. First, it was not flexible enough to give the CSRs a complete picture of customers' activities. Second, it provided CSRs with little help in identifying sales opportunities.

The old system was a typical on-line transaction processing application. It was written in COBOL, ran on an IBM mainframe, and used CICS to manage a text interface on the CSR's dumb terminals. Figure 1 shows the system's main menu. The user would enter the appropriate code to access one of the subsystems. Many of the subsystems were independent of each other, and used different interfaces.

Consider a typical usage scenario. When a call was received from a customer, a CSR would ask

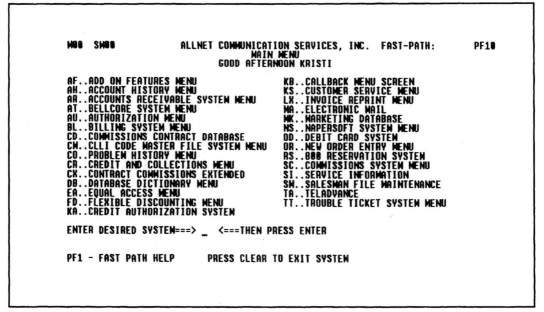

Figure 1: A menu from the Old System

```
      AUI320                    ANI INQUIRY            FAST-PATH:      PF10
      CUST NUMBER.: _      ---------BILLING--------- -----INSTALLATION--------
      AUTH CODE...:
      PHONE NUMBER:
      ANI NUMBER..:
      PORT NUMBER.:
      TRUNK NUMBER:
      ASSOC:      PACKAGE:
      PROD.:      OPTION.:
                                                  BILL START DATE:
      * * * * * * * * * * * * * * * * * * * * * * * * * * * * * * * * * * * *
      WRKING PHONE  BILL PHONE  ST TRANS DT AC SW  PROD/OPT LAST USE IP LT FX 2:3 I
      ============ ============ == ======== == === ======== ======== == == == === =



      PLEASE, ENTER "KEY" FIELD AND USE THE ENTER KEY OR APPROPRIATE PF KEY.........
         1 CELL 2 CLR 3 E/A 4 BIN 5 PORT 6 AUTH              9 ALP 11 P/H 12 MENU
```

Figure 2: Inquiry Screen From the Old System

for one of three possible numbers that could identify a customer's account: an account number, an authority number, or the customer's telephone number. Very often, the CSR would write this number down on paper, determine what type of number it was, and then enter the number into the appropriate field. The CSR's accuracy in recognizing different types of numbers increased as they gained experience. However, even the most experienced CSR would sometimes make errors. Occasionally, a CSR would have to resort to trial-and-error to determine what exactly a number was, that is, entering it into different screens and see if the system identified is as a valid number.

This procedure was clumsy and error prone. According to Cheryl Davis, an employee who trains CSRs:

> The CSR did not have the ideal method to access an account. A customer with more than one account, which is often the case, would create an even greater problem for the Customer Service Rep.

The CSRs' problems would be translated into delays and frustration for the customer.

Once the customer had been identified, the system would show the CSR one of a number of inquiry screens. Figure 2 shows a typical example. Unfortunately, only a small fraction of the data describing an account could be displayed at one time. The system also limited the ways CSRs could move from one screen to another. The CSRs often found it difficult to get a good overall picture of the circumstances surrounding a customer's account. This in turn made it difficult for the CSR to address the customer's request. Another problem was that the system did not help the CSR identify additional products and services that could benefit the customer. Management believed that the CSRs were missing sales opportunities.

One measure of service quality is the number of calls customers made to resolve a single problem. During a two-month period, 51,000 customers made 138,000 calls to the Customer Service department. Of these 51,000 customers, 20,000 called back two or more times, and 4,000 customers called back four or more times.

Allnet felt that improving service would increase customer satisfaction and reduce customer attrition. A key factor in improving service was to give the CSRs the tools they needed to do their job more effectively. This meant changing the existing information system.

Project Description

This section describes the project that resulted in the creation of the customer service workstation. The development process is examined first, followed by the system itself.

The Development Process

Allnet's management information systems (MIS) group was given the task of developing a new system that would help CSRs:

• solve customers' problems more effectively and efficiently
• promote the products and services customers already purchase
• sell additional products and services

The firm already had a system that, despite its shortcomings, did many things well. In particular, it kept track of most of the information CSRs needed (though it did not present it effectively), and was both reliable and secure. Allnet had a considerable investment in the system, and the firm's management was reluctant to allocate the resources needed to build a new system from scratch. Further, although the MIS group believed that a GUI system would help the CSRs offer better service, they had little experience with GUI and client/server technology. Note that developing a large multi-user GUI system usually involves client/server technology in one form or another, since computing power is needed both at the users' desks to run the interface, as well as centrally to manage shared resources.

Given the importance of the system and the uncertainty involved, the MIS department chose to develop a customer service workstation (CSWS) prototype to test the feasibility of their ideas. The MIS and Customer Service departments built the prototype with assistance from IBM, as part of IBM's Enterprise Alliance Services Offering.

The prototype suggested that an effective CSWS could be built by connecting PCs and the existing mainframe to a local area network (LAN). From these results, management committed to developing a new system. The plan was to continue to use the mainframe-based system to provide most of the business logic, but to present the data through a more flexible interface. Such an arrangement would achieve the project's objectives, while preserving the investment in the existing information system.

Once the overall direction of the project had been determined, joint application design (JAD) sessions helped gain a better understanding of the users' requirements (Martin, 1991). The JAD sessions brought together people from Allnet's MIS, Customer Service and Marketing departments, and were facilitated by IBM. The following requirements emerged:

• *Promotion of existing products and services.* A customer-specific promotion helps the customer feel that the CSR knows who they are and what services they use. The system should give the CSR a list of promotional suggestions based on the customer's profile, and log what was promoted in the customer history database. Future promotions could take this information into account.
• *Selling additional products and services.* The CSR should be able to establish a connection between the customer's business and the benefits that would be gained from new products and services. The system should help the CSR by examining the customer's profile and displaying services from which

the customer could benefit. The suggestions would be tailored to individual customers, based on Allnet's understanding of the their business.

• *Wrap code.* The wrap code concisely summarizes every call from a customer to a CSR. The JAD members developed a four-part code to be generated at the completion of every customer contact, consisting of a generic problem classification, a detailed problem description, the action taken, and the customer's attitude. An example would be:

> Primary: Billing
> Detail: Disputed call
> Action: Credit given
> Attitude: Very satisfied

• *Worklog.* The worklog reminds the CSR about scheduled customer activities, such as calling a customer to check on the resolution of a problem. Under the old system, this was done in an informal manner using notes on calendars. The new system should allow CSRs to enter events scheduled for a future date, including the information needed to process the request. The CSR should be able to execute the request on the specified date without re-entering the data. The system should also remind the CSR about past due and current worklog activities.

• *Alert.* The JAD members felt that the CSR should be notified of any pending requests from a customer at the beginning of a call. This would give the CSR a better understanding of activities surrounding the account. The system should also alert the CSR when the customer has been put into collection status, allowing the CSR to quickly refer them to the Credit and Collections department.

• *Jeopardy.* The JAD team also felt that the CSWS should warn the CSR when a customer might be at risk of canceling their service. Criteria for placing a customer in this category would include a decline in usage, a recent history of complaints, or payment or billing problems.

The JAD sessions provided a foundation for a high-level development plan. Although the details of the business requirements changed throughout the project, the JAD sessions set the framework for

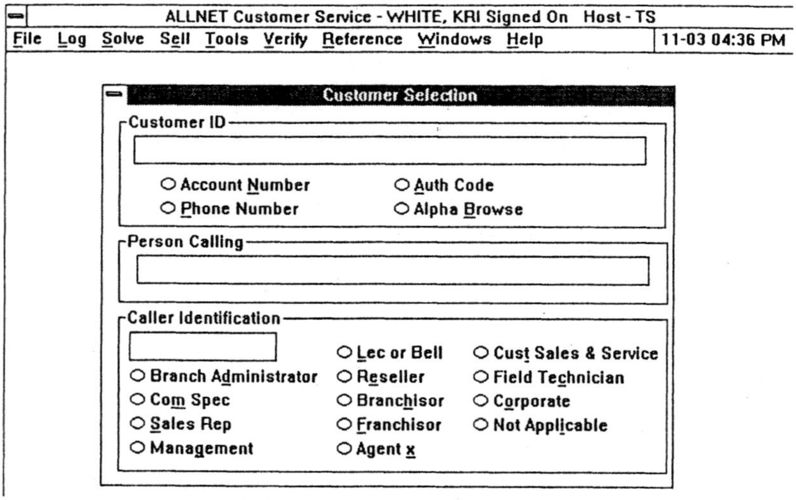

Figure 3: CSWS Customer Identification Screen

the project and established an atmosphere of cooperation between all parties involved.

After the JAD sessions, the Allnet MIS group created a project team. It consisted of an applications development manager, a project leader, three programmers, three individuals devoted to the development of specific subsystems (a reference library containing Allnet product information and files for the context-sensitive help system, a FAX server and CICS interface subroutines), and three technical support staff devoted to networking.

The Customer Service Workstation

The CSWS are IBM PS/2 Model 57 PCs running OS/2. They are linked by a token ring Novell LAN and connected to the mainframe through a gateway. The LAN also connects the workstations to a FAX server and two file servers that enforce LAN security and support the reference library. The reference library contains code and data needed to extend the functionality of the mainframe system. Easel was used to develop the client applications.

The CSRs' actions on the client machines trigger routines on the mainframe host. The routines run the appropriate COBOL programs which generate screen maps for dumb terminals. The CSWS translate the maps into GUI equivalents. The screen maps continue to serve as the I/O mechanism for the COBOL applications. This approach, called "screen scraping," limits the changes needed in the host's applications.

Figure 3 shows a customer identification screen from the CSWS. The CSR enters an identification number into the appropriate field and selects an option button to indicate which type of number it is. If the CSR does not know the number's type, he or she can ask the system to identify the number. The CSR is also able to enter the caller's name on the opening screen. The system will carry the name to every window until the transaction is completed.

The CSWS allows CSRs to view several data screens concurrently, allowing them to get a better overall picture of the customer. The system will also display account data graphically, helping the CSR identify usage trends and patterns. Figure 4 shows an example.

Sales and promotion features have been added, with the system's suggestions tailored to each customer. A CSR's typical interaction with a customer now has three stages: (1) fix the problem the customer is calling about, (2) promote existing services and (3) sell new services. Alert and jeopardy warning features have also been added to the system to support these activities. Figure 5 shows an example of a CSWS customer alert message. If a customer shows interest in a product, the CSR can click on a FAX button to send information about that product to the customer. Worklogs help ensure that promises to customers are kept.

Current Status

The first CSWS was delivered in mid-1992. Initially released in Michigan, it is now used by over 300 CSRs in Michigan, Ohio and Wisconsin. LANs in each location are connected over a wide-area network to the mainframe.

The CSWS has seen relatively little change since its introduction. It has performed well, although mainframe CPU load has become a concern with the growing number of users. In an effort to reduce the mainframe's load as well as economize on network traffic, several mainframe database tables are downloaded daily to the LANs at each site. The CSWS uses these local tables whenever possible. One other change has been to improve the CSWS help subsystem.

Future IS directions at Frontier are uncertain. The firm has grown substantially in recent years through its acquisitions. At the time of writing, Frontier is still deciding how it will integrate the

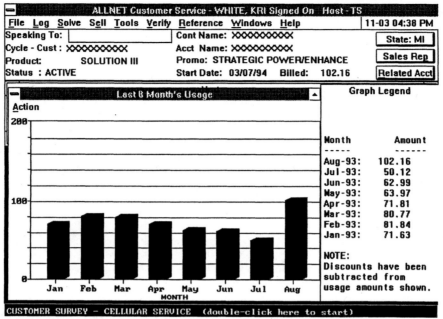

Figure 4: CSWS Graph Showing Usage Trends

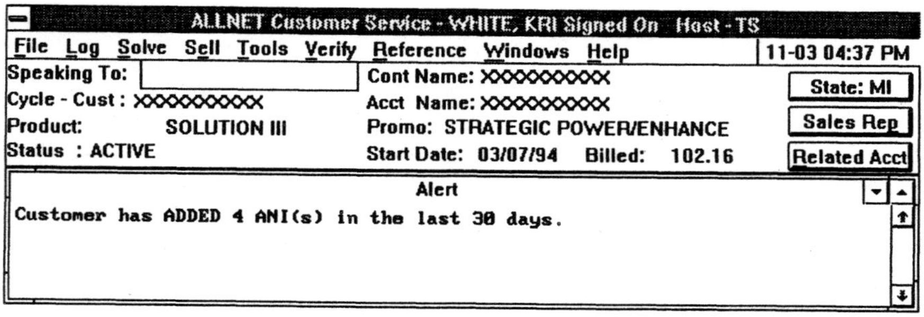

Figure 5: CSWS Customer Alert

information systems of the firms it has acquired. However, it seems likely that the CSWS will continue to provide value to the firm for some time.

Successes and Failures

The CSWS project was able to achieve its main objective: helping CSRs improve customer service. According to Gessler Walker, a Frontier employee who has been involved with the project since its inception:

The CSWS allows the CSR to compile customer information faster and in a more readable format.... The CSWS allows access to virtually everything on a customer account with the click of a few buttons, whereas the old system would take several screens as well as several different keying sequences.

The CSWS has not only improved customer service, but it has changed the way CSRs do their jobs. They are able to better understand how one call fits within a customer's history, and are able to take a more proactive approach to solving customers' problems.

The promotion and sales features have also expanded the CSRs' roles. Most sales are handled by a national sales force. However, the CSWS promotional features led to the Customer Services department increasing sales revenue by US $250,000 in the first three months of the new system's operation.

Allnet's approach is not without its costs, however. The original system ran on a single platform - the mainframe. The new system still uses the mainframe, but adds GUI workstations and file and FAX servers. This reduced the cost and risk of initial development, but increased the cost of operating and maintaining the new system. In particular, it required the firm to:

• purchase and maintain duplicate hardware (e.g., workstations/terminals and network equipment) and software (e.g., operating systems and development tools)
• train personnel on multiple platforms
• deal with the complexities of integrating multiple technologies

Of course, every MIS department faces these issues. Using a single type of computing platform is a luxury of the past for most companies. Client/server technology is becoming common, not just in custom-built systems such as the CSWS, but in off-the-shelf systems such as Lotus Notes. Even firms with mainframe-centric MIS departments still have PCs and servers scattered across their organization. The Allnet case highlights multiple-platform issues since it combines mainframe and PC technology within a single custom-built system. However, they are issues that every large firm must address.

Finally, note that Allnet used OS/2 as its workstation operating system. OS/2 has not been as successful in the marketplace as its developer, IBM, would have hoped. Its market share is considerably less than that of Microsoft Windows. There is less support for OS/2 from third party vendors (such as database vendors), less interest in the operating system from users, and it is more difficult to hire information systems professionals with OS/2 expertise.

Unfortunately, technological "Russian roulette" is part of the nature of client/server development (Orfali et al., 1994). Analysts make a large number of technology choices, including workstation and server hardware, workstation and server operating systems, network operating systems, development tools, middleware, database engines, email server packages, system management software, etc. This gives developers tremendous flexibility, allowing them to match technology and requirements to a fine degree. However, it is virtually certain that one or more of the technologies that the developers choose will not be the market leader in a few years time. The CSWS will probably continue to run under OS/2, as long as IBM continues to support the product to a reasonable extent. However, client/server developers may find it necessary to substitute technologies as the computer industry develops.

Epilogue and Lessons Learned

There are two main lessons to be learned from this case. First, information systems are sometimes developed or selected without a thorough review of their business role. Where a computerized IS replaces a manual system, it might simply automate existing work practices. Where a new IS replaces an existing computerized system, the design of the new system or its selection criteria might simply reflect the features of the old system. There may be little review of the work practices that are being supported by the old system.

In reality, every systems development project is an opportunity to examine the work that is being supported. During system design or system selection, IS and functional area staff should ask: how can existing work practices and existing technology be changed so as to better support organizational objectives? Rather than freezing work practices and choosing technology to suit, or freezing technology and choosing work practices to suit, the development team should consider the synergy that can come from fitting both together to achieve organizational goals.

This was the case at Allnet. Note that the project was motivated by business rather than technology concerns. Customer satisfaction was a problem, and management believed that the CSRs could change the way they served customers if they had better information. The development team set out to solve both business and technical problems at the same time. The result was not just a system that did what the old IS did, but a system that changed the CSRs' jobs. They are able to be more proactive and responsive to customers than they were before, researching the causes of problems, following up on complaints and promises of action, and anticipating concerns that might arise. They are also able to sell products because the new system gives them a better understanding of the customers' requirements. The CSWS works because it lets CSRs do more for customers, not because it uses new technology in an interesting way.

The second lesson is about the management of risk. Two major sources of risk in IS projects relate to (1) information requirements and (2) technology. Information requirements analysis should be thorough if the development team is to deliver a system that will have significant business value. This is often easiest if users participate in the development process (Baroudi, Olson, & Ives, 1986). Typically, the IS staff does not completely understand users' jobs or the operational constraints they face, while the users do not completely understand the opportunities created by information technology, its limitations or its cost structure. The probability of creating an effective system is increased when both groups work together.

As far as technological risk is concerned, unforeseen technical challenges can delay a project and push it over-budget. At the extreme, technological problems can lead to project termination. Technology issues were particularly important in this project, since this was Allnet's first extensive use of GUI or client/server technology. Introducing new technology can create a host of unforeseen problems, and Allnet's IS group had to manage the situation carefully. Failure of the CSWS project would have been very visible to the entire firm, including top management, because of the strategic importance of customer service.

The development team took several steps to reduce project risk. First, staff from various functional areas participated heavily in the project. The input of the CSRs and their supervisors was an important element in the success of the new system. Second, the CSWS was based on an existing system. While the mainframe system was inflexible and relatively difficult to use, it did store most of the information the CSRs required. Moreover, the system was reliable, secure, and ran on a well-understood platform. These are desirable attributes, and the development team was loathe to discard the system entirely. Completely replacing the system would not only have increased development costs, but, given the complexities and uncertainty of client/server systems (Berson, 1992), would have increased the project's risk. Instead, the core of the old system was wrapped in a new interface shell and supplemented to create the CSWS. Allnet was thus able to continue to take advantage of their investment in a stable system.

Third, Allnet involved IBM in the project. IBM has significant experience with the technical and managerial questions that arise during client/server projects. Hiring an experienced consultant can reduce the risk of dealing with new technology (Vaughn, 1994).

Finally, the development team used prototyping to test their ideas (Carey, 1990). Prototyping had two main benefits in this case. First, prototyping helps users visualize an information system (Braunstein, Lauer & Doane, 1991). It is often difficult to explain a set of information requirements, or to evaluate a design that exists only on paper. A prototype is more concrete, helping users see what a proposed design would actually be like. Second, prototyping can help evaluate the technical feasibility of a project. This was more important in this case than it sometimes is, since Allnet's development staff had had little exposure to GUI, client/server technology. Developing a prototype helped them understand the issues involved in creating these types of systems, and is commonly recommended in the client/server arena (Orfali, Harkey & Edwards, 1994).

In summary, Allnet needed to change a mission critical information system to improve customer service. The CSWS preserves the company's investment in custom mainframe applications, while giving the CSRs the flexibility they need to respond to customers' concerns.

Questions for Discussion

1. Why is customer service so important to Frontier?

2. What is the role of information technology in customer service?

3. How did the new system change the CSRs jobs?

4. How did Allnet reduce the project's risk?

5. What are some of the advantages and disadvantages of creating a new interface for an existing system?

References

Baroudi, J. J., Olson, M. H., & Ives, B. (1986). An empirical study of the impact of user involvement on system usage and information satisfaction. *Communications of the ACM*, 29, 232-238.

Berson, A. (1992). *Client/server architecture*. New York: McGraw-Hill.

Braunstein, D. N., Lauer, T. W., & Doane, D. P. (1991). Information requirements prototyping for decision support systems. *Journal of Information Technology*, 6, 26-33.

Carey, J. M. (1990). Prototyping: Alternative systems development methodology. *Information and Software Technology*, 32, 119-126.

Martin, J. (1991). *Rapid application development*. New York: Macmillan.

Orfali, R., Harkey, D., & Edwards, J. (1994). *Essential client/server survival guide*. New York: Van Nostrand Reinhold.

Vaughn, L. T. (1994). *Client/server system design and implementation*. New York: McGraw-Hill.

Chapter 12

USCInfo: A High Volume, Integrated Online Library Resources Automation Project

Mathew J. Klempa
Computer Information Systems Consultant

Lucy Siefert Wegner
University of Southern California

Executive Summary

This case sets forth automation philosophies and systems development processes associated with the University of Southern California's "USCInfo"[1], an integrated retrieval software for accessing both the USC Library catalog and periodical indexes. Regarded at its implementation as being cutting edge in library automation, USCInfo's present size is 25 gigabytes of data, with searches numbering 3,800,000 annually.

USCInfo is illustrative of "messy problems," i.e., unstructured, complex, and multidimensional, which typically involve substantive organizational issues "soft" in nature. Problem conceptualization, decision making, and solution implementations in USCInfo often are both heuristic[2] and utilize satisficing[3] decision–making processes. Such decision making deals with multiple, substantive constraints as well as conflict and ambiguity, i.e., "equivocality" [4].

Systems development concepts embodied in this case include:

• systems life cycle evolution amidst technology change and obsolescence
• systems design alternatives and end user characteristics
• management of the systems life cycle maintenance phase
• management of applications prototyping
• small design team dynamics, champions
• organizational impacts on the systems life cycle
• rational and political organization processes
• dual responsibility project management

Background

USC and Library System Overview

The University of Southern California, founded in 1880, is the oldest and largest private research university in the American West, approximately 14,000 undergraduates in a total enrollment numbering some 28,000. In the five year period preceding systems development of USCInfo, the USC library system comprised some 16 libraries, including: College Library (principle undergraduate library); Doheny Reference Center; several larger libraries – science, engineering, business, public administration and foreign affairs; and other main campus smaller libraries.

As a member of the Association of Research Libraries (ARL), there was continual pressure on resources to keep pace with a rising flood of materials, i.e., books, journals, and ever increasingly, other non–traditional media–based materials. Separately, Library administration sought to improve the quality of a collection that was historically underfunded. The USC Library budget is affected by the University's fiscal health, e.g., static or downtrending enrollment growth directly impacts library budgets.

U. S. Library Automation

Libraries make a variety of finding tools available to their users, e.g., directories, indexes, and abstracting services. Two that are ubiquitous across libraries are a library's catalog and periodical indexes. Research libraries are driven, in part, by the "information explosion," i.e., the need to provide improved capabilities for locating both catalog and periodical source material in the face of geometrically increasing numbers and types of publications.

The decade of the 1980s witnessed a concomitant rate of growth in the number of libraries digitizing catalog availability as an Online Public Access Catalog (OPAC). Digitizing a library's catalog can be thought of as an item-specific type "inventory"problem. Each catalog item's particular characteristics (book, journal, government document, etc.) must be described to an established level of detail. Item "status" must be tracked and reported for inquiry purposes, e.g., being cataloged, recalled, checked out, lost/stolen, etc. Additionally, patron data must be combined with item data.

The decade of the 1980s also witnessed increased digitization of periodical indexes by various methods such as dial-up time sharing services and CD-ROM–based periodical indexes. Prior to USCInfo, library patrons were offered dial–up periodical indexes search access. Such searches, performed at each library campus site, were librarian mediated, i.e., required to be performed by a librarian professional. Costs were subsidized by USC, patrons paid a nominal fee, and access was limited. Library automation planning documents cited the exponential growth in USC dial–up searches as a driving impetus for development of a USC–based digitized periodical indexes search capability.

USCInfo – Early Prototype Development

Formal Organization Prototyping. USCInfo began with a $1 million grant from the Ahmanson foundation. Principles embodied within USCInfo from the outset, included:

- *Unified User Interface.* Systems should support a unified user interface across all resources
- *Wide Selection of Resources.* Access should be provided to a wide selection of information resources
- *Gateway beyond USC.* Systems should provide a gateway to the information-rich environment

beyond the institution
- *Ease of Use.* Systems should be easy to use

    The USC Library wanted to provide the campus community with unlimited (free) access from any location, any time of day. In a multisite library system, the only cost effective way to provide such a capability is to 1) either purchase and modify, or 2) custom develop, both the user interface and search engine software, to be run on the university's computer. Vendor supplied periodical indexes database tapes would be "locally mounted" on the university's computer[5]. The Ahmanson project established the dual responsibility[6] of both University Computing Services[7](UCS) and the Library for USCInfo.

    The Ahmanson project began development of the formally recognized USCInfo, a vt100 version. The Library's Linda R. from the Library Automation Development Unit (LAD) and UCS (Kurt B.), working together (see Table 4), established a pilot prototype periodical index search capability, with a subsequent, second phase, small scale operation at four non–library "satellites" (computing facilities set up by the Library). The four satellite locations isolated USCInfo from USC Library personnel as a whole. Although such isolation was not desirable, both the rudimentary remote access technology and the lack of network wiring in the libraries hindered large–scale Library staff involvement.

    Informal Organization (de facto) Prototyping. Working virtually independently of, and largely unknown to the Ahmanson project for several months, Tim H. and Brad G., of the Center for Scholarly Technology (CST), undertook development of a HyperCard graphical user interface (GUI) USCInfo, i.e., Tim and Brad constituted an "informal organization" (see glossary). The "Tim–Brad" HyperCard USCInfo had similar (although not identical) functionality to the official vt100version USCInfo and was available on twenty Apple SEs exclusively in College Library, in lieu of the vt100 USCInfo. Notwithstanding frequent system crashes and reloads, the HyperCard–based front end had established preliminarily its connectivity to a mainframe. In addition, the College Library's largely undergraduate student users felt it offered vastly improved ease of use and intelligibility. HyperCard USCInfo would become a de facto pilot project for subsequent USCInfo development, and Tim and Brad its most vocal champions (see glossary).

Pro	Con
Existing relationship with vendor; would give substantial support	GEAC 9000 new machine, largely untried in marketplace
Resulting OPAC would not be "interim", but treated as longer term	GEAC 9000 incompatible with GEAC 8000 Full project migration needed
	Expense is "hard" money; university administration unlikely to approve
	GEAC 9000 solution only addresses OPAC, not periodical indexes searching
	There would be incompatible networks, i.e., GEAC 9000 – dumb terminals; USCInfo – vt100 terminals

Table 1: Upgrading to GEAC 9000 System

Setting the Stage

USCInfo Project Externalities

The paced and measured development of the vt100 USCInfo periodical indexes search capability changed with the departure of Mary L. who had established and spearheaded the early Ahmanson project, the appointment of Jim R. as Acting Deputy Assistant University Librarian for Academic Information Services (AIS), and the Library's OPAC crisis. Phased conversion of USC's manual card catalog to an OPAC (called Homer[8]) began prior to the Ahmanson Project. When Homer's public access search module was brought online, Homer experienced severe peak loading problems, i.e., searches could take minutes to complete at busy times. Deeming the Homer OPAC problem both unacceptable and untenable, senior library administration directed the recently promoted Jim R. to determine available alternatives.

In addition, the University administration was directing the Library to prepare a five year projection, with options, of totally inclusive automation costs, beyond just a combined OPAC and automated periodical indexes retrieval system. It was clear that such longer term automation planning was essential to get university backing for future Library automation proposals.

Jim R. considered his fewer-in-number alternatives. An obvious alternative was to upgrade the existing GEAC 8000 system to a GEAC 9000system (see Table 1). Considerations set forth in Table 1 notwithstanding, the senior university financial officer, citing the fairly recent $300,000 expenditure for the GEAC system, expressed very strong reservations about the approximately $500,000 "hard" money–based proposed GEAC upgrade. Another option was an "all vt100", i.e., non–intelligent terminals approach. A comparison of this approach to the Mac HyperCard approach is given in Table 2.

The Apple Appeal

The Homer crisis began both the formalization of CST's involvement with USCInfo and the emergence of Apple Computer[9]. Through CST directors, Apple Computer expressed interest in a substantial equipment grant (some $800,000) to the Library for a HyperCard–based USCInfo. This grant included 165 Macintosh SE/30 computers[10], serving as replacements for all existing 150+ OPAC terminals, as well as related hardware. In terms of economic feasibility, the Apple equipment grant

Characteristic/ Requirement	DOS/vt100	Mac HyperCard
Machines	Cheaper, but no subsidy/gift	More expensive, but substantial Apple gift likely
Interface	Quicker to adapt to existing interface, but text based	Innovative graphical user interface, requiring more extensive development
Log-on Procedure	More difficult to implement and less secure	Log–on procedure hidden in stack; more secure

Table 2: vt100 USCInfo versus HyperCard USCInfo

would make the project financially possible from the University's perspective. USC's contribution also would be substantial (approximately $500,000 total, both hard and soft monies), reflecting purchase of necessary network software, systems development costs, and implementation costs. A major portion of the $500,000 included necessary FTE systems development personnel expenses.

The perceived "availability" of a HyperCard USCInfo alternative began to influence decision making, i.e., the HyperCard–based front end USCInfo had demonstrated some capability as a network interface. No formal technical or operational feasibility evaluations of the "Tim-Brad" HyperCard USCInfo were conducted at this time, e.g., analyses of system crashes, system response times, robustness of the HyperCard interface, machine performance under conditions of poorly formed searches, etc.

Table 3 sets forth foreseen HyperCard benefits as well as drawbacks. Brad G., the early HyperCard champion, urged its use as an applications prototyping tool only, with a production version to be written subsequently in a high level language, e.g., C. In sum, the proposed HyperCard interface carried with it substantive technical, operational, and schedule feasibility issues.

Jim R. took CST's interim–step, HyperCard prototype and proposed a bold, encompassing view which reflected creativity, daring, and a willingness to take risks. The library's OPAC would be consolidated into USCInfo, i.e., an integrated on–line catalog and periodical indexes search retrieval system. Jim R. was trying to skip several iterations of system design, i.e., a Ford Taurus solution[11]. At the time, Jim R. considered the consolidation of the Library's OPAC with USCInfo as a major transition in the movement of the Library's Integrated Library System (ILS) to an IBM mainframe[12].

The principle parties involved saw the possibility of influencing national library automation trends, with concomitant future USC Library automation benefits. As stated in Jim R.'s response to Apple:

HyperCard Advantages	HyperCard Disadvantages
Sophisticated graphical design; enhanced menuing capabilities	Slower execution speed
Reduced host load; workstations do screen painting	Not suitable for multiple workstations requiring "bullet-proof" operation
More realistic distributed computing, i.e., distributed host environments	Ease of alteration makes it susceptible to corruption from a curious hacker
Capacity to install "add–on" utility programs at workstation level	Every software release requires reloading all machines, one at a time*
Workstation software can be distributed free of charge to local user population	Beta release at the time of USCInfo implementation
Ease of alteration, enables design modifications to be tried immediately	Ease with which changes can be made contributes to "project creep"

*Later, well into the USCInfo HyperCard period, capability was provided that eliminated this necessity.

Table 3: HyperCard Considerations

Participant Name	Unit	USCInfo Responsibilities*	Participant Characteristics	Previous Work Focus
Linda R.⁺	Library (LAD)	LAD responsible for Front End vt100 programming	Facilitator, good with people	Ahmanson Project vt100 USCInfo Periodical Indexes Searching
Tim H.⁺	(CST)	F ront End HyperCard Programming	Bright, unseasoned	de facto, "informal organization", USCInfo version
Brad G.⁺	(CST)	F ront End HyperCard Programming being liked	Personable. Iconoclast who didn't worry about USCInfo version	de facto, "informal organization",
Jim R.⁺	Library (AIS)	P roject Manager	Driven, heightened work pace, innovative	GEAC 8000 OPAC Implementation
Kurt B.⁺	(UCS)	Back End Database structure, maintenance, BRS Search Engine	Intelligent, skillful. His analytical abilities moved ahead of group.	Joint Responsibility with Library's LAD unit for vt100 USCInfo development.

+   See Appendix B, for Rowe Decision Style
+   Refer to Figure 2, for position on organization chart
+   These individuals were evaluated by periodic Performance Evaluation reviews

*   Library's System Support Unit was responsible for loading USCInfo databases

Table 4: Project Planning Group (PPG) Participant Characteristics

USC...has been working to develop a combined OPAC and periodical indexes, HyperCard-based, retrieval system... this innovative approach... moves beyond conventional terminal-host, ASCII-interface links

Jim R.'s radical, encompassing step would necessitate transporting the entire Homer OPAC, i.e., 8+ million items from GEAC to the VM-based USCInfo system. Jim R.'s innovative approach required multiple serial and parallel tasks (see Figure 1). Combining both OPAC and periodical indexes retrieval significantly increased the project's scope. Installation issues were also paramount, viz., Ethernet connections[13] would have to be installed in ten libraries within four months, the 165 new intelligent terminals acquired and installed, and library staff completely retrained.

In sum, acceptance of Jim R.'s proposal would commit to completion of the proposed USCInfo within eighteen months, using new machines (unfamiliar platform), a new interface, revised back-end, new communications software, and simultaneous addition of several new databases. The vt100 terminal emulation, remote user version of USCInfo, also would have to be updated concurrently, thus creating a parallel platform to be maintained until otherwise formally discontinued.

Jim R.'s proposal formally would make the three units – Library, CST, and UCS responsible for

USCInfo. Although all three units would be responsible formally, the de facto reality was that this approach would become the Library's, inasmuch as CST wanted HyperCard used only for prototyping and UCS had strong reservations about its use as a network interface (see Project Planning Group Participant Agendas section). In addition, Jim R.'s approach required the blending of differing organization cultures (Appendix A), demographic characteristics (Table 5), individuals' decision styles (Appendix B), as well as Project Planning Group (PPG) participant characteristics (Table 4). Although Linda R. served as project facilitator, she did not have authority to impose solutions when system design conflicts arose.

Jim R.'s "can–do" ebullience as well as de facto commitments made (or imposed) along the way acted like a dare on the group. Could they do it? Jim R. got a green light from the University Librarian to go ahead.

Project Description

Design Tradeoffs

Jim R.'s USCInfo design essentially traded off four considerations:

1) WHAT type of system do we want to create
2) WHO are our users
3) WHICH design factors will be given higher priority
4) BALANCING how much the system should do for the user versus how much the user should be expected to learn

Tim H. and Brad G., HyperCard champions, came down heavily on the side of ease of use,

> our goal was to create an interface readily usable by the general college student, without the student having to read a binder of instructions.

An estimated one-half to two-thirds of USCInfo users each year were either new to the system or used it infrequently. Designing for such a primary user group immediately raised screen navigation issues:

• WHAT is "intuitive" and "to WHOM"
• HOW to accommodate both the sophisticated and unsophisticated search patron, i.e., search and retrieval issues
• WHICH screen elements and their arrangement, i.e., record display issues

Both prevailing OPAC and periodical indexes retrieval designs utilized dumb terminals. In contrast, use of intelligent terminals would exploit the mainframe's retrieval power and speed, as well as the workstation's HyperCard GUI's ease of use. Longer range enhancement of a GUI–based system seemed better achievable by creating a user interface resident on the workstation, not the host. The Macintosh/mainframe design direction taken by USCInfo constituted a de facto rudimentary client–server–type architecture, thus presaging true client–server architecture in use today.

Intensive Eighteen Month Development

Jim R. projected completion in 18 months, i.e., by the September start of the coming school year. This timeline was based on very optimistic estimates from programmers as well as best case scenarios

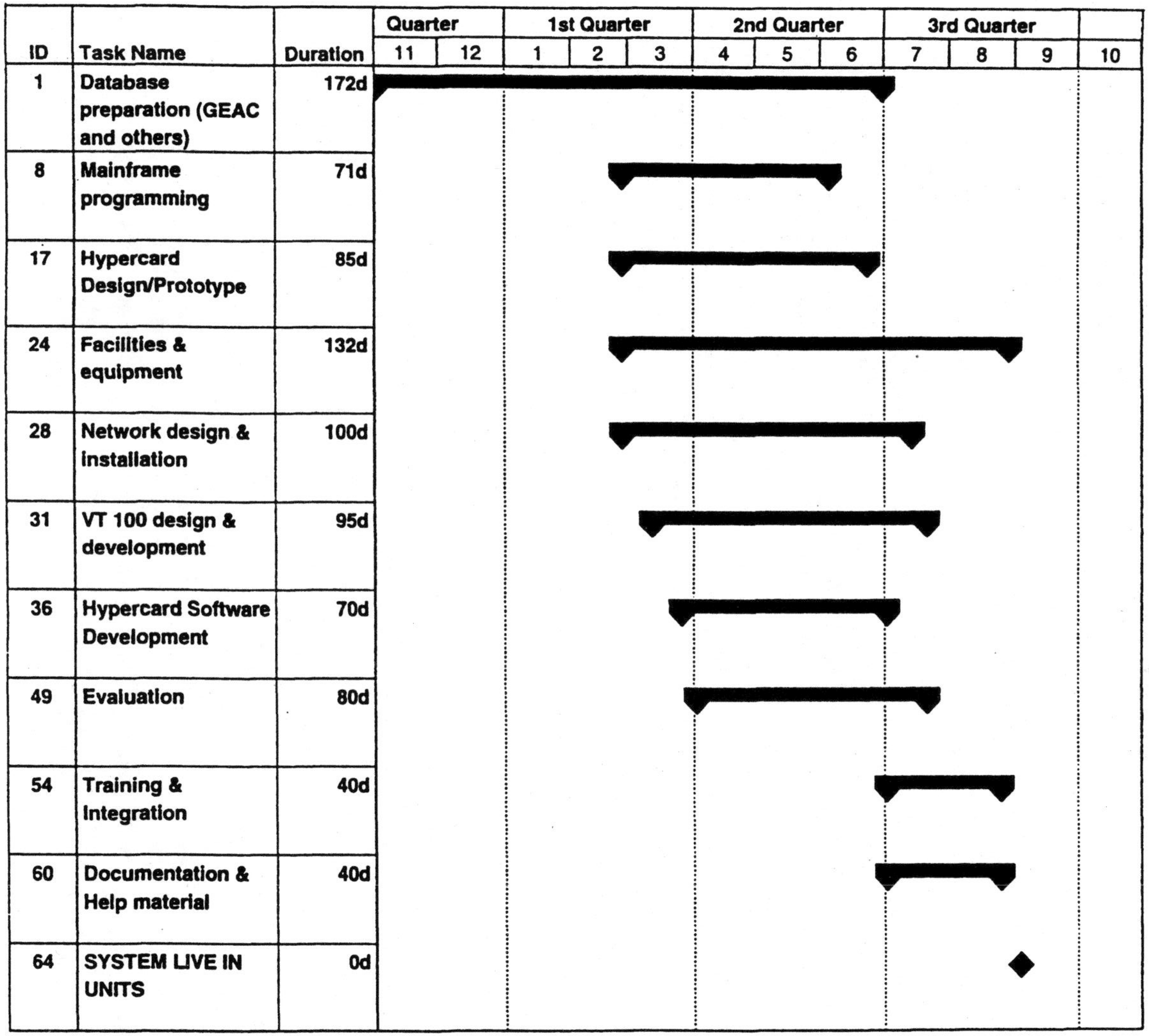
ID
Task Name
Duration
Quarter
1st Quarter
2nd Quarter
3rd Quarter
11
12
1
2
3
4
5
6
7
8
9
10
1 Database preparation (GEAC and others) 172d
8 Mainframe programming 71d
17 Hypercard Design/Prototype 85d
24 Facilities & equipment 132d
28 Network design & installation 100d
31 VT 100 design & development 95d
36 Hypercard Software Development 70d
49 Evaluation 80d
54 Training & Integration 40d
60 Documentation & Help material 40d
64 SYSTEM LIVE IN UNITS 0d

Figure 1: USCInfo Timeline

for implementation and installation. As shown in Figure 1, the original eighteen month timeline was compressed further, to eleven months (system completion date was not moved), because of delays in the start of system development. The principle parties involved did not seem as concerned about the 11 month timeline, in particular the impact of potential design bugs in elongating the 11 months and increasing frustration among the participants. After considerable discussion, a set of "basic functionality" was agreed to by all parties. Some system flowcharts and documentation were put together, although limited in nature. Development activities focused on a July 1 target date for a Beta release of HyperCard USCInfo (Figure 1, Task 36), with an almost parallel two step, four month period for design and prototyping (Figure 1, Task 17). Installation activities were geared to September 1. At the commencement of systems development, staff working on USCInfo numbered 12 (not all worked full time). During the actual 11 month development period and initial year of operation (see later section – HyperCard implementation delays), the number grew to 19 (not all worked full time). Approximately 50% of the projected person hours utilized student labor, primarily doing HyperCard coding.

Stakeholder Perspectives

Figure 2 places the Library, UCS, and CST within the overall USC organization. Table 5 synopsizes salient UCS, Library, and CST demographics. Appendix A contains brief descriptions of the organization cultures of UCS, the Library, and CST.

UCS is a masculine organization (see glossary), i.e., assertive in interpersonal dealings, with a high performance orientation. UCS' organization culture is a dyad, developmental/rational. Developmental cultures value adaptability, autonomy, and creativity. Rational cultures are less likely to engage in satisficing decision making, but rather to take a longer term, "maximize", viewpoint, i.e., long term system effectiveness.

The Library's culture is a dyad, consensual/hierarchical. Consensual cultures value cooperation, fairness, and openness. Senior library management's culture is hierarchical, i.e., oriented toward centralized control and coordination. Identifiable Library subcultures include: library administration (assistant university librarians and dean), heads of individual library units, and the divisions (public service, cataloging, AIS). Additionally, those in the "nontraditional" functions (library automation, systems development, and computer services) constituted a subculture distinct from "traditional" library functions (user services, cataloging, collection development). At the time of USCInfo development, the nontraditional subculture was poorly understood and not fully appreciated.

CST's initial umbrella–like charter as a research and development center anticipated pursuit of projects "designed to enhance the use of information technology in instruction and scholarship". CST reported jointly to both the dean of the Library and Vice Provost for Academic Computing (Figure 2). CST staff, assigned to specific projects, generally were titled "directors". CST's culture, a developmental / hierarchical dyad, valued creativity in problem solving, while at the same time pursuing coordination and control responsibilities.

The UCS, Library, and CST demographic and organization culture differences contributed to USCInfo project frictions. UCS viewed "technology" as its bailiwick. The Library staff in general viewed themselves as "different" than technology types, i.e., both UCS and CST. CST was viewed as "outside" the library, with a mission and purpose that was "fuzzy".

The Project Planning Group Participant Agendas

University Computing Services. UCS, operations and technology oriented, viewed the library as another client among many. In the role of "network cop," UCS informed the Project Planning Group of what could or could not be done on the campus network and mainframes. UCS expressed serious

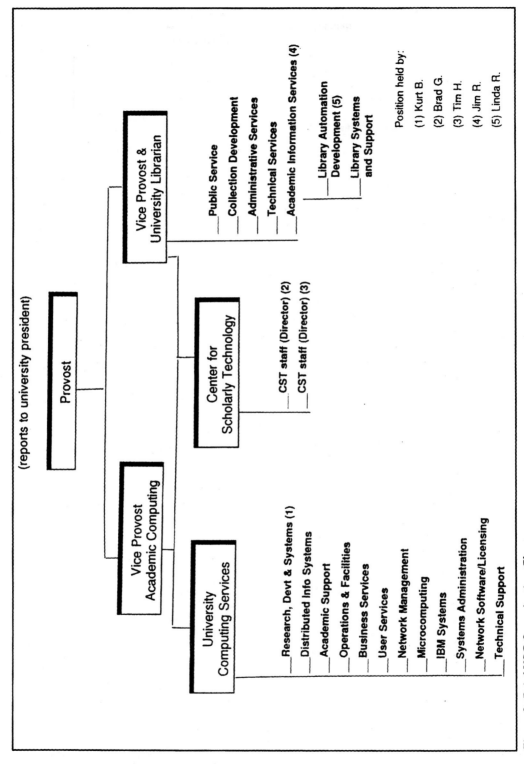

Figure 2: Brief USC Organization Chart

reservations about the HyperCard project from the get–go, centering on network behavior and robust operation, e.g., developing telecommunications software based on a beta release HyperCard[14]. UCS strongly favored developing a GUI using X–Windows–Unix only, which while platform specific at the time, was deemed by UCS as far more transferable in the future. The practical effect of UCS' "position" with respect to HyperCard implied minimal implementation support from UCS. Although UCS nominally was collaborating in the HyperCard implementation, it would have required a saint's forbearance not to be a bit gratified in subsequent months as the project implementation difficulties began to arise.

The Library. The Library was often frustrated by what it perceived as the technology's restrictions. A Library Review Committee (Figure 3), consisting of library faculty, staff, and an outside user representative, advised on interface and content issues. The Library Review Committee functioned as a "bridge", serving to both solicit end–user inputs to the design process and, when necessary, communicate design approach particulars and feedback from the PPG. Meetings were run by Linda R. or Jim R. Typical exchanges (heavily paraphrased), as highlighted below, often arose:

[Example] Committee Member (CM): **I'd** like to see all the library locations listed in a, what do you call it?, pull out menu, so the user can pick the library they want before they do a search. In GEAC, the patron chooses the library **before** searching.
Linda R. (or Jim R.): Well, that's tricky to do. We'd have to write a program to produce the pull-down menu and then send that information to the mainframe and then get the results back...
CM: Well, what **IS** possible then?

[Example] Linda R.: How about icons to represent different functions, help, quit and so on?
CM: I don't **like** icons, words are clearer. GEAC doesn't use icons and it works just **fine**.

CST. CST, the new kid on the block, was ill understood by either the Library or UCS. Some staff in UCS felt all the funds for development had been drained away to support this "isolated" unit whose responsibilities "somehow" included technology. This nebulous and isolated unit now came face–to–face with UCS within the Project Planning Group. The Library suspected that funds had been given to CST that were needed in other areas, e.g., collection development.

The Project Planning Group Dynamic

UCS	Library	CST
Predominantly male	Predominantly female	Predominantly male
Computer Professionals	Librarians	Computer professionals
Practical	Conservative	Radical
Experienced	Experienced	Creative, entrepreneurs
Many in leadership without degrees	MLS degrees + other advanced degrees	Many with advanced degrees, not MLS
Younger	Older	Mostly younger

Table 5: UCS, Library, CST Demographics

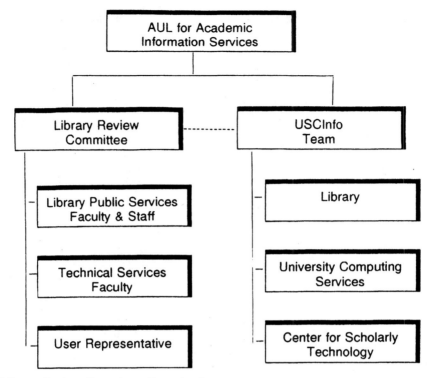

Figure 3: Library Review Committee Organization

Linda R. prepared and distributed weekly design team meeting agendas, conducted weekly design team meetings, kept minutes, and tracked implementation progress on decisions made. Linda was regarded as being able to communicate effectively with all team members, often interpreting one group to another. Jim R. was usually in attendance and also took a major role. He came into frequent conflict with both UCS (Kurt B.) and CST (Brad G).

The 11 month timeline (Figure 1), i.e., stress overload, contributed to the often tensions and disagreements between the major participants in the development process. Persistent problems generated both intense reactions, e.g., "that is unacceptable – fix it now", and often passionate responses to such reactions.

As the development process unfolded, requiring the fitting together of many untried pieces, bugs and problems arose. At times, meetings degenerated into name calling and finger pointing as each side was convinced the problem was caused by another group's sub-project. Conflicts often arose with Brad G. from CST, as in the following (heavily paraphrased) typical interchange from a PPG meeting:

Linda R: In the Mac version, records are being returned that have title in the author field, author in the title field, and aren't from the same item anyway.
Brad G.: The stack parses the data stream by pairing author (AU) and title (T) fields, starting a new record any time an AU (author) field is detected. The **problem is** the mainframe is sending data fields out of order and needs to be fixed.
Kurt B: No, **that's not it!** Some records do not have an author field at all
[draws diagram on board]:

Mainframe sends:

AT	AT	T	AT	T	AT

Mac expects:

AT	AT	AT	AT	AT

Mac displays:

AT	AT	TA	TT	AT

The Mac needs to be fixed to use the unique identifier field to delimit records, not the author field, which may not be present.

[Note: Brad G., while an experienced programmer, isn't aware that some items will not have an author field attached, something which is obvious to librarians.]

During the USCInfo development period, the small size of the PPG, its weekly and highly personal interaction modality, and its composition of highly experienced and skilled professionals, were considered as strengths. During system development, the functioning of the group could be described as "hands–on", providing both mobility and flexibility in decision making as details of design considerations arose. There were differences from the traditional systems design situation:

- Unlike the typical "end–user", Library PPG members were intimately familiar with data elements and logical processing from a librarian's point of view
- UCS PPG members were highly skilled and experienced database programmers, whose expertise could be readily applied.
- The small PPG team size, ranging between 8–12, facilitated decision–making, i.e., enabled a "strike–force" mode of operation
- The design activity sequencing incorporated a certain logical structuring of the system definition.

The weekly, personalized design interaction process was in lieu of a more formalized and elongated–in–time structured design process, which was not utilized. The limited "paper" design of the system, coupled with the weekly PPG dynamic, in part created the effect of designing for a "moving target". In addition, the PPG group had to deal with conflicting instructions and priorities from both Library and UCS administrations.

HyperCard Implementation

The PPG dynamic began to present problems during the implementation phase of USCInfo. Both a beta HyperCard USCInfo and production vt100 Version 2.0, were released in early October of the school year, one month after the targeted release. HyperCard USCInfo was available on the first thirty networked machines in College Library[15]. Each incorporated "basic functionality"[16] agreed to by all parties. Unlike the vt100 release, the HyperCard implementation was very difficult, viz., serious problems with Ethernet and the HyperCard stack involving response time for printing/downloading[17] and maintaining connectivity[18]. Most of the first several implementation months were devoted to determining problems, prioritizing them, and solving them. When operating "bugs" surfaced, causation of the problem had to be determined, i.e., a network problem, a software (HyperCard) problem, or a database problem. For multifaceted problems, e.g., connectivity between HyperCard and the network, multiple "ad hoc" meetings with smaller sub–groups, task forces, programmers, and users were necessary in order to isolate and fix these problems. The triad management responsibility – Library, UCS, and CST, impaired ability to impose responsibility for problem solutions to operating bugs.

HyperCard Interface Implementation Delays

The problems with the HyperCard USCInfo delayed development of the interface as a whole. Basic functionality was in place, but anticipated enhancements had not even been begun, including:

• LIMITS — limit a search to items with a particular characteristic, e.g., a location, language, or type of material.

• BRS SEARCH ENGINE could not distinguish if there was more than one value in the limit field. Thus, the user could only limit for the first listed location.

• HELP SCREENS — while a help command (vt100 version) and help button had been designed in the interface, the help software didn't exist.

• TRUNCATION OVERFLOW — the search engine allows truncation of search terms[19]. First partial results were given as the complete response[20].

• INSTALLATION of additional workstations was behind schedule, i.e., wiring, training and manpower problems.

Of the total programming effort, i.e., basic functionality and wish list of enhancments, the wish list accounted for approximately fifty percent.

The USCInfo implementation spotlighted the difficulty and cost of maintaining two parallel interfaces[21]. Problems in one system delayed the other's releases. Keeping functionality the same became difficult. Project creep, i.e., wish list above, coupled with the persistent HyperCard response time issues, software crashes, and HyperCard beta releases (reaching Beta version 34) placed a tremendous strain on the support infrastructure. Linda R. worked with Library Systems and Support to triage systems development responses to the wish list, "exceptions" and/or severe problems, and develop ad hoc policies and procedures as necessary. Linda R. supervised the day–to–day operation of the system, coordinated the frequent reloads of HyperCard software releases, disseminated "USCInfo bulletins" to Library staff, and worked closely with Library Support Services, i.e., "Hotline" staff.

For Whom the Bell Tolls

After some twelve months of operation, both the intractable nature of the HyperCard response time and the growth in convoluted programming using "xcommands" (see glossary), forced a decision about parallel USCInfo systems. The vt100 version, although less innovative, could be used everywhere. HyperCard, once considered promising, seemingly did not achieve operational robustness. Some supporters saw HyperCard abandonment as losing learning that had gone into the GUI as well as undermining USC's leading edge in library technology. HyperCard's champions made a spirited defense, albeit "too little, too late", i.e., attempting development of a C++ version of USCInfo called "NewInfo". UCS, strongly opposing further development using either HyperCard or C++, promised 100% programming support for a Unix–based, GUI USCInfo. Jim R. decided to discontinue HyperCard development and remove the interface by the conclusion of the current school year (summer semester). The new emphasis would be on content, i.e., not interface. The USCInfo vt100 version would be a short term vehicle, while the Library pursued development of an Xwindows graphical interface longer term. The continuing development of USCInfo was domiciled within the

Library's LAD group, until CST subsequently was brought into the Library organization and formally merged with LAD.

Preparation of vt100 Version for Library Use

Modifications of the existing vt100 version included those pertaining to printing/downloading choices, command lines, search constructors, interface, Macintosh "shell" software, and integration with UCS written software.

The plan is to treat this vt100 revision as a guerilla operation involving a small, top–level group. Please come prepared to work smart
(Team memorandum from Linda R.)

Both leveraging of the designers' knowledge base, as well as synergies from the now domiciled–in–LAD USCInfo Technical Group[22] began to emerge, as evidenced by the four month vt100 conversion and implementation.

Current Status of the Project

Migration to Unix

Planning for USCInfo's migration to Unix began almost concomitantly with the vt100 conversion effort. Unix advantages included:

• Open systems architecture
• Less expensive disk space and processors; faster execution
• Databases distributed across servers, protecting against system failure and bandwidth problems
• More compatible access to the Internet
• Potentially compliant with the Z39.50 (ANSI) information-retrieval standard
• More flexibility for future system enhancements

Disadvantages of Unix included: a complete rewrite of USCInfo, conversion of all databases and setup files, total reformulation of system maintenance procedures, retraining of both development and library staffs, and documentation rewriting. In sum, Unix presented new opportunities as well as limitations.

A tight 9 1/2 months timeline, i.e., design, migrate, implement, and test the system was completed on time as scheduled. The Unix platform–based USCInfo has run robustly, i.e., largely trouble free and its "look" has remained the same. A substantive innovation was the addition of "gateways" or links from USCInfo to external information resources. The growing availability of databases freely available on the Internet (Telnet, Gopher, other vendor–based products) has made it easier and cheaper to link to a system rather than invest in the next generation USCInfo. The concomitant growth in such external information resources has pressured the Library to take these beginning linkage steps, although budgeting and staffing for further development of this capability have not kept pace. Linking to these external resources means that the user must learn a variety of non–unified interfaces and techniques.

As of this writing, it is clear that USCInfo must be totally redesigned, i.e., the innovative character–based interface is now "old news". Acting Director of Libraries, Larry S. recently promulgated that USCInfo is a concept, not just an operating platform or interface:

USCInfo must be understood as what it has become: the campus–wide information system, regardless of how structured or administered

WWW Era

The phenomenal growth of the World Wide Web (WWW) finally brings the hope of a true graphical user interface within reach. Table 6 encapsulates WWW implications for USCInfo.

The original vision of one interface across many platforms, wide selection of resources, ubiquitous access, incorporation of information in all media and ease of use is now validated. Through many revisions and architectural changes, the goal has remained clear: to provide the user with information, whenever and wherever needed.

Successes and Failures

Successes

1. USCInfo was established, overcame earlier implementation difficulties, brought online additional databases each year, and has achieved a robust operating level. Throughout, USCInfo has been free of charge to the USC community.

Contributory factors: dedication of both UCS and the Library to make system usable and reliable; system development team composed of highly knowledgeable "doers," who were results oriented (see Successes below, academic environment).

2. Both a streamlined USCInfo development team and subsequent formalization of CST's

Pros	Cons
Combines advantages of "home grown" and vendor system; local control of interface AND support of vendor*	User needs high end machine (whatever platform), Web browser software, Internet connection, and computer skills
Multiplatform capability	
Ability to display multimedia, e.g., images, graphs, audio, video, etc.	Provision must be made for character–based access to everything now on the system
Far easier interface development and change. (Current system requires programmer time, compiling, and releasing code at slack time)	Many users not Web–capable, and never will be.
Web technology widely accepted and growing exponentially	

Table 6: WWW Interface Comparisons

position within the Library have enabled synergies and leveraging of the participants' knowledge base as both technology migrations have occurred and USCInfo functionality has expanded.

Contributory factors: Upon discontinuance of HyperCard USCInfo, shared responsibility for USCInfo was again dual, i.e., UCS and the Library (through LAD). CST, on an interim basis, was not in the picture. When brought back into the picture, CST was now domiciled in the Library with a revised and substantially clearer mission.

Throughout the post–HyperCard period, the USCInfo Technical Group has remained relatively stable, building close working relationships and facilitating migrations to new technologies as well as expansion of system functionality.

3. Management of the USCInfo project has successfully navigated the academic environment. The shirtsleeve, "doers" modality of the systems development effort described in this case, essentially supported, de facto, an "end justifies the means" approach. Collaboration in academe stems, in part, from "for the greater good." In contrast, team–based collaboration in the corporate world often is formalized through enforceable authority/responsibility boundaries and reviewable mileposts by management.

4. Senior Library management enabled the innovative dynamic to go forward.

Contributory factors: Senior Library management, recognizing Jim R.'s enthusiasm, intelligence, and drive, entrusted the USCInfo project to him. Jim R. was a still growing-and-proving himself manager. Library management approved systems development which called for more than 50% of the HyperCard programming to be completed by students. The Homer crisis created a "crash" program, which often generates "stress overload" conditions (see Failures, below, Decision–making under stress overload)

5. The combined OPAC and periodical indexes searching capability with a GUI did garner national attention within library automation literature and professional associations. Other libraries followed the lead, combining OPAC and periodical indexes searching.

Contributory factors: The Library was willing to accept the consequences of "the cutting edge is also the bleeding edge," accepting both the risks and associated implementation considerations of HyperCard as a network interface.

6. The USCInfo interface is easy to use, assures getting results, i.e., retrieval of data and not error messages.

Contributory factors: User comprehensibility, expectations, and skill levels were thoroughly addressed at each technology migration; screen presentation of results provides a cleaner, simpler screen look (see Failures below, poorly constructed searches).

Failures

1. Selection of the text–based USCInfo interface has limited kinds of materials accessible by the system. USCInfo has not kept pace with the growth curve in GUI, i.e., current advances in interface design have not been exploited.

Contributing factors: resource and funding constraints.

2. Ease of use of the interface doesn't offer any protection or warning against poorly constructed searches.

Contributory factors: non–library–based USC access means the bulk of users generally cannot consult library professionals, hence not realize that the search results are poor[23].

3. Decision making under stress overload often produces unintended consequences of varying magnitude and/or overall impact.

Contributory factors: Jim R. was willing to accept an almost thankless task, i.e., "we needed it yesterday", "monies to fix it are scarce", and "you are the wagonmaster of this 3 horse team". Both Jim R.'s and Brad G.'s decision–making styles are Conceptual / Directive, i.e., both have a big picture view, and both want results. When superimposed on the time element of "we needed it yesterday", these decision–making styles would likely contribute to "stress overload" decision making as the project unfolded.

Epilogue and Lessons Learned

Lessons Learned

1. Innovative processes within an academic environment, whose output is to be a "production" output, i.e., not pure research, need a(n) appropriate authority/responsibility mechanism(s). The particular form(s) of the mechanism(s) is(are) probably less important than the viability and enforcing processes of such mechanism(s).

2. Reward / reinforcement mechanisms need to be tailored, consistent with both the position of the person within the project and any dual authority/responsibility structures imposed.

3. The relative ages and shorter times in positions at USC, of project participants –Linda, Tim, Brad, Kurt, and Jim, to some degree contributed to both a "we can do it" spirit and, sometimes, less reliance on formal evaluation processes/methods being applied to various system development processes.

4. The basic functionality that had been agreed to was, de facto, a rather encompassing system. What had been originally thought of by Tim and Brad as a HyperCard prototype mushroomed into development of a much more complete system. Stated differently, "Think bigger longer term, prototype smaller shorter term".

Flexibility

Consensual	Developmental

Internal Focus

External Focus

Hierarchical	Rational

Predictability

Simplicity <--------------------> Complexity

Hierarchical Culture In the hierarchical culture, formal information processing (documentation, computation, and evaluation) is assumed to be a means to the end of continuity (stability, control, and coordination)

Consensual Culture In the consensual culture, collective information processing (discussion, participation and consensus) are assumed to be a means to the end of cohesion (climate, morale, teamwork)

Rational Culture In rational cultures, individual information processing (goal clarification, logical judgment and direction setting) is assumed to be a means to the end of improved performance (efficiency, productivity)

Developmental Culture In a developmental culture, intuitive information processing (insight, invention, innovation) is assumed to be a means to the end of revitalization (external support, resource acquisition, and growth)

Further reading: Quinn and McGrath (1985), Klempa (1995a, 1995b)

USC Classifications:
Library - **Consensual/Hierarchical**
UCS - **Developmental/Rational**
CST - **Developmental/Hierarchical**

Note: There is not any one best organization culture style. The four organization culture styles describe ideal style types. An actual organization's or organization subunit's culture may more or less closely resemble an ideal type. Style combinations are possible, e.g., dyads such as developmental/rational, etc. Style triads are possible.

Appendix A: Organization Culture Styles (adapted from Quinn & McGrath, 1985)

Analytic Style   This style emphasizes gathering large amounts of data so as to undertake a systematic examination, focusing on a maximum or optimal solution.

Directive Style   The directive style prefers short time lines, high certainty, values achievement, is purposive, relying on a priori logic and general principles or rules. This style makes rapid decisions, with a single purpose and focus, that are final. This style emphasizes action. Individuals often <u>revert</u> to this style, under **stress overload**.

Considerate Style   This style is oriented toward feelings. Meaning is discovered through process; the world is known through human interaction. This style emphasizes individual exceptions and spontaneous events.   This style values affiliation and emphasizes consideration of the individual.

Conceptual Style   This style prefers variation, risk, excitement, growth, and is future oriented. Idea generation is often through intuition. Problems tend to be analyzed from a dynamic, longitudinal view. Decision making has a multiple focus.   This style is oriented toward creativity, risk, adaptability and external legitimacy.

USCInfo personnel classifications:
Linda R. - **Considerate**
Jim R., Brad G. - **Conceptual/Directive**
Kurt B., Tim H. - **Analytic/Conceptual**

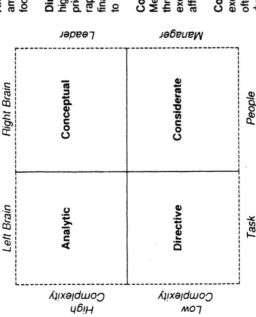

Note: There is <u>not</u> any one best style. If possible, the individual's style should be matched to the situation. The four styles describe ideal style types. An actual individual may more or less closely resemble an ideal type. Decision style combinations are possible, e.g., dyads as well as triads. Many successful CEOs' style is conceptual/directive. Under conditions of <u>stress overload</u>, individuals generally revert to the directive style.

Appendix B: Rowe Decision Styles (adapted from Rowe & Mason, 1987)

Acknowledgments

M. Klempa gratefully acknowledges the help of Lynn Sipe, who was extremely receptive to this project, as well as coauthor Lucy Wegner, who reviewed original documents and materials, drafted earlier manuscripts, responded to varied and numerous requests, and enabled the process in countless ways. Both authors generously thank the assistance of many past and present members of the USCInfo "team" who generously opened their files, shared recollections and reviewed portions of the manuscript.

Endnotes

[1] Noncopyrighted portions of USCInfo are available on the Internet at **http://library.usc.edu**. The University's home page is: **http://www.usc.edu**.

[2] A heuristic refers to a "rule of thumb" or a "rule of good guessing." Managers may employ heuristics in order to deal with decision making complexity.

[3] Satisficing means that decision makers choose a solution alternative that satisfies minimal decision criteria, even if better solutions are presumed to exist.

[4] Decision–making situations may be ambiguous and have several interpretations, i.e., equivocality. Managers reduce equivocality through shared meaning and interpretation.

[5] CD–ROM periodical index databases would not be cost effective in a multisite situation.

[6] This dual responsibility structure was cemented in a contractual agreement in 1993.

[7] UCS is responsible for providing and maintaining all campus networks.

[8] Homer was, of course, a Greek poet. USC's tradition was to use Greek names for programs, teams (Trojans), and the like.

[9] Apple Computer marketed itself, in particular, to educational institutions at all levels, K through university.

[10] During implementation the machine grant was 126 PCs, mostly SE's.

[11] Ford Motor Company touted the Taurus as "skipping several design generations and being "tomorrow's car."

[12] This plan never came to fruition. A subsequent university decision moved the entire campus from mainframes to a Unix–based client server architecture.

[13] The Library paid for Ethernet connections to ten library buildings to wiring closets. Use of Fastpath from there was a cost/speed tradeoff. Fastpath's cost was less.

[14] Both the network communication and mainframe transactions to be coded later in HyperCard were set up as X–commands.

[15] Installation of the 126 Macintoshes was phased, with thirty Macintoshes installed as of October, and installation of the remaining 96 within twelve months.

[16] For example, not until twelve months later were subject headings and browsing capabilities implemented within USCInfo, that would permit full conversion of HOMER.

[17] The HyperCard stack was very slow to process screen display results from the mainframe, i.e., Fastpath is slow, especially when busy. Mainframe response had been upgraded soon after USCInfo implementation.

[18] Prior to the 20 records at a time retrieval limit, HyperCard retrieved the entire result. Large sets created *long* waits; extremely large sets caused HyperCard to overwrite itself when it ran out of memory, thus losing connectivity.

[19] Librar$ retrieves library, libraries, librarian, etc.

[20] The iterative results problem only came to light because the Mac and vt100 versions were set to display different size partial search results.

[21] A third version, i.e., remote user HyperCard USCInfo was not released until one year later.

[22] The former USCInfo Project Planning Group's name was changed to the USCInfo Technical Group.

[23] Broad retrieval requests, e.g., "Civil War" retrieve large data sets, e.g., 2800+ hits. The user may be unable to refine the search, hence not be able to further limit the retrieved set.

Questions for Discussion

1. Evaluate the effectiveness of the shared responsibility, Library and University Computing Services, for USCInfo development. Set forth pros and cons as to the manner in which this shared responsibility was implemented. What adjustments would you have made? Why?

2. Given the organization culture styles and organization learning styles of the Library and University Computing Services, discuss the effectiveness of the Library Review Committee and its interaction with the weekly systems development process. Identify possible mechanisms that may have helped moderate the relative lack of technological sophistication of both senior library management and the larger Library staff.

3. Given the HyperCard capability to relatively quickly generate prototype inputs / outputs, discuss methods of monitoring and controlling project creep. Given the dual shared responsibility for systems development, discuss how / why your methods would work.

4. USCInfo development did not use a structured design approach. Given the small–sized PPG team composed of high knowledgeable and specialized Library, CST, and UCS personnel, compare and contrast the effectiveness of the systems development process used with the structured design approach. Would a structured design approach have improved the result, or would it have "killed the goose?"

5. Given the design trade–offs presented in the case, and the relatively slow growth in user sophistication over time, discuss the choice of HyperCard as the chosen vehicle. Could any of the parallelism problems (GUI and vt100 versions) have been anticipated and / or addressed?

6. The original Ahmanson project four principles finally are fully realizable in the mid–90s. Were the Ahmanson project's four principles visionary or premature? Discuss in light of very short technology life cycles and evolutionary versus revolutionary technology innovations.

7. Identify circumstances / situations in the case where the 80/20 concept (Pareto's Law) could have been applied in order to improve development, implementation, or operating circumstances. Be specific in your response. Show how/why 80/20 would have improved the circumstance / situation. Where there any circumstances in the case where the 80/20 concept was being applied?

8. Compare and contrast technical, economic, scheduling and operational feasibility of the three choices confronting USCInfo: the all vt100 approach, the GEAC upgrade approach, and the proposed HyperCard approach.

9. This question has two parts that can be answered either together or separately. Hypothesize that you are currently Director of Information Technology for the USC Libraries. The University's Chief Information Officer has requested an outline of your plans to move the USCInfo system into the new century, specifically considering World Wide Web access, a multiplicity of information resources, a demanding user community, and of course, inadequate time and budget. You can address this in either or both of the ways below:

A. Technical — systems analysis approach. Given user access to upwards of 100 or more databases, many of which the user knows nothing about, explain or delineate how you would go about fundamental system design so as to: 1) facilitate the novice user's search process, i.e., retrieve useful information, without a long, tedious search process; and 2) give the experienced user access to the powerful search capabilities built into the system.

B. Managerial — administrative approach. Many of the past difficulties with USCInfo development stemmed from shortcomings in the administrative structure and systems development process. Consider the following constraints and opportunities and delineate how you would structure the responsibility for and development of the new USCInfo system.

1. The system must be operational (if not fully developed) in time for the fall semester (10 months away).
2. Any money for new equipment must be taken from current operating funds.
3. Each of the three parties remains (UCS, CST, Library), albeit in revised organizational relationships (See case, Successes, #2).
4. The level of technological sophistication has risen greatly within the Library. Leadership in the digital library realm is still a major value for the Library, so some risk-taking is acceptable.

References

Amabile, T.M. (1988). A model of creativity and innovation in organizations. *Research in Organizational Behavior,* 10, 123–167.

Bartunek, J.M. (1988). The dynamics of personal and organizational reframing. In Quinn, R. & Cameron, K. (Eds.) *Paradox and Transformation.* Cambridge, MA: Ballinger Publishing

Howell, J. & Higgins, C. (1990). Champions of change: Identifying, understanding, and supporting champions of technological innovations. *Organizational Dynamics,* 19(1), 40–55.

Keon, T., Vazzana, G., & Slocombe, T. (1992). Sophisticated information processing technology: Its relationship with an organization's environment, structure, and culture. *Information Resources Management Journal,* 23–31.

Klempa, M.J. (1995a). Understanding business process reengineering: A sociocognitive contingency model. In Grover, V. & Kettinger, W. (Eds.) *Business process change: Reengineering concepts, methods, and technologies.* Harrisburg, PA: Idea Group Publishing.

Klempa, M.J. (1995b, October). Management of innovation: Organization culture and organization learning synergistic implications. In Q. Xu & J. Chen (Eds.) *Proceedings of Pan–China Symposium on Management of Technology and Innovation,* Hangzhou, Peoples' Republic of China.

Quinn, R.E. & McGrath, M. (1985). The transformation of organizational cultures: A competing values perspective. In P.Frost, L.Moore, M.Louis, C.Lundberg, & J.Martin (Eds.), *Organizational Culture.* Newbury Park, CA: Sage Publications.

Rowe, A.J. & Mason, R.O., (1987). *Managing with style: A guide to understanding, assessing, and improving decision making.* San Francisco: Jossey–Bass.

Wegner, L.S. (1991, November). Multiple resources with a unified interface. *T.H.E. (Technology Horizons in Education) Journal,* (Special Issue), 6–12.

Wegner. L.S. (1992, Fall). The research library and emerging information technology. *New Directions for Teaching and Learning,* 51, 83–90.

Wilkins, A. & Dyer, W. (1988). Toward culturally sensitive theories of culture change. *Academy of Management Review,* 13(4), 522–533.

Chapter 13

Mismanaging a Technology Project: The Case of ABC Inc.

John H. Benamati
University of Kentucky

Ram Pakath
University of Kentucky

Executive Summary

A common misconception is that technology can solve problems. Very often, the people and processes involved have significant impacts on the success or failure of a particular piece of technology in addressing a problem. This case is a classic example of how not to manage a technology project. It describes how a client, a vendor, and a sub-vendor exercised poor judgment in dealing with one another in applying client-server technology to a project of mammoth proportions. In the end, there were no real winners and the project, which came close to abortion, is now progressing to a slow finish, many valuable months and dollars behind what were originally estimated.

One learns that it is not merely enough getting a customer "involved" in a project from the very beginning. Learning who the key players are, engendering and fostering a feeling of mutual trust and commitment to the end result (i.e., a successful project-development partnership), educating the customer about technology and process re-engineering possibilities, exercising adequate authority and control, and, perhaps, iterative, multivendor-based project design and implementation are all critical elements of a successful technology venture. This case is based on reality. We have, however, changed the identities of the parties involved and other key information to preserve anonymity.

Background

The organization of interest is the State Health Services Department of a state located in the southern region of the United States. The department was formed in the early 1900s. From a 10-person,

1-office startup, located in the capitol, the organization grew over the years into a large conglomerate with 125 sub-organizations. Each sub-unit is a County Health Department, located in and serving one of the 125 counties in the state. Today, the entire operation involves 5,500 employees of whom about 900 are doctors.

The organization seeks to provide affordable health care to any and all residents in the state. While it does not deny health care to anyone, regardless of ability to pay, the decision on whether or not a patient is charged is based on the financial standing of the individual. Some patients pay the entire amount due immediately following the visit, others enter into a pro-rated payment arrangement, yet others are treated gratis.

In the urban counties, it is the underprivileged who generally frequent a county's health department despite the availability of private health care. This is so because the latter is often prohibitively expensive for the uninsured and the underinsured. In the rural counties, however, people of all income groups and social standing try to make use of the local health departments due to the paucity of private health care facilities in such areas. It is only when adequate care is unavailable here that these patients begin looking elsewhere.

While the organization's goal is to provide affordable health care to one and all, the various sub-units differ in their ability to provide quality care. A substantial part of the reason for this is the inability of the organization to attract and retain appropriately qualified medical personnel and support staff in rural areas. Even in the more urban counties, the salary differential between a doctor employed by the health department and one in the private sector tends to be quite substantial. As such, the department generally attracts professionals with a dedication to the Hippocratic oath and young interns obligated to take up the positions in order to satisfy medical study grant requirements. (Incidentally, a large number of the health department's medical professionals, particularly in the more rural counties, are also foreign medical graduates who are considerably more resilient about their living and working conditions than United States nationals. This is because, quite often, the conditions are nonetheless better than what their home countries have to offer.)

Given this disparity in medical knowledge at the various County Health departments, the supporting infrastructure also varies considerably. A large number of these units, predominantly in the rural areas, operate with a handful of general practitioners — physicians in family health care, obstetrics and gynecology, and pediatrics — and support staff. Almost all units have some kind of in-house pharmaceutical dispensary facility. The relatively larger, urban units have professionals in almost all specialties, as well as surgeons, on call. These larger units also have in-house medical laboratories, x-ray clinics, and well-stocked pharmacies.

The State Health Services Department is akin to the central office of a large corporation. Prior planning efforts by the department involved very little apart from the vision that a county-by-county, statewide presence was needed. Over the years, the 125 County Health Departments mushroomed all over the state, their growth and operational needs largely determined locally. This commitment to "state-wide presence above all else" has resulted in all 125 units remaining operational even though, as we shortly discuss, a significant proportion of the sub-units are financially weak. The central office's role in the day-to-day operations of the county units is largely limited to providing a set of general management guidelines and administering the flow of money to units through budget allocations. Each unit is essentially autonomous in almost all respects, notably in terms of interpretation of recommended management principles/practices and the disposition of allocated budgets.

Budget allocation decisions are based on the revenue generated by each unit. Essentially, this implies that a unit's budget is determined on the basis of the number of patients serviced by it and the types of services provided. As a rule of thumb, the more revenue a unit generates, the more budget it is allocated in the following year. Budgets are used by units for all of their expenses, such as the purchase of medical/office equipment and supplies, hiring and severance of employees, and salaries.

Being a government entity, the State Health Services Department is a non-profit organization. As such, apart from revenue generated in-house, it also relies on state and federal subsidies as sources of funding. The sub-units vary widely in terms of their financial strength. One of the county facilities accounts for 40% of total revenue generated. Another two account for an additional 20%. The remaining 122 county units together contribute the rest. The revenue generated by the three larger units is also used to subsidize the operations of the smaller ones.

More recently, a need for better communication and sharing of information between the sub-units had emerged. This was partly because families tended to move (either temporarily or permanently) from one county to another and sought services at their new locations. Proper information sharing would, the State Health Department felt, ensure uninterrupted evaluation of their case histories and continuance of any ongoing treatment at the new facilities. Stimulus from an external source, however, was even more compelling: new federal and state regulations for subsidies were increasingly based upon the notions of "preventive care" and "follow-up care." This thrust was primarily the result of the then-prevalent gloomy economic outlook. Federal and state funding agencies, while becoming more tight-fisted due to spending cuts, were demanding greater bang for the buck by more stringently stipulating how their shrinking funds were to be utilized.

The preventive care concept is based on the premise that taking precautionary measures while the patient is free (or in the early stages) of an affliction could curb the onset (or extension) of the condition in the future. Preventive measures are normally prescribed based on an assessment of a patient's current and past health status and the history of specific ailments in the patient's family tree (some conditions are known to be hereditary). The underlying philosophy is that the benefits of the time, effort, and money spent on preventive care far outweigh the impacts of the risks of not taking such measures. A number of studies (in highly-regarded forums like the *Journal of the American Medical Association*) have extolled the virtues of this approach.

The state and federal funding agencies had come to regard preventive medicine as being potentially more economical (in real dollars) than conventional, reactive medicine. Consequently, these agencies had begun pushing the State Health Services Department to coerce each sub-unit to comply with this philosophy by tugging on their budget strings appropriately. It was not that preventive medicine was an absolutely novel concept to the Health Department. It had always been sporadically practiced by some of the sub-unit physicians on a voluntary basis. The Health Department was now being mandated to make preventive care a key underlying philosophy of its approach to medical practice. Instituting a successful, state-wide preventive care program also meant instituting a well-designed information generation, storage, and sharing program between the sub-units.

In addition to the push toward greater preventive care, the agencies had begun mandating increased follow-up or after care in the case of certain services as a further means of conserving costs. As an example, studies have shown that it would be cheaper and healthier to retain a mother and her newborn for up to 72 hours in the hospital following a Cesarean delivery. However, common present-day practice is to rush them home as soon as possible due, quite often, to pressures from the concerned insurance company. Sometimes, a facility tends to impose upon a new mother to vacate early simply to accommodate mothers-to-be who are waiting for beds. The state and federal agencies felt that more widespread deployment of proper outpatient or at-home follow-up care would be an effective means for cutting down on the lengths of hospital stays without jeopardizing the welfare of mothers and their newborns. As with prevention, an effective, state-wide follow-up care program would require the design and implementation of a facile information generation, storage, and exchange program.

In a nutshell, a push to (a) revise current treatment philosophies and practices, (b) electronically maintain complete patient family and medical histories, and (c) efficiently share such information between county units and between the central office and these units had begun to emerge. This push was, in essence, a mandate for an evolution toward an effective and efficient "case management system" within the State Health Department That this evolution was to take place within a bureaucratic government entity did little to help matters. The prevailing culture did (and does) not allow for "big" decisions to be made relatively easily. Once made, such decisions were invariably late in being implemented.

Setting the Stage

Each patient's case history was maintained in a separate paper file folder at the County Health Department that he/she frequented. This folder had information such as the patient's name, date-of-birth, sex, social security number, address, phone number, insurance carrier, etc. It also contained a running record of the dates and facts pertaining to each affliction episode, the medical professional(s) involved, the diagnoses made, the treatment(s) recommended, the outcome(s) of the treatment(s), follow-up care recommended (if any), preventive care recommended (if any), and so on. The patient's family medical history was also contained therein. Separately, financial records pertaining to each patient were maintained in folders by the Accounts Receivable department of a unit. The formats of the information maintained by a sub-unit were determined by that sub-unit i.e., the units did not make use of documents that were standard issue.

Because federal and state subsidies were based on a number of considerations including patient-related information from the State Health Services Department, it was necessary for each unit to provide the needed information to the central office. In the early 1990s, before the deployment of the system described in the following section, the sub-units supplied their information through monthly paper reports. The central office would consolidate information received from each unit to generate a single set of monthly reports that met state and federal reporting guidelines.

The paper forms used by many of the sub-units for their reporting were also non-standard. While each contained, scattered within it, the information needed by the central office, it also contained other information of interest to the specific sub-unit involved. This is because, given the prevailing decentralized management philosophy, different sub-units had evolved their own reporting procedures over the years. Indeed, between them, the 125 sub-units had over 100 different reporting structures!

The data gathering, storage, and information generation procedures used by each sub-unit were also determined autonomously. The central office imposed no restrictions on, nor made any efforts at standardizing, these procedures. The larger, financially better-off units had acquired proprietary automated systems to facilitate this process. However, none of the units had an in-house Information Systems group or department. The platform in use at a site was supplied by some outside vendor who recommended the hardware, systems software, and the application system(s). The vendor also took care of the system installation and the initial training of one or two personnel who were to use the system. Over the years, the more knowledgeable users imparted their wisdom informally to other users. The vendors also entered into extended service contracts with the sub-units for systems maintenance (primarily, to attend to any hardware failures). The vast number of smaller clinics, however, still relied on manual processing of the forms by having dedicated personnel painstakingly fill these out using pen and ink, a typewriter, or a word processor.

Needless to say, the manually generated forms were susceptible to human errors. Correcting errors in hand- and type-written forms is a messy and/or time consuming task. This scope for human error was also present in the cases of some of the units with automated systems as we next discuss.

All of the automated systems made use of source data automation to one extent or another. For instance, the technology was used by some of the automated centers to scan credit cards for payment authorization and medical insurance cards for insurance verification. Likewise, the amounts to be charged for specific services, for patients covered by specific insurance policies, were also automatically retrieved once the service and insurance information had been captured.

However, some of the needed data had to be keyed in by humans either in real time — directly from oral responses to questions provided by a source (e.g., a patient or a doctor) — or off line, from a source document (e.g., a paper form filled in by a patient or a nurse). Not all systems, however, were equipped with appropriate key verification and control totaling procedures that would eliminate any and all errors. One might argue that such perfection is unattainable. Still, the general consensus among the users was that there was considerable scope for improvement.

For one thing, some of these proprietary systems were quite ad hoc in how user-friendly they were. Some of them did not permit a user to change a wrong entry without re-starting the entire process. Some others were at best "temperamental" in this regard. They permitted changes at certain locations but, for reasons unknown, were quite inflexible at other locations and insisted that the user either proceed with the error uncorrected or abort the entire process! For another, sometimes, a system would inexplicably "lock up," causing undue frustration to the operator. Such operational concerns apart, some of the systems were also slow and sluggish at certain junctures primarily due to poor underlying data structure and code design. Given such circumstances, it was not uncommon to hear a user occasionally complain, with a liberal dose of her choice expletives, that she'd rather be doing the whole thing by hand!

The central office was also an automated site. It had data entry personnel who, upon receipt of the completed forms from the sub-units each month, used a computerized data entry system to key in the needed information from each form into their mainframe system. This system was also equipped with appropriate report generation routines that generated the reports stipulated by the state and federal agencies. In addition, the system also generated summary reports that were distributed to each of the sub-units for their perusal. The central office system was supported and maintained by a small, in-house, Information Systems group comprised of a systems administrator, a full time programmer/analyst, and two part-time programmers.

In regard to data capture, the automated central office (which makes use of its own proprietary environment) was also susceptible to the same kinds of drawbacks as the automated sub-units in its purview. In fact, it used even less source data automation than many of the automated sub-units because it neither was the point-of-origin of the data nor was electronically linked to such points. Given that it received paper documents that had to be input, it preferred using key entry to automation like opscan for two reasons. First, the system was not designed to accept scanned data. The vendor in question had dissuaded them from pursuing this direction as the scanners then available in the market were quite unreliable in scanning even printed, leave alone hand- or type-written, information. Second, as already mentioned, many of the forms contained information irrelevant to the central office. Thus, significant amounts of post-scanning processing effort would be needed to separate the wheat from the chaff.

In addition, the central office was hampered by the variety in the form and format of information provided by the various sub-units. Hand-written forms are sometimes hard to decipher. The fact that the information of interest was located at different places on different forms meant that a data entry operator must hunt for these locations from one form to the next (the forms arrived and were processed in random order). It was generally felt that this added distraction was one more reason why the keyed-in information was sometimes erroneous or incomplete.

In a nutshell, the status quo that prevailed in the early 1990s paints a picture of a monolithic system made up of 126, loosely coupled, hybrid information gathering and report generation systems, in various stages of technological advancement, attempting to operate and communicate with one another in a smooth, seamless fashion repeatedly over time. Given the many drawbacks discussed above, this goal had always remained elusive at best. Indeed, with the passage of time, given the growth in the number of sub-units and the increasing volumes of patients processed and services offered by each sub-unit, maintaining synchronicity and cohesiveness in the total system had become a stretch. The situation had begun looking increasingly hopeless. The State Health Services Department had been aware for some time, that either something had to be done to correct the situation or total chaos, with very undesirable consequences, was imminent. So, in early 1991, the department decided to remedy the situation by hiring an outside organization to develop a solution.

Project Description

The goal of the State Health Services Department was to implement a tightly integrated, organization-wide system to replace the existing loose amalgam of sub-unit systems. The department envisaged the following broad scenario:

• Each sub-unit would no longer generate custom reports for submission to the central office. Reports would be standardized across the board.
• All sites would make use of subsystems that were both physically and functionally alike in-so-far as the needs of the central office were concerned. That is, each sub-unit would be equipped with exactly the same system in terms of inputs required, processing performed, and reports generated for the purposes of the central office.
• Over time, individual sub-units could have their systems equipped to store other kinds of information or generate other kinds of reports for their own internal needs as long as this added functionality did not in any way interfere with what was required by the central office.
• The sub-units would be able to submit the necessary reports electronically each month to the central office. These reports would contain only the right information needed by the central office system in the right format.
• Each sub-unit would be required to submit its report during a predetermined time window to facilitate processing by the central system and to distribute processing load more evenly.
• Similarly, the disbursement of the annual summary reports by the central office to the various sub-units would be done electronically at predetermined points in time.
• The sub-units would also be electronically networked with one another to facilitate easier transfer of patient information from unit to unit on an ad hoc basis. This would facilitate the appropriate and timely acquisition and processing of patient information by a county unit in the event that a patient from a different county moves into its purview.
• The entire application would revolve around a client-server data base processing system with the 125 sub-units and the central office potentially updating and accessing data concurrently through one central data base server.
• The application front end would be a workstation-resident, Windows-based, point-and-click graphical user interface with integrated word processing, document storage and retrieval, and reporting capabilities.

In fact, the above list represents the extent of in-house requirements analysis done by the State Health Department. Because its own Information Systems unit did not have the necessary manpower or expertise to tackle such a large project, the department decided to seek outside help by requisitioning bids from independent vendors. The contract was to be bid as an out sourcing contract, to include the design and development of the client-server application, the" rolling out" of the system to the various sub-units, and the running of the application system for the first five years at each unit.

An invitation to submit bids was announced during April of 1991 and seven vendors responded. After due deliberations, and largely guided by the general reputation, size, financial strength, and the bid amount, the contract was awarded, in September of 1991, to ABC Inc. located in New York city. ABC Inc., is a large, United States-based, multinational computer hardware, programming language, and systems/applications software builder and vendor. It has been in business for over 40 years and is generally regarded as one of the big players in the market with annual revenues totaling several hundred billions of dollars.

The contract was a multi-million dollar award. However, ABC Inc.'s. bid was as much as 20 million dollars less than the next highest bid! The State Health Services Department was elated with this outcome: it had managed to secure one of the best players in the business, it felt, at a considerable bargain. Being a non-profit agency, bid size was a predominant criterion in vendor selection. When news of this "coup" reached ABC Inc.'s negotiators, a feeling that they had, perhaps foolishly, grossly underbid the competition engulfed many involved. This marked the beginnings of the deterioration in the relationship between the State Health Services Department and ABC. To make matters worse, during November of 1991, one of the vendors who failed to get the contract sued the State Health Services Department in the belief that an unfair issuance of the contract had occurred. Until the case was heard in court and (as it happened) dismissed, the project could not officially take off.

Although the project officially began in March of 1992, ABC Inc. actually began working on the application design while the lawsuit was in progress in anticipation that the suit would be dismissed. During this period, ABC realized that, despite its formidable size and reputation, it was overwhelmed by what the project demanded. ABC was woefully short on knowledge needed to put together a massive client-server application.

The project, as mentioned earlier, involved the creation of a complex, geographically dispersed, client-server application system. A significant portion of the application was to run on client workstations, with pieces running on the host system. As such, the application posed several technical challenges. These included concerns related to, (a) controlling concurrency and maintaining data integrity as users checked data out and back in at the host, (b) recovering from errors, (c) distributing new code as and when developed to 1500 workstations, (d) seamlessly integrating multiple workstation tools, (e) remotely administering the 125 local area networks that would exist in the clinics, and others. However, the focus of this case is not on such technical concerns although, admittedly, they were big issues and added to the overall challenge of the project. Our focus, instead, is on the management and people issues that perhaps played a more significant role than the technical challenges.

The committed delivery date of the test system to the first site was December of 1993. ABC decided to seek the services of a better-equipped competitor to deliver the first-cut application system design while it was engaged in trying to put together an adequate design team of its own. Thus, in May of 1992, ABC entered into a contract with Why-not-Me? Corporation of Bethesda, Maryland.

Why-not-Me? Corp. is also a well-known company in the industry with a sizable reputation of its own. However, it is a smaller operation than ABC and, unlike the latter, its operations are confined to the design and implementation of client-server projects in North America. ABC's plan was to set up a management team to oversee the design efforts of Why-not-Me?. ABC felt that this would ensure its own familiarity with the design from inception and also enable it to retain full control over the project.

Why-not-me? Corp. began its first design efforts in May of 1992. While the original contract had been entered into between the State Health Services Department and ABC Inc., ABC soon began to realize that the various County Health Departments collectively exercised significant power and control over the course the project took with the passage of time. It also became evident that the extent of the power/control exercised by a sub-unit was largely a function of its revenue generation ability. The financially stronger sub-units, ABC felt, tended to muscle their way around in all dealings pertaining to the project. To be viewed as a success, the final system would need to be used by the entire organization. Therefore, ABC Inc. had been putting forth a significant amount of effort to ensure that the individual needs of each of the sub-units were met. At the same time, it was reluctant to openly confront the financially stronger units as it feared (a) an ugly, potentially unsalvageable, deterioration in its relationship with its client with the attendant risk of possibly losing the project altogether and (b) a general loss of reputation if it were to fail in what it felt was a highly visible project. Unfortunately for ABC, its dilemma was also sensed by two key players in the project — the more powerful sub-units and Why-not-Me? Corp. The two began using this knowledge to their advantage, as we next discuss.

Why-not-Me? began acquiescing to the demands of the stronger sub-units. For example, whenever one of these units approached Why-not-Me? with a request for a change in the system design parameters, it would comply even if ABC Inc. objected to the change for valid reasons. For instance, the change may have necessitated a massive increase in the scope of the application's functionality and, therefore, its cost. Or, the change may have been one that was favored by a handful of the powerful sub-units and not the others. Regardless of such concerns, the sub-units involved were getting any and all functionality they desired, with little "change control" being instituted.

Essentially, Why-not-Me? was trying to position itself as one who could provide all of the functionality desired by the bigger sub-units while undermining the credibility of, and the control exercised by, ABC Inc. Apart from enabling it to become the primary vendor for all practical purposes, Why-not-Me? also stood to gain financially. Why-not-Me? was being paid by the hour — extending the first-cut design efforts was yielding rich dividends. The stronger sub-units also recognized that Why-not-Me? stood to gain financially — but the money was coming from ABC's coffers, not theirs. Consequently, financial considerations were not a deterrent to their demanding any and all of the system functionality they desired.

This state of affairs continued through December 1992 and beyond. The relationship between the ABC and Why-not-Me? project management team leaders deteriorated to the point were they were at constant odds over project scope and credibility issues. Finally, under intense pressure from its client, ABC Inc. was forced to temporarily relinquish the overall charge of the project to its sub-vendor. Why-not-Me? now had almost unchecked control on how the design efforts progressed. ABC realized that, despite being the "primary vendor" for the project on paper, it was now actually playing second fiddle to its own sub-contractor.

One impact of the events just described was that the project's first deliverable date was advanced by an entire year, from December 1993 to December 1994. The events also left in their wake a disgruntled client, a demoralized, financially short-changed ABC Inc., and a financially content Why-not-Me? Corp. To help improve its situation, ABC Inc. entered into a re-negotiation of its contract with the State Health Services Department during April of 1993.

Two important changes occurred as a result of the re-negotiation. First, ABC Inc., was able to re-institute one of its own as the overall Project Leader and, thus, be in a position to regain control of the project. Second, ABC was able to reach an agreement with Why-not-Me whereby the latter would undertake a re-design effort with the objectives of cutting back on application functionality to the extent possible and advancing the deliverable date. As a result of such moves, the target deliverable date was advanced by two months to October 1994 and a 3-month project re-design effort began.

Despite this shaking of hands, Why-not-Me? completed the re-design only in December of 1993, about five months behind schedule. To make matters worse, despite the time delay, the functionality of the system had actually marginally increased, rather than decrease! ABC and its sub-contractor were once again in disagreement. During early 1994, a second re-negotiation effort began between ABC, its client, and its sub-contractor with a view to de-scoping system functionality to that proposed originally. ABC Inc. felt that this was the only course of action that was fair to all concerned. ABC emphasized that it would still be meeting its contractual obligations to its client. However, the resultant uproar in the ranks of the State Health Services Department brought the entire project close to abortion. In the end, ABC was able to prevail upon its client to agree to a de-scoped implementation and also convey that they would be better off dealing with one another directly by eliminating what it viewed as the troublemaker — Why-not-Me? Corp. ABC would undertake to complete the de-scoped project on its own.

ABC completed the de-scoped re-design in March of 1994 and began implementation efforts. At about the same time, the client began claiming that the de-scoping had actually resulted in a system that was far inferior to that originally proposed. It even hinted at a possible law suit. Fortunately for ABC, it was able to convince the client to settle things out of court. The implementation of the de-scoped system proceeded even as re-negotiations were in progress. The implementation was completed and delivered for user test in December of 1994. The client, however, was far from happy and unwilling to settle for something less than what it now thought it was entitled to.

Current Status of the Project

The course of events until the deployment of the test system had left ABC in a state of utter chaos. Internally, no one involved with the project in any way was willing to assume any responsibility for what had occurred. In the ensuing period of finger pointing and buck passing, ABC's original project management team was dismantled and a new one put in place. In early 1995, ABC Inc. and the State Health Services Department shook hands on yet another contract by which all of the functionality that had been removed during de-scoping would be added back. Fortunately for ABC, the client also agreed to share in the financial losses incurred over the many months of going around in circles.

Re-design efforts began and ABC decided that it would opt for a phased re-design and implementation approach rather than deliver a complete system for testing and conversion. ABC envisaged a 2-phase design/implementation effort with Phase II implementation being completed by March 1995.

Unfortunately, ABC had once again underestimated the task. Phase I re-design was completed only in 1995 August. Its implementation took about 3 months. During that period, Phase II re-design was also undertaken. Thus, by 1995 November, Phase 1 implementation and Phase II re-design were both completed. It is now March of 1996. Phase II implementation is still in progress. To further complicate the situation, the client has again requested functionality over and above whatever had been last agreed to, thus necessitating additional design work as well. ABC, not wanting to make matters any worse, has quietly acquiesced.

Successes and Failures

In a nutshell, from ABC's perspective, there were few successes of any kind through much of the project apart from the costly lessons that it learned. The client views itself as being successful insofar as it has succeeded in getting all of the functionality that it had hoped for although, financially, it has had to share in ABC's losses. The biggest "winner," financially speaking, is Why-not Me? Corp.

From the perspective of an outside observer, however, the entire effort was peppered with failures of omission and commission by all involved. First, ABC Inc. failed to recognize (or acknowledge) its own weaknesses in needed expertise at the time that it first bid for the project. It was, in a manner of speaking, saddled with the proverbial Trojan Horse! Likewise, the client, the State Health Services Department, did not make sure that ABC could deliver on its promises. Perhaps, one might argue, every client cannot be expected to have the needed expertise in house to make such judgment calls and the State Health Department ought not to have been put in such a position by ABC.

Having realized its mistake, ABC should have ensured that its contract with Why-not-Me? clearly stipulated their respective roles and the scope and timing of the project. This would have closed what proved to be costly loop holes.

There is also clear indication that ABC failed to exercise appropriate authority over its sub-vendor. This is reflected in that ABC could not control the sub-vendor effectively, manage customer expectations being inflated by the sub-vendor, nor control the scope of the run-away project through rigid change control processes. Perhaps ABC's project management team and its Project Lead were to blame. Perhaps, those who had the authority to assemble the team were also responsible for having exercised poor judgment.

The client also exercised poor judgment in assuming an adversarial position with ABC. Again, perhaps ABC was partially to blame — after all it had brought on much of the mis-happenings upon itself and others by hiring Why-not-Me? Nonetheless, the client ought not to have acted myopically by pitting itself against its contracted partner while aligning with Why-not-Me? Clearly, the client was motivated by less than honest intentions. In the end, Why-not-Me? Corp. walked away with a lot of money. The client had to assume some of the financial losses and also settle for a system delivered very much behind schedule.

For its part, all indications are that Why-not-Me? had practiced poor business ethics. No business ought to be driven by the sole motivation of making extra dollars at any cost. The continued goodwill of enterprise partners, customers, regulatory bodies and the like is essential for longevity in any enterprise. Despite its financial gains, Why-not-Me? had created an extremely poor impression of itself with ABC and, in hindsight, with the State Health Services Department. It had also risked having this negative impression spread to others by the injured parties, notably by ABC Inc. which still enjoys a formidable reputation in the business.

Epilogue and Lessons Learned

As mentioned in Project Description, technology is a big part of this project. However, as many have now come realize (usually, the hard way), throwing technology at a problem is rarely in itself a solution. People and processes have significant roles to play. Client-server technology is cutting-edge technology. Technical complications have historically impeded successful migration to client-server from centralized or other forms of distributed processing. Adding poor judgment and interpersonal strife to the mix can only complicate things further. This case is a classical example that demonstrates that no technology can be any better than the humans involved, their management principles, and their business ethics.

People are an organization's most valuable resource. They often make or break an organization. The same is true of a venture involving enterprise partners as is the case here. The partnership is also an organization. As such, the venture's success or failure rests ultimately with the people involved to a substantial extent. Some who serve an organization's goals in a less than optimal fashion do so out of ignorance, others due to inefficiency, and yet others with malicious intent. In the scenario described herein, human behavior encompassing all such behavioral elements played a part at various junctures.

The resultant negative impacts affect not only those directly involved with the project but all employees of the concerned organization (and, by extension, society itself) to one extent or another.

Four other insights concerning the situation are worth special mention. First, it is important to spend adequate time to get to know who the key players are when entering into a joint venture. Any contract entered into must recognize the potential roles played by all such players. ABC's contract was with the central office. Yet, it turned out subsequently that the central office was completely subservient to some of its sub-units. These units used their financial clout as a weapon by threatening to boycott the original system. The central office had no power to force them to use the system. Apart from the fact that such a boycott would negatively impact the overall effectiveness of the system, the central office would also appear ineffectual in the eyes of the state and federal funding authorities.

Second, it is critical to not only involve client participants in a project from the very beginning but also to educate them to enable them to make more informed decisions. The Health Department representatives were very knowledgeable about the business processes that were to be automated but more or less at a complete loss on different ways in which technology could be exploited toward this end. As a result, everybody's focus was merely on automating existing manual processes using client-server technology. It would have been preferable to redesign each process around the capabilities of a set of candidate technologies. This would have helped to not only assess multiple technologies meaningfully, in terms of their inherent efficiencies and inefficiencies, but to reassess one's own operations in light of each one's capabilities.

As the client's representatives became more educated about client-server technology, their demands of the technology also increased. ABC Inc., itself being a novice in the nuances of the technology, was in no position, from the very beginning, to educate the customer. It was only committed to the terms of the contract — automating existing manual processes — and felt that the customer was making unfair demands.

Third, given that both the client and the primary vendor were learning the technology being used, it perhaps would have been better for all concerned to commit to developing and implementing the system incrementally. This approach calls for a greater degree of trust between the parties involved. Notably, the client ought to have some assurance that the vendor would not abandon the project after having delivered a partial system. Likewise, the vendor should be willing to commit itself to the project in incremental steps and not be concerned that the client may parcel out any and all of the subsequent phases to other vendors.

Fourth, from a vendor's perspective, there is no way that it can generate a reasonable estimate of what it would cost to create an unfamiliar system using unfamiliar technology. It is in a position where it must bid to stay in business and yet be a low-cost provider. Naturally, it tends to underbid very heavily to be awarded the project and then must exercise very strict change control. Neither party can emerge a winner under such circumstances. Perhaps a better strategy would be for a client to ask various vendors to demonstrate how they would put together the proposed system, approach the processes of implementation and conversion, what they estimate the cost of each component of the system to be and why, and what the overall project would cost. Vendors could then be compared on these attributes and contracted to do only what they are perceived as being good and cost-effective at.

This strategy is not without its potential pitfalls, however. The client must now be willing to coordinate the activities of a variety of vendors and have the know-how to determine whether the work performed by the different vendors is technically integratable into a cohesive whole. While what we described in this case could well happen with any of these vendors, both the client and the concerned vendor are only risking a small portion of a mammoth project and not the entire project. Re-negotiations, replacements, etc. can be more easily accomplished given the smaller scope of each sub-project.

Questions for Discussion

1. What factors prompted the State Health Services Department to begin considering applying technology to a perceived problem?

2. How did the department go about seeking a technology solution?

3. What specific difficulties did the department encounter in getting the chosen solution implemented?

4. How did the department handle itself and its interactions with others involved when such difficulties arose? Could it have handled things differently?

5. What suggestions would you have for organizations wishing to undertake a technology solution to fix a problem?

Chapter 14

DSS for Strategic
Decision Making

Sherif Kamel
American University in Cairo

Executive Summary

This chapter describes and analyses the experience of the Egyptian government in spreading the awareness of information technology and its use in managing socio-economic development through building multiple information handling and decision support systems in messy, turbulent and changing environments. The successes over the past ten years in developing, implementing and sustaining state-of-the-art decision support systems for central governmental decision making holds many lessons for the implementation of sophisticated systems under conditions of extreme difficulty. The experience offers insight into a variety of problems for designers, implementors, users and researchers of information and decision support systems. The chapter focuses on two main themes; the use of information in development planning and the use of decision support systems theory and applications in public administration. These themes reflect the government attempts to optimize the use of information technology to boost socio-economic development which witnessed the initiation, development and implementation of a supply-push strategy to improve Egypt's managerial, technological and administrative development. The chapter demonstrates how the nature of decision making at the Cabinet and the information needs related to such a strategic level necessitated the establishment of an information vehicle to respond to the decision making requirements. Finally, the chapter provides some case analysis showing the implementation and institutionalization of large information and decision support systems in Egypt, their use in unconventional settings and their implications on the decision making process in public administration.

Background

The importance of information technology has been greatly emphasized in most developing countries (Goodman, 1991; Lind, 1991) where the government has played a vital role in its diffusion

(Moussa & Schware, 1992). These governments, through their policies, laws and regulations, still exert the largest influence throughout various organizations and entities (Nidumolu & Goodman, 1993). Recently, the extensive benefits of information collection, analysis and dissemination, supported by computer-based technologies have been sought to enable decision makers and development planners to accelerate their socio-economic development programs. Thus, many developing countries have been embarking on medium and large scale information technology and computerization projects. In practice, most of these projects have sought to introduce computer technologies to realize socio-economic development. However, frequently, it concentrated more on large scale capital expenditures rather than on human capital investment such as training and human resource development (UNESCO, 1989), and therefore, failed to achieve their goals resulting in a generally negative conventional wisdom which defined information technology as inappropriate to developing countries.

Consequently, developing countries, gaining from the experiences of the past, have been extensively investing in training, consultancy and the establishment of a strong and efficient technological infrastructure that could move them into a state of self sufficiency and help build an information infrastructure that could help boost their socio-economic development efforts. However, to realize concrete benefits from the implementation of information technology, there was an ultimate need to apply the appropriate technology that do fit the country's values, social conditions and cultural aspects as well as the identification of information technology needs, and its related policies and regulations that could provide the proper environment for its implementation.

Realizing the enormous impact of information technology and its important role in socio-economic development, the government of Egypt has been striving to implement a nation-wide strategy to support the realization of its targeted objectives. Therefore, it adopted since the mid 1980s a supply-push strategy to improve Egypt's managerial and technological infrastructure. The objective was to introduce and diffuse information technology into all ministries, governorates, and government organizations which necessitated the development of an infrastructure for informatics and decision support, a software service industry and a high-tech industrial base in the areas of electronics, computers and communications. Consequently, the government, late in 1985, established the Cabinet, Information and Decision Support Center (IDSC) to support the Cabinet and top policy makers in key socio-economic issues through the formulation of information and decision support projects reaching 600 in 1996.

Setting the Stage

Decision support systems (DSS) imply the use of computers to assist managers in their decision processes in semi and ill-structured tasks, support rather than replace managerial judgment, and improve the effectiveness of decision making rather than its efficiency (Keen & Scott Morton, 1978). Decision support systems were mainly developed and applied in profit-oriented organizations which are managed through market constraints and trends. However, IDSC experience suggests new areas of applications for decision support systems which are based on developmental objectives for socio-economic improvement, governed by country-wide laws and regulations and regarded as systems which ought to fit within developmental contexts, policy decision making and supporting management problem solving.

While there are examples of successful decision support systems used for strategic decision making by top management in such decision contexts as mergers and acquisitions, plant location and capital expenditures, these systems tend to focus on limited and well-structured phases of specific decisions. However, when supporting the comprehensive strategic decision making process over a longer span of time with competing and changing strategic and socio-economic development issues, multiple decisions and changing participants, much less progress has been made. A large part of the challenge comes from the messy, complex nature of the strategic decision making process and the related issues that it brings to the design, development and implementation of decision support systems. This could be attributed to the nature of strategic decision making which is usually murky, ill structured and drawn out over a long period of time through requiring rapid response capabilities in crisis situations (El Sherif & El Sawy, 1988). It is usually a group rather than an individual effort involving cooperative problem solving, crisis management, consensus building and conflict resolution (Gray, 1988). It involves multiple stake holders with different assumptions (Mason & Mitroff, 1981). The information used is mostly qualitative, verbal and poorly recorded (El Sherif & El Sawy, 1988) and its HH unlimitedness causes not only an information overload with multiple and conflicting interpretations but also the absence of relevant information (Zmud, 1986). Finally, the formation of strategic decisions is more like an evolving and emerging process where the supporting requirements are difficult to forecast (Mintzberg & Waters, 1985). There are also some challenges that are associated with the nature of the decision maker such as difficulty in contacting due to his valuable time, unwillingness to spend time learning, preference to rely more on personal experience and intuition rather than on information technology tools and techniques, and resistance to changes.

In the case of Egypt, strategic decision making at the Cabinet level provides an opportunity for the design and delivery of information and decision support systems that differ from other conventional settings. The inadequate reliability of the information infrastructure coupled with the need for crisis response led to prototyping the design and delivery processes which was based on an issue-based rather than an organizational decision-based approach to fit the decision making environment. There are many similarities that could be mapped between the Cabinet and organizational decision making where the use of issues management is not alien to corporations (King, 1981) and was applied in the planning for various management information systems organizations (Dansker, et al., 1987). Table 1 provides a comparison of the conventional decision-based approach and the issue-based approach to decision support systems as identified by IDSC and which has been successfully implemented during the last decade in response to the need for supporting strategic decision making at the Cabinet level (El Sherif & El Sawy, 1988). The table is useful for information systems researchers and practitioners in determining the advantages and constraints of the issue-based approach to various organizational and decision making environments. The approach's life cycle is highly iterative and consists of nested and intersecting process loops. It includes; the issue requirements definition loop, involving cycles between structuring the strategic issue and defining its requirements, the support services definition loop, involving cycles between defining information support services and decision support services, the prototyping design and delivery loop, where the design prototype iterations are nested in a delivery process that is also prototyped. The process iterates with the support services definition loop and the institutionalization loop, which includes both adoption and diffusion in addition to the establishment of an issue-tracking system which iterates with all other loops.

Project Description

Overview of the Project

The decision making process at the Cabinet addresses a variety of socio-economic issues such as balance of payment deficit, high illiteracy rate, housing, health, public sector reform, administrative reform, debt management, privatization and unemployment. The decision making process involves much debate, group discussions, studies development and is subject to public accountability and media attention (El Sherif & El Sawy, 1988). Figure 1 shows a model of the Cabinet of Egypt decision making

	Conventional	Issue-Based
Focus	• decision maker • single decision • decision making • alternatives generation	• issue • groups of interacting issues • attention focusing • agenda setting
Favored Domains	• tactical & operational decisions • one-shot decisions • functional applications • departmental applications	• strategic decisions • recurring strategic decisions • cross-functional applications • trans-organizational applications

Design & Delivery	• promotes customization to
	  individual decision maker
	• interaction between decisions
	  not incorporated
	• prototyping design
	• design approach becomes
	  the system
		• promotes consensus around
		  group issue
		• integration and consensus
		  drives process
		• prototyping design & delivery
		• delivery approach becomes
		  the system

EIS Readiness	• no tracking component
	• emphasizes convergent structuring
	• major transformation
		• incorporates tracking
		  component
		• balances divergent exploration
		  and convergent structuring
		• easy transition to EIS

Emerging
Leveraging
Technologies
	• expert systems
	• artificial intelligence
		• idea processing & associative
		  aids
		• multimedia connectivity
		  platforms

Table 1: Conventional versus Issue-based Decision Support Systems Approach

process prior to the establishment of IDSC including key participants and the information use within the context of the Cabinet decision making.

The Cabinet decision making process is usually seen in terms of its mission, objectives, and outcomes. However, extensive observations revealed that the decision making process is better viewed by its stake holders as a process of attention to sets of issues with varying and changing priorities. These issues circulate continuously and are liable to political manoeuvring and situation changes until they are managed over time. The issues are usually complex, ill structured, interdependent and multi-sectoral with strategic impacts at the national, regional and international levels. The decision making environment at the Cabinet level could be characterized by being data rich and information poor due to the lack of proper data analysis, the isolation of the information and decision support experts from the decision makers, the use of computer systems as ends rather than tools supporting in decision making and the focus on technical issues rather than on decision outcomes [Figure 2].

Management & Organizational Concerns

IDSC's mission is to provide information and decision support services to the Cabinet for socio-economic development and to improve the country's managerial and technological infrastructure

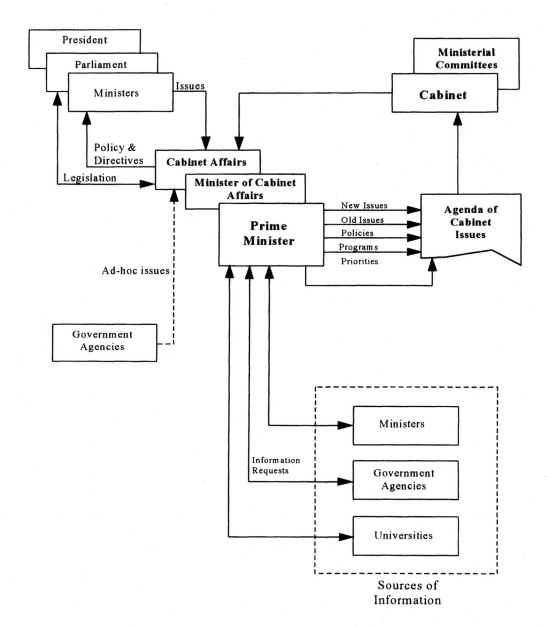

Figure 1: The Cabinet Decision Making Process before IDSC

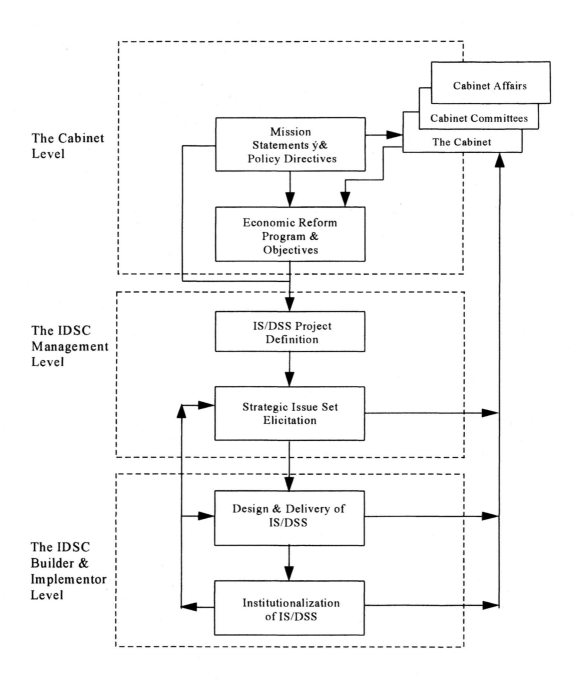

Figure 2: Supporting Strategic Decision Making Through Information and Decision Support Systems

through enhancing the decision making process. To realize its mission, IDSC objectives included: developing information and decision support systems for the Cabinet and top policy makers in Egypt, supporting the establishment of decision support systems/centers in different ministries, making more efficient and effective use of the available information resources, initiating, encouraging and supporting informatics projects to accelerate managerial and technological development of various ministries, sectors and governorates.

IDSC interacts in three main directions for data accessibility and information dissemination. The first direction represents the Cabinet base where information and decision support systems are developed to support the strategic policy and decision making processes. The second direction represents the national nodes where IDSC links the Cabinet with data sources in Egypt within different ministries, public sector organizations, academic institutions and research centers. The third direction represents the international nodes where IDSC accesses major databases worldwide through state-of-the-art computing, information and communications facilities. IDSC's scope of activities extends to four levels: the Cabinet, sectoral, national and international. At the Cabinet level, it provides information and decision support, crisis management support, data modelling and analysis, multi-sectoral information handling and databases development. At the sectoral level, it provides technical and managerial assistance in the establishment and development of decision support centers/systems, advisory and consultancy services, and sectoral information systems development. At the national level, it provides assistance in policy formulation and drafting, legislative reform support and in the technological infrastructure development. Finally, at the international level, IDSC acts as a window for technology transfer to Egypt, establishes decision support systems models for developing countries and formulates cooperation links and communication channels with international informatics organizations.

The organizational structure was developed to fit IDSC's environment of operations in terms of the required human and technological infrastructure to accommodate such a dynamic environment. It comprises three hierarchical levels, the top management and executive level, the experts level consisting of two remote teams; the crisis management team and the priority assessment and quality control team which are formulated from IDSC's experts in addition to other consultants and researchers in different disciplines related to the organizationís activities. These teams on the one hand support requests coming to IDSC and set priorities for their implementation and on the other hand, monitor, follow-up and assess the performance of different departments throughout the development and implementation of various activities. The third level represents IDSC's different departments interacting in parallel to realize projects design and implementation, data collection and verification, issue formulation and decision support, training of staff, and other administrative functions. They include: (a) decision support services to respond to different information and decision support requests including the identification of users needs, issues formulation, definition of information and decision support requirements and the provision of possible sets of solutions and recommendations to these issues; (b) Information resource management focusing on information systems design, development, installation and maintenance; (c) Projects development to plan, control and manage various projects implemented; (d) Human resource development to train the organization's staff as well as the staff of various partner organizations with which IDSC has joint projects.

Technology Concerns

IDSC evolved quickly from three people in 1985 to over 1,000 managerial, technical and administrative personnel in 1996. The staff is composed of highly trained and qualified professionals including over 150 Ph.Ds, 280 Master Degrees and 75 Diplomas. Moreover, over 100 staff members are currently engaged in post-graduate studies. The staff's background varies in areas of interest to social sciences and technological issues which facilitated IDSC's mission in meeting its different objectives.

IDSC's technical infrastructure witnessed a dramatic growth both in quantity and quality. Thus, from one site of 200m2 and 3 XT 8088 personal computers in 1985, the organization's technical resources now occupies twelve sites across the city of Cairo, with accessibility to a heterogeneous, well integrated, multi-platform environment that comprises mainframes, several high-end UNIX workstations, and a multitude of personal computers and macintoshes all connected using different connectivity protocols with seamless internetworking between the different sub-networks. Furthermore, the organization has become a leading government entity in introducing Internet in Egypt with its ability to provide several services and Internet Protocol addresses of its class B set.

The profile of human resources comprises the traditional mix of titles in most informatics organizations such as programmers, database administrators, application developers, systems analysts, decision support systems builders, network specialists, end users, consultants, trainers, technical group leaders and project managers. However, based on the organization's experience in designing and delivering a large number of informatics projects in a rapidly changing environment, such mix of titles was not useful to fulfil the requirements of its projects and activities. In that respect, IDSC characterized its human resources profile in terms of its organizational roles where there was a mixture between technical and non-technical roles in addition to a hybrid representing selected individuals who had acquired a combination of technical and non-technical skills.

The role mix was multi-dimensional and helped capture both the organizational and cultural impacts caused by the introduction, use and diffusion of information technology. Therefore, IDSC started to characterize its human resources profile through more differentiated roles that were defined through an intersection of client, organizational, cultural and information systems role demands which later on helped manage the career path development of IDSC staff which was respectively translated into a remarkable improvement in the organizational performance (El Sherif & El Sawy, 1990).

Throughout the development phases, a set of human resource management strategies were implemented to assess the improvement of the staff's skills and knowledge and to leverage IDSC's capacities to formulate world class information systems professionals. These strategies included; cross-fertilization through visiting expatriates, consultants and experts, tracking emerging technologies, and networking with leading centers of excellence; focusing on promoting and financially rewarding customer-responsive skill hybridization through the development of two-tiered teams which led to the continuous and smooth communication with various customers; intensively investing in the staff's growth through academic and professional development; fostering expertise infusion and diffusion through in-breeding by carefully selecting the staff and incubation through encouraging the staff to spin-off new projects and ventures and finally; formulating excitement over the information systems career as part of the organizational culture which has resulted in creating a positive image of information systems careers across the country at large.

The most direct and cumulative impact of the human resource management profile was reflected through three main indicators; the information systems turnover rate was 2 percent in a locally competitive environment, the education and human resource development program, apart from the staff members pursuing graduate studies, has gone up from 72 training hours in 1987 to 250 training hours in 1995 and finally there was a growth in the number of IDSC staff members who are being transformed from a technical or non-technical focus into a hybridized multi-dimensional focus which helped improve their potential skills and knowledge to better respond to changing user demands.

Current Status of the Project

As of November 1985, IDSC started providing information and decision support services for the Cabinet positioning itself as a facilitator, integrator and expediter of information from various sources to the Cabinet by providing access to different national and international information sources and databases through cutting-edge computer-based facilities [Figure 3]. The design and delivery of the information and decision support systems capabilities was developed using a non-conventional process to be able to accommodate the strategic decision making environment. It evolved around three main concepts; the need to improve the fit among the users in their decision making context, the form of support provided and the technologies used, and the use of an iterative prototyping strategy for information and decision support systems design and delivery.

While the decision making at the Cabinet revolves around issues, they are translated outside the Cabinet as programs and policies and are handed to IDSC in a mission-driven form such as "we need to build a decision support system to help formulate, develop and monitor the industrial sector strategic and tactical plans," or in a directive data driven form such as "we want to establish an information base about all companies in the industrial sector in Egypt." At the IDSC management level, these requests are translated through interactions with policy makers to a set of articulated strategic issues around which information and decision support systems are defined.

The design and delivery of such systems are carried out at the IDSC builder and implementor level within the decision support services and information resources management departments where the process goes through a series of iterative prototyping cycles. IDSC's experience in implementing decision support systems made it clear that managing institutionalization is as important as model building. Thus, it should be explicit, complementary and an integrated process that accompanies systems development and model building (El Sherif, 1990).

Managing the design and delivery of information and decision support systems at IDSC follows two phases. First, the implementation phase which including; the identification of policy needs and the full mobilization of human and technical resources to be able to achieve effective response and support, the identification of decision areas and information requirements which deal with the translation of the planned policies into specific issues of concern to the Cabinet, and the formulation of projects with specific goals and dedicated human and technical resources for each potential area of policy and/or decision support. The implementation phase consists of two parts: strategies and tactics (Shultz, Slevin & Pinto, 1987). The value of education, local development, defining user involvement and obtaining top management and decision making levels involvement is crucial for successful implementation (Keen, Bronsema & Zuboff, 1982). Finally, the importance of the non-technical component in avoiding implementation failure must be recognized (Ginzberg, 1981). Therefore, IDSC's project teams were selected to provide fast response, focus on results and actions and consists of two-tiered teams comprising government civil servants, information technology professional and technical staff to deal with administrative as well as technology oriented staff. These two-tiered teams represented one of the key success factors in bridging the application gap between systems builders and applications users. Second, the institutionalization phase consisting of: adaptation, diffusion, adoption, monitoring and tracking, value assessment and evaluation of decision support systems. Adaptation deals with various modifications needed to fit the contextual and cultural characteristics of the environment of application. Thus, IDSC designs and develops Arabised software tools and utilities to support and facilitate the use of various software which represents the cultural interface. Diffusion deals with spreading the use of decision support systems at various organizational levels. Therefore, the IDSC approach is built on developing the information technology infrastructure across all organizational levels through the diffusion of personal computers which represents the organizational interface. Adoption deals with the personalized use of information technology tools and

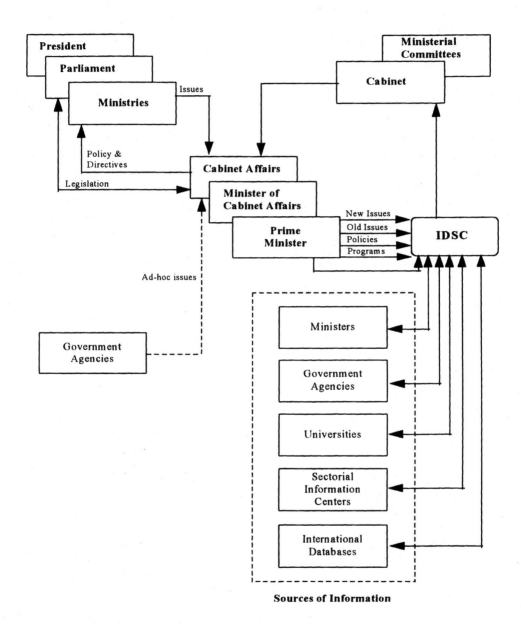

Figure 3: The Cabinet Decision Making Process after IDSC

techniques by decision makers and their support staff. Therefore, decision support systems are customized and adjusted to the users' needs which represents the user interface. Monitoring and tracking deals with the parameters of critical issues, assumptions, priorities and information and decision requirements in addition to the changes in the technology and their impacts on the decision making process. Value assessment deals with how decision support systems have greatly improved strategic decision making including the tangible and intangible benefits such as improving decision making at the Cabinet level and making better use of the available resources. Evaluation deals with the appraisal, analysis and validation of the value added benefits of decision support systems on socio-economic development.

Successes and Failure

Developing countries represent a challenging domain for information and decision support systems. The characteristics of the country, the problems faced and the opportunities are among the challenges. Examples of these challenges include: the lack of informatics infrastructure, the use and availability of information is still limited, the lack of technical expertise and the application gap between existing information and decision support systems innovations is widening. Moreover, the experience of IDSC in Egypt with regard to the development and implementation of large information and decision support systems projects helped identify new challenges. These challenges relate to: strategic decision making, decision support systems, implementation of decision support systems and its institutionalization process. In strategic decision making, the challenges related to the ill-structured nature of processes extending over long periods of time, the involvement of many stake holders, the need for conflict resolution, consensus building and crisis management, the efficient and effective use of scarce resources, and the turbulent and dynamic environment in which the decision making process occurs.

In decision support systems, the challenges related to managing the development of multiple information and decision support systems, their institutionalization within their application contexts, the development of appropriate interfaces, the availability of tools and generators relevant to different industries, supporting rather than replacing managerial judgements, fast response and prototyping the design and delivery phases.

In implementation, the challenges related to the lack of user involvement, inadequacy of model evaluation, lack of problem definition, resistance to change, and the difficulty to diffuse new model-based systems. It also included; untimely, unresponsive and inadequate information and non-responsiveness to user needs, lack of top management support, lack of vital continuous communication, poor documentation, and language problems (Gass, 1987).

In institutionalization, the challenges included: overcoming resistance to change, adapting model-based systems to the context of work and formulating documented procedures, managing the process of change, information technology diffusion and adoption and their impacts on the individual and the organization.

Managing the implementation and institutionalization of decision support systems required facing all the challenges which represented, within the strategic decision making level aimed at realizing socio-economic development objectives, one of the most difficult and challenging context for implementation and institutionalization due to the messy, ill-structured, dynamic and turbulent environments.

The scope of IDSC projects are grouped along four dimensions which encompass its activities. These dimensions are decision support systems for strategic issues, building sectoral decision support centers, management and technological development and information infrastructure development. Following are selected decision support cases that were implemented by IDSC aiming at socio-economic development, structuring the decision making process and supporting the technological development of the country.

In decision support systems for strategic issues, recent economic rebuilding efforts required Egypt to accumulate a foreign debt of about US$ 33 billion covered in 5,000 loans. These loans needed to be monitored for debt services, payments, terms re-negotiations, interest rates, management of payments schedules and transactions. The magnitude of the debt burden led its reform program to become among the top priority issues at the Cabinet level. Hence, IDSC has initiated, developed and implemented the debt management project aiming at the rationalization of debt utilization, reduction and rescheduling. The project was developed to provide a management tool to support and facilitate the registration, monitoring, control and analysis of Egypt's debts. Over a period of 18 months a national comprehensive database was developed by IDSC technical staff and was located in the Central Bank of Egypt. The database included the government loans in addition to a transaction-processing system for debt management that was built with decision support systems capabilities to be able to test the implications of different debt management scenarios. Throughout the development phase, a number of problems arose which caused delay and frustration. These problems were related to both technical and language issues. The impacts of the project through the implementation of the decision support system included: the success in the rescheduling negotiations with 14 countries which was smoothly managed through the provision of a solid grounded information support that was made available to the negotiators. Moreover, loans have been viewed ever since as part of a comprehensive, integrated and dynamic portfolio rather than being managed on an isolated case by case basis which was in favour of the economy, its debt rescheduling status.

In building sectoral decision support centers, the increasing cost and subsidy on electricity were continuously enlarging the balance of payment and adding to the burden of the economy. Thus, IDSC developed the ministry of electricity decision support system to assess the impact of tariff changes on different income groups, to provide statistical data on power and energy generation including the distribution and consumption of electricity, and to aid in pricing and managing the loans of the electricity sector. A joint team was formed from IDSC and the ministry of electricity. The ministry staff collected data from different sources while the IDSC staff focused on issue structuring, systems and human resources development and more importantly on managing the process of developing and delivering the decision support system. Along the implementation process, a strategic issue emerged that related to drought in the sources of the Nile River. It caused a dramatic drop in the hydro-electric power generated by the Aswan dam and necessitated the provision of millions of US dollars to build 3 power generating stations. Thus, the ministry of water resources had to take part and contribute to the project since it became a stakeholder in the decision support system design process. The team, as of that stage, included a third group from the ministry of water resources to cover the issues that related water resources to electricity. The impacts of the ministry of electricity decision support system came out mainly in the implementation phase which included the ministry of water resources as a stakeholder in energy generation related issues, the issuance of a new tariff after assessing the possible alternatives generated by the decision support model and the evaluation of their impacts on different income groups. The case showed that implementation and design processes are inseparable and evolutionary throughout all phases.

In management and technological development, Egypt formulated a comprehensive plan to improve its development and growth in the world market place using the latest emerging information technologies. The use of information technology aimed at supporting the countries' socio-economic development programs and boosting its economy through the development of a high-tech industry as well as through increasing its software development and exportation in terms of technical expertise and software applications through the optimum utilization of its resources, mainly expertise, low-cost labour and a flourishing business and investment climate. The IDSC's Pyramid Technology Valley program is one such effort to improve technological infrastructure. The program was launched through an international conference held in Cairo in 1989. It aims at creating a suitable environment for Egypt's high-technology industries with an emphasis on developing electronics and software industries, attracting new foreign investment, assisting in the creation of new opportunities for small business enterprises, and exporting high-technology products to various countries. The expected impacts of the program showed that a developed information technology industry in Egypt could achieve an annual production value of about US$2.5 billion of which US$1.5 billion will arise from exports revenues. Moreover, the program will create annually around 15,000 jobs for a period of 5 to 7 years which could have a direct effect on Egypt's growth national product (GNP).

In information infrastructure development, realizing the enormous impact of information on decision making and its vital role in socio-economic development, IDSC adopted a strategy to restructuring public administration at the governorates level through the use of information and decision support tools and techniques. IDSC developed a comprehensive information base at the governorates level through the establishment, in each governorate, of a Governorate Information and Decision Support Center (GIDSC) to introduce and diffuse information technology, and to restructure the role of the governorates in socio-economic development planning. The project since its inception aimed at rationalizing the decision making process of the governors through the use of state-of-the-art information technology.

Epilogue and Lessons Learned

Based on IDSC's efforts in the design and delivery of 600 informatics projects in Egypt targeting socio-economic development, the following is a set of lessons learned that could be generalized to the implementation of decision support systems in similar environment and that represent potential areas for future research.

- Structuring of issues is an integral part of the design and implementation of decision support systems dealing with socio-economic development .
- Providing decision support systems for development planning is often coupled with both urgency and criticality of the issue. Therefore, decision support systems design should allow for crisis management to be able to respond to crisis requests which entails the preparation of crisis teams with their managerial and technical support capable to operate in such situations.
- Providing decision support systems requires much time and effort in building and integrating databases from multiple data sources and sectors.
- Developing a decision support system for one socio-economic issue might affect other issues which should be put into consideration during the design phase to save time and effort and avoid duplication of activities.
- An effective decision support system depends on the availability and accessibility of timely, relevant and accurate information.
- Successful implementation of decision support systems is a necessary aspect but not sufficient condition for successful institutionalization, both processes should be well integrated.
- Prototyping decision support systems should be reflected during the design, development and delivery phases.
- Providing decision support systems requires textual and document-based information sources capabilities which should be reflected in the organizational design.
- Recurring decisions related to certain issues need to be monitored through a management system for

tracking the changes in the critical parameters of these issues.

- Successful design and delivery of decision support systems is based upon top management support during implementation and organizational support during institutionalization.
- Evaluation and assessment of decision support systems is a vital process that should accompany all phases of implementation and institutionalization in order to realize on-line response to changes occurring in the environment.
- Continuous multi-level training of human resources leads to the adaptation, diffusion and adoption of decision support systems within various organizations.

In summary, the experience of such new form of information-based organization in Egypt led to the improvement of the decision making process at the Cabinet level and supported in the socio-economic development programs. The new opportunities developed from the use of decision support systems in such an environment have increasingly contributed to the conviction of the top level policy making level of the advantages of the use of various information technology tools and techniques for development purposes.

Questions for Discussion

1. Examine the organizational implications of the use of decision support systems at the strategic national level and its effects on the decision makers and the decision making process.
2. Identify what changes need to be made at the organizational and decision making levels to optimally benefit from the output and deliverables of decision support systems.
3. Compare the conventional and the issue-based approach in the design and delivery of decision support systems and their impacts on the decision making process in the corporate versus public administration domain.
4. Examine the value-added benefits of a decision support system within the context of socio-economic development based on the decision support cases described in this chapter
5. State the future research areas and directions for the implementation of decision support systems in public administration in light of the research findings and lessons learned from the Egyptian experience.

References

Berman, B.J. (1992). The state, Computers and African Development: The Information Non-Revolution. *MicroComputers in African Development.* (Lewis & Samoff, eds). Westview Press, Inc.

Dansker, B., Hansen, J.S., Loftin, R., and Veldweisch, M. (1987). Issues Management in the Information Planning Process. *Management Information Systems Quarterly.* 11(2).

El-Sherif, H. (1990). *Building crisis management strategic support systems for the Egyptian Cabinet.* Maastricht School of Management Research Papers. 2(2).

El-Sherif, H. (1990). Managing institutionalization of strategic decision support for the Egyptian Cabinet. Interfaces. 20(1).

El-Sherif, H. and El-Sawy, O. (1988). Issue-based decision support systems for the Cabinet of Egypt. *Management Information Systems Quarterly.* 12(4).

El-Sawy, O. (1985). Personal Information Systems for Strategic Scanning in Turbulent environments: Can the CEO go on-line? *Management Information Systems Quarterly.* 9(1).

Gass, S. (1987). *Operations research-supporting decisions around the world. Operational Research '87,* Edited by G.K. Rand. Amsterdam: Elsevier Science Publishers.

Ginzberg, M.J. (1981). *A perspective model for system implementation. Systems, Objectives, Solutions.* 1(1).

Goodman, S.E. (1991). Computing in a less developed country. *Communications of the ACM.* 34(12).

Gray, P. (1987). Using group decision support systems. *Decision Support Systems.* 3(3).

Gray, P. (1988). Using Technology for Strategic group decision making. Working paper, Claremont Graduate School.

Hirschheim, R.A., and Klein H.K. (1985). Fundamental Issues of decision support systems: A conquestialist perspective. *Decision Support Systems.* 1(1).

Housel, T.J., El-Sawy, O. and Donovan, P.F. (1986). Information systems for crisis management: lessons from Southern California Edison. *Management Information Systems Quarterly.* 10(4).

Keen, P.G.W. (1980). Information systems and organizational change. Working paper, International Center for Information Technology.

Keen, P.G.W. (1975). Computer-based decision aids: the evaluation problem. *Sloan Management Review.* 16(3).

Keen, P.G.W. and Scott Morton, M.S. (1978). *Decision support systems: an organizational perspective.* Reading: Addison-Wesley Publishing Company.

Keen, P.G.W, Bronsema, G.S and Zuboff, S. (1982). Implementing common systems: One organization's experience. *Systems, Objectives, Solutions.* 2(3).

King, W.R. (1981). *Strategic Issues Management. Strategic Planning and Management Handbook.* W.R. King and D.I Cleland (eds.). New York: Van Nostrand Reinhold Co.

Lind, P. (1991). *Computerization in developing countries: models and reality.* London: Routledge.

Mason, R.O. and Mitroff, I.I. (1981). *Challenging Strategic Planning Assumptions.* New York: John Wiley & Sons.

Moussa, A. and Schware, R. (1992). Informatics in Africa: Lessons from World Bank Experience. *World Development.* 20(12).

Nidumolu, S.R. and Goodman, S.E. (1993). Computing in India: An Asian Elephant Learning to Dance. *Communications of the ACM.* 36(4).

Nidumolu, S.R., Goodman, S.E., Vogel, D.R. and Danowitz, A.K. (1996). Information Technology for Local Administration Support: The Governorates Project in Egypt. *Management Information Systems Quarterly.* 20(2).

Scott Morton, M.S. (1971). Management decision systems: computer-based support for decision making. Working paper, Boston: Graduate School of Business Administration, Harvard University.

Schultz, R. L., Slevin, D.P and Pinto, J.K. (1987). Strategy and tactics in a process model of project implementation. *Interfaces.* 17(3).

Sprague, R.H., Jr. (1980). A framework for the development of decision support systems. *Management Information Systems Quarterly,* 4(4).

Sprague, R.H., Jr. and Watson, H.J. (eds.). (1986). *Decision support systems.* Englewood Cliffs: Prentice-Hall.

United Nations Educational, Social and Cultural Organization. (1989). *World Communications Report.* Paris: United Nations Press.

Zmud, R.W. (1986). Supporting Senior Executives through Decision Support Technologies: A review and directions for future research. *Decision Support Systems: A decade in perspective.* E.R. McLean and H.G. Sol (eds.). Amsterdam: Elsevier Science Publishers.

Chapter 15

End-User Computing at BRECI: The Ordeals of a One-person IS Department

Kathleen Moffitt
California State University, Fresno

Executive Summary

Small business is frequently touted as the fastest growing part of our economy. In the 1990s, a small business can easily use technology to its advantage. This has been made possible by the rapid and significant drop in the cost of hardware and networking, the availability of a wide-range of cost-effective software packages, and the escalating computer and information literacy seen in executives and the general workforce. In spite of this, and contrary to what is reported in the general and computer press, the application and understanding of technology is lacking in many small businesses that could benefit greatly from its use.

In contrast to the success stories seen in the press, the intention of the case study presented here is to show a less than successful attempt at the introduction and use of information technology in a small business. The business was a multi-state consulting firm with a highly educated workforce, geographically-dispersed projects, and demanding customers. Information technology offered the promise of significantly reduced administrative and communication costs; improved document production, distribution and management; and improved internal communication. The benefits stalled just as they were beginning to be realized, because executive management lacked the necessary understanding and failed to provide the support that was needed to fully realize the benefits. In addition, end-users failed to understand their role in supporting the introduction and implementation of information technology, and thus sealed the fate of the overall implementation.

IS staff hiring and transition planning, training, software selection and piracy, ergonomics, managerial support, and end-user involvement are examined in this case. While the details have been disguised to conceal the identity of the company and individuals involved, the case is an accurate depiction of end-user computing at "BRECI" and many other small businesses.

Background

Basin & Range Environmental Consultants, Inc. (BRECI) provides a limited number of highly specialized environmental consulting, planning and impact mitigation services to clients throughout the western United States. Most work done by the firm is the result of the requirement to conduct environmental impact studies for, and mitigate adverse impacts from, projects funded or licensed by public agencies. The entire industry tends to move through feast and famine cycles with numerous projects authorized within short periods of time and then nothing for extended periods. While an occasional large-scale project is approved, it appears that the days of numerous simultaneous large-scale projects is over. In the western US in the last 10 years, there have been only four large projects which needed the type of consulting services provided by BRECI. BRECI had successfully bid two of these.

BRECI has offices spread throughout the Rocky Mountain and Great Basin states of Idaho, Utah, Colorado and New Mexico. The corporate office was moved from Boulder, Colorado to Colorado Springs, Colorado in the late 1980s. This was done because a major career opportunity became available for the spouse of BRECI's president. The physical location of the corporate office is of little concern as long as it near a major airport and has easy access to the interstate highway system. The administrative activity remained in Boulder after the move because employees preferred Boulder and did not want to move to Colorado Springs. The Boulder office also became a field projects office and had a small staff of environmental specialists. An executive secretary, graphic artist and eventually an administrative assistant were hired for the Colorado Springs office. An environmental specialist with an interest in business administration became the Colorado Springs business manager and took over some corporate administrative functions. The corporate office also became home to four high level environmental specialists who were charged with overseeing various parts of a large project that was under way.

A major field project office was maintained in Salt Lake City, Utah. The purpose of field offices was to service major projects and clients. While these offices were originally intended to be temporary, they took on a life of their own due to the multi-year projects they serviced and the number of highly skilled staff who were, over a period of years, converted from temporary to permanent status. The philosophy of BRECI was that field offices would remain if they could bring in enough work to be self supporting. The attitude in the field offices was that they were too important to be disbanded. In addition, field office staff failed to recognize that the large projects would eventually wind down and did little to market themselves and thus ensure their survival. Luckily, a large project near Las Vegas, New Mexico was gearing up at about the same time the Utah project was beginning to wind down. Project transfers were offered to and declined by most Salt Lake City project office staff. The Boise, Idaho, office was a one-person show run by an environmental specialist who wouldn't leave Boise because of the wonderful job held by his spouse. On occasion, a few temporary staff were hired to assist him. Overall there were approximately 40 permanent employees and from 60-120 temporary employees.

Hiring of Chief Administrative Officer

By the end of 1991, the strain of a split administrative function was obvious. The business manager was doing a reasonably good job considering her lack of formal training in the area but was constantly caught in battles between the Colorado Springs and Boulder offices because of loyalty the president had to his former staff. In fact, the administrative assistant and bookkeeper in Boulder were jokingly referred to by many as the people who ran the company because they always got their way, right or wrong.

By early 1992, the Board of Directors had advised the President, Jim Morris, to hire a Chief Administrative Officer and begin efforts towards consolidating some activities. By late spring they had hand picked a personal friend to be put in the position but the placement was resisted by Morris. A short time later Morris saw opportunity knocking. An old friend who had left the environmental consulting field to get an MBA was moving to Colorado Springs for a 15 month period while her husband was on special assignment to the US Air Force Academy. This person not only had an MBA, work experience, an extensive background in computers but also knew the environmental consulting business. It was an opportunity he couldn't turn down and offered the position of Chief Administrative Officer to Karen Connolly without consulting with the Board of Directors. The Board was unhappy and retitled the position Director of Administrative Services.

Case Description

Specific directives given to Connolly were to improve the administrative function, improve the information systems, and teach the President how to use a computer. In reminiscing this, Connolly remembers,

I didn't realize the humor in the last directive (to teach the president to use computers) although the staff in general found it very funny. I eventually discovered that just about every computer that was in the corporate office had originally been purchased for and placed on the president's desk. They never even got turned on and when someone needed a computer, his was simply loaned, never to be returned. A few weeks later, a new electronic desk ornament would arrive. It even happened to me (the president's computer was offered to me while I decided what to purchase for myself). After seeing, literally, the quality of the monitor, I brought in my old COMPAQ Plus luggable from home until my new computer arrived. My old computer was eight years old and had a little tiny screen but was easier on the eyes. This unfortunately was my first indication of the "quality" of the equipment the business manager had been purchasing.

Connolly made visits to each field office to make or renew working relationships with the consulting staff. While there she assessed the local administrative function and technology-base. The administrative function was extremely inefficient and while there was a significant amount of technology in place, the quality, inter-operability, connectivity, backup, security and employee skill level were seriously lacking and causing major inefficiencies. There was no overall plan or coordination to hardware or software purchases and no training. Everyone was doing their own thing. A significant problem with software piracy also surfaced. Connolly describes what she found:

I firmly believe that with organizational computing, you pay now or you pay later where quality is concerned. It appeared that the sole selection criteria for everything had been cost; the cheaper the better. I could barely find a piece of equipment where I even recognized the brand name; many things literally had no labels at all. There were no manuals anywhere but I was expected to magically fix problems just because "I knew something about computers." It reminded me of Johnny Carson holding the envelope to his head on the Tonight Show and guessing what was inside it. It was funny, but it was a frustrating and very serious problem. Any corporate MIS manager will tell you that IS/IT purchases made in this manner are exactly what not to do. The job was quickly looking like far more than one person could reasonably handle.

Addressing Identified Problems And Opportunities

Standards and Upgrades

The first step after the initial assessment was to standardize all new hardware and software purchases. Connolly chose Gateway because it was a good product, with good pricing, performance, quality, documentation and support. The pre-installed software was also legal, thus helping to begin addressing the software piracy problem. The Salt Lake City office was networked. Unfortunately the equipment selection and network installation were based on a bare-bones, shoestring budget and the result showed in slow response time and down time. Connolly made plans to increase hard drive capacity, upgrade the operating system to Novell 3.11, and send a knowledgeable and reliable employee to Novell training.

Ergonomics

Out of the three administrative staff at the corporate office, one, the executive secretary, had already filed a worker's compensation claim for repetitive stress injury. She was having extreme pain in her arms, neck and shoulders but the examining physician stated that she had not worked there long enough to have a repetitive stress injury and recommended relaxation exercises.

When Connolly first interviewed with BRECI, she noticed the workstation layout for the executive secretary and cringed. The computer monitor was on a shelf well above the proper eye height and was directly facing a large picture window. There was no glare screen. The keyboard rested on a flimsy pullout drawer that provide no support at all. It was no wonder she was in pain. Connolly discussed rearranging the work space but the executive secretary liked it and didn't seem to believe it could possibly be causing her problems. Within a few weeks her symptoms had become so severe she was nearly unable to perform her job but stubbornly refused to let Connolly rearrange her work area. Connolly took matters into her own hands, went in on the weekend, rearranged everything, and made sure to get to work before the executive secretary did on Monday morning. The executive secretary was not happy when she saw her "new" office but she did agree to try it for a week and if it did not help, the workspace would be returned to the way it was. Within two days the pain and headaches were gone as was her desire to return to the original arrangement. Word spread and Connolly was soon asked to rearrange other employees' workstations as well. It was clear Connolly would need to take an active part in furniture selection and placement for the new office BRECI would be moving to. The move was three months away. This was only the beginning of the resistance to change that would become a continuing problem for Connolly.

Accounting Information Systems

A nearly immediate request was made by the bookkeeper in Boulder. The custom-made accounting software, in use for many years, needed to be modified. It had been developed by a consultant when the company was very small and had been modified, presumably by the same consultant, over the years. No one remembered the name of the consultant, the software or language it was developed in, what modifications had been made to the system (although they knew that modifications had been made), why it occasionally spit out really strange results, or where the documentation was (actually no one remembered any documentation at all). Connolly, being the "computer guru" was expected to solve the problem. Connolly remembers her reaction, "I refused to make any changes and was prepared to quit if anyone tried to force me into it. It was then that I learned about the expensive accounting package that had been purchased a year earlier, but never installed, and the $10,000 in upgrades that had been ordered for the uninstalled system immediately prior to my arrival."

In spring of 1991, the Board of Directors had decided to purchase a modern accounting package. The only analysis conducted was that a member of the Board had heard it was a good package. The basic package cost $20,000 and this did not include the modules that were needed to make it do what a normal person would expect an accounting package to do. Whether due to basic human resistance on the part of the Boulder bookkeeper or sheer inappropriateness of the software package, the new accounting package was never implemented. Consultants specializing in this package were brought in from Denver shortly before Connolly arrived. The consultants recommended the purchase of the upgrade to the package. The upgrade alone was $10,000 with the functional modules additional. Connolly immediately had questions regarding the appropriateness of the accounting package since it was designed for a manufacturing environment with an order taking and inventory emphasis. The concern grew after working with the consultants who, while highly skilled in their knowledge of the software package and accounting, did not seem to understand BRECI's needs. BRECI needed a simple, integrated and flexible accounting system which was affordable. The proposed system needed expensive add-on modules to do much of what BRECI needed, used a complicated scripting language to create reports, and was not expandable/flexible enough to handle the rigors of multi-state payroll and typical client requests.

Morris was becoming alarmed at the feedback Connolly and Stacey Janus, the new corporate office accountant, were giving him regarding the inflexibility of the accounting package and the real cost of using it. Even with his limited knowledge of accounting, he understood the system lacked the flexibility his clients demanded and he needed. He was reluctant to take on the Board of Directors, however. Connolly, stating this was her area of expertise, said she would be the "bad guy" for the Board and do what was in the best interests of BRECI. In October 1992 she announced to the Board that she was abandoning the system, and with Janus' guidance and leadership, brought in an accounting package designed for construction (which had accounting needs analogous to the industry BRECI was in), implemented it over a period of months, and actually pleased a Board that was on the verge of firing her a few months earlier. The new system cost $5,000, did everything that was needed, was easily modifiable for unusual client accounting and multi-state reporting requirements, and had very attentive local support. It was also able to handle multi-state payroll, something the payroll service had extensive trouble with and the scuttled package was incapable of handling. Payroll was brought in-house providing far better support and accuracy than provided by the payroll service which had been used. The accounting function was incrementally moved from Boulder to Colorado Springs and Colorado Springs was solely responsible for all accounting functions by May 1993.

Networking: Transition Through Sneaker Net, Novell Lite and Novell 3.11

The end of September, 1992 brought the much awaited move into the new corporate office. Connolly could now effectively address many problems that were put on hold while in the old location. "Sneaker Net" had been the internal data sharing method for the old office. It wasn't too serious when the corporate office was small, but as corporate functions began to be consolidated in Colorado Springs, more and more problems arose. The entire report production function was moved to Colorado Springs about six weeks before the move to the new location. The head of production, Carrie Phillips, had been promised, as a condition of her agreeing to the move, that a LAN would be in place. Phillips had spearheaded the drive to install the LAN in Salt Lake City. Unfortunately the loan for the building purchase was delayed while there was a determination of whether or not BRECI still qualified for a SBA-backed loan. BRECI had made just under $5 million in 1991 and this was very near or above the limit. It was settled favorably but the purchase and move were delayed by two months. Connolly knew that document and hardware sharing capabilities were essential infrastructure and without these the reasons for consolidation became moot. Morris did not understand that the IT infrastructure needed to support the report production operation was critical to its effectiveness and insisted, in spite of considerable discussion with Connolly and Phillips, that the consolidation take place as planned and not be delayed. Connolly ended up with a demanding and impatient production supervisor who simply did not want to wait for the LAN and networked printers she had been promised. Connolly immediately took steps to put a quick, easy, inexpensive and portable infrastructure in place to cool down the situation. Report production went operational with a Novell Lite peer-to-peer network and an additional printer. These would be transferred to a field office at a later time.

The move, combined with the up-front cost of starting the Las Vegas project, put a real crimp in BRECI's cash flow for a short while. But even after the cash flow improved, Connolly found it difficult to get a spending authorization for the LAN, as Morris was showing declining support for the planned IS/IT installation. Bids had already been solicited and a consultant had been selected by Connolly. After what seemed like endless justifications, Connolly finally received authorization from Morris to proceed and the LAN was installed and functional by the end of the year. The delay actually provided time for Connolly to address other parts of her job. She was, after all, Director of Administrative Services, and was in charge of all administrative, accounting and human resource functions and had a staff of five: Stacey Janus, the accountant; an accounting assistant; an executive secretary; a receptionist and an administrative assistant. The business manager had resigned in October, shortly after the move. An executive decision had been made to not refill the business manager position and Connolly had to take over these duties. This included administering the employee benefit package. It was an extremely generous package, especially for an organization as small as BRECI. The employees had no idea how good they had it. This was a direct reflection on Morris. He truly believed in being fair to his employees and frequently paid wages well above going rate. Unfortunately, some employees were not as generous in return. Although employees were paid for every hour they worked, a complaint regarding excessive overtime had been filed. The investigators from the Department of Labor were very helpful and recommended ways to improve overall labor management, documentation and compensation in the firm. Connolly had the unfortunate job of implementing changes no one was particularly happy with, some resisted, and some were outright hostile towards. The changes were only temporary though because Connolly received no support in enforcing the new policies. In addition, in early spring BRECI failed the non-discrimination test for contributions to its 401k. Connolly planned and successfully implemented an enrollment campaign. By May, all but two permanent staff were active contributors to the 401k.

Database Implementation

Connolly and Janus were carefully tracking administrative costs and looking at areas for improvement. Actual project overhead costs were nearly twice what were being charged to clients. Morris insisted that clients would not agree to larger overhead percentages, so the problem had to be addressed solely from an internal cost cutting perspective. Significant inefficiencies in internal procedures provided good material for Connolly and Janus to work with. Together they devised new administrative and accounting procedures. The LAN, while expensive to install, helped reduce costs by providing a means to share hardware, software and data. It also enforced security and backup which had been absent in the stand-alone environment. Small databases were built in Paradox to automate routine tasks that had been done manually. Reports could now be produced in a matter of minutes rather than days. The cost savings were amazing: administrative costs dropped close to forty percent between December 1, 1992 and March 31, 1993.

Project Budgeting

Project budgeting was an area that was perfect for technological support. Morris developed all budgets by hand with pencil and calculator but frequently delegated individual sections to various section heads. The administrative assistant was then asked to recheck all figures. Connolly developed spreadsheet templates to help the section heads with their budgets. They were warned not to change the templates and Connolly promised to make whatever changes they needed. Connolly recalls,

> I already had a President who didn't trust spreadsheet output and along comes this rush project. The section heads all used the spreadsheet template to build their sections of the budget but someone made a modification to the original template without telling anyone. This created an error of almost $100,000 in the submitted budget. When Morris found out I practically needed a straight jacket to control him. Luckily the client didn't like the budget and asked that it be reworked and reformatted before resubmission. By coincidence, the format they wanted was almost identical to the template I had developed. It was a simple matter to make a few modifications. Morris insisted on doing the entire budget by hand calculator. I paralleled him with the spreadsheet. Our final numbers differed by $3500. I prayed the mistake was his. The administrative assistant found the error in one of Morris' calculations and he asked her to recalc the entire budget a second time. The client accepted the budget but asked for a few minor changes. Morris conceded to allowing me to make the changes in the spreadsheet.

LAN Physical Security

The staff quickly became reliant on the network and were downright unforgiving on the two occasions the network went down during the nine months it was under Connolly's supervision. Connolly muses,

> The employees ended up loving the network. I thought two crashes in nine months was an outstanding track record but tell that to the users and you would get dirty looks. Luckily, a production typist hired for report preparation had prior experience on a LAN and openly shared that the LAN at her former place of employment was down between four and eight hours a week. That put things in perspective real fast. In retrospect, one of the crashes was really quite funny. I came into work at 7 a.m. one morning to find a frantic accountant telling me she couldn't get on the network. The network was not only down, it was also off. The power switch on the server had been turned off. I brought the system back up but it was unstable and knew we were in for an interesting day. It ran for about an hour and then crashed. The problem was clearly beyond my skill level so I put in a panic call to the consultants who installed the network. They were wonderfully responsive and had the "rescue squad" there within an hour. The volumes were really a mess and it took quite a while to rebuild everything. Interestingly, the power had been turned off about seven minutes after I left the previous night. Morris was the only person remaining when I left and the security alarm records showed that he exited the building a minute after the network went down. He never admitted that he turned the file server off, was incensed that the UPS hadn't protected the system (a little hard since it was between the server and the outlet), and felt someone was trying to destroy his business with downtime. Everyone knew he had turned off the server because he was always going around turning off things that weren't in use. Unfortunately, the servers were not in a secure location.

I did lose my cool once, a few weeks after the above network crash. The server room also had some storage and a small copy machine in it. Morris had decided to buy storage shelving and was in the process of installing it but had never said a word to me. He was dragging the file server off one table and onto another as I walked into the room. I just lost it. He had no idea how sensitive the equipment was or how much damage he could have done.

Survey of End-User Needs and Satisfaction

In March 1993, data was collected by questionnaire to determine end-user satisfaction with the network and to identify future needs and direction. The results identified three areas needing attention: statistical analysis, word processing upgrade and inter-office communication.

Statistical Analysis Software: The user survey had identified some employee interest in obtaining a statistical analysis package. A group of end-users was assigned the task of identifying the types of statistical analyses that were or might be needed and then to identify packages to meet those needs. The analysis appeared biased and incomplete and the recommendation, to buy the most expensive PC stat package available, was not well justified and would cost in excess of $30,000 to place a fully-loaded single user copy at three different locations. Connolly turned down the request and encouraged the user group to consider a wider range of alternatives including high quality spreadsheet packages which had powerful statistical analysis functions built in.

Word Processing Upgrade: The report production staff requested that BRECI move to Word Perfect 6 when the software became available. They presented a well developed justification which related their needs to new software features. Connolly approved the request and knew the upgrade would address another problem as it fit in with her overall approach for addressing the software piracy issue. The President did not understand why he couldn't buy just one copy of a piece of software for the whole company. A little help from the corporation's attorney helped convince him of the serious nature of the problem. He really wanted to do everything by the book; Connolly just had to get him to the right page. It was quite an outlay of cash, but after the Word Perfect 6 purchase, BRECI was legal on all networked software. There was still a constant battle keeping pirated software off individual machines. BRECI had policy on the matter but Morris did not support Connolly when problems arose. But Connolly knew full well she would be held responsible if the Software Publisher's Association paid a little visit.

Inter-office Communication: A few people were requesting modems. A continuous problem had always been sharing information with field offices. FAX and overnight delivery were used extensively. The Salt Lake City office had a modem but always had problems getting it to work. Installing a separate phone line had helped to some degree. One of the local employees kept "adjusting" the telecomm software and this may have contributed to the problem. The corporate office also had a modem but no separate phone line. The likelihood of successfully transferring a document between the two offices was so low and the software so user nasty, that the few who were willing to try quickly gave up.

Adding to this is the fact that Connolly had been tracking the administrative phone activity for some time. Over 80 percent of administrative calls made to field offices were for one way communication of information or to request a piece of non-time-critical information. Figures were not available for project-related calls. She had purchased Microsoft Mail when the network was installed and felt this was the right time to implement e-mail connections with the field offices. E-mail would solve several problems. Administratively, it would get people off the phone except for time critical requests, reduce interruptions, solve the problem of people being out of the office and others having to take messages for them, provide user-friendly software for attaching and transferring files, and require only one modem and an e-mail server.

Connolly ran a demonstration on the corporate LAN to show the ease of transferring documents from one location to another. Everyone was enthusiastic except Morris. He had read an article on how employees did nothing but play on e-mail. Connolly remembers the frustration of trying to convince him of the value of e-mail. She had used it at several other jobs and considered it the No. 1 time savings tool she had used. It reduced interruptions to work, reduced communications cost, improved internal communications, and made document transfer a breeze. Her cost/benefit analysis was not believed because the benefits were hard to quantify, and the costs, as usual, were quite evident. Morris saw nothing wrong with the way they had been doing their work (FAX and overnight delivery were just fine with him). He thought e-mail would increase their already astronomical phone bill, rather than reduce it. He simply could not see the value of receiving a document in machine readable form. FAX was just fine. The typist was fast so if the document needed to be reentered at the other end, it wouldn't take that long. Many of BRECI's documents were over 20 pages in length. Connolly finally conceded defeat,

By late April, we were clearly at a stalemate. I finally gave up. On top of that, Jim had authorized the purchase of two more laser printers for employees who thought they were too important to have to walk a few dozen feet to one of three network printer sites in the 4000 sq. ft. corporate office. When I approached him about this he said that a $1500 printer was an inexpensive way to keep an employee happy. I told him it was $1500 he might need to pay their salary with some day and defeated a main purpose of the network. It was clear that little additional progress would be made in information systems so I spent the remainder of my time at BRECI improving the overall administrative function. There was more than enough to keep me busy. I would deal with IS issues as they arose but not beat my head against the wall any more.

Training

Connolly's attitude toward training was that within reason, there was no such thing as too much training. The problem at BRECI was that there was absolutely no training and no support for training in anything, not just software. A "portable" concentrator had actually been purchased so that the lab could be turned into a six person training center when needed. Classes on Quattro and Paradox were arranged but somehow the attendees were always pulled off for more important things. No training ever managed to be conducted. Connolly jokingly referred to this as "training by osmosis. You hope something eventually sinks in; the problem is, you never know what sunk in." The need for training escalated as user confidence with software increased. Connolly clearly knew that user over-confidence was one of the biggest problems in end-user computing. Being able to find the on/off switch does not make someone computer literate.

Current Status of Case

Connolly's Departure From BRECI

August was quickly approaching and Connolly was preparing for her departure and trying to get everything in order for her replacement. An excellent candidate, Robert Simms, was identified and hired. Connolly's only concern was his lack of experience in information systems. Morris assured her it would not be a problem. Although Simms showed up for work about a week after Connolly's last day, the two were able to have a few transition meetings before she left town. The first meeting centered on the newly and discretely hired IS staff member Simms would be supervising. He had not been informed of this employee or position when he interviewed for the job. Connolly knew nothing of the new hire. In discussing this with Simms she explained that Morris really was a wonderful person, but he (Simms) should expect that Jim would sometimes not consult with him, even on issues of key importance that were directly under Simms' supervision.

Paul Morris, Jim's son, was the newly hired IS staff member. His sole computer experience was selling Macintosh computers and testing Mac software. He had never worked on PCs or on a PC network. For the first three weeks Connolly received almost daily calls for help with the network, which was crashing regularly. Paul was learning the network during operating hours. Connolly suggested he do it at night and on weekends; he didn't want to work nights and weekends. BRECI standards on hardware were broken with the first purchase that was made and the company returned to a buy cheap philosophy. Connolly recalls,

> A non-standard network interface card was purchased to attach Paul's new, non-standard PC, to the network. It was a $10 savings over what I had been purchasing so it looked like a good idea. Well, it just wouldn't work. Paul spent at least two days tinkering with it before calling me for help. I recommended calling the network consultants since Paul needed to establish a relationship with them too. The consultants were unsuccessful in getting it to work properly. It was finally discovered that an interrupt conflict between the card and the inexpensive CD-ROM Paul had installed was causing the problem. The consultants installed the BRECI standard network interface card and had it running in minutes. Paul also purchased another laser printer. His intention was to network it but unfortunately it was a non-networkable personal model and could only be used as a stand alone printer. Penny wise and pound foolish aptly describe the situation.

The Word Perfect 6 software arrived and it was Paul's job to get it installed. An emergency request came in from a client the morning after the install. The manager in charge of the client's project immediately jumped on the request and found his trusty Word Perfect 5.1 and his painstakingly developed macros gone. The school of hard knocks was quickly teaching Paul that preparing his users for changes on the network can be the difference between life and death (his life). Paul was unaware that the macros could be recovered from the archived network backups.

Attempts were made to modify the databases developed in Paradox. Unfortunately, the restructuring caused significant problems with the underlying scripts and destroyed their usefulness. No one on the staff had the skill to rebuild the scripts or develop alternative solutions. Report preparation returned largely to manual mode.

The Boulder office was closed in Fall, 1993. While all staff were offered positions elsewhere in the company, only one accepted. Major layoffs began in Salt Lake City and Colorado Springs in Spring 1994. Paul was included in the layoff. Although BRECI had considerable work in progress, its bids on several new projects were not successful. There were no more large projects and BRECI had evolved into a large project company and couldn't afford to bid on small projects because of low profit margins. In essence, it had lost the flexibility that had made it what it was. Minority, small business and WOBE (Woman Owned Business Enterprise) set asides were eating into BRECI's traditional market and were blamed for much of their problem. The company's assets were sold in January of 1995.

Successes and Failures

The installation of the LAN which provided for data sharing, software management, and improved backup and security was the most important success. Along with this came an awakening among employees to the power and capability of computers. The accounting, administrative and report production functions experienced the greatest benefit from the LAN. The failures centered on the inability to improve internal communication through e-mail connections among the offices. While administration would have benefited from this, the greatest loss was to the improved project management and client support that was foregone by failing to improve internal communication.

Epilogue and Lessons Learned

This case is presented from the viewpoint of Karen Connolly, the Director of Administrative Services. Connolly, in retrospect, identifies the following as two of the key lessons she learned:

The job was simply too big for one person to handle. Adequate staffing with skilled people is a necessity but is frequently a problem for small businesses. Taking on more than one can possibly handle properly means that many things cannot be given the attention they deserve and that there is no time for the endless process of dealing with and playing company politics.

Failing to obtain or maintain the support of high level management, especially the president, is a real "deal killer" for information systems. If more time had been available, more effort could have been expended here. But it also needs to be recognized that some individuals will always mistrust computers and/or be computer phobic no matter what is done or said. When this occurs, the Director of IS is in a most difficult situation.

Questions for Discussion

1. How typical is the above situation for very small businesses like BRECI? At what point should a small business consider hiring a full-time IS staff person? What alternatives are available to full time staff support? Can small businesses use IS/IT strategically without guidance from IS/IT knowledgeable staff/consultants?

2. How might Connolly have educated Morris to make him more computer literate and supportive of the role IS/IT could play at BRECI?

3. Is software piracy, such as portrayed here, common in small business? What leads to software piracy and what can IS staff and general management do to prevent it?

4. Succession planning is very important in IS. Discuss what Connolly could have done to help with succession planning and reduce the problems that occurred after she left. How could this have helped keep the systems and procedures she installed/implemented in working condition?

5. Look at BRECI from today's perspective. Is this company a candidate for becoming a virtual organization? If yes, what organizational and technological changes would be needed to be successful?

Endnote
[1] Details have been disguised to conceal the identity of the company and individuals involved in this case. The case is, however, an accurate depiction of end-user computing at "BRECI."

Chapter 16

Evolving Organizational Growth Through Information Technology

Ira Yermish
St. Joseph's University

Executive Summary

The Service Employees International Union, Local 36 Benefits Office, provides service to over 3,500 union members in the Delaware Valley area. In addition to managing the collection of dues and other funds through employers, the Benefits Office administers several insurance programs and funds. From 1979 until 1996, this office has grown in sophistication and service efficiency primarily through the leadership efforts of Joseph M. Courtney, its only Administrator during this period. Starting with an organization with no technical sophistication, Courtney identified critical areas where technology could make a difference in service levels to the Local membership.

This case study describes the gradual evolution of the use of information technology, first to support basic transaction processing, and ultimately to support the strategic issues that such an operation faces. Through the careful use of a number of outside vendors and consultants, and through the slow growth of internal talent, Courtney was able to shepherd the operation from a purely manual system to one where every employee has a PC workstation connected to a network of internal servers and external services.

Issues that will be raised in this case include questions of internal versus external development of applications, the relationships among various vendors and consultants, and the growth of internal expertise without significant information technology staff. As the case closes, a new Administrator, Michael Ragan, looks at the operation and considers alternatives. He is very much concerned that their primary vendor, Benefit Systems, is no longer responsive to Local 36's needs.

Background

As March 1996 comes to a close, Joseph M. Courtney looks back on his twenty years as the Administrator of the Benefits Office of the Service Employees International Union (SEIU) Local 36.

Retirement approaches and this former steam–fitter can look back with pride on his accomplishments and the services that been extended to the members of the Union. From a completely manual operation, the Benefit Funds office has been transformed into an efficient operation using multiple computer systems to perform the various operations on behalf of the membership.

The Local

The Local 36 Benefits Office provides a number of services to over 3,500 active union members and 2,000 pensioners in the Delaware Valley area. Of primary importance is the collection of dues through the member's employers. What makes this so much of a challenge is the nature of this union. The Union represents janitorial, window cleaning and maintenance workers, many of whom are on the bottom of the economic ladder and who frequently do not speak English. Exhibit 1 shows the relationship of the Benefit Office to the Local. In addition to being responsible to the Union, which is part of the International Union, two boards of trustees are responsible for oversight of the two major Funds managed by the Benefits Office: Building Operators Labor Relations, Inc. (BOLR) and the Building Maintenance Contractors Association (BMCA). These two funds represent different contracts and groups of employers. The two contracts have different characteristics and benefits, the results of separate collective bargaining agreements. Exhibit 2 shows the organization structure of the Union and the Benefits Office. Exhibit 3 contains an excerpt and the contents of the BOLR collective bargaining agreement.

The Benefits Office must provide services to the members that have been negotiated for in the agreements. In addition, the Trustees of the Funds must be convinced of the fiscal soundness of the operations and their ability to supply the services to the members. Clearly, there are a number of

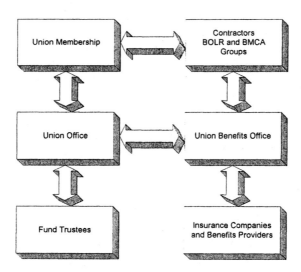

Exhibit 1: Organizational Relationships

pressures that the Benefits Office must face. First, they are responsible for collecting dues and fees from the Employers (contractors). Employers are responsible for identifying new employees, making dues and other payments. Given the nature of the industry, there are many opportunities for abuse. The Benefits Office is responsible for identifying these abuses and making sure that all members have been properly identified and that the moneys have been collected.

On the other side of the operation, the Benefits Office is responsible for administering the various insurance programs and pension plans. There are questions of eligibility and abuse by service providers and members. Contractual relationships between these providers, e.g. Blue Cross, is based upon utilization. The Benefits office must be sure that the services provided are appropriate and cost effective. The rapid growth in health care costs affectsits members more severely than many other cohorts.

The Funds represent large sums of money maintained on behalf of the membership. Some of these funds provide for self–insurance coverage for some of the benefits. These funds must be tracked and analyzed to be sure that the investments are safe and meeting the needs of the membership.

Exhibit 4 outlines most of the major functions of the Benefits Office. Activities on behalf of the members and their direct employer relationship are handled by the Union Office. The Union Office is responsible for organization and contractor–member conflict resolution.

Looking back on his tenure as Administrator, Courtney realizes how important information technology was to making the Benefits Office a model of responsible and fiscally sound operation, recognized by others as forward thinking and creative.

Developing Information Technology in the Benefits Office

The history of information technology in the Benefits Office tracks the use of technology in other organizations. First, basic transaction processing is automated. Next, tactical management issues are addressed and finally, strategic planning issues are attacked. A timeline of hardware and software developments are summarized in Exhibit 5. Exhibit 6 describes the current hardware configuration and Exhibit 7 outlines the distribution of applications on the various hardware platforms.

In 1979, a consulting company, MagnaSystems, Inc., was asked to review a contract for a new software system to be installed at the Benefits Office. Up until that point, the office had been completely manual, with file cabinets full of documents, slow processing and meager services. They were swamped and were looking forward to getting out from under the piles of paper. They had looked at a number of software systems and had identified a package appropriate for managing union benefits operations. The vendor, Benefit Systems, Inc., was located in Baltimore and had already installed their software at a number of offices, one of which was in the Philadelphia area. Given that the Benefits Office had no experience whatsoever with information technology, it was important that they install a system that did not require in–house expertise. The staff did not include any college graduates, but given the leadership of the Administrator, they were loyal and willing to move forward. After some negotiations and plans for some modifications to meet the specific needs of Local 36, the contract for a mini–computer based system was awarded and work started on building the database of membership, contractor and contributions. Within a very short period of time it became evident that they had made the right decision. The tedium of tracking thousands of contribution records was handled well by the system.

Courtney had gambled that the technology would work and he was right. Contributionswere processed more efficiently, benefits were distributed more rapidly. After a year or so of operation, getting the initial bugs out of the system, and making it meet the Local's specific needs, he identified another area where the technology could be of some help. It was well known that the contractors could

SEIU Local 36

March 1996

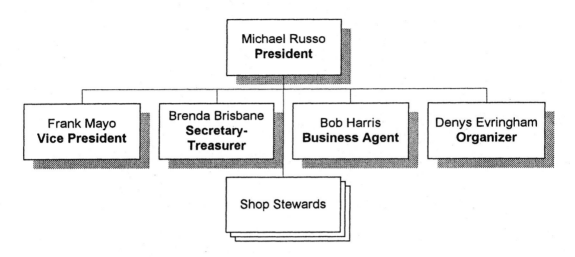

Benefits Office

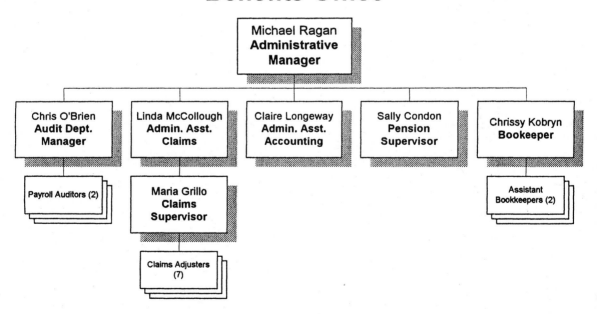

Exhibit 2: Organization Charts

Agreement

(Office Buildings)

This Multi–Employer Agreement, entered into the first day of November, 1993, by and between BUILDING OPERATORS LABOR RELATIONS, INC. (hereinafter called the "Corporation"), acting for and on behalf of such of its Member Buildings as are listed in Schedule "A" attached hereto (each of whom is hereafter referred to as "Employer"), on the on hand, and SERVICE EMPLOYEES INTERNATIONAL UNION, Local #36, AFL–CIO (hereinafter called the "Union"), on the other hand.

ARTICLE I   RECOGNITION

Section 1. The Employer recognizes the Union as the sole and exclusive agent for the purpose of collective bargaining and for those of its employees in the following classifications:

> Janitorial Employee, Class 1
> Janitorial Employee, Class 1 (Day Matron/Day Attendant)
> Janitorial Employee, Class 2
> Janitorial Employee, Class 2 (Lobby Attendant)
> Elevator Operator
> Elevator Starter
> Combination Elevator Operator and Job Class No. 2 Cleaner
> Foreperson
> Mechanics and Maintenance Workers
> Licenses Engineers and Operating Engineers

Such definition shall exclude supervisors, clerical employees, confidential employees and armed guards as defined in the National Labor Relations Act, and whose operating engineers and maintenance mechanics who are covered under a separate collective bargaining agreement. Whenever the word "employee" is used herein, it refers only to those employees for whom the Union is the recognized bargaining agent.

Section 2. The Employer Shall have the right to hire new employees from any source whatsoever. All new employees shall be on probation for ninety (90) days after employment and during such probationary period the Employer shall be the judge as to whether or not such new employee is qualified to continue in its employ and the Employer may discharge such employee for any reason at its discretion. Employees hired on or after November 1, 1993, shall not be entitled to holiday pay, paid funeral leave or jury duty benefits during their probationary period.

ARTICLES

II	UNION SECURITY AND CHECK–OFF	XX	SPLIT SHIFTS AND ASSIGNMENTS
III	RIGHTS OF MANAGEMENT	XXI	GRIEVANCE AND ARBITRATION
IV	NO DISCRIMINATION		PROCEDURE
V	WAGES AND OVERTIME	XXII	GOVERNMENT CONTRACTS
VI	HOLIDAYS	XXIII	SUBCONTRACTING AND
VII	VACATIONS		REDUCTION OF FORCE
VIII	CONVERSION AND SEVERANCE PAY	XXIV	NO STRIKES OR LOCKOUTS
IX	FUNERAL LEAVE	XXV	OTHER LEGAL ENTITIES
X	JURY DUTY PAY	XXVI	MOST FAVORED EMPLOYER
XI	UNIFORMS	XXVII	INSPECTION OF RECORDS
XII	TEMPERATURE WORKING CONDITIONS	XXIX	SAFETY
XIII	HEALTH AND WELFARE PLAN	XXX	SEPARABILITY
XIV	PENSION PLAN	XXXI	HOURS
XV	FAILURE TO REMIT DUES OR TRANSMIT	XXXII	PREPAID LEGAL SERVICES PLAN
	WELFARE AND PENSION CONTRIBUTIONS	XXXIII	BREAKS
XVI	INDUSTRY PROMOTION FUND	XXXIV	JOB POSTING
XVII	SENIORITY	XXXV	TOOLS
XVIII	DISCHARGE AND DISCIPLINE	XXXVI	TERMS OF AGREEMENT
XIX	UNION ACTIVITIES IN BUILDINGS		

Exhibit 3: BOLR Collective Bargaining Agreement (excerpt)

Dues and Contribution Collection
Each month the bookkeeping department sends a remittance form to each of the contractors, showing all of the known members and the required dues and fund contributions. The contractors are responsible for remitting the appropriate funds which they are responsible for and the funds that are supposed to come out of the employee's pay. They are also responsible to update the list with terminations and new hires. The remittance form is then processed into the transaction processing system to maintain a complete record of all fund contributions which is used for benefits eligibility.

Insurance and Benefits Claims Processing
The major function of the Benefits Office is to coordinate the member insurance and benefits services. Some of the insurance services are provided by third party insurance carriers such as Blue Cross and Blue Shield. Other services are provided through self–insurance programs that are funded by the members' contributions and administered by the Benefits Office. The Claims processing operation is responsible for determining eligibility and appropriateness of benefits. Each month the office sends out checks to providers and members for benefits not covered through the third party insurance providers.

Coordination of Benefits Processing (COBRA)
Occasionally, a member may have other insurance outside of the Union plans. Furthermore, the insurance must be provided for a period of time after a member leaves the employ of a contractor in the system.

Pension and Disability Processing
At this time, the Benefits Office keeps track of those members on pension and disability but contracts out to a bank for the processing and distribution of the monthly checks. Pension benefits must be determined for members and surviving spouses.

Investment Tracking
Millions of dollars of member's funds are invested to provide the long–term viability of the welfare and pension funds. The funds are also managed by outside investment firms, but it is the primary responsibility of the Administrator to see that these funds are invested wisely and in a way that will make it possible to improve the benefit packages to the members.

Bookkeeping and Fund Accounting
This activity coordinates each of the above to keep track of all of the transactions and fund balances.

Contractor Audits
It is important to make sure that each of the contractors is making the appropriate payments to the Benefits Office on behalf of the membership. There are many opportunities for fraud and for honest mistakes. This activity attempts to match up the actual payroll records at the contractor sites with the records processed by the Dues and Contributions activity described above.

Provider Audits
Third party insurance carriers are responsible for checking the validity of claims submitted by hospitals, physicians and other service providers. However, there are many opportunities for abuse. One of the Bookkeeping Department's functions is to audit the activity in these areas to determine if duplicate payments have been made or if inappropriate services are provided. Since the costs if insurance are directly determined from actual usage, it is important to keep the costs as low as possible by the constant audit of actual service. Once offending institutions and providers are identified, it is possible to automatically monitor these for subsequent problems.

Planning and Negotiation
As each collective bargaining agreement nears its end, the process of renegotiating on behalf of the membership begins. The Union constantly strives to enhance the pay and benefits to for its members. The Contractors try to keep their costs down through pay and benefits reductions. One of the planning functions of the Benefits Office is to determine the impact of possible benefit changes on fund viability. Given the complex relationship that exists between the Union, the Contractors, the Fund Trustees and the Benefits Office, these negotiations can be quite complex. The Benefits Office has developed the tools to test the effects of changes in benefits over time to determine the changes in employee or employer contributions needed.

Exhibit 4: Benefit Office Operations Summary

exploit the system because of the nature of the workforce and the kinds of work involved. It was not unusual for contractors to hide workers in their payrolls and thus avoid some of the employer based contributions. It was also possible for employers to pocket contributions from members and not forward them in a timely fashion to the Union. The system was based upon the good faith of the employers to provide the information and contributions in a timely and accurate fashion; a dubious assumption if there ever was one. Courtney saw the volumes of data on contributions that were accumulating and wondered whether this data could also be used to improve the collection process. In other words, could the data be matched against actual employer records to confirm that all contributions were accurate? He was faced, however, with a problem. Who could do these *audits* and with what tools?

It was 1983 and the IBM PC and its most interesting competitor, the COMPAQ portable, were just starting to make their presence felt in industry. The consultant was asked to examine the feasibility of using these tools in conjunction with the minicomputer to provide an audit capability. Certainly, it was technically feasible, but who would do the work? No one in the organization had any experience with personal computers or the new software technology: *spreadsheets*. For the first time, the Benefits Office hired a college graduate with accounting and computer background to perform the audits. A special program was supplied by Benefit Systems to download contractor data to a COMPAQ portable, and the consultant wrote a Lotus 1–2–3 macro to transform the downloaded contribution data into a standardized spreadsheet format. With these software tools and the "portable" computer, the auditor started visiting contractors, causing quite a stir. It wasn't long before the Benefits Office was able to recoup its investment with adjustments and settlements.

In 1995, for example, there were thirty–six audits resolved, with a total of nearly $200,000 recovered. One audit alone was resolved for a total of $87,000. Recent years were even more dramatic:

Year	Audit Resolution
1990	$182,832
1991	$113,650
1992	$435,863
1993	$310,410
1994	$359,887
1995	$199,008

Today, the audit professional staff includes a manager and two auditors who, using notebook computers continue to guarantee that the contractors are meeting their obligations. All of the contractors are visited on a regular basis. Young college graduates with MIS or accounting degrees have filled these positions admirably over the years, some moving on to other areas where their acquired expertise has been valued. However, it has been clear to Courtney that these young people have provided a significant path of professional growth for the organization and its relationship with the contractors and service providers. The initial hardware and software investment has paid for itself many times over.

The next several years saw a continued dependence on the technology. After about seven years with the initial system, a major CPU upgrade was required. The platform on which the software was running (McDonnell–Douglass minicomputer with the Pick Operating System) was well suited to meet the needs of the basic centralized processing environment. Using the built–in report writer, ENGLISH, it was possible for at least one of the Local 36 staff to generate specialized management reports. The hardware and software were not inexpensive, but could be justified on the basis of their cost–effectiveness. There were concerns, however about the proprietary nature of this environment. At that time, given the software involved and the lack of real alternatives, the upgrade was made but

1979   Initial Hardware/Software Installation
A Microdata minicomputer was purchased to run the standard union office package supplied by Benefit Systems., Inc. (now BASYS). This system handled the processing of dues collection, fund tracking, benefit eligibility and claims processing. The software was written in a business dialect of BASIC and included some report writing capabilities.

1983   COMPAQ Portable and Contractor Audit Software
A transportable computer was purchased to be used by the first payroll auditor hired by the Benefits Office. Benefits Systems provided some customized software to permit the downloading of contribution data to the portable computer through a direct serial port connection. A consultant developed a series of data translation programs and LOTUS spreadsheets to assist in the preparation of the audits.

1987   Minicomputer Upgrade
As additional services were provided to the membership, the original system became inadequate to meet the needs of the Benefits Office. More terminals were required and additional storage was required to maintain the growing historical database of fund contributions. A McDonnell–Douglas system based on the PICK operating system was purchased and the existing software and databases were ported to the new environment with little problem. The vendor, Benefit Systems, Inc. provided the necessary support for this transition.

1988   Planning Model Development
The Administrator with the help of the consultant, developed a planning model for the larger fund (BOLR). The model was implemented in LOTUS 1–2–3 and installed on a 386. There was extensive testing of the model before its acceptance by the Union as part of the negotiation process. A model of the smaller, but more complicated fund, BMCA quickly followed.

1989   Insurance Subrogation Tracking System
Another standalone PC system was purchased and database software (using Foxpro) was developed to handle the Insurance Subrogation Tracking function of the Claims Department.

1990   Provider Audit Software
Another standalone PC system was purchased and software was developed to provide more extensive analysis of the claims handled by the minicomputer system. A procedure to transfer the Blue Cross claims information from the minicomputer to the PC was implemented. Subsequent software was developed to analyze the Prescription claims and the Blue Shield claims.

1993   PC Network
As the number of standalone PCs grew, it made sense to connect them with a Novell network. The installation of the network coincided with a move to new, expanded quarters. The planning model, subrogation system, provider audit software, contractor audit software and standardized word processing and spreadsheet software were installed on the network.

1994   Sun SparcServer Upgrade
Again, to meet the growing needs of the base contribution and claims processing system, the centralized minicomputer was upgraded to a Sun SparcServer. The software was directly ported to the new environment. Unlike the prior systems, this system used the UNIX operating system which promised more flexibility.

1995   Network Integration
Using the TCP/IP options of the Sun SparcServer, the Novell network was integrated with the BASYS applications software. Dedicated terminals were eliminated in favor of PC workstations connected to both systems for transaction processing, word processing and other functions. Using Windows 3.1, clerks could process data on the transaction processing system, use the network word processor, or perform other complex reports using the data warehouse functions available on the Novell network.

Exhibit 5: System Implementation Timeline

with the concern that we would monitor the environment carefully for changes.

Adding to this concern a problem arose that frequently plagues users of vendor supplied application software. The vendor wants to keep each of its customers happy, but there is also the pressure to maintain a standardized, maintainable package. Each of the vendor's customers may see its case as being unique even though, in this case, they are all Taft–Hartley union operations supporting benefit operations. The vendor is responsible to maintain the software in light of changing government regulations and passing these changes to the customers in a timely fashion. But how do these changes get installed when many of the users have requested and gotten special modifications to the software? As a vendor grows, each of the customers becomes a smaller share of its business and apparently less critical for the vendor's survival. This may translate to a perception of indifference and alienation. On the other hand, the vendor is critical to the success of the customer, having become strategically dependent on that vendor for its basic operations.

At that time (1988), there didn't seem to be any other reasonable choice. It often took a long time to get specialized reports programmed. The programming charge for these reports and updates required hard negotiations. The "captive audience" expressed concern but could do nothing but maintain vigilance.

Around this time, Courtney also began to address other strategic issues. One of his primary responsibilities at contract negotiation time was to determine the feasibility of new benefits and contribution structures. These were often complex negotiations where fund viability could be jeopardized by an overaggressive negotiator. The fund trustees were often faced with emotional decisions and could not see the financial implications. Courtney came to the consultant with the idea for a planning tool that could be used directly in the negotiation process. He wanted to be able to play "what if" games to determine the effects and contribution requirements of the decisions. A 386 PC was purchased and a planning model was developed for the BOLR fund. This model forecasted the results of decisions based upon the actuarial forecasts of expense changes and contribution commitments. Fund balances were displayed and presented. The model was very effective in negotiations and planning. Over the year the model was updated on a quarterly basis with actual results. This helped spot possible expense trouble spots before they could become a real problem. After the BOLR model was tested and used successfully for a year, a similar model was built for the smaller, but more complicated BMCA fund. This planning model operates as a central repository for the operations staff to record quarterly summaries of operations. Exhibit 8 contains a summary of the Benefit Offices welfare operations and forecast as extracted from the planning models.

Evolving Information Technology

In 1988 Courtney looked carefully at his operations, trying to identify where information technology could further enhance his operations. The terminals attached to the mini–computer were doing the routine transaction processing, posting collections, identifying eligibility, processing insurance claims. One of the first additional applications that he saw involved the tracking of insurance subrogation cases. In these cases where a member may have been involved in an accident, claims against other parties must be tracked. Some of these cases involved very large insurance claims that could severely impact the rates paid to Blue Cross and Blue Shield. Of primary concern was the exposure for not being able to collect the funds from other insurance carriers.

The manual system previously maintained by Linda McColllough, the Administrative Assistant for the Claims operations, was unable to generate timely status reports. Several choices for this system were identified. The primary vendor, Benefit Systems proposed a solution to be integrated with the mini–computer system. However, the consultant pointed out that there was really little connection between the data tracked in that system and the requirements for the application. Instead, the

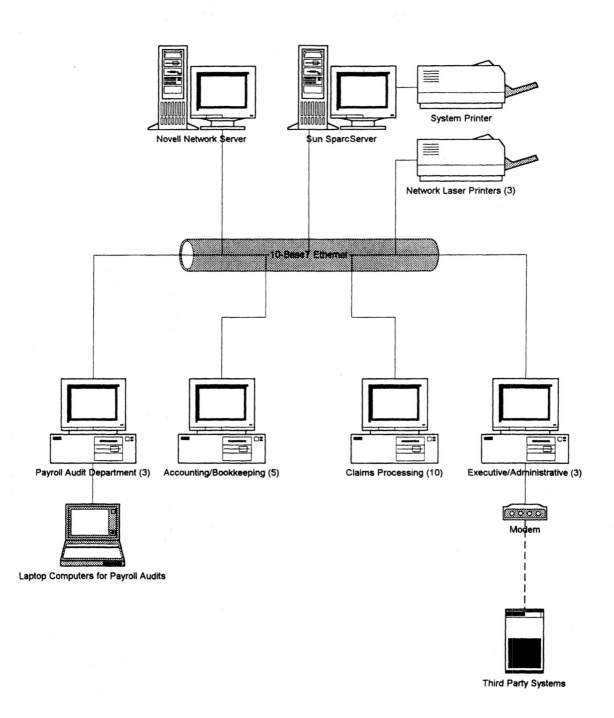

Exhibit 6: Current Network Configuration

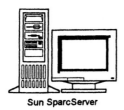

Sun SparcServer

- Standard Union Office Software (BASYS, Inc.)
- Custom Reports for Local 36 (BASYS, Inc.)

Novell Network

- Word Processing (WordPerfect 6.1)
- Spreadsheet (Lotus 1-2-3)
- Basic Accounting (Quicken)
- Planning Models (Consultant)
- Insurance Subrogation System (Consultant)
- Contribution/Funds Data Warehouse (Consultant)
- Payroll Audit System (Consultant)
- Provider Audit System (Consultant)
- Investment Tracking System (Consultant)

Standalone PC Systems

- COBRA Tracking (Benefits Consultant)
- Pension Tracking (Benefits Consultant)
- Office Security System (Security Vendor)
- Prescription Claims Transfer (Provider)

Auditor Laptop Computers

- Spreadsheet (LOTUS 1-2-3)
- Word Processing (WordPerfect 6.1)

- Payroll Audit Software (System Consultant)

Exhibit 7: Current Software Configuration

	Actual					Estimated				
	1991	1992	1993	1994	1995	1996	1997	1998	1999	2000
BOLR										
Number of Participants	3,192	3,115	3,084	2,949	2,820	2,820	2,820	2,820	2,820	2,820
Contributions	11,168,395	11,550,627	11,380,577	11,684,595	12,839,586	13,163,760	13,163,760	13,163,760	13,163,760	13,163,760
Interest Income	209,812	161,905	50,935	40,619	139,989	645,930	765,904	844,901	876,301	852,633
Total Income	11,378,207	11,712,532	11,431,512	11,725,214	12,979,575	13,809,690	13,929,664	14,008,661	14,040,061	14,016,393
Blue Cross Expenses	5,351,621	5,354,700	5,701,999	4,143,611	3,998,150	4,308,632	4,647,997	5,018,670	5,424,353	5,869,308
Blue Shield Expenses	745,797	1,020,545	1,449,933	1,373,234	1,458,993	1,619,482	1,797,625	1,995,364	2,214,854	2,458,488
Prescription Plan (PCS) Expenses	1,238,934	1,343,472	1,287,407	1,264,839	1,313,455	1,455,714	1,613,510	1,788,547	1,982,716	2,198,114
Self-Insured Plan Expenses	1,301,745	1,466,646	1,240,701	1,236,984	1,158,197	1,262,009	1,377,126	1,505,002	1,647,296	1,805,913
Medical Center	333,423	344,493	348,516	337,068	302,661	338,400	338,400	338,400	338,400	338,400
Loss of Time Disbursements	646,816	652,047	659,273	657,276	648,412	687,317	728,556	772,269	818,605	867,721
Administrative Expenses	629,194	755,585	852,757	851,629	1,229,115	1,290,571	1,355,099	1,422,854	1,493,997	1,568,697
Total Disbursements	10,247,530	10,937,488	11,540,586	9,864,641	10,108,983	10,962,125	11,858,313	12,841,106	13,920,221	15,106,641
Net Change Gain/(Loss)	1,130,677	775,044	(109,074)	1,860,573	2,870,592	2,847,565	2,071,351	1,167,555	119,840	(1,090,248)
Adjustments	470,732									
Year-End Fund Balance	5,414,362	6,189,406	6,714,203	8,995,196	11,817,782	14,665,347	16,736,697	17,904,252	18,024,093	16,933,844
Months of Reserve	6.3	6.8	7.0	10.9	14.0	16.1	16.9	16.7	15.5	13.5
BMCA										
Number of Participants	654	596	563	491	420	424	424	424	424	424
Contributions	439,921	706,697	747,471	644,158	649,260	582,072	607,512	607,512	607,512	607,512
Interest Income	46,351	16,459	11,385	16,977	21,654	28,050	21,241	11,356	(2,650)	(21,345)
Total Income	486,272	723,156	758,856	661,135	670,914	610,122	628,753	618,868	604,862	586,167
Benefit Expenses	542,762	614,522	475,684	481,116	516,606	576,716	632,973	693,077	758,419	831,871
Administrative Expenses	102,307	136,992	139,804	137,214	138,305	154,174	163,424	173,230	183,623	194,641
Total Disbursements	645,069	751,514	615,488	618,330	654,911	730,890	796,397	866,307	942,042	1,026,512
Net Change Gain/(Loss)	(158,797)	(28,358)	143,368	42,805	16,003	(120,768)	(167,644)	(247,439)	(337,180)	(440,345)
Adjustments	(45,547)									
Year-End Fund Balance	401,674	317,857	549,625	620,223	639,289	437,546	289,902	22,463	(314,717)	(755,063)
Months of Reserve	7.5	5.1	10.7	12.0	11.7	7.2	4.1	0.3	-4.0	-8.8

Exhibit 8: Summary of Benefits Operations (Welfare Only)

consultant developed a stand-alone PC based application (using the Foxpro database application language) to track these cases. A PC was purchased for McCollough and the database application was developed and operational within a few months.

In this time frame, the actuarial consultants and auditors, the Wyatt Company, provided two other stand-alone applications to support the Benefit Office. The first of these helped Sally Condon, the Pension Supervisor, track the status of pensions. This is critical for testing the viability of the pension funds. Identifying the ages and status of the pensioners determines the funding requirements for the pension funds.

Chrissy Kobrin, Bookkeeper, was a heavy user of the Benefit Systems transaction processing system. Her department was responsible for the processing of dues and fund contribution collection. She developed the skills to generate special reports from the mini–computer system using the ENGLISH report writing language. In addition, she was given a PC and some basic accounting software (Quicken) to track some of the funds. Furthermore, her department's responsibilities included the tracking of the coordination of benefits (COBRA). The Wyatt Company provided a stand–alone PC application for the tracking of these cases.

Another major responsibility that Kobryn's department has is the identification of insurance claims problems. In essence, they were also responsible for the auditing of the third party carriers and the service providers themselves. For example, hospital billing departments would submit the same claim more than once which might not be picked up by Blue Cross. A physician might submit a claim based upon a diagnosis that was unacceptable to the plan which might not be identified by Blue Shield. At first, Benefit Systems provided a number of reports to assist in this process, but they lacked the flexibility needed to meet their needs. The ENGLISH report writer was too difficult to use for the current staff. Benefit Systems was reluctant to provide changes to their basic system. Given the proprietary nature of their software and the operating system, Courtney expressed concerns about the future of the operations, particularly with respect to the flexibility needed.

In 1990, Courtney met with the consultant to explore the possibilities. The information industry pressure was away from proprietary minicomputer platforms and towards industry standard platforms based upon UNIX. Unfortunately, Benefit Systems could make no commitments that they would "port" their system to this platform. Furthermore, the sharing of applications and data via PC local area networks had become routine. The Audit Department manager at that time, John Matekovic, had an undergraduate degree in Management Information Systems. Perhaps his background could be used to support additional internal development to meet the long–range needs of Local 36's operations.

It was agreed that it was too early develop a complete operational system in–house. The costs would be too great and the expertise was not there. However, to meet the needs for the third party audit operations, a large amount of the data captured on the minicomputer system needed to be processed. The most critical area was in identifying problems with Blue Cross payments which were being loaded monthly onto the minicomputer system from tapes supplied by Blue Cross. Benefit Systems was asked to provide software to extract this data from their system and supply it in a form that could be loaded directly onto a PC. This became the first step in a possible transition to a completely home–grown operations system. At this time the design was to include the capabilities for multi–user processing. Matekovic, Kobryn and her assistants, helped prepare a list of the kinds of functions and reports neededto improve their operations. Given the years of experience they had gained with the minicomputer system and their familiarity with more current, mouse driven, PC based software, they were quite efficient and doing this design work. The consultant developed a standalone PC application (in Foxpro again) to provide for the much more powerful and user–friendly analysis programs needed for the third–party audits. This system would be flexible enough to provide for the audit of other insurance providers such as Blue Shield and Prescription Claim Services (PCS).

The Third Generation of Information Technology Growth

In 1993, the Benefits Office was contemplating a move to new, larger quarters. As part of this move, the technology issues were identified. Though they had not done so yet, it was clear that additional networking capabilities would be desirable. However, they were faced with a problem, the need to provide the cabling for the minicomputer system as well as a possible PC network. The consultant recommended a parallel path. Both serial (RS–232) cables would be run to meet the needs of the minicomputer system and twisted–pair (10BaseT Ethernet) cabling would be run for the PC network. Most of the workstations were "dumb" terminals for claims processing and bookkeeping. Other stations would be PCs with both a direct serial connection to the minicomputer and a LAN connection to the PC network. At this point, a user could, within the Windows 3.1 environment, have a terminal connection to Benefit Systems software and connections to the PC LAN software.

Finally, recognizing the industry trends, Benefit Systems implemented their software on a Sun SparcServer using Solaris, the Sun version of UNIX. This opened up a number of interesting opportunities. First of all, it was possible to eliminate the serial connections and provide all of the terminal TCP/IP connections from the PCs to the Sun and the PC network. This notably improved the terminal response time. It also simplified the connections to the systems. Finally, it improved dramatically, the connection abilities for transferring data between the Benefit Systems software and the PC network applications.

Through 1994 and 1995, additional applications were installed on the network and others contemplated. At his retirement banquet at the end of 1995, Joe Courtney was able to look back with pride on his accomplishments and the growth his organization. Much of the success he attributed to information technology. Only one member of his senior management was not with him at the beginning of this growth back in 1979. Each of his staff was routinely using the technology for reporting and analysis purposes as well as standard word processing. New applications for pension processing and for investment tracking were on the boards. Fund balances were well under control and the relationships with other organizations were strong.

Future Growth and Development

As Michael Ragan, the new administrator sits in his office, his PC connected both internally to the computer networks and externally to data information services, he could foresee many ways to improve the operation and gain further control. He expresses concern over the unresponsive character of their primary information technology vendor and is looking at alternatives. His strong educational background and experience as Administrator of the Operating Engineers gives him some confidence to take additional steps. In his former position he led the way for the internal development of operating software over which he had complete control. He looks forward to the possibility of developing more efficient claims processing software, of building stronger relationships with vendors via information links, and perhaps, developing more internal information systems expertise. Looking down Chestnut Street there are many avenues open and potholes to contend with.

Epilogue and Lessons Learned

The Union Benefits operation continues to operate efficiently using the technologies that it has acquired over the period described in the case. There is special emphasis in improving the access to the claims data supplied by the insurance providers (Blue Cross, Blue Shield, and PCS). There is also a serious consideration for switching primary software vendors based upon the high cost for custom software modifications and the lack of responsiveness. This step, however, must be taken very carefully because of the tremendous economic and operational impact it would involve.

The staff has grown comfortable with the Windows 3.1/Netware/Unix environment, switching easily between applications running on the Netware fileserver and the Unix server. CD–ROM databases are being used for research and external access to the service providers is improving. Throughout the case, the consultant and management were careful to implement software and hardware tools gradually. Each incremental step has met with little resistance because the normal flow of work was not changed significantly, though over time, the changes have been dramatic. Within the staff, the skills needed to use the new tools were acquired as they were needed to assure productivity. For example, when a switch from Word Perfect for DOS to Windows was made, staff were given the opportunity to take courses on the software during work hours.

The technology provided the basis for organizational improvement, but it was the management style that encouraged the growth of the staff's use of that technology that has been instrumental in the success of this operation.

Questions for Discussion

1. What are the similarities and differences that organizations such as the Benefits Office face compared to typical for–profit operations? What forms of executive motivation are appropriate for an organization like the Local 36 Benefits Office?
2. In this case, how has productivity been affected by the growing information technologies? How should this productivity be measured?
3. Up to the end of the case the Benefits Office has not had a formal internal information systems staff, though most of the Audit Department has some MIS education. From both the organization and the individual perspective what would be the advantages and disadvantages of such a staff? When, if ever, should such a staff be developed?
4. Consider the dual role that the consultant took, both as an expert to help identify and evaluate alternatives and as a supplier of some of the software and hardware solutions. What are the operational and ethical considerations of such a relationship?
5. What are the pressures on the primary software vendor who develops "vertical market" applications? How does the relationship between vendor and customer change over time? Consider the relative growth rates of the vendor and its clients.
6. What direction should the new Administrator take to assure continued organizational growth? To what extent should he institute changes to demonstrate his own talents and experience?

References

Fitzsimmons, J. A., and M. J. Fitzsimmons, *Service Management for Competitive Advantage,* McGraw–Hill, New York, 1994.

Inmon, W. H., and R. D. Hackathorn, *Using the Data Warehouse,* John Wiley & Sons, New York, 1994.

Keen, P. G. W., *Shaping the Future, Business Design through Information Technology,* Harvard Business School Press, Cambridge, MA, 1991.

Chapter 17

Integrating Information Technologies into Large Organizations

Gretchen L. Gottlich
John M. Meyer
Michael L. Nelson
NASA Langley Research Center

David J. Bianco
Computer Sciences Corporation

Executive Summary

NASA Langley Research Center's product is aerospace research information.   To this end, Langley uses information technology tools in three distinct ways. First, information technology tools are used in the production of information via computation, analysis, data collection and reduction. Second, information technology tools assist in streamlining business processes, particularly those that are primarily communication based. By applying these information tools to administrative activities, Langley spends fewer resources on managing itself and can allocate more resources for research. Third, Langley uses information technology tools to disseminate its aerospace research information, resulting in faster turn around time from the laboratory to the end-customer.

This chapter describes how information technology tools are currently cutting cost and adding value for NASA Langley internal and external customers. Three components from a larger strategic WWW framework are highlighted: Geographic Information Systems (GIS), Integrated Computing Environment (ICE), and LANTERN (Langley's Intranet). Based on experiences with these and related projects at Langley, we suggest that there are four pillars of information technology project success: training; provision of useful services; access to enabling tools; and advertising and advocacy.

Background

Established in 1917 as the first national civil aeronautics laboratory, Langley's mission is to be a world leader in pioneering aerospace science and innovative technology for U.S. aeronautical and space application.   The Center is dedicated to serving traditional aerospace customers and to transferring aerospace technology to non-traditional customers in response to changing national priorities.

More than half of Langley's effort is in aeronautics, improving today's aircraft and developing ideas and technology for future aircraft. The center's wind tunnels and other unique research facilities, testing techniques and computer modeling capabilities aid in the investigation of the full flight range — from general aviation and transport aircraft through hypersonic vehicle concepts.

The Center manages a dynamic program in atmospheric sciences, investigating the origins, chemistry and transport mechanisms that govern the Earth's atmosphere. A key component of this study is to understand the impact of human activity on our planet. Langley is also contributing to the development of the Earth Observation System (EOS), a major part of the international Mission to Planet Earth.

To better reflect the needs of its customers the Center has recently implemented a major reorganization of its management and operating structure consisting of: customer interface groups; a Research Group and an Internal Operations Group. Langley Research Center is a world class research laboratory which has a staff of well trained and highly productive scientists, engineers and support personnel, as shown in Tables 1 & 2 (Office of Public Affairs, 1995).

Other pertinent workforce facts include:

• Civil Service Employees 2,508 (Fiscal Year 1995)
• Contract Employees 1,975   (Fiscal Year 1995)
• Fiscal Year 1994 total procurements: US $525,000,000
• Fiscal Year 1995 Payroll: US $144,500,000 (includes all compensation)
• Total Program Year 1995 Budget: US $643,700,000

The NASA Langley Research Center occupies 787 acres of government-owned land and shares aircraft runways, utilities and some facilities with neighboring Langley Air Force Base. The center's

Function	Number	% of Workforce
Scientific/Engineering	1,256	50.0%
Administrative	271	11.0%
Tech/Craft/Production	757	30.1%
Clerical	224	8.9%

Table 1: Skill Mix (1995 data)

Degree	Number	% of Workforce
Doctoral	282	11.2%
Master	573	22.8%
Bachelor	647	25.8%
Associate	469	18.7%
Some college	260	10.4%
H.S. Diploma	268	10.7%
Other	9	0.4 %

Table 2: Formal Education Distribution (1995 data)

more than 220 buildings represent an original investment of $687 million and have a replacement value of over US $2 billion. Langley's experimental facilities are: aerothermodynamic, subsonic, transonic, supersonic and hypersonic wind tunnels as well as scramjet engine tunnels. Langley's unique facilities include:

• Nation's only large flight Reynolds Number transonic tunnel
• Nation's only transonic dynamic loads/flutter tunnel
• Nation's only aerodynamic spin tunnel
• Nation's only high-Reynolds Number supersonic quiet tunnel
• Nationally unique aircraft landing loads and impact dynamics facility
• Highly specialized aero structures and materials research laboratories

Langley's 30 wind tunnels cover the entire speed range from 0 mph to nearly Mach 25. In addition to these unique facilities, Langley houses facilities for structures, materials and acoustics research, flight electronics, flight systems, simulators, simulation facility components, and a scientific and general purpose computing complex.

Setting the Stage

NASA Langley Research Center's product is aerospace research information and its production can depicted by the data relation model in Figure 1. Due to the technical nature of Langley's work, use of some information technology tools at Langley was already common place. A campus-wide Transmission Control Protocol / Internet Protocol (TCP/IP) network, known as "LaRCNET" (Shoosmith, 1993), has been in place since 1986, and use of e-mail, USENET news, file sharing, and other electronic communications were wide spread.

Langley uses information technology tools in three distinct ways in the production cycle of aerospace information. First, information technology is used in a variety of methods during research: computation, analysis, data collection, data reduction, etc. (Wieseman, 1994). Second, Langley uses information technology tools to assist in streamlining its business processes, especially those that are communication based. By applying these information tools to administrative activities, Langley spends fewer resources managing itself and can allocate more resources for research. Lastly, Langley uses information technology tools to disseminate its information. Depending on the media format, security classification, and targeted customer, the end product can be a technical report, software and data sets, or general technology availability notices. Distribution is by traditional hard copy and Internet publishing methods. NASA Langley technical publications are currently distributed on the World Wide Web (WWW) by the Langley Technical Report Server (Nelson et. al., 1994) and the NASA Technical Report Server (NTRS) (Nelson, et al., 1995); some software via the Langley Software Server (LSS); and technologies available for licensing via the Technology Opportunity Showcase (TOPS) (Nelson and Bianco, 1994).

This work relation model for aerospace information requires: (1) *people* to do the work (2) *tools* to do the job (3) and *facilities* to house the tools and people. Managing the research and technology process involves allocating varying resources to achieve the optimum relationship between these unique data sets.

However, decreasing workforce and budgets, coupled with increasing workloads has forced Langley to investigate technologies with a non-linear return on investment. Based upon the success of earlier experiments of using WWW for electronic publishing, increasing WWW usage and focusing it on a few core functionalities was seen as a method to achieve the desired cost savings and efficiency gains.

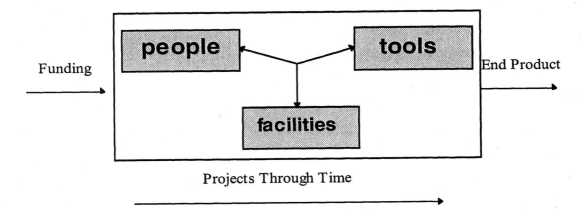

Figure 1: Simple Work Relation Model at Langley

Project Description

Overview

The desire was to build upon the existing TCP/IP infrastructure and budding WWW user community to provide universal access to key services at Langley. The World Wide Web (Berners-Lee, 1992) is a TCP/IP based, wide area hypertext information system that is available for all popular computer platforms: Mac, PC, and Unix. In June 1993 Langley became the first center in the Agency to have a World Wide Web home page for distributing information internally and to the public. Growth of home pages at the center and throughout the world was rapid; Langley web space currently consists of 17,000+ pages, and the entire web is estimated at 50 million pages (Bray, 1996). The rapid growth at Langley, however, was due to the efforts of a few World Wide Web enthusiasts. In early 1995, NASA Langley dedicated 1.5 full-time equivalents to officially handle the integration and coordination of WWW services and facilities. Membership in the team is dynamic and is a grass roots effort, with new members constantly being recruited. The team consists of 13 additional members from across the Center and has occasionally grown to 126 for events such as Internet Fair 2 (See Appendix A for Uniform Resource Locators (URL's)). Under this Center-Wide Self-Directed Team approach the WWW team provides vision, develops strategy, and procures resources to implement its mission. The WWW team's mission is "To implement an integrated, easy to use, and cost efficient information environment."

There were a number of distributed WWW activities occurring simultaneously, but there were three that benefited from central coordination and provided significant savings: LANTERN, Langley's Intranet; Cicero, a software distribution mechanism; and an on-line version of the Langley Master Plan, a facilities and physical plant reference guide. Each of these significant activities corresponds to a component in the work model in figure 1: LANTERN is an asynchronous communications tool for people, Cicero provides point and click access to software tools, and the on-line Master Plan is a continuously updated record of the physical center and its facilities. Although the 3 projects did not run concurrently, they form the foundation of a holistic information technology strategic plan for Langley.

Technology Concerns

Technology was not a limiting factor in any of the projects. Aside from having a large pool of creative technical talent at Langley, most of the tools involved in the Master Plan, Cicero and LANTERN were developed wholly or in part by the Internet community at large or were commercial-off-the-shelf (COTS) tools. By leveraging the output of a world-wide development team, creating WWW services becomes largely systems integration, not systems development. Turn-key solutions do not exist freely on the Internet; but their components do. The following is a summary of the technical challenges for each of the project components, with the details appearing in the next section.

For the Master Plan project, the technical challenges were largely database integration, and converting legacy hard copy information to electronic format. Once the information had been extracted from closed, proprietary databases, or converted to electronic form, manipulation of the data is a well understood process.

Cicero required the innovative application of existing Unix tools, with some Perl script "glue" to hold it all together. The technology for Cicero has existed for some time, its the defined process available through a well-known, consistent WWW user interface that makes it a full product.

LANTERN required the least amount of additional technology of all. The very nature of an Intranet dictates the reuse of wide area networking tools in a local area networking scenario (Auditore, 1995; Sprout, 1995). The challenge in establishing a successful Intranet is the social and political groundwork, not the technology.

Management and Organizational Concerns

Management, organization, and logistical concerns are by far the biggest challenges to an information technology project. In fact, solving the "technical" part of a project is often the "easy" part. Information technology projects impact existing processes and must overcome both those that have a real or perceived interest in existing processes as well as the inertia of human nature. They key to mitigating the resistance to the projects is to involve all stake holders of the existing process early in the planning and development of the information technology project (Moreton, 1995).

In the case of the Master Plan, this involved working with those that operated and maintained hard copy drawings, maps, and various proprietary databases. By involving the current information holders early in the process, resistance to creating an on-line version was minimized.

Cicero illustrates a socio-management challenge on multiple levels. There were many people that had wanted Cicero-like functionality for some time, and eagerly embraced it as soon as it was available. Others were won over through several demonstrations, seminars, and referrals from other users. Even though Cicero is widely praised by all that use it, it has the side effect of serving as a catalyst for existing, unresolved debate in how to handle distributed systems support. So even though a product can meet customer expectations, its impact has to be understood within the larger organizational context.

LANTERN's challenge was similar to Cicero's, but on a larger scale. Not only was a new communications process introduced, but its impact on existing processes had to be clearly communicated to all involved. The LANTERN team accomplished this by first gaining the support of a senior member of management, then publicizing and then holding a number of informal design shop meetings that encouraged employees to contribute suggestions for process improvement at Langley. The suggestions that were within the scope of LANTERN were addressed, and explanation was given for why the remainder were outside the scope of LANTERN. In addition to the design shop meetings, feedback was encouraged via e-mail, hard copy, and telephone.

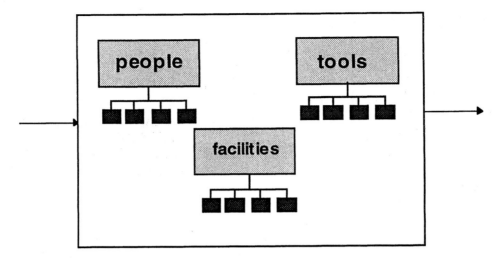

Figure 2: Non-Integrated Databases for Each Component

Current Status of the Project

This section introduces the history and current details about each major component of the WWW project at Langley.

Master Plan

A 1994 survey of the Internal Operations Group identified many problems associated with how institutional information at Langley was gathered, stored, updated, distributed and used. One of the most significant challenges found was that large volumes of data were held in many different formats. As many as 95 different management information systems were in use in the Internal Operations Group (Ball, et al., 1994). The survey found that these systems were developed with a, "variety of software packages on a variety of platforms." The study also noted, "Many are standalone and unique to functional organizations" and with regard to these systems, "There is a large amount of manual data entry." This diversity in the location and formats of data as well as the lack of integration of the various systems (as illustrated in Figure 2) makes complex queries (i.e., across multiple databases) very difficult and time consuming. One of these databases was the Master Plan, the architectural blue prints of each building and total center layout for Langley. The Master Plan is a benchmark when new construction or changes need to be done to any of the buildings or adjacent land area. The Master Plan includes data such as underground utilities, building dimensions, ground composition, title, and abstract data.

The Langley Master Plan had traditionally been produced by hand as a collection of sheets or "plates" which were duplicated and distributed in hard copy form using offset printing. Approximately 70 copies of these tabloid sized booklets consisting of 150 color plates each were distributed for each release. In 1979, the cost for producing the Master Plan was approximately US $500,000. Because of this costly and labor-intensive process, the document was only revised every 5 - 10 years. This update schedule was typically "crisis-driven," by events such as major building additions and other large construction projects. Because of this haphazard revision cycle, and because of the document being almost always out of date, the Master Plan was only used as a sort of "coffee table reference" to be marked up by planners wishing to make changes. Actual site planning was done with separate drawings for Preliminary and Critical Design reviews. The nature of the data in the document limited its usefulness as well. The plates, existing only as pictures on paper, could not contain or effectively reference other attribute data. This static format did not enable "what-if" planning or make it easy to visualize or analyze different options. This format also dictated that a completely separate database, existing totally on paper, be maintained for the Master Plan and individual building site plans, since the Master Plan was not drawn to sufficient levels of detail or accuracy to be used as an engineering working document. The level of effort required to produce the Master Plan increased dramatically in 1986 because of escalated requirements for documentation of environmental and historical information. In order to make the Master Plan more current, cheaper to maintain, and carry additional information, it was converted to CADD (Computer Aided Design / Drafting) electronic format beginning in 1989.

The development of this electronic version took place between 1989 and 1992 with a total cost (including printing and distributing 60 copies) of approximately US $300,000. The required number of complete copies distributed was reduced by making the electronic drawing files available over the Langley computer network. The level of detail and accuracy of these drawings allowed them to be used for engineering planning, both in the creation of proposed site plans and for discussion in design reviews. This alleviated the need for separate drawing databases and the extra maintenance associated with multiple copies.

The ability to associate these drawings with additional features such as environmental and historical data allowed other organizations outside the Master Planning office to use them for reference and analysis. This electronic Master Plan was demonstrated to a NASA-wide "lessons learned" conference as a model for the other centers to strive toward. Even though this migration to electronic files was a necessary and cost-effective step, the emergence of new technologies for handling spatial data would prove to eclipse this version with even greater savings and more useful data. This new technology, Geographic Information Systems would revolutionize the way planners at Langley thought about maps.

Begun around 1993 as a prototype of a future Master Plan, this transition to GIS has been accepted as the latest incarnation of this "document." Actually, Master Plan is really a database, tying together electronic drawing sets and tabular data into a seamless hierarchical system of information gathering, display, and analysis. Unprecedented accuracy is possible through the use of digital aerial photography and Global Positioning System (GPS) data, which can be readily assimilated into the system. Through the use of appropriate queries, the separate plates of the old Master Plan can be generated, but the real power of this system is to allow detailed analysis and scenario planning using any number of variables, data relationships, and constraints.

By integrating the graphical databases of underground utilities, building layouts, environmental zones, roads, etc., with tabular databases such as personnel information, space utilization, energy metering, and real property, the GIS Master Plan allows complex analysis and planning to be easily performed in a fraction of the time. This data can now be used for tasks which were all but impossible before. The system was recently used to settle a 20 year old dispute over some remote property used by Langley for drop model testing. Using the aerial photos, GPS surveys, and property and tax maps digitized into the system, property boundaries were precisely located, and plots generated which convinced a Federal judge that Langley was the legal owner of the property in question. During the threat of hurricane Felix in September of 1995, flood contours and building outlines were used to determine where to place sandbags, and what equipment to elevate and how high, to minimize water damage.

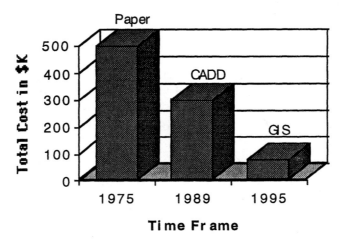

Figure 3: Decreasing Master Plan Cost

Not only has the Master Plan database become a much more useful planning and response tool, it has truly become the most current source of spatial information at the center. Because live links to various databases are used to gather information on demand, every query is answered with the latest data from every source. The GIS version of the Master Plan was developed between 1993 and 1996 at a cost of less than US $70,000. The decreasing cost of producing the Master Plan in various formats is shown in Figure 3. The ability to perform queries and view result over the LaRCNET network has drastically reduced the need for printed copies. Individual users can print a report as needed at their local printer, and almost no one needs a print of the entire database. Although network access has made the Master Plan available and useful to a much greater user community, some training and computer expertise is required to effectively use the system. That is changing rapidly through the development of World Wide Web based tools and services.

Cicero

Historically, distributed computing at Langley has been a collection of small groups of computers, separately maintained and staffed by individual branches or projects, held together by a center-wide TCP/IP backbone. Little work sharing existed between the individual system administrators, especially those employed by different organizations. The Langley Computer Users' Committee (LCUC) was established to provide a unified voice for Langley users to provide their requirements to the computing center. Under its auspices, the Distributed Systems Subcommittee provided a way for system administrators to get to know each other and to cooperate in order to provide better service to their users.

The LCUC and its various subcommittees have proved enormously successful. LCUC-sponsored user's groups and initiatives have helped individual system administrators stay current with the important computing issues at Langley. In addition, they offer a repository of sources and binaries for popular software packages, which has been one of their most successful offerings. It represents a form of load-balancing among the system administrators. Unfortunately, the software is considered "unsupported." Anyone at Langley who wishes can contribute to the archive, but there is no way to determine if the software they configured and compiled will work on any other given system. The system administration methods at Langley vary widely, and software configured for one set of machines may not be suitable for another. Thus, the load-balancing provided by these software archives, while useful, is not quite as useful as it could be if common configuration differences were overcome.

To help overcome these problems, Langley formed the Integrated Computing Environment (ICE) team in late 1993. ICE's objectives are twofold: the first is to provide a common computing environment on each of the major platforms in use. By providing a common set of software tools across all platforms, users will feel comfortable no matter what hardware or OS is being used. The second objective is to ease the administrative burden on the maintainers of these systems. We accomplish this by serving as a clearinghouse for important tools and information for example, vendor security information and by providing optional standards for system installation and configuration.

In February 1994, the ICE team started to look seriously at the problem of providing stable, pre-configured versions of its Unix software for use by the Langley community. Learning from and building upon the success of the LCUC software archive, the ICE team offered a set of applications and software that is made available on each of the widely used platforms at Langley. The team projected that some system administrators would prefer to get their entire /usr/local partition from ICE through a method such as Rdist (Rdist is a Unix program to maintain identical copies of file over multiple hosts) that are executing that would serve to keep them tightly in sync with the latest supported versions of the software for their platform. The ICE team recognized, however, that this would not be the normal case. Most system administrators would prefer to retain the privilege of determining exactly what software is present on their systems rather than trust an automated method. Cicero was born out of this need to provide a solution that would address those concerns, while still providing an easy, semi-automated method of acquiring supported ICE software.

Using the WWW method, administrators can use WWW clients to browse the list of supported software for their particular hardware and operating system combination. Clicking on the software's name will download the package information file and cause ciceinst (Cicero install) to run on the local machine. Because the package files have digital signatures there is no possibility of accidentally installing malicious software. If the package is not signed correctly, ciceinst refuses to proceed with the installation.

LANTERN

NASA Langley Web activities prior to the summer of 1995 were largely constructed for external customers. However, a growing number of information resources that were not appropriate or applicable for external dissemination were becoming common. At that time, the WWW Team decided that a separate information space was necessary dedicated to the business of doing business inside Langley. WWW and computer networks were no longer the domain of the computational scientists, but all organizational users could now access information of interest to them on the internal web pages (Sprout, 1995). LANTERN is Langley's Intranet (LANgley inTERNal home page.) LANTERN's value is that an employee can access institutional knowledge and initiate processes from their desktop 24 hours a day seven days a week ("is Bob in this week?") and "storage" of information ("Where did I put that notice, I can't find anything on my desk?") is provided in a single well known location. In order to build an effective Intranet the team also recognized that there were a number of activities that needed to be done to ensure successful integration of an Intranet into Langley's work environment, most importantly training.

The WWW team developed a 2 hour training class taught by volunteers to give instruction to the entire center on the fundamentals of the Internet and WWW browser Navigation. During the first offering of classes 288 slots were filled in less than 2 hours and 265 people were place on a waiting list. The team then scheduled two 1 day retreats. On May 23, 1995, the WWW team met to develop the design requirements and work out the process methodology for gathering for customer requirements for the center's Intranet. The three significant design goals that came out of the process were: it must be easy to use by all; it must be easy to maintain; and it must provide useful information that employees want.

To gather data an electronic message was sent to the entire center explaining what an Intranet was, how it would streamline administrative processes, and how they could participate. The team also scheduled five 2 hour round table discussions open to the entire center for requirements gathering. Equipped with the data from the first retreat, collected e-mail, and data gathered from the round table discussions, the team met two weeks later for an all day retreat to analyze and process all data into categories and develop the initial architecture for LANTERN.

The WWW team felt that it needed to inform most potential users and so the Researcher News, the center's bi-weekly publication was asked to participate in the design process. Timed very closely with the first release of LANTERN, June 13, 1995, was a two-page article in the center's *Researcher News* explaining LANTERN, its scope, and how interested employees could participate.

Successes and Failures

Master Plan

In 1995, Langley was beginning to use the Web as an Intranet tool for many of its internal data services. It was apparent that the ideal way for the largest number of users on various computing platforms to use the Master Plan and other GIS data was to make them accessible through WWW browsers. The first such a service was the Langley Building and Room Locator. This interface presents a form to the user into which a building number and room number are entered, and maps of both the building and room are pulled from the GIS database and presented on the user's WWW browser.

This service has been made a part of the Langley electronic post office, also Web based, which allows a search by name, e-mail address, etc. and after presenting the address, organization, phone number, and other pertinent contact information, the user can access the Building and Room Locator to find that person's office. Since live database connections are used, and the maps and building drawings are generated on the fly, the system automatically shows the current room assignment, correct building, etc. This is a limited use of GIS on the Web, but it is a proof of concept for the eventual interface to the Master Plan. Users will be able to perform complex queries on multiple data sets and generate specific graphics that show the relationships between those data sets. Information such as energy use by building, maintenance costs per organization, population density within buildings, and even combinations of those data will be available, forming the core of a decision support system for downsizing, building closure planning, consolidation of similar spaces, personnel relocation planning, etc.

With sufficient "hooks" into many databases, the types of information available are nearly unlimited. Eventually, updates to the database will be possible using advances in WWW technology and digital signature and authentication techniques. This will allow anyone to maintain their data with little training. Because of this universal accessibility, the data will converge to greater accuracy, since each user will be interested in correcting the particular information associated with their facility or function. It is anticipated that a significant number of possible queries will be available over the WWW before 1997. Hopefully, with easy access to the Master Plan, hard copy distributions will be not be needed again. The Master Plan will evolve into a complete, detailed virtual model of Langley that is always up to date, available to everyone, and sophisticated enough to answer any question about the people and infrastructure of the center.

Cicero

Cicero has been very well received by the Langley community. There was, however, one unanticipated objection to providing this service. During an informal presentation of Cicero to one of the LCUC subcommittees, it was pointed out that we had perhaps made software "too easy" to install. System administration methods vary widely at Langley. In many places, users have root access in order to perform certain tasks relating to their research (e.g., loading a real-time sensor device driver). If Cicero provided an easy to use "Click to Install" method of updating system binaries, would the users not be tempted to install any piece of software that looked interesting to them? Potentially, this could cause such problems as filling up available disk space or catching other users by surprise when a piece of software is suddenly upgraded to a newer, slightly different, version.

This is, unfortunately, a symptom of a more serious problem: users who have root access yet cannot be trusted to use it wisely. For Cicero, a compromise was available. Cicero uses the syslog facility to log a message each time a software package is installed. While this does not prevent users with root access from installing software on their own, it does provide a useful audit trail.

The system administration community gives Cicero high acclaim because saves significant time and frees them to do other work without worrying about the chore of software installation. In the 10 hours it takes to build and install X Window System, they can help users, re-configure workstations, etc. Users also are pleased with this concept, since it means they receive much more personal attention from their system administrator. Package installation systems like Cicero are time savers for large sites with distributed system administration tasks. Langley has already seen significant cost savings. Packages that used to take 3 hours for an experienced system administrator to install now takes 2 minutes.

LANTERN

LANTERN quickly integrated into Langley culture. Through the outreach efforts, people took ownership in LANTERN and enthusiastically contributed to the services available, a sample of which is in Table 3.

In November, 1995 the weekly newsletter ceased hard copy circulation and is available only through LANTERN, at an annual cost savings of US $25,000. In addition, the editor of the newsletter has reduced preparation time of each issue from 1.5 days to 2 hours. The center is also transitioning all small purchases to a WWW transaction based system. This service will become available in April 1996 and the estimated annual cost saving is US $100,000. Significant cost reductions are being realized from the elimination of redundant paper processing with the center's Management Instructions Manuals. Secretaries no longer have to spend time replacing outdated sheets in the Management Instruction Manual binders with updated versions. This is significant in that there is at least 50 copies of the Management Instructions Manuals across the Center and each need to be kept up to date. On average a secretary spends an hour a week on this activity. Keeping all 50 sets up to date used to consumer nearly a collective person-year! Also eliminated are costs incurred from making the initial copies and mailing them to all offices that have manuals.

New communications tools create new communications patterns (Evard, 1993). The most obvious communications shift caused by WWW and LANTERN is that people are comfortable with passing pointers to information collections, instead of trying to pass entire data object(s) through e-mail, hard copy, conversation, etc. This lessens the effort required for certain communication tasks

1.	Forms (81 currently used Center-wide)
2.	Health Services
3.	Holiday and Payroll dates
4.	How Do I ? (by subject, computers, procurement, printing; publishing, scheduling; reservation)
5.	Idle Property Screening List
6.	Instructions for putting a paper on Langley Technical Report Server (LTRS)
7.	Intranet feedback form
8.	Inventory Database
9.	Job Order Numbers
10.	Langley Activities Association (Intramural Activities)
11.	Langley Child Development Center
12.	Langley Federal Credit Union
13.	larc.announce (newsgroup which archives all messages sent Center-wide)
14.	LaRC Street Map
15.	LaRC This Week (Weekly Newsletter)
16.	LaRC Townmeeting Question Form
17.	Institutional Studies Library
18.	Recycling Information
19.	Services Directory
20.	Software License Information

Table 3: 20 of the 60+ LANTERN Services

and encourages more data sharing. There has been a tremendous growth of sharing of information in the past year. Many databases where information was solely the domain of a particular organization are now available to the entire Center. For example, there is an equipment database that tracks who owns what equipment and where it is located. Previously an employee had to call the inventory office or and fill out a form to request an inventory of equipment. Now it is possible to query the equipment database in 12 different ways and get the data on-line in a matter of seconds.

Another time saving device is the Center's electronic post office which started out as an X.500 server then subsequently was ported to the Web with necessary common gateway interface (CGI) scripts to incorporate the building and room locator service (Master Plan data). Currently, the electronic post office has 10,000+ accesses weekly. It is also noteworthy that the Center telephone directory is printed once every year and half at a cost of US $15,000 and is out of date the moment its printed. However, the electronic post office receives weekly downloads from the Personnel database and automatically does its updates at virtually negligible cost. Its these types of efficiencies that is maximizing information sharing among employees and increases work productivity while cutting costs.

Not exactly a failure, but a situation to be aware of is the cost of success. LANTERN has been successful, but it also raises expectations in the user community. Users, encouraged by the usefulness of the initial Intranet, expect that anything can be done for everyone. Setting priorities and curbing expectations are difficult management tasks that occur in the wake of a successful project.

Epilogue and Lessons Learned

Through the Master Plan, Cicero, LANTERN, and the other related WWW projects, we have found that there are 4 pillars that are key to information technology project success (Figure 4):

• *Training*— How to use emerging information technology tools
• *Providing Useful Services*— Services Langley's staff needs and wants
• *Enabling Tools*— Providing information access tools to the customers
• *Advertising and Advocacy*— NASA's products and services around the nation and internally

By applying resources equally across each pillar, the Master Plan, Cicero and LANTERN have been successful individually, and have provided the foundation for a large strategic information interchange infrastructure for the center. Table 4 shows major activities for each project component and it is measured impact for people at Langley and the external customers.

The WWW, GIS, and ICE project teams have already been introduced. TAG and K-12 refer to the technology transfer and educational outreach project teams, respectively.

Specific lessons we would give to others considering integrating information technology into their business environment include:

Get a strong Senior Management sponsor with resources
WWW efforts have the highest probability of success when they begin as grass roots efforts, develop a small number of success stories, and then sell the concept to a sympathetic member of senior management. It is inevitable that WWW successes will be viewed as threats (real or imagined) by other members of the organizations, and a sponsor offers a greater level of protection.

Find someone who is a WWW evangelist with leadership skills
Until a WWW effort is institutionalized, success is dependent on generally a single person who can both produce useful WWW services with limited resources while enduring changing perceptions of WWW technologies, from "when will this silver bullet fix my problem" to "WWW is a waste of time."

Train everyone how to use your tools and services
Just as nearly all employees are both consumers and producers of information in traditional

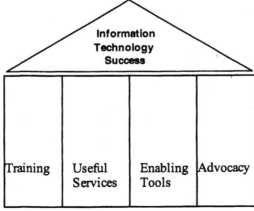

Figure 4: Four Pillars of Information Technology Success

Area	Activity	Participating Team	Number of People Reached
Training	WWW browser training classes	WWW, GIS	750
	3 WWW reference sheets	WWW	1,500
	WWW browser training video	WWW	500
Services	NASA Technical Report Server	WWW	100,000
	Langley Software Server	WWW, TAG	1,000
	Technology Opportunity Showcase on-line	WWW, TAG	15,000
	LANTERN - Langley's Intranet	ICE, GIS , WWW	5,000
	WWW caching server	ICE	5,000
	Building & Room Locator	GIS	15,000
Enabling Tools	Netscape Site License	WWW	2,500
	MacHTTP Site License	WWW	300
Advocacy	TOPS '95	WWW, ICE, GIS, TAG	2,500
	Oshkosh '95	WWW, K-12, TAG	10,000
	Internet '95	WWW, GIS, ICE	400
	Internet Fair 2	WWW, GIS, ICE	2,000

Table 4: Activities and the Impact Chart (March 1-, 1995-December 1, 1995)

media formats, the same holds true for electronic format. It is everyone's responsibility to both use and contribute to an organizations information space.

ADVERTISE, ADVERTISE, ADVERTISE and then ADVERTISE some more

Advertisement and outreach is a never ending effort. The resources required will go down when critical mass is required, but it is never "done." A danger to watch out for is that the technical organizations that generally assist in the development of WWW resources are generally unskilled in the advocacy of such resources, especially to non-technical customers.

Find and GET the best technical support you can find

Services that are down, unavailable, or stale can do more harm than good. Enlist the best technical people possible, but ensure they have the commitment necessary for information mainte-nance.

World Wide Web has been the catalyst for many Information Technology projects at NASA Langley. The Master Plan, Cicero, and LANTERN are selected because they support each segment of the NASA Langley Work Relation Model; Facilities, Tools, and People respectively. For providing useful services, the focus for the future is to integrate more Master Plan data, push for wider application of Cicero, and transition more hard copy administrative data to LANTERN. Langley's Intranet continues to grow, with even more procurement and tracking services slated for WWW interfaces. For training, in March 1996 the Center began HTML authoring classes. For enabling tools, an Agency-wide site license for Netscape has been purchased. Advertising and outreach continues at every possible center event and at a personal, one-on-one advocacy and education. How do you know you have succeeded? When phrases such as "Well we can just put it up on LANTERN" are commonly overheard in the cafeteria.

Questions for Discussion

1. The focus of this paper has been mostly applicable to large organizations. How would the issues, resolution, and services presented here be applicable to small organizations? What would be the same? What would not be applicable? What new challenges would exist that large organizations do not face?

2. WWW and related technologies are often applied to integrating a number of legacy database systems. If an organization could start with a clean slate, what would be an appropriate Information System architecture and what role would WWW play in the new system?

3. The Master Plan and related geographic information systems showed a clear path of evolution from hard copy to initial WWW interface. Discuss how a traditional Management Information System would make such an evolution. What additional security or privacy issues are introduced by the switch to Management from Geographic data?

4. The NASA Langley WWW Team proposed the "Four Pillars of Information Technology Project Success" which are: Training, Developing useful services, Providing enabling tools, and Advertising available resources. Discuss this 4 pronged model. Are there additional pillars? Could the model be simplified to fewer pillars? Are there cases where the 4 pillars could be fully satisfied, but a project could fail?

5. The concept was introduced of a grass roots team or project transitioning to official status with senior management approval and sponsorship. What is the best time for this transition to take place? What are the dangers of it occurring too early? Too late? What (if any) about this concept is applicable only to Information Technology projects?

References

Auditore, Peter (1995). "Weaving a web inside the corporation: The future of collaborative computing," *Computer Technology Review*, Summer-Fall 1995, pp. 14-17.

Ball, W. Brad, Meyer, John M., Gage, Robert L. & Waravdekar, Jay W. (1995). "GIS Business Plan", NASA Langley Research Center. URL: http://gis-www.larc.nasa.gov/bplan/

Berners-Lee, T., Calliau, R., Groff, J. F., & Pollermand, B. (1992), "World-Wide Web: the information universe," *Electronic Networking: Research, Applications, and Policy*, 2(1), 52-58.

Bray, Tim (1996). "Measuring the Web", *World Wide Web Journal*, 1(3), pp. 141-154.

Evard, Remy (1993). "Collaborative networked communication: MUDs as system tools," *Proceedings of the 7th System Administration Conference* (LISA '93), Monterey, CA, November 1-5, 1993, pp. 1-8.

Moreton, Robert (1995). "Transforming the organization: the contribution of the information systems function," *Journal of Strategic Information Systems*, 4, pp. 149-164.

Nelson, M. L., Gottlich, G. L., Bianco, D. J., Paulson, S.S., Binkley, R. L., Kellogg, Y. D., Beaumont, C. J., Schmunk, R. B., Kurtz, M.J., Accomazzi, A. & Syed, O. (1995). "The NASA Technical Report Server", *Internet Research: Electronic Networking Applications and Policy*, 5(2), pp. 25-36.

Nelson, Michael L. & Bianco, David J. (1994). "The World Wide Web and technology transfer at NASA Langley Research Center," *Proceedings of the Second International World Wide Web Conference*, Chicago, IL, October 18-20, 1994, pp. 701-710.

Nelson, Michael L., Gottlich, Gretchen L., & Bianco, David J. (1994). "World Wide Web implementation of the Langley Technical Report Server ", NASA TM-109162.

Office of Public Affairs, NASA Langley (1995). "NASA Langley Fact Sheet" URL: http://www.larc.nasa.gov/org/pao/PAIS/Langley.html

Shoosmith, John (1993). "Introduction to the LaRC Central Scientific Computing Compex," NASA TM-104092.

Sprout, Alison (1995). "The Internet inside your company," *Fortune,* 132(11), pp. 161-168.

Wieseman, Carol D. (Ed.) (1994). "The role of computers in research and development at NASA Langley Research Center," NASA CP-10159.

Appendix A: URLs of Listed Resources

Resource	Uniform Resource Locator
Building and Room Locator	http://gis-www.larc.nasa.gov/cgi-bin/locator
Cicero	http://ice-www.larc.nasa.gov/ICE/doc/Cicero/
Integrated Computing Environment	http://ice-www.larc.nasa.gov/ICE/
Internet Fair 2	http://www.larc.nasa.gov/if2/
Langley Computer Users Committee	http://cabsparc.larc.nasa.gov/LCUC/lcuc.html
Langley Home Page	http://www.larc.nasa.gov/
LANTERN	(restricted access)
Master Plan	http://gis-www.larc.nasa.gov/
Post Office	http://post.larc.nasa.gov/cgi-bin/whois.pl
WWW Training	http://boardwalk.larc.nasa.gov/isd-www/training.html

Chapter 18

Developing Effective Computer Systems Supporting Knowledge-Intensive Work: Situated Design in a Large Paper Mill

Martin Müller
University of Zurich

Rolf Pfeifer
University of Zurich

Executive Summary

The case to be discussed is a joint project between the university of Zurich and "Swiss Paper"[1], a large paper mill in Switzerland. The paper mill had recently undergone deep structural changes after an investigation of by of the world's leading management consulting companies. Our project is mainly concerned with support of energy management by means of computer technology. There were essentially three goals. The first one was to minimize energy consumption while keeping it at a constant level. The second goal was the exploration of a scientific hypothesis, namely that expert behavior cannot be adequately explained in terms of "information processing," but is more adequately seen as "situated action." The latter emphasizes the actual organizational and social circumstances. The objective of Situated Design— a particular project methodology that we have been developing in our group at the university over the last few years—is to support "situated action" by means of computer technology, rather than to formalize human expertise. Applying and refining this methodology is the third major goal of the project. In this paper we will discuss our experiences with Situated Design at Swiss Paper.

The software industry's biggest problems are well known - projects arriving late, over budget or not delivering what is needed. We will argue that one of the main problems is a misconception of human cognition and behavior. We claim that this misconception is at the source of the problems of software development in general. We suggest an alternative approach which has grown out of our experience with many projects in the area of 'work place design by means of computer technology.'[2]

One of the underlying assumptions that we will discuss in the paper is that the goal of software engineering is support rather than automation. Thus, we do not intend to develop software packages that will take all the design decisions for the software engineer. This position can be contrasted with, e.g., the conviction underlying CASE systems, where the design process and the whole software life cycle can be formalized. All the designer has to do is apply the detailed recipes prescribed by the CASE software. What we have in mind contrasts sharply with this view. It is our belief that an answer to the so-called "software crisis" is to optimally exploit human expertise, not automating it. Furthermore, design involves a lot of communication. The software designer has to listen and observe carefully, in order to better understand the latent user's needs. The aim of Situated Design is to stimulate the designer's awareness of the issues involved in the design process, such as the expertise used in daily work. It should encourage the discussion and confrontation of these issues from different perspectives among all members of a project team, designers as well as the people concerned. The goal is not to provide "canned" solutions, but to optimally bring to bear the user's as well as the designer's knowledge. The success of the project depends on the human designer's experience in perceiving related issues which are not optimally exploited.

In order to test and refine the methodology of Situated Design we have defined a project with Swiss Paper. The investigation of one of the world's leading management consulting companies has been the first consequence of a preceding declaratory capital reduction. Though the company's interest in the project is energy management, our approach will rather emphasize the communication between all workers about energy issues than to understand the energy process itself.

Therefore, the objective is to improve or, respectively, to enhance the existing computer infrastructure in a way that the communication process about the energy issue will be improved. Finally, we expect that an improved communication will enhance the paper mill workers' understanding and mastery of the energy management.

Background

The holding

Swiss Paper specializes in high-quality paper production with a total annual production of 300'000 tons. Swiss Paper is one of two paper mills belonging to the "Swiss Paper Holding"[3] with a total production of 450'000 tons. The second paper mill produces newsprint. In 1994, the business volume of the holding was roughly US $ 600 million with a loss of US $ 50 million. This has to be contrasted with the mid 1980s, where Swiss Paper Holding made large profits (in 1989 they still had a surplus of 13 millions) and accounted a very high liquidity (60 %).

During the period of 1994/95 two subsidiary companies engaged in paper manufacturing and paper trading were sold as a result of restructuring. With the attempt to increase productivity the work force of the holding was reduced from former 3295 to 1675 persons. At Swiss Paper itself there was a reduction from 1300 to 900 employees. Both paper mills have a function-oriented, hierarchical organizational structure (see figure 1).

Our partner: "Swiss Paper"

The main activity of Swiss Paper is the production of high-quality paper. In addition to the paper production itself, it manufactures high-quality paper into semi-finished levels (cut-size sheeting and packaging). A total amount of 300'000 tons is produced by three independent paper production lines with different production capacities (49%, 29%, and 22%). However, the primary raw material, the pulp, is not produced by Swiss Paper itself, but bought from independent deliverers.

Until 1988 there was a shortage of high-quality paper on the European market. In 1991, after a

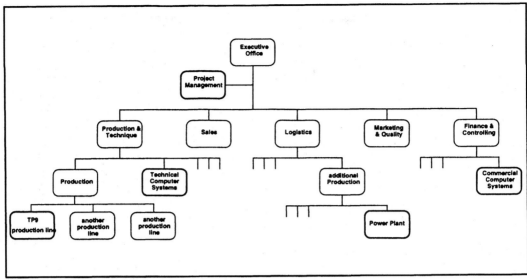

Figure 1: Organizational structure of Swiss Paper

market analysis of future developments, Swiss Paper invested US $ 400   million into a paper production line of the newest generation. Nowadays, this production line is producing nearly half of the total amount of paper. At about the same time, strong German and Scandinavian competitors were making similar investments which lead to a significant over-capacity of the whole European paper industry around 1992/93 (there was a previous over-capacity of 25% in 1991). As a consequence, the price for paper dropped. However, European paper production capacity was still rising, which was probably the reason why the pulp price increased also. This market development caused difficulties for Swiss Paper.

There were a number of additional, specific factors contributing to the already difficult situation of the company. First. the European market within the European Union had become well established, making it more difficult for a company in a non-member country like Switzerland to compete. As a side effect of the European alliance, there were large fusions going on. During 1994 the ten biggest European paper mills were producing two-thirds of the total amount of European paper. Second, there had been some unfortunate investments. For example, Swiss Paper decided to assign the contract for the development of the control system of the new paper production line to a new-comer in paper industry. This decision lead to a lot of system crashes during the first two years. These frequent crashes had an immediate negative impact on the production capacity and on the quality of the paper. 1993 was a bad year for the company: the holding's losses totaled US $ 100 million. Also, there is the general phenomenon that the market has become more dynamic. For example the price of the pulp increased from October 1994 to October 1995 from US $ 380 to US $ 1000 per ton. This was another unfortunate development for Swiss Paper, because there was a practice of making contracts with their customers for a period of one whole year in advance, based on the current pulp price.

In this kind of new market situation companies not only have to be able to produce efficiently, but they must react dynamically to unforeseen changes. Last but not least, there was also the great danger that the company would have to file bankruptcy. It was obvious that something had to be done to get the company back on track.

At the end of 1994 Swiss Paper had to write down the capital. Additionally, in early 1995 a consortium of banks launched a far-reaching restructuring operation - just before our project had been approved by the CEO. While the management consulting company was focusing on the overall organization, our project was focusing on a more operative level.

Setting the Stage

The operative level

Our efforts are centered around the complex issue of energy management. This focus was chosen for several reasons:

(a) Energy costs for paper production amount to approximately 10% of the total production costs. Energy is a strategic factor for the paper industry, first because of the high energy costs, which can be expected to increase in the future. Moreover, currently the average cost for electricity in Switzerland is extremely low as compared to the surrounding countries. It can be expected that this situation will change in the near future. Second because of ecological considerations that will become even more relevant in the future.

(b) According to one of our hypothesis, energy consumption is linked with paper quality. Thus, if we get the energy situation under control, the paper quality will also be improved.

In 1994, for example, Swiss Paper expended about 228 GWh of electrical energy (68% were produced by Swiss Paper's own power plant), and about 495 GWh of thermal energy. The total cost of the company's energy consumption amounted to US $ 21 million, including the cost for additionally purchased energy. The cost for the 72 GWh bought from an external electricity provider totaled US $ 7 million. Energy required for the production of one sheet of paper is equal to the amount of energy expended if you leave a bulb of 60W on for 12 minutes (see figure 2).

To convey a flavor of the situation of the company at the operational level, we will emphasize some characteristic "cultural" points. Now we present a short overview of some managerial, organizational and technical concerns, which are important for understanding our project partner's situation.

Fields of investigation

Because of our focus on energy, the investigation could be constrained to the company's own power plant as the energy supplier and the three paper production lines as the main energy consumers. 84% of the company's total electricity production, and 81 % of the company's total steam production is consumed by the paper production lines. Our research capacities were too low to handle all three production lines, so we decided to concentrate on the most advanced and most energy consuming one, called TP9. TP9 is Swiss Paper's ninth paper production line since its foundation in 1862. Geographically, the power plant and TP9 are at a distance of one kilometer from each other with several buildings in between them.

The power plant

As mentioned before, Swiss Paper runs its own power plant which produces most of the paper mill's energy demand (e.g., 68% of the total electricity consumption). Both gas and liquid fuel are used for producing electricity and steam (see figure 3).

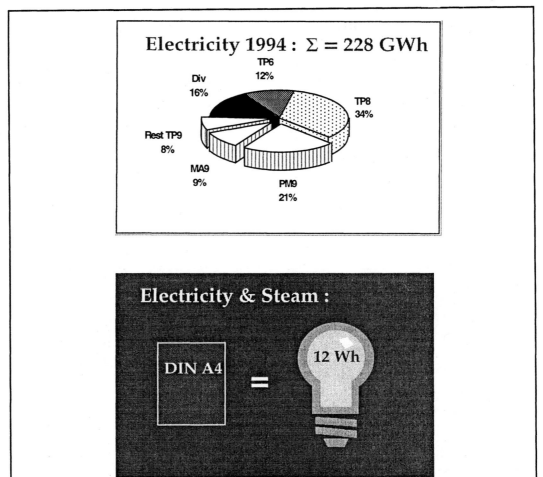

Figure 2: Top-Total consumption of electricity in 1994 subdivided into the three main consumers (the paper production lines TP9, TP8 and TP6) and various others; TP9 is subdivided into the paper machine (PM9), the grinding system (MA9) and various (Rest TP9). Bottom-Energy costs for a sheet of paper (for explanations see text).

An advanced gas turbine produces electricity and heats a boiler. The boiler in turn produces high pressure steam. In addition there are four older boilers running by gas and liquid fuel which also produce high pressure steam. The high pressure steam from all the boilers is used to drive two steam turbines producing electricity. The resulting low pressure steam is subsequently used to dry paper.

A large part of the electricity is produced by means of the steam turbines. A second part is produced by the advanced gas turbine. A third part, however, is bought from an external electricity company (see Figure 3 & 4).

The staff and the paper machine

The production of paper, and consequently the energy production as well, run 24 hours a day and 7 days a week. In the control room of the *power plant* there are two operators working in each shift of eight hours. During the day, the manager of the power plant is present as well.

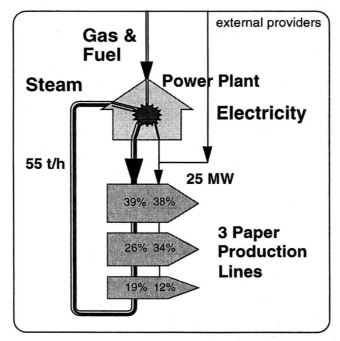

Figure 3: Energy flow at Swiss Paper (for explanations see text). Also indicated is the maximal load of steam flow (55 t/h) and electricity (25 MW).

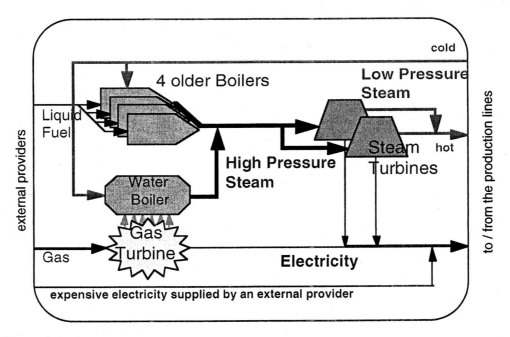

Figure 4: Technical situation at the power plant of Swiss Paper (for explanations see text).

jobs	task
'paper makers'	mainly being responsible for fulfilling the production planning guidelines and monitoring paper quality.
'1st engineers'	controlling the machine process and enforcing quality norms
'2nd engineers'	supporting the '1st engineer'
handymen	doing the work assigned to them by the engineers
shift manager	maintaining the communication between the three parts of the production line; belongs to a shift.
line manager	responsible manager of the whole paper production line, only present during the day.
two additional persons	at the production quality laboratory, also belonging to a shift.

In order to run the *paper production line* TP9, there are 30 workers present in each shift. The production line is divided into three consecutive production parts, namely the *paper production* itself in the paper machine, the *processing of the paper for improving its quality* (surface and whiteness), and the slitting system for producing smaller reels. Unlike the operators at the power plant, each worker at the production line has a certain specialization:

The main part of the paper production process takes place in the first third of the paper production lines, in the paper machine. The paper machine itself has two main sections. In the first one, paper pulp, a quite liquid substance, is poured on a large plane, 30 meters long and 5.68 meters wide. This plane is in fact a sieve which slides with a velocity up to 1000 meters per minute over tens of bars, extracting the most part of water from the pulp. That means that after less than two seconds the 5.68 meters wide paper strip is already strong enough to withstand tension without the support of a carrying   plane, which facilitates movement around 39 cylinders. These cylinders are heated with the low pressure, but hot steam originating in the power plant. The function of this second section of the paper machine is, of course, to dry down the paper strip to the expected value. At the end of the paper machine the paper strip is rolled up on a huge reel of final weight about 20 tons. Now the main paper production process is finished. The paper on the reel is now ready for further manufacturing, mainly concerned with quality improvement and cutting into customizable sizes.

The dynamic interrelation between steam consumption and electricity production

There is a mutual dependency of steam consumption and the production of electricity, which is caused by the steam turbines: the higher the rate of paper production, the higher the rate of steam consumption, the higher the plant's electricity production.

There is a paradoxical phenomenon that occurs here where the paper strip inside the paper machine is torn for any reason (thus interrupting the flow of paper production), the machines of the paper production line continue to run (thus still requiring current). However, steam is no longer required because there is no paper to dry. As most of the electricity is produced by steam turbines and as steam is no longer needed, the power plant's steam production is consequently reduced which

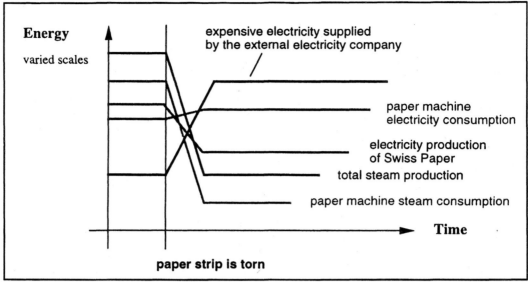

Figure 5: Interdependency of electricity production and steam consumption at the moment when the paper strip is torn.

implies that its electricity production will also go down. As a result, electricity may have to be purchased from the external electricity company. Due to specific contract issues in which the electricity company *guarantees* to supply any amount of electricity to Swiss Paper at any moment, this additional electricity can be very expensive, even if the actual amount of electricity consumed is relatively small. The account Swiss Paper has to pay for the purchased electricity is two-fold. Besides the cost for the total amount of electricity consumed during a month (counted in MWh), Swiss Paper is likewise charged with respect to the highest peak they reached during the same time (counted in MW), independent of how low the next lower peak is. That means that two months with the same total consumption of electricity (MWh), in one case with a stable consumption over time (hardly any peaks), and in the other case with a dynamic, unstable consumption (high peaks), can result in vastly differing amounts. For example, if the company is able to bring its monthly highest electricity peak down by 3 MW, given the same total consumption, it will save four hundred thousand dollars a month. The development of some of the key variables is shown in figure 5.

The understanding of the interrelationships between the various processes are so far understood by Swiss Paper's experts as they are displayed in figure 5. Most of the workers aren't even aware of these facts. Further considerations about this financially crucial process, such as how electricity cost could be reduced by appropriate reactions at the three paper machines, have not been regarded by Swiss Paper's engineers. It was assumed that the interrelationships are too complex to be handled appropriately. Furthermore, it was stated by managers that any possible alternatives - should any exist, would probably have unwanted, negative consequences on the logistics of the whole production process.

Other dynamic aspects

There are two other dynamic aspects worth mentioning. Firstly, because pulp is a natural product, it is very hard to predict how actual pulp suits the requested paper quality standards. Pulp contains various types of wood fibers and other components. For example, there can be remarkable differences between fibers of Canadian and Australian pine resulting in a different paper production process, even if the trees have the same age. Moreover, the quality of the pulp is strongly influenced by hardly accountable measurements, for example, by the amount of sunshine the trees were exposed to. The paper maker uses his experience to decide on the pulp mixture, which has a strong influence on the quality of the paper.

Secondly, the paper quality cannot be objectively defined. It also depends on the customers' subjective impression. For example, although the paper may fulfill defined standards, some customers will complain. This is so, because, for example, during an economic recession customers are less liable to accept the average paper quality. Or take the example, that if the picture printed on the paper has a blue area in it, e.g. a part of the sky, paper imperfections will be detected more easily and become a source of complaints. If the picture does not have any blue in it, the paper can be sold even though it does not fulfill the defined quality standards. In this case, the customers accept or do not even notice the imperfections, which still exist from an objective point of view. Consequently, the quality standards are designed in a way to meet an   average of the customers' expectations. In fact, the crucial decision whether a reel of paper is qualitatively acceptable even though the paper does not meet defined quality guidelines, lies in the hands of the workers at the production lines.

The current standard of computer systems

Swiss Paper's computer infrastructure is two-fold. On the one side, there is a computer infrastructure for the support of commercial and financial tasks. These systems constitute a kind of MIS (Management Information System) consisting of financial programs, data bases, production planning utilities, and general managerial support tools. On the other side, there is a huge and highly complex real-time system which is needed for monitoring and controlling the sophisticated paper production lines and the power plant machinery. It is, in essence, based on signal processing systems technology.

Many of the computer systems are insufficiently supported by the technical staff of Swiss Paper, in particular the exchange and interrelation of the two kinds of computer system infrastructures. The staff supporting the real-time system, the 'Technical Information Systems Department', consists of four persons. They are responsible for maintaining the four independently running process control systems of all three paper production lines and the power plant. This number should be compared to the 20 people which are available for the maintenance of the MIS, the so-called 'Financial Information Systems Department'. Five years ago, the 'Technical Information Systems Department' consisted of 14 employees. Probably because of the massive investments in advanced machinery, the technology had become too complex for the average systems engineer to handle. The company had to hire external expertise. Then for financial reasons it had to reduce its own staff. Today, there is a serious lack of know-how in building and maintaining the complex process control systems by the 'Technical Information Systems Department' (cf. figure 1).

The real-time computer systems at Swiss Paper are more or less independent of each other. There is only one computer per production line connecting the company's real-time systems to the network of the MIS. The connection between the two computer systems is a known source of problems.

The integration of the computer systems

There is a need for data exchange between the MIS and the process control computer systems. Some of the data required for running the process control system at TP9, is produced by the MIS. For example, data about planned production capacities which is generated on the commercial side, has to be transmitted to the process control system. Likewise, data collected by the process control system has to be transferred to commercial departments which monitor the progress of the paper production process and the extent to which the customer orders have been fulfilled.

This interface is realized by just a few computers. They have to handle the different technologies and protocols. The maintenance of these protocols is known to Swiss Paper's computer engineers as being very problematic. A known source for these problems are release updates with changes in data structures. Interestingly enough, neither the manager of the MIS,   nor the head of the real-time systems are willing to assume the responsibility for the maintenance of this interface. Because the connecting software system has been developed by a third party, this interface is poorly understood and therefore not well maintained.

The data situation

At the power plant control room, a lot of data about boilers, turbines and other machines are displayed on two screens. This data represents the operational state of the power plant machinery. In their daily work the operators also have to monitor and adjust the controls located directly next to the boilers. Note that the boilers are a ten minute walk away from the control room.

No data about the energy consumers (i.e. the paper production lines) is available at the power plant. There is even no data about production planning and none about the current state of the production process available. For example, the actual electricity and steam consumption of the various production lines is not available at the power plant. Although, there is an optical fibre cable belonging to the data processing network (part of the MIS) going through the power plant, there is no computer attached to it. There are two alarms indicating when the paper strip is torn at one of the two older production lines. Interestingly, such an alarm is missing for TP9, the most advanced production line.

One of two screens at the control room of the power plant summarizes the data about steam production, the other displays an overview of the electricity production (MW) of the gas turbine and the two steam turbines. The rate of electricity consumption for the electricity supplied by an external provider, is also shown. All data of the process control system at the power plant is electronically stored for three days.

At TP9, the most highly computerized production line, the process control system continually collects thousands of data records: quality data, such as the whiteness or the thickness of the paper, production data, such as the number of tons of paper produced, and finally process control data, such as the current steam consumption or the flow of pulp and water. All data collected at TP9 is electronically stored for seven days. Although the US $ 7 million control system of TP9 is collecting and displaying data on the current electricity consumption of hundreds of single engines, pertinent summary data about electricity consumption is missing. It is not surprising then that there is a lack of awareness about electricity use among the production line workers, and that the electricity consumption does not influence their working activities.

The distribution of competence and communication

The only communication device connecting the paper production lines and the power plant is a telephone. The workers at the production lines are instructed to inform the operators at the power plant about planned activities such as the start of the machinery, changes in the production plan, and incidents that interrupt the paper flow, such as when the paper strip is torn. Incidents of this sort require the full attention of the operators at the power plant. They have to readjust the controls of boilers and turbines to comply with the changed energy demands. Nevertheless, the line manager of TP9 has forbidden his line workers to do the requested phone call when the paper strip is torn, because the line workers have to do a lot of hurried work and have no time for other tasks such as calling the power plant. Of course, this is only justified as long as energy cost is ignored.

When the paper tears, it is also possible that the power plant is not able to produce enough steam which in turn may lead to a total system crash. Further detail about this matter are omitted here, because technical explanation is required. However, a reduction of the current steam consumption at the production lines could prevent such crashes, for example by reducing the speed of the paper machine.

Thus, it would be advantageous if the operators at the power plant could demand changes in the operation of the paper production lines and vice versa. However this would demand a better understanding of the interrelationships in order to define action alternatives applicable to daily work. That means that such instructions must be interpretable by the workers with respect to current problems. Yet, as we already outlined earlier, Swiss Paper's managers don't believe in the possibility to reach a better understanding than described above and are therefore not willing to invest in respective investments. Moreover, they force their workers to act in just the opposite way.

The Project Description

The methodology

At the outset of Situated Design, a vision has to be created which is shared by all participants (by us as Situated Designers as well as by the involved management and the selected workers). The vision that has been implicit in what has been said so far is the overall improvement of the energy situation. The vision can be vague and overly general and should not specify concrete aspects of the project. Although the vision must be shared by all project members, it should leave open the operative details. It is reasonable to start with a general analysis about the current state of the art. Of particular interest are contradicting results and opinions. The second step consists of a complete analysis of the working place with respect to the defined vision (c.f. the 'Setting the stage' section). The collected data and observations have to be evaluated and discussed in order to define an operative starting-point (see below: "Conclusions of the first analysis").

The third step is to define a small project that can be realized within a short time (a few weeks or months) and quickly yields payoffs. The "art" of Situated Design is to find small projects that are immediately of use, but at the same time do not compromise the original vision. Then the systems developed within the projects have to be introduced into the working situation. Finally the effect on the whole work place has to be evaluated and the cycle can be repeated starting with new projects. All developments have to be made together with the staff that will have to deal with the system. The idea is to get the staff interested and to bootstrap a process. Thus, the main task is the initialization of a process of continuous learning and change, rather than a product. To support learning is the key point here, not rationalization. This seemed to be   the underlying problem of Swiss Paper: many insufficiently understood, relatively isolated phenomena. In Situated Design, the computer scientists in the project team have the function of a catalyst or a moderator. Eventually their function will be reduced to one of informing the company on new developments.

The general stages are: 1) Developing a vision of where you want to go, 2) Analysis of the complete working situation; Initialization of the process, 3) Designing the initial system, 4) Introduction of the system into the working environment, and 5) Evaluation (take into account new working environment; generate ideas about new system).

This procedure hardly differs from the current understanding in software engineering and organizational design. However, Situated Design emphasizes a quite different view on particular aspects of how to improve work places by means of computer technology. For example, the understanding of the dynamic characteristics of the "real world" (see Pfeifer & Rademarkers, 1991, and Pfeifer, 1996), the social nature of knowledge and communication (see Heath & Luff, 1996 & unpublished), and the situation of human expertise (see below) result in different understandings about a) the necessary focus of analysis, b) the possibilities of computer technology, c) the nature and ability of human expertise, and d) the situated character of the design process itself.

Further, these steps are formulated in a fairly abstract manner. The methodology of Situated Design is almost by definition a methodology that cannot be couched into very precise terms. Making things much more precise would defeat the whole purpose of situated development. Because adaptability, interactivity, and change are the main issues of concern, it is virtually impossible to precisely define all the details in advance. This is in contrast to traditional CASE-like approaches. CASE tries to formalize all the steps in a project development process. The underlying assumption of CASE is the controllability of the entire process. If your main concern is budget and deadlines, CASE seems like a good solution. However, the real world is different. Because during the project the ideas, goals, and attitudes change, it is clear that predictability is only limited. The introduction of a new computer application not only changes the way in which a particular task is performed, but it changes the whole work place. And over time, the computer systems are used in different ways and their results are interpreted differently. The methodology of Situated Design tries to take this into account.

The goal is not to develop a kind of an expert system. Rather, Situated Design can be seen as an instance of user-centered software engineering. But in addition to traditional, user-centered approaches, Situated Design intends to bootstrap a process of organizational learning and enhanced communication among the company's workers and mangers, rather than to develop fancy software. The goal is not to build a sophisticated 'Decision Support System' (DSS). The work of an expert is not sensibly characterized by a series of decisions. A better conceptualization is in terms of 'situated actions' (see below). In the context of DSS - as well as in the context of any traditional software engineering approaches - the experts (synonyms: users, workers) are treated as information-processing entities; as well as the computer itself. Consequently, there is, firstly, no substantial difference recognized between the nature of human cognition and the computer's computational power. Secondly, the situated nature of human behavior is totally neglected. And finally, social processes are reduced to a kind of cybernetic system.

To define a small project, we started by looking at the individual work place of the employees while keeping the company as a whole in mind. The design process is largely bottom-up. Having the employees at the very bottom of the ladder involved seemed very important. First, because we hoped to generate enough motivation for the project in this way, second, because we see the workers as main holders of knowledge - they are the real experts of the domain concerned. The real experts have to have a strong say in what the new system should look like - not only we as designers. They have to compare the trial results achieved with the new system with the previous situation, based on their professional experience.

Theoretical considerations of Situated Design

On the one hand Situated Design implies a critique of the most widely held misconceptions of human expertise and the power of computers, and on the other - as a consequence - an alternative approach in designing work places. The fact that other methods are needed has been argued by many other authors (see, e.g. Landauer, 1995, Winograd & Flores, 1988, Suchman, 1987, Dahlbom & Mathiassen, 1993, Ehn, 1988, Greenbaum & Kyng, 1991, Pfeifer and Rademarkers, 1991). We will first briefly summarize the theoretical foundations and then we will discuss the implications for a design methodology.

In order to understand the misconceptions let us start by looking at the concept of "knowledge".

For the purpose of this case description, let us define knowledge as the experience that guides an expert's behavior as she or he interacts with the environment. This characterization has to be contrasted with the view of knowledge endorsed in the expert systems literature. There, the aim is to formalize knowledge, to make the knowledge explicit. Formalizing knowledge implies that knowledge has the same quality as data. By data, we mean entities that can be syntactically manipulated. Data differs from information in that the latter implies interpretation by an individual. A similar argument has been made by McDermott (cf. "Artificial Intelligence meets Natural Stupidity", 1976). In this paradigm - the one underlying expert systems -knowledge can be "extracted" from an expert like coal from a coal mine (cf. the `knowledge mining' metaphor). There is a strong belief underlying this paradigm, namely that knowledge can be reduced to (possibly complex) representations (e.g. formulas, algorithms, plans, plain text etc.). However sometimes the term `tacit knowledge' is used to indicate that knowledge cannot be reduced to representations (e.g. Polanyi, 1967). Dreyfus & Dreyfus (1986) characterize, in essence, knowledge as "tacit" and not amenable to rationalistic description.

• Knowledge

Reducing knowledge to representations, however, neglects the fact that there has to be an individual, who is a member of a community and therefore able to interpret the meaning of the representation with respect to the community's agreements on and use of the representations. Formulas, algorithms, plans, and the like in and of themselves do not constitute knowledge - representations represent the knowledge only with respect to social agreements. The real knowledge - so to speak - is and can only be defined in terms of the particular situation in which an individual is behaving and with respect to community members.

Knowledge can be communicated without the need for explicit representation. For example, masters are able to teach their apprentices by referring directly to reality. They can use the world as its own best model (Brooks, 1991). Second, a group of people are able to cope with the real world in a more effective way than one person alone. Of course, a group will normally be faster on a particular task than one person alone. But this is not the point here. The point is that the motivation for group work is, among other things, that the product of the group will be qualitatively better.

Let us illustrate these rather abstract reflections by an example. The main concern of our project is "energy management". Obviously, both parties, the energy producer (power plant) and the energy consumers (production lines) are influencing the result, i.e. how much energy is finally consumed and how expensive it has become. Today, both parties have only limited knowledge of the task. The power plant operators know how to drive the boilers and turbines. But they do not know how to react to the specific circumstances at the production lines. They do not have the appropriate information at their disposal (except for information about the current steam and electricity consumption by the whole company). For example, they rarely know why one paper machine is currently using less steam than a short time before. At least a phone call would be necessary to find out.

Similarly, the paper machine workers do not really know anything about energy production. Neither do they know when the problematic situation of a lack of steam comes up, nor are they aware of the current electricity consumption of their machines. As mentioned earlier, there exists no data about the current energy consummations (e.g. which production line is producing what kind of paper quality and therefore is consuming how much energy for how long). The idea is now that if more data about energy are available to all the workers, energy will be used more effectively - if workers knew how to read (interpret) the data. In other words, they learn to communicate with each other about energy issues. This implies that the interpretation of the energy data (the task of defining the meaning of the representations pertaining to energy) cannot be performed by the members of one party alone —both the members of the power plant as well as the members of the production lines have to communicate their ideas about the meaning of the new data (with regard to the current situation and to the common and individual goals etc.). Only when this kind of organizational learning is supported will there be a fair expectation of improving the company wide energy task.

- **Situated actions, situatedness**

Suchman (1987) introduced the concept of 'situated actions' which brings us a step further towards a better understanding of human expertise.

One of the assumptions underlying all of our work on designing computer systems is that if we have a better understanding of what people do, we can design better systems. In our theory, we argue that the classical view of humans as 'information processing systems' (or, more accurately `data processing systems') is inappropriate. An essential point of criticism is that the classical view does not explain how data becomes meaningful. We point out that meaning can only be understood in terms of —typically implicit— social conventions. In other words, we have to look at entire communities, not only individuals. We also introduce the term `tacit knowledge', meaning that knowledge is not an explicitly available "substance" that can be seen, formalized, stored, and manipulated in a computer system. Rather, it is whatever guides the individual's actions in a particular situation. `Situated action' means that the agent brings to bear its own experience - in the form of (socially shared, tacit) knowledge in the present situation.

Note that the action the actor takes in a particular situation, e.g. increasing the speed of the paper machine, depends on the context (customer demands, general economic situation), on the operator's experience, and on the specific situation (paper quality, state of various machines, etc.). Because the real world is indefinitely rich, unanticipated situations can always occur. A complete description of all the potential situations is not possible. Coping with novel situations implies adaptability, which in turn implies taking the (novel) general context and the (novel) specifics of the situation into account. Humans are adaptive in the physical and social world because they have grown up in it, because their 'tacit knowledge' has been acquired in the continued interaction with it. This kind of adaptability is another essential factor of situated action. An additional aspect of situated action is the so-called "indexicality of language" (Suchman, 1987), which means that otherwise ambiguous expressions acquire unique meaning within a situation. The simplest example is the use of terms like "this one", which can only be disambiguated in a particular situation.

We mentioned that the action a human takes depends strongly on the particular situation. Humans very strongly interact with their environment: they are, in a sense, coupled to it. In case of an emergency, e.g. a torn paper strip, the operator will move into a position where he has a good view of the machine, where he can perform the required actions. These actions will be different on every occasion (even though they share some similarity). Rather than basing their actions on elaborate internal models, the current real-world situation is exploited in the decision process.

There is another central aspect of a situated actor. Situated action also implies that the actor perceives the situation locally. His actions are based on what is currently available to his sensory system. This aspect of locality is particularly important for systems design. It provides us with strong heuristics on where the human could be supported (see below).

The goal of Situated Design now, is to develop computer technology (or technology in general) in order to support a human, now conceived as a 'situated actor'. In the paradigm of Situated Design behavior is not sensibly conceived as process of abstract "decision making," as argued above. Note that this notion of human expertise sharply contrasts with the classical one. Behavior (and decision making) is no longer based on detailed plans, elaborate internal models, or sophisticated rules for logical inferences, but on "situated action." Needless to say, the nature of the support will be very different.

Implications for systems design

Given that systems must function in the real world, and given that human experts are situated actors, we can draw the following conclusions about the goals of the system to be designed, its technical characteristics, and about issues to take into account when designing systems. For further discussion, the interested reader may be referred to Pfeifer (1996) and Müller (in preparation).

The goals of system development that we pursue with computer technology support are: short-term practical utility, maintenance and improvement of expertise, support of exploration, support of creation of external representations, support of communication and cooperation, and support for adapting to change.

There are certain relatively obvious technical characteristics systems must meet if they are to support the above- mentioned goals. They are: transparency, easy manipulation, flexibility, "what-if" tools, graphical tools, and tools for communication and cooperation.

A good example of a type of system that incorporates many of the features mentioned is a spreadsheet. People use them in many different ways, they do a large variety of things with them from financial planning, to producing nice graphics, to normal statistics, to simple bookkeeping. The concepts of spreadsheets have been around since 'Visicalc' in the late seventies, early eighties. Essential success factors are the large variety of things people can do with them, and the powerful "what-if" facilities.

Tools and techniques

Situated Design is a method for bringing computer technology into the real world, i.e. into companies. Situated Design projects are computer projects and therefore computer tools, as in any other project, will be an essential part. We have tried to characterize the sorts of tools we are looking for. The means for developing these tools are standard prototyping tools, code generators, or whatever. We will not go into them, they are well-known from standard software engineering practice. The book by Greenbaum and Kyng (1991) is a rich source of tools and techniques that can be applied to systems development. Some tools and techniques that are not so common are outlined in Pfeifer (1996). Some examples that a discussed there earlier originate from the field of 'knowledge acquisition', like the user dialogue, or "expert-guided novice problem solving".

Other approaches

There are a number of approaches in modern software engineering aiming in a similar direction. Examples are 'Cooperative design' (Kyng, 1991; Greenbaum & Kyng, 1991), 'Participatory design' (also called the "Scandinavian school", see Ehn, 1988; Floyd, Zullighoven, Budde & Keil-Slawik, 1992; Schuler & Namioka, 1993), 'anthropological a roaches' (see e.g., Zuboff 1988), 'Philosophical approaches' (see e.g., Dahlbom and Mathiassen 1993), 'Human-computer interaction' (HCI), and 'Computer supported cooperative work' in general. It comes as no big surprise that the first four are highly compatible with our own views. Their work, like ours, has been strongly influenced by Lucy Suchman's seminal book, "Plans and situated action" (Suchman, 1987). The "Scandinavian school" (e.g. Ehn, 1988) is based on the ideological assumption, motivated by the strong position of the trade unions in Scandinavian countries, that the people affected by a certain technology should have a say in it. We feel that this ideological assumption is not necessary, but the approach can be justified by considerations about the real world and situatedness.

The field of human computer interaction or HCI is focusing on developing computer systems with which humans can interact in natural and efficient ways. This perspective is important and should be given serious consideration in every project. However, HCI - in its traditional form - isolates the user-system dyad. Even the term "user" is somewhat inappropriate since it views the world through the perspective of the computer system. The "user" of a computer system has a job to do which implies many activities, some of which are supported through the computer. But it also requires making phone calls, interacting with a physical process, interacting with other employees, drinking coffee, going to meetings, talking to customers, etc. Viewing system development in this more global context brings new perspectives into the design process and defines new requirements for the systems to be developed. This is why the formerly rather narrow field of HCI has now, for the better part, adopted a more broad perspective, compatible with Situated Design.

Finally, CSCW has been a buzzword for quite some years now. The overall goals go in a similar direction. To our knowledge, the focus has been on providing tools. The best-known tool in this area is probably 'Lotus Notes'. We have been experimenting with 'Lotus Notes' in this project and we have come to realize that there is much more to cooperation than connecting workstation via a network. The chemistry within the project, and the entire work situation of the participants has to be taken into account. But it is very likely that within a Situated Design project, CSCW tools can be employed beneficially.

Situated Design of the energy support system

The project team

The project, we started with Swiss Paper, was funded for three years by the National Energy Research Foundation of Switzerland[4] (German abbreviation: NEFF). The scientific team, lined up by members of two independent research groups at the University of Zurich and the Federal Institute of Technology of Switzerland respectively, mainly consists of three graduate students. The academic research group is extended by two Ph.D. students acting as project managers and the two leaders of the involved research groups.

At Swiss Paper the project manager is a member of the executive board (cf. figure 1). Five managers are reporting to him, namely the line manager of TP9, the manager of the power plant, the manager of the 'Financial Computer Systems Department', the person responsible for ecological concerns of the paper mill, and an additional member of the executive board. After a year, the manager of the 'Technical Computer Systems Department' was also invited to participate in the project team meetings. Swiss Paper's CEO is not a member of the project team, but he was one of the initiators of the project.

Even though one of our main methodological concerns is to involve the end-user, i.e. the power plant operators and the workers at the production lines, none of them was a member of the project team. However, we strongly assume that the line workers are the real experts, because they decide "which button has to be pushed in which situation" - according to their knowledge and experience. They hold the operative (tacit!) knowledge we want to support with computer systems in order to enhance the quality and effectiveness of their work. So, they still remain to be the main target group of our intended process.

It is also one of our main methodological concerns to start a project by accepting the project partner's values. Unfortunately, this implied that the line workers have not been involved in the project team meetings (cf. the discussion in the section on 'successes and failures'). For the discussion of theoretical reasons why workers must be continuously involved in a project, the interested reader is referred to, for example Greenbaum & Kyng (1991).

Conclusions of the first analysis

Given this above background on the operative situation of the company (c.f. the section 'setting the stage') we can identify some problems. For the next step of Situated Design, this first analysis has to be evaluated by all members of the project team in order to find a common, more focused project goal.

Five important issues have been identified. First, there is a general lack of understanding of the interdependencies of different processes. Second, there is a lack of communication between departments. Third, there is a lack of expertise concerning the different kinds of computer systems. Fourth, data resources are not coordinated and not explained. And last, but not least, the possibilities for change are underestimated by the staff of Swiss Paper. Let us briefly discuss these points in turn.

• Lack of understanding of interdependencies and understanding of possibilities for change
Although some managers are aware of the interdependence between steam consumption and electricity production, the details are not well understood. Moreover, this insight is not generally known. But there are additional reasons that prevent operators from taking measures to save energy. On the one hand, the managers and the operators doubt that there is any way in which the energy consumption can be influenced. On the other, because of the unsatisfactory economic situation, the focus is entirely on fulfilling the customer orders. One straightforward way to reduce the peak load would be to lower the velocity of the machines. But this option is not even considered. The situation is perceived as unchangeable.

• Lack of communication between departments
Because the 'Financial Computer Systems Department' and the 'Technical Computer Systems Department' do not communicate well, there is a lack of understanding of each other's problems. Managers even explicitly refuse to communicate. As we have seen, one of the results of this lack of communication is that nobody is willing to assume the responsibility for the interface between the MIS and the real-time systems.

There is also a lack of communication between the energy consumers (the production lines) and the energy producer (power plant). Let us illustrate this point with an example. There is an official guideline that emergency situations at the production lines have to be reported by phone to the power plant operators. As opposed to the official policy the TP9 line manager does not allow his workers to make this call. The explanation given by the manager is that at this very moment he needs all his workers to get the machine back to normal. There is no time to lose, least of all to make a phone call which is considered unnecessary, anyhow. This argument illustrates the general environment. Although the manager of TP9 and his colleague at the power plant often have lunch together, they do not really understand each other's reasoning. It seems that current function-oriented hierarchical organizational structure does not encourage the communication. At one of our project meetings the TP9 manager explained his motivation for the ban on phone calls to his managerial colleague - apparently for the first time. It is obvious that if the energy costs are to be reduced the knowledge about the actual energy situation has to be improved, which implies that the communication between the energy producer and the consumers has to be intensified.

• Lack of knowledge about computer systems
There is strong evidence that there is a lack of knowledge about the company's computer systems (hardware and software). There is a general reluctance to touch anything that might interfere with the real-time system. For example, even a simple operation like extracting data from the real-time system

is considered a delicate matter. Let us again explain this point with an example. In order to learn more about the work of the TP9 workers, we observed them on several occasions during our investigation. We compared statistical data about the process with our own observations. This task was very tedious because the data was only available in printed form. Several reasons were given for this problem. First, the 'Technical Information Systems' staff justified this obviously unsatisfactory situation with the expected costs for reprogramming the complex signal processing systems to make electronic data available. Second the real-time systems do not have the capacity to store this mass of data. And because the real-time systems are principally isolated they cannot resort to the MIS for this purpose.

- **Uncoordinated data resources and a lack of system integration**

An enormous amount of potentially useful data is generated continuously. Thousands of signals are produced by the control systems at TP9 every tenth of a second. However, they are not systematically recorded. Between the consumers and the supplier there is practically no exchange of data. An exception are the alarms indicating that the paper strip has been torn. But these data items do not indicate, e.g., the location at which the paper strip was torn in the production line. This location could be used for estimating the expected time of interruption. It would also be of interest to power plant operators to know about the so-called grade (gr./m2) of the paper under production. This would enable them to better approximate the expected reduction on steam consumption during an interruption. Most important of all would be data about the current steam and electricity consumption of every single production line. The current rate of steam consumption is available to workers at TP9 but not to the power plant operators. Moreover, the actual power consumption is totally unknown.

- **Unclear ideas about "autonomy" of workers and processes**

An important topic at the project meetings was the question of how autonomous the workers at the paper production line are in their decisions. To what extent can they influence energy consumption? Some experts in the company maintain that there is hardly any "autonomy" for the workers at the production lines. They claim that technology is so dominant that the production processes have no independence, and that there is no room for individual decisions. Others claim that the opposite is true, arguing that there are, for example, clear differences in quality between shifts. The argument for limited autonomy was primarily made by leading managers who normally do not directly interact with machinery. The line manager of TP9 agreed with this opinion although he is concerned with instructing his workers day by day. He also made contradictory statements with respect to the "autonomy question". Actually, he was the one who made a proposal to improve the awareness of the TP9 workers about the actual power consumption. He suggested to install a kind of "light column". This "light column" should visualize the current electricity consumption of the entire production line, or of particular machines. A the moment of our first analysis the workers had no idea about the impact of their activities on energy costs.

Such contradictory situations are normally not intrinsically "bad". On the contrary, they can be fruitfully exploited. They provide an excellent starting-point for potential innovation.

The first operative steps

After a long period of discussions of the previous issues with the people at Swiss Paper, we decided to focus on the communication problem between the paper production lines and the power plant with the intermediate goal to produce a load management support system. In a first phase, the data about electricity and steam consumption should be made available and displayed in intuitively comprehensible form on a computer screen in the power plant. In this way, the energy producers should be able to handle situations of high load in the very short and intermediate term, by communicating their capacities to the energy consumers. An important aspect of load management is the assessment of the "autonomy" of the various processes: which processes can be delayed without problems (e.g. starting up a pulper, or the slitting machine). This should lead to a reduction of the peak load and thus of the electricity consumption from external providers.

The second phase then, should be a more complete energy information system. This should enable the company to perform some kind of more long-term planning, leading to a more stable energy consumption rate. Moreover, and that is an extremely important factor, it should lead to a better understanding of interrelated processes and variables, and, last but not least, of the needs of the other employees. From an organizational point of view, the hope is that this enhanced understanding will lead to a more adequate communication between the operative workers about the energy concerns of the paper mill, and finally will lead to process of continuous learning of the two working groups themselves. It is no coincidence that these objectives are quite similar with the ones which are well known in the context of 'Total Quality Management' .

Current Status of the Project

In order to define a small initial project, as required by the methodology, we engaged in a number of activities. We had a lot of discussion with Swiss Paper managers. We conducted many interviews and so-called participant observation sessions at the work places of the power plant operators and the paper machine workers. We also organized quite a few workshops with the people concerned. We produced many protocols summarizing our observations and conclusions.

Moreover, we did a lot of statistical analysis of collected data, etc. As a result we proposed two complementary projects:

Project "Power Plant"	The first is aimed at fulfilling the information requirement of the power plant operators by providing refined information about the company's energy situation. This requirement is to be satisfied by additional data transferred from the production lines to the power plant in order to enhance the "autonomy" of the operators when dealing with boilers and turbines.
Complementary Project "Production Line"	The second project is to fulfill the complementary information requirement of the paper machine workers by further data about the current energy consumption rate in order to influence the paper machine workers with regard to current and expected energy costs.

At a project meeting it was decided to pursue the first proposal to begin with. The hypothesis that load management could be improved if more data about future energy demands were available, was considered to be plausible. The other hypothesis, namely that enhanced awareness of energy-related issues of the paper machine workers could improve the energy   situation, was met with a certain amount of skepticism.

For us, it was clear from the start that both projects would have to be realized, otherwise the intended communication support between the two parties could not be fully successful. We were convinced that cultural changes would also be required. The intention was to promote and support this cultural change by means of computer technology, rather than by "preaching".

Project "Power Plant" in progress

The goal of project "Power Plant" is to support the load management task at the power plant. The idea is to provide more data about expected demands of steam and electricity. Remember that currently, the power plant is only re-acting to production lines demands. It tries to satisfy every request. This means that the boilers and turbines have to be controlled in such a way that every demand can be satisfied in a short time. This control strategy is certainly not optimal with regard to energy consumption. Being ready for any kind of change implies having, e.g., two boilers running continuously although one boiler could supply the current energy demand. But two boilers running simultaneously typically have lower efficiency coefficient characteristics than one boiler alone.

This situation is to be improved by providing three sorts of data:
1. *Energy data*: Data about the current steam and electricity consumption of each single production line and each single paper machine respectively.
2. *Process data*: Data about the current process situation, such as the velocity of the paper stream, the type of paper (i.e. the grade), an indicator signaling a torn paper strip, and the location where in the paper machine this has happened. The aim of this indicator is to forecast the time of interruption depending on, for example, the place where the paper strip was torn. In forecasting, it is always a difficult task to determine the relevant factors. The necessary data must, of course, be available for statistical analysis.
3. *Planning data*: Data about the production planning, such as "which grade of paper ("quality") should be produced when and by which paper machine?". Together with the second sort of data, statistical data can be calculated - once more - forecasting the consumption of steam and electricity depending on, for example, the paper grade and the velocity of the paper machine.

At the moment no algorithm or statistical procedure is known (yet) to make the predictions. As we have discussed, the interdependencies of the various subsystems and the dynamics are very complex. Even the weather, the quality of the pulp, and the staff can have an influence on energy consumption. And there may well be other unknown factors. But the operators have a lot of experience - there is a lot of distributed 'tacit knowledge' present. Giver the right kind of data, the operators will be able to optimally bring to bear their experience in the current situation. One crucial condition is that the workers do communicate with their colleagues about the particular circumstances and potential future developments. Together, they have a higher chance of being successful because every individual taken for him or herself knows too little. Additionally, we could say that a lot of knowledge about the energy management task is only "alive" and reachable if it is actively communicated during and with respect to the current situation and therefore shared by all involved experts, power plant operators and paper makers, a clear case of 'socially shared knowledge'. And this is compatible with our original design goal, namely to optimally exploit human expertise.

In addition, on the basis of statistical data, we expect to better understand the relationship between velocity, paper quality, and steam consumption. With enough empirical data a more sophisticated paper production planning process could be realized. Given this additional information, the distribution over the three production lines could be carefully planned in order to minimize energy costs.

At the moment project "Power Plant" is in the implementation phase. Among other things, we are evaluating possible human-computer interfaces in collaboration with the power plant operators. In the discussions with the operators, there are already new ideas popping up which were not present before we started the project. We take this to be an indication that the methodology is beginning to work - even before the first small system has been installed.

Complementary Project "Production Line"

The further analysis of project "Production Line" and its realization is deferred until after a first re-evaluation of the project "Power Plant". We are convinced that the full benefits of the project

"Power Plant" will only become obvious if the project "Production Line" is also realized. We hope that through the implementation of the first system, the motivation to develop the second one will also increase. For example, the paper maker must be able to compare similar situations to each other, so he can test the influences on energy cost, e.g. when he changes the velocity of the paper machine, and learn for future times. The ultimate idea is to develop a so-called "expenses tracking system" (cf. Zuboff 1988). The idea is not to totally automate a seemingly well-defined task, but rather to support the learning process of the individual workers and of working groups. This objective should be reached through the implementation of the "expenses tracking system", because it provides the necessary data and supports the communication between the workers involved. To us (the computer scientists, or better: work place designers by means of computer technology), the main goal is not to find the "right" data structures and their "correct" algorithmic relationships, but rather to learn and to experiment what implementation, what design has the highest value with respect to the organizational goal. Because this kind of work place design is understood with respect to its intrinsically social nature, it must start and regularly be re-evaluated on an empirical basis.

Presumably the production line workers would need data about the power plant and the other production lines. Moreover, they would need support from the experts at the power plant to interpret the data. Imagine that there is evidence of an impending expensive electricity peak. The normal reaction is to lower the velocity of the machinery. If the paper machine operator communicates with the power plant operator they might decide that, this single time, it would be unreasonable to slow down, because this would set off a highly complex dynamics that might make matters even worse. Of course, such a conclusion can only be made by the experts based on a analysis of the situated circumstances.

It is crucially important to involve those concerned into the design process in order to determine the information requirements. The adequacy of the data that is put at the operators' disposition is an empirical question. But note that the needs of the operators change over time because in the real world, there is always change. One important type of change is the introduction of a new artifact (here: new software or new computer system). As a result the situated interpretation of the data changes, too. These changes may in turn induce requirements for new or differently presented data.

In addition to the information requirements about the energy costs, we found that some emergencies at the power plant should be communicated to the energy consumers. For example, a serious emergency that rarely occurs is when the power plant is no longer able to produce enough steam. If the consumers do not reduce their steam consumption, they run the risk of a total power plant breakdown. A total breakdown would result in a loss of at least half a million dollars because of a production interruption for at least eight hours and high repair costs. Currently, the workers at TP9 do not fully understand the importance of such considerations.

Successes and Failures

At the moment we are not able to report successes and failures of a finished project, because it is still in progress. We will simply report some of our experiences so far.

First of all there is the fact that the cost for project "Power Plant" is US $ 100 thousand compared to an estimated savings in energy cost of US $ 250 thousand per year. These figures are based only on an estimate of potential improvements due to a more optimal working point of the boilers and turbines. The estimate does not yet include returns, due to a reduction of the electricity peaks. Overall we predict that with the realization of project "Power Plant", 2.5 % of the actual energy consumption can be saved.

Another positive effect is that since our project was launched, the issue "energy" has become an important topic at Swiss Paper. Here is an episode that illustrates the point. Once we were interviewing operators at the power plant during their normal work. Accidentally the advanced gas turbine had a serious crash. The influence of this crash on the production lines was so strong, that the paper strips were torn. As pointed out, the power plant operators were not used to receiving phone calls from the paper machine workers. Of course, the paper machine workers did not know anything about the reason for this incident at the time. But this time the operator whom we were just interviewing, received calls from two of the paper production lines. Both callers were telling him about their own accident, as it had been demanded from them for a long time. After responding to the calls the operator showed us his honest surprise, assuring us, that these had been the first calls for months. This episode happened about one month after we had conducted regular interviews with employees at the production lines.

As is typical of user-centered methods, Situated Design is to involve those concerned from the very beginning. In this way, discussions about visions (like the energy topic) and about their concrete work situation can be initiated. These discussions should be continued when we, the university partners, leave the company. The new computers and the newly developed software will still be there and have to be maintained and enhanced. The process which has been initiated during the project has to "survive" our involvement in the cooperation.

Partly, this strategy has been successful. It has been successful because of the TP9 line manager. He was the person who created the idea of the "light column", an indicator of the electricity currently consumed by the paper machine. It was thought of as an actual "light column" because it should have a strong presence in the workers control room, indicating the importance of its message. Somehow it was the starting point of project "Production Line". This kind of involvement is necessary if our methodology is to work.

Partly, our strategy has not been successful. Our aim to involve the front line workers into the decision process has failed so far. Even though they participated in our interviews and the workshops, none of them were permanent members of the project team. Additionally, most members of the project team were asked by the management to participate. They had no choice. As a consequence, not all the participants were very motivated. Moreover, the unfavorable economic situation was not conducive to a positive mood. These are all reasons why progress was relatively slow. We hope that this situation will change in the future.

On the other hand there is the story of how the load management support system got off the ground. It was necessary to have the data about the different boilers and turbines in the power plant control room. Some of them were missing. This required a bit of hardware (some cables, a board), and a bit of programming. Originally this was seen as a real problem. Finally, it was done by one of the operators at the power plant in a few days on the side, i.e. during his normal working hours while performing his job as an operator. The fact that the relevant energy data could now be displayed, aroused the interest of others and demonstrated that with relatively little effort, a lot can be done.

Finally, as mentioned above, the ideas about the "autonomy" of individual processes and employees were contradictory. The project made them explicit and we found that there is much more room for individual decision making than the engineers - and sometimes the operators themselves - were aware of. For example, it could be demonstrated that steam consumption, which is considered as given by the technical requirements of the production line, could be increased by the operator by nearly 50%, at least for a short period of time.

In summary, we have been confirmed in our intuitions, that with Situated Design a lot can be achieved with relatively little effort, few resources, and only small financial commitments. Given the dramatic situation of the company, the achievements seem even more relevant. We plan to finish the first phase by the end of this year. We are convinced that this will lead to a process that is mostly driven by the employees of the company. At some point, our task will only be to keep the company up-to-date on recent developments in computer science, and the continuous learning and development process will have become autonomous and running on its own. But even now, we feel that we have succeeded in being the catalysts.

Epilogue and Lessons Learned: Challenges for Project Management

Situated Design represents a challenge for project management. The traditional view is focusing on a product: the goal of an computer technology project is the development and installation of a particular product. In recent years, computer technology has been used as an enabler, as a kind of vehicle to support the restructuring of companies. But even there, a goal   state is defined as clearly as possible at the very beginning of the project. The experience with BPR ("Business Process Redesign") projects has shown that on the one hand the clear definition of the goal state is far from trivial and that it is entirely open how to achieve the goal state. The situated perspective suggests that typically the goal definition has to be adjusted as the project evolves.

Situated Design does not start with a clearly defined goal state or product specification. Rather, it starts with a vision and then tries to initialize a process. The focus of the methodology is on this process. The conviction is that innovation requires a process of continuous change and learning. This point has been made very nicely by Peter Senge in his book about the learning organization (Senge, 1990). Situated Design is compatible with this philosophy of the learning organization. One of its main goals is to support "learning" in its many forms.

But if we do not start by defining concrete goals, how should we measure progress in the project? Where are the milestones? How do we know how much the project is going to cost? How can we make a budget? How do we know how to allocate personnel to the project? If it is a process and if the goal is that the process evolves on its own, how do we ensure it is going in the right direction? How do we know what the right direction is? These questions are all justified and we must somehow find an answer for them. Otherwise, the methodology will have a hard time being accepted by companies.

At the moment we really do not have good answers to these questions. It will be particularly hard to provide quantitative measures for success. Partly we will have to rely on common sense, partly we can use tools from work psychology. If there are a few factors that are generally accepted as indicators for progress, this is a lucky coincidence. If they can be found that makes the approach much more convincing, even if improving this particular quantity may not be all that central to the overall vision. Cutting the costs through load management system is a case in point, the expenses tracking system will be another.

There is an additional difficulty. Because of the involvement of the people and because of the initial investigation of the working environment, the situation is already changed. Thus, it is hard to have an exact before-after evaluation. But our goal is inducing change.

Dialogues at all levels, intensive communication, carefully performing the evaluation step (step 4, above), will be extremely consequential for the project. Our experience has shown that this continued interaction of the management and the project developers with the user, quickly shows whether the project is going in a desirable direction. Moreover, during the process, very often many new ideas emerge. Again, measuring ideas quantitatively is very hard, but it is obvious when the atmosphere is conducive to creativity.

Coping with change and uncertainty is the main point. Perhaps the control and evaluation of a Situated Design project might require more time from both the participants in the project and the management responsible for it. But the hope is that this additional effort is more than compensated by the quality of the results: innovation does not come for free.

Computer technology, if applied wisely, might just provide the right tools for project management in rapidly changing, highly unpredictable environments. Imposing strict guidelines with the goal to make everything controllable seems to be defeating the point.

We are optimistic that courageous and innovative students and practitioners of management will take up these ideas and investigate more thoroughly the issues raised by such an approach. A prerequisite is, of course, that they accept the basic assumptions of Situated Design.

Questions for Discussion

1. Characterize the term *knowledge*!

2. What are the main points distinguishing Situated Design from traditional software engineering methodologies?

3. Where do you see the main problems of Situated Design?

4. Given the background in this case description, why do you think so many expert systems failed?

5. In your opinion, what will be the effects of an 'expenses tracking system' once implemented?

Endnotes
[1] Name changed.
[2] We prefer this term as opposed to 'software engineering' because of the too restricted meaning of the latter.
[3] Name changed.
[4] Grant-No. 356.

References
Brooks, R. A. (1991). Intelligence without Representation. *Artificial Intelligence 47,* 139-160.

Dahlbom, B., & Mathiassen, L. (1993). *Computers in Context: The Philosophy and Practice of System Design.* Cambridge, MA: Blackwell.

Dreyfus, H. L., & Dreyfus, S. E. (1986). *Mind over machine: the power of human intuition and expertise in the era of the computer.* New York: The Free Press.

Ehn, P. (1988). *Work-oriented design of computer artifacts.* Stockholm: Arbetslivscentrum.

Floyd, C., Züllighoven, H., Budde, R., & Keil-Slawik, R. (Eds.). (I992). *Software Development and Reality Construction.* Berlin: Springer.

Greenbaum, J., & Kyng, M. (Eds.). (1991). *Design at Work: Cooperative Design of Computer Systems.* Hillsdale, NJ: Lawrence Erlbaum Ass.

Heath, Ch., & Luff, P. (unpublished). *The Social Organisation of Complex Tasks: the naturalistic analysis of human conduct and computer system design.* Private collection.

Heath, C. C. and Luff, P. K. (1996). Convergent activities: collaborative work and multimedia technology in London Underground Line Control Rooms. In D. Middleton and Y. Engestrom. *Cognition and Communication at Work: Distributed Cognition in the Workplace.* Cambridge: Cambridge University Press.Kyng, M. (1991,). Designing for Cooperation: Cooperation in Design. *Communications of the ACM, 34,* 65-73.

Lamberts, K., & Pfeifer, R. (l993). Computational models of expertise: accounting for routine and adaptivity in skilled performance. In K. Gilhooly & M. Keane (Eds.), Advances in the psychology of thinking. New York: Simon and Schuster.

Landauer, T. K. (1995). *The Trouble with Computers: Usefulness, Usability and Productivity.* Cambridge, MA: The MIT Press.

McDermott, D. (I 976). Artificial Intelligence meets Natural Stupidity. *SIGART Newsletter 57,* p.4.

Müller, M. (in preparation). *Situated Aspects of the Software Engineering Process and the Work Place Design.* AI- Lab Reports, AI-Lab, Department of Computer Science, University of Zurich, Switzerland,1997

Pfeifer, R. (I996). *Real World Computing.* Unprinted lecture notes, Department of Computer Science, University of Zurich, Switzerland.

Pfeifer, R., & Rademarkers, P. (1991,). *Situated adaptive design: toward a new methodology for knowledge systems development.*   Paper presented at the Verteilte Künstliche Intelligenz und Kooperatives Arbeiten, Proceedings des 4. Internationalen GI-Kongress Wissensbasierte Systeme, Munich, Germany.

Polanyi, M. (1967). *The Tacit Dimension.* London: Routledge & Kegan Paul.

Schuler, D., & Namioka, A. (Eds.). (1993). *Participatory Design: Principles and Practices.* Hillsdale, NJ: Lawrence Erlbaum Associates.

Senge, P. M. (1990). The fifth Disci line. *The Art & Practice of the Learning Organization.* London: Century Business (Random House).

Suchman, L. A. (1987). *Plans and situated actions: the problem of human-machine communication.* Cambridge: Cambridge University Press.

Winograd, T., & Flores, F. (1988). *Understanding computers and cognition : a new foundation for design.* Norwood, NJ: Ablex.

Zuboff, S. (1988). *In the Age of the Smart Machine: the Future of Work and Power.* New York, NY, Basic Books.

Chapter 19

Business Reengineering at a Large Government Agency

Nina McGarry
PRC Inc.

Tom Beckman
Internal Revenue Service

Executive Summary

A team of consultants undertook reengineering the delivery of compensation and benefits at a large quasi-governmental agency. Benefits included six programs which accounted for several time intensive processes such as "cafeteria plan" options for individual and family health coverage, a health benefits open enrollment period where information is dispersed to assist employees in plan selection; thrift spending account; and retirement accounts. In addition to the benefits portion, a myriad of compensation programs existed. Many of these hadn't been used in years, although available to all employment levels in the agency. In all, thirteen programs were to be reengineered in a twelve week period.

A complicating factor was the structure of the organization. The organization included five senior vice presidencies, ten area vice presidents, eighty-five district managers, and many more levels of functional managers. The many levels and sheer number of vice presidents created overlapping spans of control stretching across the agency's domain with regard to people management, resulting in a negative effect on operations.

Notwithstanding some of these factors that were outside the dominion of the reengineering team, the team created its own set of obstacles. Personalities, management styles, skill levels, expectations, waffling team membership and leadership were shared concerns among the team members. However, these concerns remained largely unspoken and certainly were not resolved.

Despite what could have become a disastrous experience, the core team survived to build a telephone call center that will one day grow into a national center, handling all the compensation and benefit needs of this organization.

Background

A team of highly trained consultants was hired to direct and facilitate the reengineering process for a compensation and benefits program supporting nearly 800,000 employees across the United

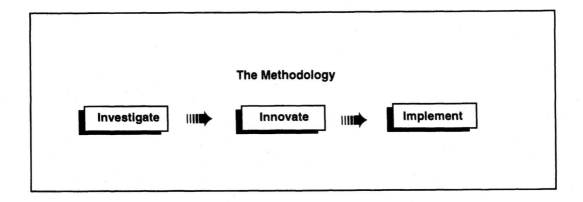

Figure 1-1: Methodology

States.

Due to the efforts of several managers, the agency had already developed a reengineering methodology of its own that became known as *The Methodology*. A merging of Hammer's *Business Process Reengineering* (BPR) (1993) with Tom Davenport's Process Innovation (1993), the company's methodology blossomed into a three phase design consisting of Investigate, Innovate and Implement. Company team members were supplied with a copy of Hammer and Champy's (1993) book and encouraged to read it during the week before the contractors reported to the assignment.

When the three contractors arrived, two of three team members had returned to their offices to finish a few last minute responsibilities prior to participating in the very exciting task of improving the workplace. One of the three team members would be absent for two more weeks. Project duration was scheduled to last three months. The task was to reengineer compensation and benefits delivery for the company's very large workforce.

The team room was a well appointed and outfitted area. Four desks outfitted with personal computers networked via a LAN to a small server. The server housed software that was used throughout the project to record progress and store data. The L-shaped room afforded a place for a conference table, removed from the work area and yet accessible should team members want to continue working and participate in meetings which may be taking place. In the conference area were several white boards and a memory-write white board.

The Reengineering Project

Overview of the Client

The client is one of the largest employers in the United States. Education levels of employees spanned a continuum from high school degrees to doctorates from Ivy League schools.

The company advocates promoting from within the organization. In fact, the company is very proactive in this regard. Many employees are promoted to higher level staff jobs for various reasons. The employee may have attended a successive number of courses, spent time-in-the-job, or has the necessary number of hours in a requisite job.

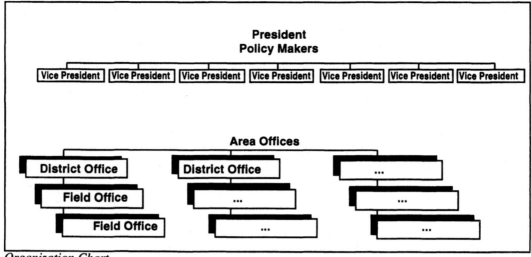

Organization Chart

Organizationally, the company has several layers of management. Following is the company's organization chart.

All policies and procedures are issued from Headquarters with information disseminated to the field offices through two other levels of management. Naturally, before the information is received in the field where policy is implemented, the news is old news, having traveled faster by "grapevine" to reach the field units. Often, Headquarters has refined and reissued the edict before it has arrived in the field initially. Sometimes the information never officially reaches the field —instead a summary is passed along from the second tier management structure. It is safe to make the judgment that communication in this very large organization is convoluted.

This helps to create a dysfunctional culture where Headquarters personnel are held as suspect by field personnel, while Headquarters views field personnel with impudence. This imbalance in relationships and conflicting perspectives played a significant role in hindering the documentation of the "AS-IS" process necessary for developing improvements.

Purpose of Study

Team members were charged with developing work flows of current processes surrounding the delivery of twelve separate compensation and benefits programs. Once documentation of current processes was complete, the team was to engage in "out-of-the-box" thinking, develop improved processes, summarize the benefits, and provide an explanation of the improved processes. And finally, the team was to develop an implementation plan for future delivery of employee programs.

To assist in the above process, the team was to use the company's in-house reengineering methodology. A binder with the methodology was presented to each team member. For further education, company team members were presented with a copy of Hammer and Champy's *Reengineering the Corporation* (1993).

Company team members were brought into the project two weeks prior to the consultants. Since most of these team members were subject matter experts and unfamiliar with reengineering methodology, they were instructed to become familiar with the company's methodology and to read the BPR textbook.

Once the consultant team arrived and most of the company's designated members were in attendance, the team began work on a variety of tasks: sorting through available information; determining who is the client and what would be investigated; assigning tasks; and the documenting the current workflow processes.

Software tools were provided to expedite process mapping. In addition to email, other software supplied included word processing, project plan, and a simulation tool. Four desks were outfitted with desktop PCs and a laptop was provided to augment any shortages. Two consultants had PCs of their own.

Immediately, the team realized that investigating all thirteen processes to the detail expected by the company within the allotted twelve week period would be impossible. In fact, one consultant was adamant that the time period allotted was totally unrealistic

An complicating factor in the reengineering effort was the knowledge that the company was recovering from a recent reduction-in-force (RIF). Many of the company team members had seen friends of theirs pushed out of jobs or offered lucrative retirement packages. The effect of the RIF was low morale, furthering suspicions toward anything Headquarters did, and cynicism of the new BPR agendas. In fact, many of the company team members explicitly stated that they wanted to participate on the project just to make sure their job was not in jeopardy—not exactly conducive to radical redesign of processes and jobs.

Organization/Hierarchy of Team

A team of highly skilled consultants was brought in to facilitate the reengineering process with the client. Additional team members of subject matter experts were selected by the company from field units. Selecting consultant team members was the responsibility of one office, while selecting company team members was the responsibility of the office managing the compensation and benefits programs.

The consultant team was selected in three steps: 1) Provide the solicitation; 2) Submit a proposal; and 3) Interview teams by the contracting officer.

Everyone on the consultant team had a master's degree or higher. The designated project leader had a doctorate in organizational behavior. Of the remaining team members, one held a master's in Human Resources, and the other had a master's in Management Information Systems.

Selection of company team members was more involved. The selection process involved company sponsors soliciting participation, waiting for a response, interviewing prospective participants, making a selection, arranging for the detail begin date and duration, arranging for accommodations, sending an acknowledgment letter to the participant and their manager. From the start, acquiring company team members was difficult.

Requests were sent to all Area Offices. The Area Offices were requested to solicit District and Field offices for recommendations. From ten Area Offices and 80 District Offices, only seven applicants were found. Of the seven interviewed, two asked to have their application rescinded. Of the remaining five, three were selected. From these three a project team leader was appointed.

The selected team members were considered subject matter experts in compensation and benefits. All three had worked their way into their current positions. One had a college degree. The college educated person and one other person were at the same pay and responsibility level. The third member was one pay level lower and ostensibly, had less professional responsibility.

When the two teams met for the first time (the consultants and the company), only one company team member was present. Of the other two, one member was on home leave to acquire personal effects to make the stay away from home more enjoyable; the other would arrive in two weeks due to work related responsibilities which precluded BPR participation.

Although only one company member was present, the team began its mission — to document current delivery processes for the compensation and benefits programs.

The core team comprised more than just these team members. To manage the project, a company project team leader was appointed. In addition to the company appointed project team leader, the consultant team also had its designated team leader — as determined by the contracting officer. Furthermore, the sponsors also designated a project team leader. The team consisted of six present members, one member in route, one member who dropped-in, and three project leaders.

It's no wonder that from the beginning ownership of the program was confusing. While the consultants were instructed to provide weekly reporting to their contracting officer, the company team members felt allegiance to their Headquarters manager — the one ultimately responsible for their jobs. To add to the mixed bag, the Headquarters designated project team leader was also the manager responsible for one of the programs to be reengineered.

One of the project teams first tasks was to introduce itself to the management team. The management team was selected by the contracting officer and the sponsoring organization. The management team consisted of interested parties from the legal, information technology, labor union, accounting, and payroll divisions in the company. Although none of the management team were vice presidents, they were only two levels removed from the policy makers, and were therefore considered influential.

Regrettably, as the BPR team discovered later, these same management team members were management team members for nearly all BPR projects undertaken by the company. What resulted was a lack of freshness and enthusiasm for redesigning the processes. What occurred was a reluctance to give credence to another BPR project.

Sponsors for the team communicated via the Headquarters project team leader. On two occasions team members were able to make presentations to the sponsors. These mock presentations were requested so that the sponsors could anticipate questions and avoid any potential difficulties with senior management. It was made very clear that access to the sponsors was only through the Headquarters project leader.

Building the Project Plan

As was stated earlier, the team began the project feeling pressed for time. The breadth of the exploration, the size of the organization, the limited resources available to the team added to the sense of desperation. From the outset, the team knew that to understand the processes, visits would have to be made to field units.

However, before anything could be approved, including travel, the contracting officer had to receive a project plan. Although the entire team was not yet assembled a project plan had to be devised. Only two of the six team members had computer experience. The most computer-experienced team member was tasked with completing the project plan on available project scheduling software.

Attempts were made to develop cohesive team behavior in order to capture the steps necessary to successfully complete the project. From the onset, it was very difficult to get the group to focus. The team was seeking a leader and several had stepped forward to claim the role. Attempts to develop a timeline without facilitation from the designated group leader were cumbersome.

Furthermore, clear comprehension was lacking regarding the BPR process. The group proved unable to develop a project plan and schedule, issues were discussed again and again, absent members caused reluctance to commit to any timeline, and drop-in leadership by the sponsor designated project leader was disruptive.

Atempts at decision making resulted in one of the team members stating that the team should wait until the sponsor designated project leader arrived in order to win approval. The sponsor designated project leader was unpredictable in arrival times, limited in the amount of time spent with the group, and nearly always recommended reviewing alternatives.

The team agreed to address milestones. What were the immovable dates? For one, three Management Review Board (MRB) meetings were mandatory. Is it reasonable or responsible to schedule a meeting when there was nothing to report? And, by the way, one team member was still missing.

Three dates were selected from the remaining calendar. The sponsor project team leader agreed to take the lead in securing a time, place and forwarding announcements to the MRB members. A timeline for these activities was created. As responsibilities started to be assigned, the team became aware of other tasks that had to occur in order to prepare for the MRB meetings.

It was understood that at the first MRB meeting the team would present its scope and charter as well as propose a plan of action to investigate the AS-IS delivery process. However, the team also realized that to acquire a full understanding of the processes, a variety of offices would have to be visited. In addition, to fully understand the processes, visits would have to be made to management centers in other parts of the country. A considerable amount of travel was mounting. Placing travel on the project timeline shortened even further the remaining time for the full project.

Despite the team's perceived schedule, the contracting officer insisted that his schedule also must be met. Milestones on the contract officer's time line which directly impacted the first three weeks of project work included an MRB meeting, conducting team building exercises for two days, and initiating change management. All of these activities are reasonable as long as nothing slips prior to these tasks. Our team, however, was still missing a team member. We had yet to define our scope. Definition of scope and charter was delayed because one team member was adamant that the project could not be finished in the allotted time frame. Team morale was slipping fast.

Teambuilding

Team building finally occurred well into the project. As a matter of fact, the team was six weeks into the project. During the prior six weeks, we had acquired three new team members — two were designated as advisors. Team members had very strong feelings towards these new members. Two were viewed as agents spying for other divisions.

By the time the team building activity was undertaken, the consultant team leader had been removed from the job, a new consultant team leader had been designated, the sponsor project team leader realized that more attention needed to be spent on this BPR effort, a new team member from one of the very political regions was assigned, and two additional team members arrived from another division within the company. Team composition had expanded to ten.

The team was told to participate in team building exercises. The exercises were completed off-site, away from the office and phones. We were encouraged to wear casual clothes. Prior to scheduling the sessions, each team member had to complete a lengthy personality test survey. The results would be presented at the session. The team building exercises consisted of visualization, dividing into teams, developing a vision, brainstorming relationships, and reviewing survey results.

To say the team was cynical would truly be an understatement. We were civil during the first session. When it came to presentation of personality survey results, the team became very disjointed. The recommendation of the analyst was to display the team survey results so that each member would better understand how to interact with other team members. Several team members were receptive to this idea. Several team members were adamantly opposed to the whole idea of personality tests and particularly opposed to having the results posted on the wall for all to view. As a result everyone went home with his own results and never shared the outcome with each other.

In some strange way we did coalesce. The team yelled because an intruder to our group. The intruder told us we were ill and instructed us on how to cure our illness. Many of the members felt pressured to select an allegiance to one group or another. Hurt feelings continued that stemmed from the quick dismissal of the previous consultant team leader. The new consultant team leader began with numerous obstacles to overcome from the consultant team as well as the company team. And now during this team building exercise we were to discover the blocks and overcome the barriers.

Documenting the AS-IS Process

Early on, the initial five team members determined that in order to acquire a fair and comprehensive perspective of the full spectrum of programs, local viewpoints and process variations would have to be addressed. Therefore, geographic locations, size of organizations, and political sensitivity would influence any process mapping that would occur. Immediately, the team set-about identifying locations to visit.

The team split into three subteams based on geography. One team would focus on the West/Northwest area, another team would direct its attention to North/Northeast, and the third team would focus on the South/Southeast. In each area, a team would visit a large, medium and small installation. And at each site, compensation and benefits delivery processes were to be mapped. The intent was to discover a best practice process being used in the field which would shorten the lengthy delivery time frame.

In all, eighteen sites were visited. However, selecting eighteen sites took well over two weeks. In a task scheduled for twelve weeks, one fourth of its duration was already spent. Additionally, site selection had to be modified as two sites were considered excessive travel and removed from the list. Further, the one team member still not on site had refused to travel to certain locations causing reassignment of travel plans. And one more wrench, one team member refused to travel on weekends further delaying completion of site visits.

Nevertheless, the team now felt as though it was moving in a direction. The consultants developed a list of questions to be used as a guideline while visiting the sites. Instructions were to map the delivery process and timelines at the site host, and bring back the data and reconvene as a team. The trip was scheduled for six days, analyzing and summarizing data was allotted three days, and further discussion one day. The team was on a roll.

Each site was contacted by telephone and a follow-up letter was sent securing a time and date and delineating the purpose of the meeting. The members set off on their investigation. Prior to making travel arrangements, the core team members met with Headquarters subject matter experts who were not on the team to map their perspective of the delivery process for each of their respective areas of expertise. Three days were devoted to this endeavor with four hours allocated to each area of expertise. A Headquarters review process was included.

Just as the team was to embark on its lengthy and extensive travel, two Headquarters experts raised doubts regarding the consultant team leadership. These experts felt that their processes were not adequately captured, and that this was undoubtedly the result of poor information exchange. The core team members agreed to not use Headquarters processes as a talking point while on travel but rather would conduct a full field investigation.

Midway through the trip, the North/Northeast team was informed that a new team member would be joining them in New York City. The remainder of the trip would be made with this new member.

All teams were instructed to let the company team member ask the questions while the consultant team member captured the data using the authorized process mapping tool. All team members were told to reassure the host sites that this was purely an investigation, that site cooperation and data were essential to success, and that the results would be shared with the sites. In addition, after each site visit, each team member was to jot down their impressions of the site visit, the perceived comfort level of participants, any other observations worth sharing.

When the teams reassembled it became apparent very quickly that everyone used a different data collection methodology, that not everyone completed an after site visit narrative, and that our consultant team leader was being released from duty.

One team used the computer technology exclusively for collecting and documenting the AS-IS process. The response from the field to this team was favorable. The site host was actively involved in creating the map, assigning time frames, and assuring the accuracy of the data. Conversation was open and comfortable. The team introduced the site team to the tool being used, proposed a method for data collection, and positioned the computer so that all could easily view what was being developed. As a result, this team's process maps needed very little modification upon returning to Headquarters.

The second team, however, did not use a computer. The company team member handwrote all processes in shorthand and came back to Headquarters and transcribed the notes. Little, if any, confirmation of processes occurred. Additionally, due to the lack of computer experience of the company team member, all notes were transcribed into a word processing program and then transcribed again into the process mapping tool. The Headquarters project team leader was a member on this site visit team and as a result, extensive amount of time was spent addressing the subject area of expertise and little information was gathered in other areas of interest.

The third team did not use a computer, nor did they take adequate notes. Each night, this team returned home. During the evening, one member would try to capture the day's events.

All told, site visits to capture field unit processing of delivery compensation and benefits was dismal. The only reliable data was from the one team that captured processes using the software tool. However, at one of their site visits, the host read from the Headquarters manual. Many of the participants at this site were unfamiliar with the required forms. It was doubtful that a process was even in place, let alone followed.

Presenting Process Findings/Recommending Change

With site visits now complete and new team members added, including a new consultant project leader, it was now time to document the AS-IS process flows. As was already mentioned, before the team set off on its journeys many of the process flows had been reviewed by the Headquarters subject matter expert. One expert was extremely dissatisfied with the process flow and refused to let it be used during the field sites.

Once the teams began amalgamating the flows from each site, many similarities were noticed. In spite of poor data collection, the team was able to document excessive forms handling, incomplete employment history which affected benefits, non-productive tasks, numerous sign-offs, and confusing forms.

Each company team member was assigned at least one benefit program to investigate. The tasks were to: develop the process flow for the assigned program, determine through telephone interviews the amount of time and resources needed for each process in the flow, develop a matrix of every step involved providing details, time allotment, cycle time and to what process the step was allocated — either service delivery, forms handling, error correction, wait state, or miscellaneous. Software tools, access to a computer attached to a network and a printer were available to each team member.

There was now about one week to prepare for the first MRB presentation. The team requested indulgence from sponsors due to team membership changes to combine the first and second MRB presentations. Therefore, the scheduled MRB agenda would address the project scope and charter, present AS-IS findings, and ask for permission to continue the reengineering project to the next phase, Innovation.

Realizing that a lot was riding on this initial MRB, the team drove themselves especially hard. Since most had no computer skills, paper and pencils were used to draw the process flows. The one computer literate member of the team was assigned the tasks of inputting all the hand-written notes into the tool, verifying the accuracy of data, making any changes as needed, creating the associated matrix of data, again verifying accuracy, printing the data, and providing a printout to each company team member. This process was repeated for the number of processes being mapped.

However, before the next process could begin, the previous team member had corrections. Furthermore, the Headquarters experts wanted to review the field work flows. As a result, additional changes were made. The outcome were process flows representing transactions in the field, sanitized by Headquarters staff, and released as original work. One flow was changed so many times that in the end it looked nothing like what the field sites reported but had a striking similarity to the steps provided in the policy and procedure manual.

The team grew more frustrated as the days progressed. Lack of computer skills prevented all but one team member from inputting data. This person assumed the role of typist. One team member made gallant attempts to help but regularly deleted files to the complete dismay of both consultant team members. One company team member cooperatively typed data only to have files lost on the network. The other company team members tried to understand what was transpiring but they had all they could handle trying to remember how to use the mouse.

In addition, presentations had to be assigned. Clamoring for who would present and what would be presented at the MRB consumed team members attention. Some expressed a desire to not present to the MRB while others felt that all company team members should make a presentation. It was determined that all company team members would present their assigned process flows. During presentation, the flow would be presented, business concerns and impacts identified.

The MRB had agreed to meet for no more than two hours. The agenda was a combination of the first and second MRB and, therefore, a lot of issues had to be discussed. It was agreed that all team members would present their process flow but only one would address the business concerns and impacts.

In hindsight, this selection was not a bad choice. Presenting the process as defined showed that 67% of a staff person's time is spent completing forms. The pie chart depicting time allotted to each step had "wow" affect. The MRB was very impressed. Another team member presented the scope and breadth of investigation. The MRB was again impressed. Finally, the consultant team leader presented the scope and charter of the project and asked the MRB for guidance on how to proceed to the innovation phase for so many programs in such a short amount of time.

The MRB agreed to reduce the number of programs investigated, extend the project to 16 weeks, and approve the scope and charter. The team was empowered to move forward with their investigation. The presentation of the next phase was scheduled for a future MRB meeting.

A celebration luncheon was held and the team rejoiced. What the team didn't realize was that the hard work was just about to begin.

Delivering compensation involved not just the agents who met with the employee, completed forms, and entered data into a computer database; it also involved payroll department's database and human resources' database. Because benefits were being addressed, union officials became very interested in the project. The sponsors insisted that everything that transpired in the room must be kept within the room. Shortly, rumors erupted and staff members worried about job security.

If there was a single pivotal point in the project it would unquestionable be at this time. It was the managers sitting at the MRB table who chose to avoid change. It was this very group who chose to not launch the experimental voyage. These managers need to learn how to improve through "personal bests"; to give up the security of tidy charts; to immerse themselves in the culture of learned willingness and individual accountability; and to gain control by relinquishing control.

Thinking "out-of-the-box"

The team allocated two days for developing an innovative approach to resolving the identified business issues. Team members became combative with each other. The consultant team was also splitting. Subcontractors were overheard questioning the abilities of team members. The creative process began with team members suspicious of each other.

A vain attempt was made to develop team cohesiveness using one of Peter Drucker's (1995) metaphors — baseball, football, or tennis teams. None of these approaches worked. The prevailing attitude among the company team members was a gross lack of trust. All members not only wanted to know, but in fact needed to know, what other team members were doing. This need was taken to extremes. If a member went to the company store to purchase supplies, a general announcement had to be made. An atmosphere of paranoia clouded the room.

The contractors moved the group towards using a groupware software tool hoping to build on other team member ideas while maintaining open communication. The reaction to the one day in which the tool was used was very disappointing. The team members opined that the groupware tool was being used as a guise to hide behind.

Next the consultants moved to a traditional, facilitated session. An agenda was proposed to the team, times for each segment were agreed upon, a timekeeper was responsible for keeping the schedule, and work began. A combined total of four hours was allocated to the process. Two hours in one afternoon, a night to think things over, and another two hours the following morning were agreed upon. In this brief span of time, the team worked cohesively. All goals and objectives were met. This was undoubtedly a rewarding time the team spent together.

Upon conclusion, the team had created its mission statement. Using the existing mission statement, expanding upon this theme to incorporate new found knowledge from field visits, the team developed a thorough and comprehensive mission that everyone agreed upon.

When the group moved to consider ideas for providing *customer-first* service, the euphoria dissipated. If a similar company was mentioned, nearly every voice from the company would claim that processing couldn't occur that way because "they aren't like us." Even though it was emphasized that the intent is not to emulate but to extrapolate best practices and make them better, the team members were in disagreement. In reengineering, it is the responsibility of the consultant to recommend what the "to be" conditions ought to look like, without spending much time understanding the reasons for the "as-is" conditions. The credo of reengineering is to forget what you know about your business and start with a clean slate to "reinvent" what you would like to be. After an additional two hours the team decided to put future consideration to rest. The team report would address the mission statement and leave the process vision untouched.

Developing an Implementation Strategy

During the next phase, the team had completely dissolved to the point where polarized groupings occurred. The sides split among those who were a certain grade level or higher, those who were males or females, those who were contractors not from the West coast, and an infinitesimal number of other groupings.

With time running out and many tasks remaining, the contracting team decided the best approach for them was to create and sell. As a result, one contractor was given the task of creating an implementation plan. This contractor was selected because of the perceived acceptance by all team members. The task was to investigate and document financial rewards and risks associated with automating compensation processing.

The contractor worked over the weekend developing formulas for implementing a plan. Never mind that the plan had not been agreed upon. This was a doable plan from the contractor's perspective. The contractor felt confident that what he would propose would be endorsed by company team members.

Instead, what transpired was two days of coaching the contractor in how to develop an implementation plan. The first hurdle was assessing the business impact. Who would be affected, how to account for change, and the cost of implementing a change management plan were just a few of the oversights. In the end, the three contractors spent all night before the final MRB meeting throwing together a plan, designing graphic representation, and attaching language for the 9:00 a.m. presentation.

Last and Final Phase

The final outcome was no surprise. The company was dissatisfied with contractor performance. The contractor was dismayed by the persistent resistance of team members from the first day. One company member was incensed that someone else was selected as team member and took every instance to insinuate that it was a gender choice. The irony was that company team members each received a reward for their participation and contribution, but another contractor received the follow-on work.

Several attempts have been made to review the process and discuss areas of improvement. The company has been reluctant to this point. However, we believe that one day, after much consideration, the company will redress the work completed and once again begin process improvement for the benefit of their customer.

Business Reengineering Methodologies

Business process reengineering first burst on the management consulting scene in 1990 through the work of two pioneers: Michael Hammer (1993) and Thomas Davenport (1993). Hammer coined the term "Reengineering," while Davenport preferred "Process innovation." Originally the focus was on dramatically improving the performance of business processes. During the last three years, many practitioners have expanded reengineering to include an organization's entire business system. Occasionally, products and services were also redesigned. Infrequently, market and customer relationships were influenced or redefined.

The field's most ardent and influential proponent, Michael Hammer (1993), defined reengineering as "The fundamental rethinking and radical redesign of a business process to achieve dramatic improvements in critical measures of performance." Beckman has expanded this definition as follows: "The fundamental rethinking and radical redesign of an entire business system to achieve dramatic improvements in critical measures of performance and customer value." This definition embodies the most important concepts in reengineering:

• Fundamental Rethinking:
   ■ Means challenging existing assumptions and biases, and reformulating the business strategy

■ Not just accepting existing perspectives and culture, and existing markets and customers
- Radical Redesign:
    ■ Means creating innovative designs by applying IT, creative thinking, and best practices
    ■ Not just incrementally improving the existing system
- Entire Business System:
    ■ Means redesigning most components such as product, service, process, management, IT, expertise, and workforce
    ■ Not just redesigning the process
- Dramatic Improvements:
    ■ Means achieving measureable gains of at least 50% in organizational performance and customer value
    ■ Not just 10 – 20% gains in organizational performance

Fundamental Rethinking

The first concept in the definition involves two types of fundamental rethinking. Hammer's (1993) "Thinking outside–the–box," challenges habitual and comfortable thought patterns and actions based on rules, policies, assumptions, biases, and culture — and replaces them with a new attitude that promotes learning, creativity, and receptiveness to new ideas.

The second type of fundamental rethinking involves strategy. According to Beckman, an organization's business strategy must be formulated before proceeding with the reengineering initiative itself. Otherwise, considerable resources might go into redesigning a product or service that the marketplace cannot support or available customers do not want. First, an environmental assessment analyzes the market/industry, customer, competitor, stakeholder, and socio/political/economic forces. Next, the following questions are answered: what industry should we be in; what customers should we serve; and what products/services should we offer. Then the overall business strategy is formulated, consisting of the grand, competitive, market segment, and resources strategies. Finally, the proposed reengineering project is examined to ensure that it is aligned with the business strategy.

Innovative Redesign

The second part of the definition, radical and innovative redesign, has been the weakest aspect of most reengineering methodologies, although it is critical to success. According to Beckman's methodology (1996), creating superior designs requires the following activities and enablers:

- Identify customer groups
- Assess customer needs, values and expectations
- Identify industry and work system component best practices
- Determine gaps between current and desired performance
- Transform customer needs and gaps into business requirements
- Surface and challenge rules, assumptions, and biases
- Apply creative thinking methods
- Apply design guidelines to each work system component
- Apply innovative IT to each work system component
- First, create an ideal or highly desirable future state and only then apply resource and feasibility

1) Customer	Needs, values, perceptions, expectations
2) Market	Competition, strengths/weaknesses, strategy
3) Environment	External influences, impact, trends, regulatory, social, political
4) Product	Features, service, price/cost, net-value-added
5) Expertise	Theory, experience, learning, innovation, problem-solving
6) Process	Inputs, resources, controls, procedures, outcomes, triggers, cycle time
7) Management	Workflow, workforce, resource, change, measures, rewards
8) Workforce	Empowerment, development, motivation
9) Structure	Organization, center of expertise, teamwork, job profile
10) Technology	Computing, communication, interfaces, tools
11) Culture	Values, beliefs, norms, biases, assumptions, expectations

constraints.
• Create several promising design alternatives.
• Develop and test designs jointly with customers using iterative prototyping

Work System Components

The third aspect of the definition involves the redesign of an entire business system. This involves more than simply mending the process or automating the work. The decomposition of a business system into its constituent components is one of the most powerful concepts of the reengineering approach. Most analysis, design, and development work is first organized around components and only later integrated during testing. With the exception of IT and the organizational culture, this compartmentalization strategy works very well.

Hammer's methodology lists four work system components:

• Processes
• Management and measurement systems
• Jobs and structures
• Values and beliefs

In addition, Hammer considers IT to be the most important enabler of design. Based on his experience and a review of the reengineering literature, Beckman's methodology (1996) consists of eleven components depicted in the table following.

Improvement Dimensions

The final aspect of the definition focuses on improvement. Organizations should look for dramatic improvements in performance and customer value in one or more of the following areas:

• Increased product functionality
• Improved customer service
• Reduced costs
• Increased productivity
• Improved quality
• Reduced cycle time
• Increased flexibility and customization
• Improved customer satisfaction
• Increased revenue
• Increased market share
• Increased learning and innovation

Hammer's reengineering methodology (Hammer and Champy, 1993) consists of four phases:

1) Mobilize (establish project governance and assign team members)
2) Diagnose (understand current system and set targets)
3) Redesign (design, test, iterate)
4) Transition (implement through pilot and rollout)

Beckman's reengineering methodology (1996) is similar although it places more emphasis on formulation strategy, determining customer and business requirements, and creating a robust, innovative, detailed design through exploring promising design alternatives:

1) Determine strategy
2) Assess current state
3) Determine business requirements
4) Develop conceptual design
5) Build and test detailed design
6) Implement design

In addition to the sequenced phases, most reengineering methodologies also include several additional continuous activities that span the life of the project:

• Manage project
• Manage change
• Ensure alignment (to the business direction and other change initiatives)

Reengineering Life Cycle

In the abstract, reengineering methodologies are rather similar to System Development Life Cycles (SDLC), and perhaps more specifically, to Systems Engineering (SE). Reengineering deals with business systems, rather than information systems (IS). Both reengineering and SDLC/SE have a structured process consisting of a series of phases, and both are often decomposed into components to more easily deal with system complexity.

The traditional SDLC decomposes into five phases:

1) Analyze
2) Design

3) Build
4) Test
5) Implement

The main distinction between the IS and reengineering approaches is the importance accorded executive sponsorship, commitment, and involvement in the reengineering model. In Beckman's Phase 1, Determine Strategy, business executives validate or create the mission, vision, and values statements, as well as explore and determine the preliminary project scope and deliver a signed charter approving and funding the project through its next three phases.

For IS, Alter (1995) proposes a comprehensive System Life Cycle model consisting of four phases:

1) Initiate
2) Develop
3) Implement
4) Operate and Maintain

A related Enterprise Life Cycle (Beckman, 1996) can be conceived that integrates four complementary business improvement methodologies:

1) Strategic Management (direction, vision, and change initiative portfolio)
2) Business Reengineering (radical change)
3) Business Process Improvement (incremental change)
4) Systems Management (operations and continuous improvement)

One of the main distinctions between reengineering and IS development is a matter of scope. Reengineering is conceptualized at an enterprise level, where IS is simply one component in a business system. In similarity, business systems are comprised of from five to 14 components; IS are usually subdivided into hardware, telecommunications, and software. Software can be further divided into several subdisciplines (Beckman, 1996):

• Numeric computing
• Symbolic computing (expert systems)
• Repositories/stores
• Human/machine interface
• Operating systems
• Perception
• Language

And expert systems, for example, can be further classified as case-based, rule-based, or model-based.

Futuristic Design Example for Workforce Management

In 1993, Tom Beckman and Rick Schreiber were asked by the IRS Assistant Commissioner for Management and Administration to develop a detailed future vision for management systems (Beckman and Schreiber, 1993) in six areas: workforce management, training, logistics management, acquisition, financial management, and management reporting (MIS). Beckman also articulated visions for workload management, assessment, research and analysis, planning and policy formulation, and management/office support. Both Beckman and Schreiber had extensive background and experience in artificial intelligence (AI) and IS applications. As a result, they developed a revolutionary design that made extensive use of AI, specifically expert systems, as well as sketching out the necessary data stores and more conventional IS applications needed to support these futuristic concepts of operation.

What is presented here is the workforce management component of this vision. The creativity of Rick Schreiber is responsible for the great majority of the ideas presented here. This example presents the reader with one possible design alternative that the case study reengineering team might have achieved if their members possessed the necessary AI and IS expertise, and if the team was receptive to such ideas.

Employee

The workforce management system of the future should empower the individual employee in a variety of ways. The employee will be able to directly enter transactions of interest. This includes changes to the payroll system (health benefit plan, amount of withholding, leave bank, bond selections, combined federal campaign, insurance, etc.). The system will serve as a focus of communications with the employee being able to examine mail (preferable with a filter) to learn of meetings, training sessions, health appointments, open seasons, job announcements, etc. Employees will have electronic access to their own personnel folders and may supplement the electronic drop file maintained by the manager.

Expert systems will provide a variety of on-line advise. These systems will enable the employee to obtain advice about benefits, payroll options, retirement planning, grievances, leave and hours of duty, EEO programs, employee assistance, individual career development, training, making suggestions, selecting an insurance program, etc. The expert systems will replace routine counselling from managers and resourcing specialists. Managers and resourcing specialists will still be available for non-routine counselling.

Employees will express their preferences for training courses, details, and job vacancies to a data base that can be examined by system programs whenever courses, details, or job vacancies occur. The job vacancy system, in particular, should be well developed. The employee will be able to express an interest in specific positions as well as in general types of positions.

The employee should also have access to limited cost and performance data for those process in which the employee is involved. This will enable the employee to establish a frame of reference for his own performance and may also serve as analytical data for improvements and, changes suggested by the employee.

The employee locator system will help communication with other employees. The locator system eliminates the need for telephone lists, voice mail, and other cumbersome locator systems. The employee will be able to key on employee name (approximate spellings also permitted), the employee's organization, or the employee's job title. The locator system will return the sought employee's telephone number, electronic mail address, voice mail number, physical location, or organizational location as appropriate.

Manager

The manager will have greater control and more current information about the workforce management programs of interest. In particular the manager will have access to current performance data, to the local financial plan, and will be not only to compare plan and performance, but will be able to make what-if assumptions and replan given changes in staffing, workload, training, logistics, acquisition, financial constraints.

System applications will enable the manager to have more direct control over functions currently performed mainly by resourcing specialists. The manager will be able to initiate some functions directly. For example, the task of developing position descriptions and justifications should be largely automated although it will require interactive input from the manager mainly to identify the major tasks to be performed in the new position. A simplified or broad-based approach to position descriptions will reduce the need to a large number of PDs. For tasks that require direct participation of resourcing specialists the system will provide systematic status and tracking information to the manager.

For a task like an accession, the manager will be able to determine from the local financial plan if the resources are available to fill a vacancy. The manager will input a request to fill the vacancy. This will cause an automated system agent to be established to control and track the status of filling the vacancy. An Expert System using rules established by the Resourcing Specialist can make routine determinations about the proper source for filling the vacancy. The expert system may routinely help the manager to consider the diversity or developmental implications of certain types of announcements. In more complicated cases, the job of making this determination will be automatically assigned to a resourcing specialist. Automated system agents can prepare the vacancy announcement, identify and notify the individuals who have expressed an interest in the specific position or in a position of that type. After a specified period of time an automated system agent may ask the manager for selection criteria, of course, after proposing some standard criteria. Another automated agent may request evaluations or may extract them from the on-line employee file. Yet another automated agent may perform a preliminary ranking of candidates for review by a review panel automatically selected from a pool of reviewers. An automated scheduling agent may schedule interviews and notify employees selected as best qualified. The status of the process will be tracked and electronically available at any time to the manager. The appropriate training, financial, and logistics subsystems will be notified.

The process described above is not completely automated but is designed to provide a controlling framework and to minimize the administrative details and tasks to which all parties currently involved are now subject.

Expert advisors provide counselling and advice to employees. This will not eliminate the consultative role of the manager, but will reduce it and will allow the manager to focus on consultations that really do require managerial input. By the same token a variety of expert advisors will be available to the manager. These advisors would include grievance advisors, awards advisors, suggestion advisors, adverse action advisors, etc.

Because routine decision making will be invested in the system it will be necessary for manager to establish rules, to set parameters, or to specify their policies. For example, a manager might specify the organization's leave policy leaving an automated system agent with the task of approving or disapproving leave and notifying the manager and the employee. Most useful to the manager will be a schedule prepared by another automated system agent which incorporates all leave decisions and graphically shows available work force or the whereabouts of all employees. Such a schedule will include details and training as well as leave.

The manager should be equipped with a variety of tools that enable analysis of staffing, training, workload, etc, within the managers area. These include standard reports periodically generated and distributed to the manger, the ability to generate special reports based on selection from a report library, and the ability to input ad hoc queries and to specify statistical analyses.

Resourcing Specialist

Many of the functions of current resourcing specialists will be invested in the system either in the form of specific programs or as expert systems. Counselling, advising, process verification, and routine decision making will be delegated to a certain extent to expert systems. Employees or managers will enter the data to initiate a process while the system will control and track each process.

Resourcing specialists will need to develop the rules for the expert consulting and counselling systems and develop the rules or criteria for the systems performing routine decision making. This includes such systems as those provide counselling on retirement, adverse actions, grievances, etc. In a sense, the rules and procedures that would go into Internal Revenue Manuals will be input to the system in the form of rule bases or other system specifications.

Related to establishing knowledge bases for expert systems is the translation of policies into system parameters. For example, definitions are needed for open seasons, cutoffs for initiating acquisition actions, the length of time a vacancy announcement is open, etc. Rather than directly compiling these into program they should be contained in separate knowledge bases. The programs using this information should refer to the knowledge base when they are run. Updating such a knowledge bases should be made through a user interface that controls access to the knowledge base and maintains a complete audit trail of updating transactions.

Resourcing specialists will be furnished with the same statistical and analytical tools provided to managers. These tools will enable a Resourcing Specialist to analyze staffing, diversity, grievance, employee assistance, benefit, or organization needs, etc. at a selected organizational level. Resourcing specialists will also have access to the same planning and scheduling system available to managers.

The resourcing specialist will still have a role to play in a variety of semi automated processes. For example, although many parts of the accession process will be controlled and performed by automated system agents, the resourcing specialist will be particularly active in processes such as recruiting. This will require establishing and having access to a variety of local and external data bases.

Since the system will contain a variety of text retrieval systems, it will fall to the Resourcing Specialist to obtain or create the electronic text to input to these systems. In the workforce. management area, text data bases will primarily include Internal Revenue manuals and policy statements. Other text files will include data from vendors about health plans, insurance, IR regulations, etc. Although information from these source will be incorporated into the advisory expert systems, the complete text may also be made available in text retrieval systems.

One of the roles played by resourcing specialists will be to enter into agreements that enable an exchange of data or the furnishing to the IRS of data bases and text *corpora*.

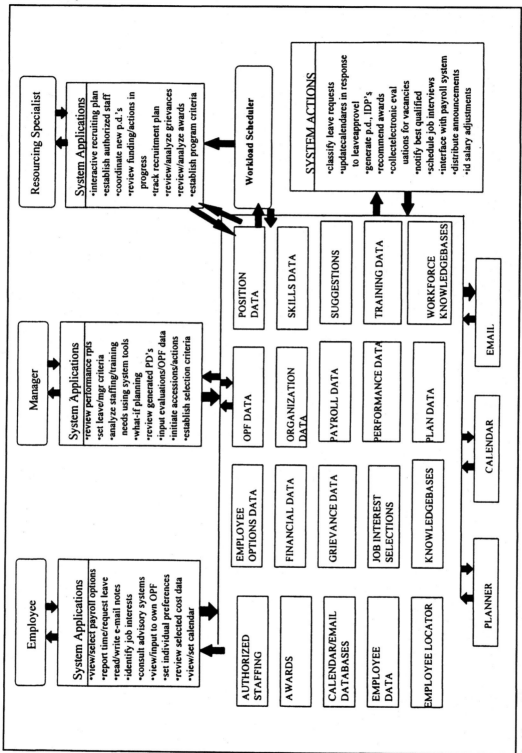

Workforce Management

Workforce Management
Major Tasks

Major Task	Support System
Requirements Planning Established authorized staffing Prepare recruiting plan Overall planning for IRS	Requirements Planning System Recruitment Plan System Requirements Planning System
Staffing Process personnel actions Identify applicant sources Verify staffing authority and funding	Personnel Action Processing System Staffing System Organizational System
Performance Maintain EPF and OPF Process awards and suggestions Advise on appraisals Career counselling	Personnel Action Processing System Performance System Performance Analyzer & Awards Processor Retirement Planner
Labor and Employee Relations Manage grievances Advice on adverse actions Track negotiations	Grievance Tracking LMR Advisor LMR Hypertext System
Employee Benefits Advise on benefit Inform about benefits	Employee Benefits Advisor Personnel Action Processing System
Position Manager Adjust organization structures Conduct desk audits Develop position descriptions Position Classifier	Organizational System Position Management System

Work Force Management

Important Data Stores

Authorized Staffing. For each organization identifies the authorized staffing.

Awards. A data base of all awards in process. Also a data base of historical data.

Calendars/E-Mall Data. Each individual will have a calendar and access to e-mail. The data bases of these programs may be accessed by a variety of other applications and system functions.

Employee Data. Employee personnel file. Contains all information about each individual employee. One sections includes evaluations and can be updated by the employee's manager. Another section includes both the managers and employee drop files. The employee drop file section permits the employee to make the manager aware of events the employee believes are significant to the appraisal process.

Employee Locator data. A data base of employees which includes all information associated with finding and communicating with the-employee including telephone number(s), electronic mail address, voice mail address, organization, office location, and current location.

Employee Options Data. A data base of options available to the employee. This data base includes the background, explanatory information about various options available to the employee.

Financial Data. The financial plan data relevant to each level of the organization.

Grievance Data. A data base of all grievances in process. Also includes a case base of historical data.

Job Interest Selections. This data base represents the interactively selected job preferences of each employee. May be viewed by employee, by preference, or by position. Enables employees to identify a variety of preferences including specific positions, general types of positions, geographical constraints, time constraints, grade level of interest, etc.

Knowledge Bases. Knowledge bases used by the various expert system programs. Organization Data. Fully describes each organizational component.

OPF. The official personnel file of data. Contains a record of all the administrative actions pertaining to each employee.

Payroll Data. A local copy of data available in the payroll system. Includes time reported, leave requested and taken, work schedule, etc.

Performance Data. Volumes and times by program, rates, errors, imported from the tax processing system. Some local data may be accessed by the employee.

Plan Data. Local planning information. Contains all information needed for local workforce planning and includes training, logistics, and acquisition data.

Position Data. Describes the major tasks associated with each position. Describes the skills requires to perform each task. Describes the training required to achieve each skill or task.

Skills Data. Data base of organizational skills. Relates skills to programs, tasks, training, and positions.

Suggestions. A data base of suggestions in progress. Includes historical suggestions that can be reviewed by an employee making a suggestion.

Training Data. Data identifying the training received by all employees. May also separately identify scheduled training, needed training, and forecasted training.

Workforce Knowledge Bases. These knowledge bases include both parameters and rules input by Resourcing Specialists. The data represents the specific policies and regulations which the workforce management process are subject to. Data in the knowledge bases is compiled into or used by other programs and expert systems accomplishing workforce management functions. Access to these knowledge bases is restricted and a completed audit trail of transactions is maintained.

Work Force Management

AI Systems

Employee Benefits Analyzer: Given data about benefit plans, prepares a graphic comparison. Reaches no conclusions, but presents a feature check list. Might require providers to submit electronic data corresponding to a number of attributes.

Employee Benefits Advisor: Presents the data analyzed by the Employee Benefits Analyzer. Responds to what-if inquiries by employees.

Employee Benefits Hypertext. A hypertext component of the Employee Benefits Advisor. In response to keywords, retrieves plan sections of selected plans.

Grievance Classifier. A case-based reasoning application. Given a series of attributes the system retrieves the past grievances that most closely resemble the described case. Can be used to play what if by assuming certain findings of facts.

Retirement Planner. Provides advise to employees on retirement questions. Uses data from the employees personnel file and from payroll as a basis for computation. Also presents a spread sheet of information to enable the employee to ask what-it questions.

Position Classifier. A mature version of the prototype in joint development by IRS and OPM. Enables a manager to classify a position. Prepares the position description and the justification.

LMR advisor. Provides a manager with advise about Labor/Management Relations (LMR) questions, for example adverse actions. Also connected to a case based reasoner which allows a manager to retrieve sanitized cases when compared to a set of described attributes. Is also connected to a hypertext scanner that returns manual sections in response to keyword selections.

Organization Advisor. Analyzes the organization structure of a selected organization in accordance with established rules of thumb. Suggests organizational changes.

Performance Analyzer and Awards Proposer. Analyzes individual performance data and compares it to peer performance using criteria defined by the manager. Suggests awards or adverse action as appropriate.

Performance Management Advisor. Used to analyze group performance. Analyzes group performance in terms of tasks performed, skills required, training received, and performance achieved. Suggests problem areas, training needs, etc.

LMR Hypertext System. Delivers text retrieval capabilities of drafts of documents currently being negotiated.

Workforce Management

Automated Information Systems

Employee Locator System. A tool used to locate employees. Using name, organization, or title, enables a user to identify an employee, determine the employee's telephone number, electronic mail address, organization, office location, etc. Can be updated by the system or by the employee. Also permits an employee to give temporary location such as on leave, in travel status, on detail, etc. information of this type should be optional.

Grievance Tracking. System to input and track open grievances. Open and historical grievances should be available for analysis by managers and resourcing specialists.

Organization System. Displays selected information about an organization. Represents the staffing and structure of each organizational component.

Personnel Action Processing System. Processes all personnel actions. Provides an interface to the Payroll and Time tracking systems. Any actions sent to the Payroll System should also be posted to the local payroll data base.

Position Management System. Supports the Position Classification System described above. Provides retrieval of position description components.

Performance System. Adds or updates information on the employee master file. Includes a set of tools for the manager including an electronic drop file. Includes a set of tools for the employee, so that the employee may see the activities for which he has been credited and allow the employee to note activities for which he should be credited. Includes the automatic transfer in of performance data, training data, details, letters of appreciation, awards, etc.

Recruitment Plan System. A system for handling block recruitments. Provides convenient facilities for a manager to initiate and track the recruitment of blocks of employees.

Staffing System. Process personnel actions. Causes new records or updated records to post to the payroll personnel system. Also provides for the tracking of actions in process. Any actions sent to the Payroll System should also be posted to the local payroll data base.

Workforce Requirements Planning System. The planning component needed for workforce management should be build on a more general planner as described below under Requirements

Planning Tools. Enables a manager to interactively develop a work plan by playing what-if. Once completed the planning system should be available to the manager for short-term replanning.

A Personnel Specialist Scenerio

Paul Schnell, a personnel specialist, signs on to his personal system the morning of January 15, 1998. His electronic mail filter identifies 2 messages with today's action date. One is a note from an automated Health Unit agent reminding him that he is scheduled for a physical examination the following day at 10:30 a.m. The other is a note from an automated evaluation-collection agent notifying him that one electronic evaluation was not received by the final action date for the Tax Market Segment Analyst vacancy announcement he is responsible for. Before taking action he checks his daily calendar and is reminded that he is scheduled at 1:30 p.m. to give a segment of a teleconference briefing/training session for a group of new compliance specialists who will be working off site. Next he checks his overnight phone log and finds that a new IRS university instructor has been unable to have his electronic deposit rerouted to a bank in the university area. Finally, he checks his work queue. He has received his periodic report on the status of hiring temporary personnel to work the image scanners. In addition there is a request from the chief of personnel asking him to analyze the problem of why the response to our temporary image scanner position is less robust that in the previous year. It looks like it will be a slow day.

Paul calls up the evaluation section of Lorraine Lento, the manager whose evaluation is late and finds this has happened on several occasions. The most recent problem was because Ms. Lento was on detail. Ms. Lento is not at her desk, but Paul leaves voice mail explaining the need for the evaluation. He wonders if this is an individual problem or a group problem? To find out he sends e-mail to a specialist who prepares SQL inquires and asks for a report on late evaluations. What is the average for the entire organization? for Ms. Lento's organization? He calls up the automated evaluation retriever agent's user rule base and enters a rule that says if Paul Schnell is the personnel specialist, and a manager has two or more late responses to a request for evaluation, and a first request for an evaluation has been sent, and a second request for an evaluation is being sent, then Paul Schnell should be notified.

Paul doesn't think the reduced number of applications indicates a problem. The increased use of co-op students and the use of 4-hour student shifts has enabled vacancy announcements to be more targeted. Hopeful, he sends another request for an SQL report to determine the average examination score of this years applicants. If he is right the score will be higher, indicating that even through the quantity of applicants is reduced, the quality of the applicants is, in fact, higher. Not to mention a reduced advertising budget. Come to think of it, it would be useful to have that score on the recruiting report. He checks the recruit file dictionary interface and finds that the data he needs is available, so he goes into the report interface and adds it to his copy of the report. Of course, he could have asked a report analyst the change the parameters, but this is an area he knows well, so he made the change himself. The new field proves useful, he will send an e-mail to the specialists and managers who might be interested in this change.

P.S. Then on to problem solving that university instructor's situation...

Questions for Discussion

1. How might reengineering and SDLC methodologies learn from each other? For example, might CMM key practices such as configuration management and requirements management be applicable to business systems? Could analysis and design of IS be improved by importing business best practices such as process design guidelines and the concept of Performance Support Systems?

2. What are the similarities and differences between reengineering and project management methodologies?

3. An ongoing problem for the IS organization is quickly getting correct and complete requirements from the users/clients. For large new systems, most clients do not know what they want until they see it. IS usually expected clients to hand over requirements without much interaction. Is this fair? Do you see how reengineering might improve requirements determination process?

4. Can IS development work be better performed in cross-functional teams? Is individual expertise and performance or collaboration the best way to go?

5. How far can a methodology be bent/modified before it "breaks"? Must a methodology be followed to the letter, or is it simply a set of guidelines and tools to be used at the whim of the developer? Should high-performing experts be forced to follow the same methodology as everyone else?

6. Do the lessons learned in this reengineering project about executive sponsorship, commitment, and involvement apply to IS projects as well? In what ways are they the same? Different?

7. How strong do you think the organizational culture is in shaping and limiting what is acceptable in terms of behaviors, values, beliefs, best practices, and innovative IT design?

References

Alter, S. (1992). Information Systems: A Management Perspective. Addison–Wesley.

Beckman, T. and Schreiber, R. (1993). *Management Systems Concept of Operations*. IRS.

Beckman, T. *Applying AI to Business Reengineering Tutorial*. World Congress on Expert Systems III.

Davenport, T. (1993). *Process Innovation: Reengineering through Information Technology*. Harvard Business School Press.

Drucker, P. (1995). *Managing in a Time of Great Change*. Truman Talley.

Hammer, M. and Champy, J. (1993). *Reengineering the Corporation: A Manifesto for Business Revolution*. Harper–Collins.

Selected Bibliography

Aaker, D. (1995). *Developing Business Strategies*, 4th ed. John Wiley & Sons.

Andrews, D. and Stalick, S. (1994). *Business Reengineering: The Survival Guide*. Yourdon Press.

Band, W. (1994). *Touchstones: Ten New Ideas Revolutionizing Business*. John Wiley.

Cross, K., Feather, J., and Lynch, R. *Corporate Renaissance: The Art of Reengineering*. Blackwell Business. 1994.

Martin, J. (1995). *The Great Transition: Using the Seven Disciplines of Enterprise Engineering to Align People, Technology, and Strategy*. AMACOM.

Tobin, D. (1996). *Transformational Learning: Renewing Your Company through Knowledge and Skills*. John Wiley.

VanGundy, A. (1992). *Idea Power: Techniques and Resources to Unleash the Creativity in Your Organization*. AMACOM.

Vollmann. (1996). *The Transformation Imperative: Achieving Market Dominance through Radical Change*. Harvard Business School Press.

Winslow, C. and Bramer, W. (1994). *Future Work: Putting Knowledge to Work in the Knowledge Economy*. Free Press.

Woodruff, R. And Gardial, S. (1996). *Know Your Customer: New Approaches to Understanding Customer Value and Satisfaction*. Blackwell Business.

Chapter 20

The Clinical Information System: A Case of Misleading Design Decisions

Gurpreet Dhillon
Cranfield School of Management, UK

Executive Summary

The case study described in this chapter concerns the introduction of a new computer based integrated Clinical Information System (CIS) into a British National Health Services Trust—the Sunrise Trust. At the time of the study most of the system modules had been developed and were being tested largely for technical aspects. The system was being introduced during a period when the organization was experiencing significant changes. It was an environment where new structures were being created and the existing ones changed. Indeed, the case study was selected primarily because of these factors. The analysis of these structures, formal and informal, provides insight into the management of information systems.

Various stakeholders in the Hospital Trust felt that a computer based information system would facilitate the change process. However the analysis and design of the system posed its own problems. The system turned out to be inflexible with respect to the core health care delivery process. It was also non–responsive to the needs of the key stakeholders. Analysis of the case shows that clearly the formal methods adopted by the system analysts fell short of determining the rapid changes required for care. In particular this was an important issue, since the context of the British National Health Services posed pressures on individual trusts to be cost effective. This resulted in long term patients being moved out into the community. However, this richness in the context was overlooked by the analysts. They developed "logical" models of the system, which ended up in being "tidy pictures of reality" and were prescriptive and utterly inflexible. Structured Systems Analysis and Design Method (SSADM) was used as a modelling tool, which amplified the rational view of decision making and information technology (IT) applications (for more details on SSADM see Downs et al., 1988).

The interpretations identified in the case show a clear mis–match between the formal models and perceptions of the system users who inevitably reflect a more informal and pragmatic approach to their own organizational realities. The analysis of the case poses a number of interesting issues. It questions the relationship between the complexity of the social relations and systems design. Furthermore it brings to the fore the paradoxical viewpoints of different stakeholders and the emergent concerns for a system analyst. The chapter also identifies the impact of an "over–formalized" information system on the integrity of an organization. In doing so it evaluates the nature and significance of social power structures in systems analysis, design and implementation.

Background

In order to gain an understanding of the wider context of organizational events and actions, it is necessary to evaluate the environment of the Trust. This is because organizational processes, structures and information systems have largely been determined by the wider contextual changes in the British NHS.

The changes in the organization of the British NHS prompted by the Griffiths report of 1983 and the Community Care Act (1990), have inspired the NHS Management Executive and the individual Hospital Trusts to reassess their information needs. These have, to a very large extent, been determined by the introduction of general management principles. Apart from matters of firm leadership and corporate structure, the question of controlling the cost and quality of the service came to the fore. This also meant that the new managers had to know what they were doing and also to have more power and control over the resources. Crucial to improved organizational performance was the need for better NHS information.

There was however a problem in judging organizational performance. Though most of the managers had the best motives, few understood the "product" itself. Consequently there was a lopsided emphasis on maintaining the efficiency of the health care delivery process as opposed to quality considerations. The health service therefore saw an increased demand for information. As Scrivens (1987) notes:

> The greed of the NHS for information has grown rapidly in the last decade because of increased pressures from the central government to increase the accountability of the service in its use of public money, to rationalize its resource allocation procedures and to maximize value for money. Recent changes in the management style of the NHS towards general management have increased further the desire for more information about the running of the health care service. The information needs of the NHS are closely related to its concerns about limited resources, increased demand for services and a lack of management in the past (p147).

In response to the increased need for information at different levels in the NHS, the NHS Management Executive formed the Information Management Group. In addition an Information Management and Technology strategy was developed. The purpose of the strategy has been to assist the Management Executive to achieve the aim of creating a better health service for the nation. The business goal of the Management Executive forms the basis of the Information Management and Technology strategy. In pursuing these goals the strategy aims to create a better health service. The Information Management Group considers that the Information Management and Technology strategy will help in realizing the strategic vision of the NHS which is to support better care and communication. The emphasis therefore is to develop such an environment, where staff use information regularly in the course of providing services. Furthermore the environment should facilitate the sharing of information smoothly, effectively and securely. If such a sub–culture develops, the NHS will see enhanced quality, responsiveness, targeting and efficiency of its healthcare service.

The responsibility for assessing the information needs has been devolved to individual units, but the NHS Management Executive has imposed some strategic thrust on developing computer based systems in the NHS. The case study described in this chapter is part of one such thrust area – the development of integrated solutions within hospitals for people with learning disabilities.

Case Description

The Sunrise Trust is a specialist one which currently provides services to approximately 1,500 people with learning disabilities. Although at present about 9,000 people feature on the District registers in the Trust catchment area, it is envisaged that between 14,000 and 17,000 people from the catchment population could be receiving services. These services are provided through four large hospitals. In the future, the Trust plans to rationalize these sites and services, and introduce a geographically dispersed community–based health service.

Organizational Structures

Health services to people with learning disability within the catchment area are provided through the "Community Mental Handicap Teams." These Teams show variation in orientation depending on whether they are run with a social services orientation or health service orientation. The Teams also vary significantly in their composition, some lack members from basic disciplines such as psychology and nursing, while others benefit from a good multidisciplinary staff complement. There are a number of districts within which these Teams operate. A majority of the Sunrise Trust's "business" comes from the districts.

In providing services, the Sunrise Trust has adopted the model of systematic monitoring, a single line of command and an integrated structure. It is evolving towards being an organization which is run by generalists rather than specialists. As a consequence there is a move towards developing hybrid staff members who know something of everyone's job. Such hybrid staff members are developed under five different directorates, viz. Nursing, Finance, Service Development, Medical and Human Resources.

The five directorates manage the health care delivery process through mutual adjustments across departments and divisions and direct supervision within specified functions. Some of the work practices at the service delivery level have been standardized and routinized, consequently it has become relatively easy to monitor them. The process of therapeutic monitoring for instance is a standardized process where drug prescriptions are checked for their compliance to very strict formal rules. However much depends on informal communication among specialties which helps in achieving co–ordination of work. Within the particular specialties of nursing and medical, the prevalent ethos is that "knowledge develops as the work unfolds." So the success of a diagnosis or a treatment plan of a patient is largely dependent upon the ability of the specialists to adapt to each other. However within each speciality, there is a significant element of direct supervision. A consultant doctor, for example, directly supervises the registrars and senior registrars.

The Health Care Delivery Process

The ultimate objective of the administrators of the Sunrise Trust is to help people move from hospitals into the community. In doing so the emphasis is to provide the best possible services to people who come to stay in the hospitals for short periods of time before being relocated into the community. In providing these services, the administration aims to develop and manage high quality specialist health care.

The health care delivery process is viewed as a dynamic system where people with mental health problems enter the hospital, are offered treatment and discharged into the community (Figure 1). The emphasis is to encourage patients to stay in the community. The health care professionals consider the advantages of this to be two fold. First, the patients are able to experience and live in a natural environment. Second, the overhead costs of a hospital are substantially reduced. Thus a concerted effort is made to treat the traditional "long–stay" patients in the community. They are only admitted to a hospital if their condition deteriorates or when they need urgent specialist medical attention. Consequently most of the patients of Sunrise Trust are being transformed into "short–stay" patients.

Health care is provided through a "service specification," which describes a service that is available for use by one or more clients. A service is made up of a number of elements called "care packages." A number of service specifications may have care packages which are common to them. The service specifications are specified in the contracts agreed between the purchasers and the providers. The Sunrise Trust views the health service as a menu in a restaurant with each dish being a care package. Dishes are chosen for customers (i.e. the care packages) to make up their meal (i.e. the service package). When a client is referred to the Trust, a needs assessment is done and an individual care plan is developed (Figure 1). The needs assessment and the subsequent care plan implementation is realized by a multidisciplinary team constituted of nurses, physiotherapist, dieticians, doctors etc. The Sunrise Trust model for service planning considers multidisciplinary teams as central to the success of the health care delivery process.

A key problem with health care delivery is the timely availability of information. This was

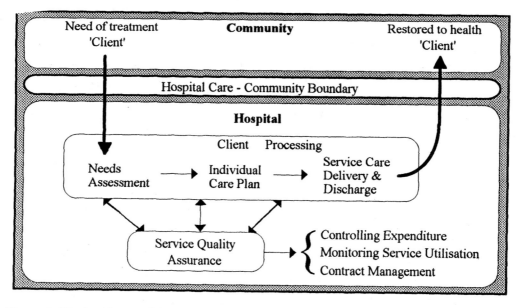

Figure 1: The health care delivery process at Sunrise NHS Trust as envisaged by the management

particularly the case in the Sunrise Trust. A computer based information system was seen as a means of filling this information gap. It was thought that such a system would not only help the Trust to adapt to the macro environment (where there is an increased pressure on the Trusts to provide precise information on its activities), but also to add value to the health care delivery process. With respect to the recent changes in the health services, the traditional health care management system had certain shortcomings. For instance it was not possible to give due consideration to isolated "encounters" which could subsequently be consolidated into health plans. It was also not possible to perform audits and assess the effectiveness of resources used. In response to such criticisms a typical integrated information system at this NHS Trust would incorporate care planning functionality in itself. Furthermore it would also allow case mix management and have clinical audit functionality. Such a system would help the Trust to adapt better to the existing environment. This facilitates the meeting of demands by purchasers to provide information for assessing the quality and effectiveness of services delivered. Such information can be drawn through a process of constant monitoring of care delivery, recording of assessment details and measurement of outcomes. This logic formed the basis of system development activities at Sunrise NHS Trust.

The Key Players

The Sunrise Trust is characterized by three distinct stakeholders groups: the clinicians, the nurses and the administrators. The Trust has experienced significant changes in the way in which the three "specialist" groups are organized. Traditionally, in the pre–internal market era, the doctors were a dominating force. This was by virtue of their clinical expertise, and practically nothing used to happen without the consent of the Consultant Doctors. Major hospital decisions were generally initiated and executed by them. The doctors' expertise prevailed because of their professional attainment. Therefore they drew power from the formal authority vested in the same role. At a formal level however there existed a "triumvirate" arrangement where a senior consultant doctor, a senior nurse and a senior administrator took formal responsibility. However, the senior doctor invariably would exercise influence over the other two members of the team. Consequently the doctor, generally of a consultant level, emerged as clear top decision maker.

Besides the system of expertise, the doctors dominated because of two other factors. First was the system of authority, which gave legitimate power (or formal power) to the role. Second was the system of politics. The system of politics generally operates to displace legitimate power (Mintzberg, 1983). However since authority and expertise lay with the same role, the system of politics further strengthened it. Thus, because of the operation of all these systems, the role exerted tremendous influence. With the changes at the national level, hospitals were amalgamated into Trusts, being headed by a chief executive. This was also the situation at Sunrise Trust. In the Trust a senior doctor has now assumed the role of a medical director and a senior nurse that of a nursing director. The role of the directors is to advise the chief executive on the various top management decisions, but the ultimate authority rests with the chief executive.

The Sunrise Trust doctors today experience increased pressures on their authority and expertise within the Trust environment. Traditionally, because they were experts in their fields, they were allowed considerable discretion in performing their tasks. This meant that most hospital work came under their direct control. Though an administrative hierarchy existed in the hospital, it had to surrender a lot of power to this elite group. The hospital functions were conducted more by mutual adjustment and less by formal bureaucratic rules. Work was carried out in small teams, members of which used to change over a period of time. This is especially true of junior doctors (Registrars), who generally come on a teaching rotation of one year duration. Different Consultants were in charge of different wards, their work being co–ordinated informally.

In the new set–up, the former authority and power of the doctors has now formally been placed in the hands of the Chief Executives. They also hold all the budget strings. Consequently the system of expertise that gave tremendous power to the doctors is also diminishing. A concerted effort is being made by the Sunrise Trust administrators to minimize the role of doctors even in the health care delivery process. The formation of multidisciplinary teams and attempts to capture the knowledge of doctors in the integrated computer based information systems are steps in that direction. The success or failure of these efforts is subject to debate, but such actions mark a trend towards a situation where the chief executive wields a lot of power and authority and is able to promote his ideologies in Sunrise Trust.

Current Status and Evaluation of CIS

Like most health care establishments, Sunrise Trust, is characterized by three professional groups: clinicians, nurses and managers. The three groups represent their own power structures in the organization. Interviews with members of the these groups revealed conflicting ideologies (i.e. organizational and professional ideologies). The doctors and nurses believed in the profession and its norms more than the new goals and objectives being enforced by the new IT infrastructure. The managers on the other hand wanted to derive business value out of the health care delivery process. Though the nurses and doctors agreed with this in principle, they had their own ideas of the manner in which this could be achieved. The doctors in particular felt that at a clinical level the system could not be utilized effectively. This was largely because the care planning module of the system was geared for "long–stay" patients. The needs of these patients are very different from those who come to the hospital for a "short–stay" (this is typically the case in hospitals for people with learning disabilities). In this respect the objective of the clinical system was clearly in conflict with the organizational policy. The National Health Service in general and the hospital in particular were striving to move the "long–stay" patients out into the community. The parent Trust was also in the process of closing three of its constituent hospitals in the next three years. Thus the need for an over–emphasis on long–stay patients seems unnecessary. The managers, though agreed that patients were being moved out into the community, were not convinced that IT system was solely geared for the needs of "long–stay" patients. Further investigations revealed that in fact the user requirement analysis was flawed. The system developers had been short–sighted in their approach and only the "long–stay" wards (which were due to be closed in the very near future) had been sampled for requirements analysis.

There is a strong likelihood that the IT system will neither contribute towards enhancing the productivity nor towards the effectiveness of the organization, rather it may make the organization highly vulnerable. This is because there is a mis–match between the actual practices and the formally designed information system. There are two contributing reasons. First, since the organization represents a split hierarchical structure (i.e. between clinicians and managers), the informal organizational norms are very weak, indicating the prevalence of an informal environment where the clinical and business objectives do not support each other. This has resulted in a remarkable difference in roles created by the formal system and as they actually exist. Second, though all stakeholders (doctors, nurses and managers) agreed that ideally the system would be a boon to the organization, there was disagreement on the manner in which it had been developed and implemented. The emergent organizational work practices were technology driven, i.e. it was the computer system that was determining the formal reporting and authority structures. Moreover, it was also forcing unrealistic informal social groupings on to the members of the organization. Since the key players were unhappy with the change process, there is the risk of the information system not being used.

An illustration

The issues related to the viability of the changes will be left for the students of politics and government. Our immediate concern here is to see, at a micro level, the factors considered in implementing an information system in the NHS Trust. To do this we have taken the issue of controlling a staff member session schedule. Controlling such a schedule poses a complex managerial situation, especially when a computer–based system is used to carry out the task. The staff scheduling module is not just another duty roistering mechanism. It gives a graphical display of the "free" and "busy" times of each staff member. This allows the service point manager to plan the use of staff effectively. However the system analysts and the designers have not related the procedures and structures so created in the technical system to the meanings and intentions of the users and the staff who are being controlled. Thus the syntactic domain so created in the computer system does not represent the semantic domain (activities of the real world). An understanding of these issues is of significant importance for the success of the information system. This will help us to decide the boundary between the formalizable and the non–formalizable aspects of the management systems, especially when our concern is with evaluating complex managerial situations. It would also be possible to prioritize the system development tasks, especially when the scale of the project is of significance.

With respect to our particular illustration, of relevance are the two roles of a service point manager and the nurse. The service point manager of the hospital is responsible for allocating work to another role, a nurse. Thus, for all necessary activities, the role of the nurse draws authority from the service point manager. The particular activity in question is to provide therapy to a specific patient. In the normal situation, a nurse would allocate (book) time for the therapy sessions and would be held responsible for the activity. With the implementation of the computer–based information system the situation has changed. Not only would the nurse be held responsible for the activities, but the time allocations, free times, number of sessions per day/week etc., would all be monitored. The computer has indeed emerged as a new supervisor.

The development of a module controlling a staff members session schedule is a typical example of a poor system specification. It should be the endeavor of the system analyst to relate the syntactic domain (i.e. the formalizable aspects of the problem) to the semantic domain (i.e. to ask the question: what would it mean in the real world?). In other words, consideration has just been given to the *form of* the problem and not to the *content*. Such a design, which concentrates on the surface structures only, not only leads to the development of systems that cause problems (e.g. staff morale) but also lack vigor. Consequently such projects are seldom abandoned.

Logical Service Specifications at the Hospital Trust

In the particular case of the information system at Sunrise Trust, the system developers and the project team regarded Trust activities as an input–output process. Therefore they considered the health care process in terms of patients coming into the hospital, being treated and then discharged into the community (also depicted in Figure 1). This conception helped in modelling the systems development tasks by using SSADM. The first phase of SSADM, analysis of the current system, identified eleven sub–systems within the hospital environment. These sub–systems interact with each other to transform patients so as to improve their learning skills. The eleven sub–systems are: Client Admission; Care Provision; Client Administration; Client Resettlement; Contract Management; Staff Deployment and Duty Rostering; Pharmacy Management; Monitor Service Quality; Staff Training and Development

Provision; Budget Management; Ward Management. In conducting the analysis of the current system, SSADM requires an analyst to investigate into problems, bottlenecks or dissatisfactions amongst users. This is an important stage since the very success of the final product may depend upon correct requirement assessment. The analysts for the integrated information system were supposedly directed by the Planning Manager to key personnel in each of the functional areas. Discussions with different people revealed that these personnel were not rightly placed to provide the required information to the analysts. Two interesting issues emerge. First, either the Planning Manager purposefully directed the analysts to these individuals or there are doubts about his competence. Second, the analysts (who were outside consultants) should have taken the initiative to define the problem domain adequately. The result of this is that though various processes had been identified, there was no consideration given to user reactions. A careful interpretation of such reactions helps in the development of a rich picture and assess the cultural and meaning content of the decisions.

The second stage of SSADM provides a logical view of the required system. The system analysts identified five core activities, *viz.*: Client Administration; Care Provision; Trust Administration; Client Resettlement; Management of Staff Deployment. The logical structure was again based on the input–output model. The underlying presumption in this case is that if the needs of individual sub-systems are being met, then the needs of the overall system are also being fulfilled. The logical view of the system has problems at two levels. First, it is based on an inadequate systems requirement, which is an output of the first stage. Second, the control transforms introduced in the data flow diagrams do not represent the real operations. The reason for this is also related to the problems in requirements analysis. Implementation of controls at this stage is a very sensitive issue. These become apparent once the system is automated. Because the nature of logical controls does not match the prevalent structures, there are problems of incoherence. This becomes clear from the structure of the "Care Provision" sub-system of the information system. The module is central to the health care delivery process and its successful operation depends on the construction of an individual care plan for each patient. However the analysts do not consider the relatedness of individual care plans and the organizational functions. The formal model for developing an individual care plan is based on the notion of choosing dishes from a hospital menu, a concept which does not consider the needs of the doctors. This notion is related to the ongoing conflict within Sunrise Trust regarding whether an individual care plan be drawn out of a ward round or *vice versa*. Such a discordance becomes more obvious in a hospital that provides care to the mentally ill. Individual care plans work well in residential wards, but those wards are being closed by the management. What would be left will be the acute wards. Consultant doctors within Sunrise Trust are of the opinion that in this new setting primacy cannot be given to individual care plans. Judgements about care plans are largely dependent on ward rounds. In fact they proposed the merger of wards rounds and care plans when considering health care provision for acute wards. The logical model of integrated information system simply considers the existence of a care plan and bases the controls (error handling routines) and security mechanisms around them. The "Care Provision" module typically is constituted of six processes: assess needs; construct care plan; plan care delivery; review care; monitor care; implement care. Each of the processes gets constant input from the individual care plans for the purpose of monitoring and control. The quality of the logical model can well be imagined since there is an over–reliance on individual care plans which necessarily do not represent the real world situation.

The second stage of SSADM also looks into the new requirements of the users. These are then included into the logical models. However because of requirements analysis problems such new needs have not been met. In one particular case the requirements of some doctors have simply been ignored. The Hospital Trust is a centre of post–graduate training of psychiatrists. The Medical Federation, that provides funding, had requested the consultants of the Trust to develop an IT infrastructure to better manage the training function. The consultants approached the project team in this regard but the

Planning Manager declined to provide any system support in the short term. The consultants could not wait for years for such a system being developed, so they bought some custom software from a vendor. Such a requirement should not have been ignored by the planning department for a number of reasons. First, since it is a user requirement it should have been considered adequately. This would have also prevented independent system developmental activities at the unit or departmental level. Second, inadequate management of the training schemes would affect the quality of the training process which in turn means that funding may have been withdrawn. This could result in loosing accreditation for the training programs resulting in the loss of manpower. Had the system analysts been aware of the consequences, they would probably have considered this new requirement more sympathetically.

Other stages of SSADM have had problems as well. The final set of formalisms selected by the users also do not represent the real environment. A feasibility study of various options for implementation was carried out and later presented to the users. Two interesting issues emerge. First, the users selected do not represent the real setting of Sunrise Trust. The ward managers involved in the study specialize in long stay residential care and non–acute illnesses. Consequently the focus of the information system is skewed in that direction. Second, the residential non–acute specialities are being relocated from hospitals to a community setting. The requirements in the new environment will be substantially different from what they are at present. The system developers have not considered this aspect. The reason is that none of the users from the acute mental illness units have been involved in selecting options for the system. The underlying intentions for such a situation are more political than indiscreet. Had the system analysts been aware, consideration would have been given to these factors. The remaining stages of SSADM though having been carried out adequately are insufficient because of inconsistency problems highlighted above.

Synthesis

A number of key issues emerge from the case. One of the main objectives of the hospital management was to make sure that the planned IT system was successful. However, as it has been made clear from the description above, little attempt was made to understand the interplay between IT and the culture of the hospital. This would have been one of the key factors determining the appropriate exploitation of technology. Clearly, the management failed to interpret the various power structures that existed within the hospital. A careful analysis would have indicated that there were a number of informal, but important, professional ideologies at play. There was a significant incongruence between various stakeholder groups which led to some disagreement on the objectives for the IT system. For example, the care planning module of the system, which is unique in terms of administrative support, was differentiated between "long stay" and "short stay" patients by each professional group. The hospital managers considered the computer system as a major investment which would yield high added value to clinical care. The doctors and nurses on the other hand were consistent in their view that "short term" care was equally important and therefore should be the focus for system usage. One interpretation of these events is the managers perception of the long term investment potential of the computer based information system, while the medical staff were looking for short term operational advantages.

A further significant interpretation of events within the Hospital is the activities associated with systems development. The traditional method of determining a requirements assessment for the users involved was very much at variance with the real organizational situation at the time. The stakeholders identified were not the people who were the main participants in implementing the IT system. Consequently, the problem domain was not accurate with the result that important processes were not developed and exploited. The tools employed using SSADM techniques were clearly inadequate in addressing the rich organizational realities involved.

Success and Failure

The purpose of this section is to relate the findings of the case study to the mainstream information systems literature. This will enable us to interpret the dominant paradigm that was at play when the clinical information system was being conceptualized, analyzed, designed and implemented. This interpretation will also help us to analyze the relative success or failure of the clinical information system.

A useful proposal for an organizational analysis of the impact of IT is offered by Kling (1987) who refers to the vulnerability of individuals who are involved with problems relating to change. This could, for example, include managers who are experiencing externally driven change and are attempting to match resources to potentially conflicting demands. Early attempts to articulate the organizational influences upon IT development were proposed by Kling & Scacchi (1982). They argued that much of the analysis of IT in organizations is narrow. The boundaries which analysts place around organizational studies often fail to capture the important social relationships which are critical for the successful development of IT. The systems developmental activities, as described in the case, illustrate this aspect. Kling & Scacchi (1982) conceptualize their approach as "discrete–entity" and "web" models of organizational analysis. For example, discrete–entity models again focus on formal-rational considerations of IT use in organizations. They do not generally consider the social context in which IT based solutions are developed, rather they concentrate on the economic, physical and component parts of the technology. With respect to the CIS case, the attitude of the Sunrise administrative staff could be termed as formal–rational.

Since the nature of IT exploitation within organizations is based on the formal–rational models, analysts tend to study only the defined and official roles specified through job descriptions, etc. They do not consider the informal social relations, for example through coalition formulation, which are common in complex organizations (Kling, 1987). The clinical information system described in the previous section is a clear example where a formal–rational perspective was taken at every stage of the project. The analysts failed to evaluate the context. Viewing organizations from a formal–rational perspective results in inter- and intra-organizational social relationships being considered as incidental. Had the analysts involved in the clinical information systems project evaluated such relationships, the system would have had been more acceptable to the various stakeholder groups. A similar viewpoint is also propounded by Kuhn & Beam (1983) who give "substantial attention to the importance and inevitability of informal organization within the formal and of making the informal work with, or at least not against, the formal." Understanding the informal aspects of an organization is of even greater significance today. This is because of the *informatization* of most activities (Zuboff, 1988). The health services sector typifies such a move. In this changed environment, where information technology has extensively been used, it is important that a multi–perspective viewpoint of organizations is developed. Morgan's (1986) work on *Images of Organisation* is one such example. In recent years Walsham (1993; 1991) has used Morgan's metaphors in studying IT usage in organizations. This has resulted in developing a good understanding of the complex managerial situations arising with an increased use of information technology.

The IT literature generally does not consider the potential of the changing priorities of managers, the different values they hold, the relative complexity or uncertainty of the tasks they perform, their dependency upon and interaction between each other and, in many cases, the influence of senior managers. Clearly there are a number of gaps in our knowledge of the impact of IT on organizations. The extent of the complexity and variety within organizations cannot easily be quantified into a finite number of contingency factors. Doing so gives a "functionalist" understanding of organizational context " where an organisation is split into two conflicting factions, management and end users. Hence the management is viewed as dominating end users and hampering their development and that of the organisation at large. A more fruitful approach is to attempt to subjectively identify issues which can be interpreted from the business processes involved. Hence, any attempt to quantify a given set of tightly defined variables can not hope to cover every eventuality. In other words an over reliance upon situational factors alone is problematic. This view has important implications for considering the impact of IT as it reflects the social actions of the managers themselves. It is these perspectives which were not considered in the analysis, design and management of the information system in the hospital case study. Consequently the "soft complexities" of the development of a clinical information system were ignored. In fact these form the basis for any successful development.

Epilogue and Lesson Learned

The case presented gives an opportunity to examine the relationship between the use of IT, the integrity of the information systems and the associated risks (see Table 1). In the case of Sunrise Trust the integrity of the organisation is in question because a flawed technical system is being implemented and is forcing a new formal structure onto the existing work practices. The findings support the theoretical notion that though information technology is considered to be a means of enhancing the efficiency and effectiveness of an organisation, in practice an inconsistent use is counter–productive (Brynjolfsson, 1993; Weill, 1993). The case study clearly illustrates the implications for information system failure when the use of IT is restricted just to the technical components (i.e. formalizable processes) of the organisation. Hence when computer–based systems are imposed onto the informal environments the wholeness of information systems is affected. As a result, organizations run the risk of system under utilization, non achievable system objectives, or even complete system abandonment.

It becomes clear that in minimizing risks, managers in organizations will have to devise appropriate ways of coping with the use of IT and hence maintain integrity of the enterprise. While there is no universal "recipe" for achieving success, IT professionals will have to evaluate the nature of the organizational environment before considering to implement any IT based solution. Consequently they will have to address issues arising at three levels: technical, formal and informal. At a technical level the choice of an appropriate technology and design methodology is very important. The use of a hard approach such as SSADM, limits the consideration of the "real world" issues. This is

	The CIS project at Sunrise Trust
Purpose of IT infrastructure	To add value to the health care delivery process.
Semantics of IT infrastructure	The IT infrastructure is interpreted differently by the various stakeholders.
Form of IT infrastructure	An integrated system where rules and procedures do not represent the "real world."
Means of achieving the purpose	By introducing a computer–based information system and expecting formal and informal work practices to adjust accordingly.

Table 1: Summary of Findings

especially the case when the problem situation is characterized by conflicting objectives (as illustrated in the case study). Equally important is choice of hardware and software which would allow interconnectability and media independence.

At a formal level an organisation needs structures which support the technical infrastructure. Therefore formal rules and procedures need to be established which support the IT systems. This would prevent the misinterpretation of data and misapplication of rules in an organisation and help in allocating specific responsibilities. If a new technology is being implemented, there is a need for a formal team which gives strategic direction to the project. Finally, a clearer understanding of the structures of responsibility, existing and new, formal and informal, needs to be developed. This would facilitate the attribution of blame, responsibility, accountability and authority (Backhouse & Dhillon, 1996).

The informal level needs to address more pragmatic concerns. It is often the case that a new IT infrastructure is presented to the users in a form that is beyond their comprehension, causing problems of acceptance. Users should be made aware of all the features and this should be supplemented by an ongoing education and training program. The emphasis should be to build an organizational sub–culture where it is possible to understand the intentions of the management. An environment should also be created which is conducive to develop a common belief system. This would make members of an organisation committed to their activities. All this is possible by adopting good management practices sensitive to formal and informal dimensions of the organisation. Such practices have special relevance in organizations which are highly decentralized and thus have an increased reliance on third parties for infrastructural support.

Questions for Discussion

1. If you were a chief executive, how would the above analysis affect your information systems related plans and policies?

2. Given the complexity of the social relations within the hospital trust, what should you as a software engineer be aware of in designing information systems?

3. In determining the success of the information system, what organizational and system design aspects should the planning manager have taken into account?

4. The case study identifies the impact of an "over–formalized" information system on the integrity of an organisation. How would you address this issue? Would you redesign the social power structures prior to systems analysis, design and implementation? Discuss.

References
Backhouse, J., & Dhillon, G. (1996). Structures of responsibility and security of information systems. *European Journal of Information Systems*, 5(1), 2–9.

Brynjolfsson, E. (1993). The productivity paradox of information technology. *Communications of the ACM*, 36(12), 67–77.

Downs, E., et al. (1988). *Structured systems analysis and design method: application and context.* Hemel Hempstead, Herts: Prentice Hall.

Kling, R. (1987). Defining the boundaries of computing across complex organisations. In R. J. Boland &

R. A. Hirschheim (Eds.), *Critical issues in information systems research.* New York: John Wiley & Sons.

Kling, R., & Scacchi, W. (1982). The web of computing: computer technology as social organisation. *Advances in Computers,* 21, 1–90.

Kuhn, A., & Beam, R. (1983). *The logic of organisation.* San Francisco: Jossey–Bass Publishers.

Mintzberg, H. (1983). Power in and around organisations. Englewood Cliffs: Prentice–Hall.

Morgan, G. (1986). *Images of organisations.* London: Sage Publications.

Scrivens, E. (1987). The information needs of district general managers in the English National Health Service. *International Journal of Information Management* (7), 147–157.

Walsham, G. (1991). Organisational metaphors and information systems research. *European Journal of Information Systems,* 1(2), 83–94.

Walsham, G. (1993). *Interpreting information systems in organisations.* Chichester: John Wiley & Sons.

Weill, P. (1993). The role and value of information technology infrastructure: some empirical observations. In R. D. Banker, et al. (Eds.), *Strategic information technology management: perspectives on organisational growth and competitive advantage.* Middletown, PA: Idea Group Publishing.

Zuboff, S. (1988). *In the age of the smart machine.* New York: Basic Books.

Chapter 21

The Managerial Challenges in the Transformation of the Danish Geodata Sector

Erik Frøkjær
University of Copenhagen

Helge Korsbæk

Executive Summary

The organizational transformations in the Danish mapping, charting and geodata sector from the mid eighties to the mid nineties are summarized. New products and possibilities raised by information technology were the driving motive behind the ambition to develop an integrated national geographical information system (GIS). The visions and commitment of key people, especially the Director General of the National Survey and Cadastre in Denmark, seem to have been decisive in this, for the government, uniquely successful development within the Danish public administration in which also private enterprises have taken part. Guidance from specific systems or organizations development methods has played no role in the process of change, and the study of the present case suggests that such guidance is of minor importance compared to professional insight, visions and leadership.

Background

The application area of concern is land surveying and geographical information systems (GIS). From an informatization point of view the measurement of land gives scope for large data systems, with intimate connection to the science of geodesy. The basic data, obtained by measurements in the field, have an indefinite lifetime. They consist of alphabetic location names, descriptions and numeric coordinates. The volume of data grows steadily as new measurements are made. Surveyors take part in the collection of new data, and ordinary people take part in the over-all process every time they use a map produced by the systems. There exists a broad variety of data that can be localized, directly or relatively, within geographical reference systems as points or areas at the surface of the earth. Such data, which can be presented in maps, are termed geodata. Computers may be used for checking and conversion of the raw data, for preparing the field work, and for converting the data for geographical information systems, e.g., in the form of maps.

Cartography and mapping have always called for the most advanced equipment and techniques for measurements and calculations, a fact connected with the importance of having correct and updated maps in societies where ownership to land and the shape of landscape are crucial in many relations, in both times of peace and of war. This application area was among the first to utilize the computing machinery when it appeared after the second world war. In Denmark, the first industrially produced computer GIER was developed in 1958-60 in a close collaboration between the research institution Regnecentralen and the Geodetic Institute (Sveistrup et al., 1976). Also today we see how mapping institutions and defense organizations in all the industrially developed countries demand the most sophisticated computing and satellite technology to produce maps adequate and convenient in a large variety of contexts.

Here we will summarize the organizational transformations in the Danish mapping, charting and geodata sector since the mid eighties until the mid nineties. The pivotal effort was the merger of three governmental mapping institutions. Based on an account of this merger given by its leading personality, Peter Jakobsen, Director General of the new National Survey and Cadastre, we will discuss what seems to be essentials in major organizational and technological transformations.

The Original Three Mapping Institutions

The three institutions involved were: the National Land Registry (Matrikeldirektoratet), the Geodetic Institute (Geodætisk Institut) and the Nautical Archives (Søkortarkivet).

The purpose of the National Land Registry from its start was to lay down two sets of facts: (a) the ownership of the land, and (b) the size, position, shape and yielding capacity (land valuation) of the individual properties. This required maps in a fairly large scale that were currently updated with changes in the circumstances just mentioned. The National Land Registry comprised in its latest analog state in the mid eighties of about 18,300 maps in scales from 1:500 till 1:4,000 covering approximately 2.9 million title numbers. In Denmark the cadastral work has traditionally been entrusted to licensed surveyors under the supervision of the National Land Registry. In the two metropolitan municipalities of Copenhagen, the cadastral administration has for historical reasons been left to the local government. In the southern part of Jutland, which was under Prussian/German administration from 1864 until 1920, the Prussian system with state-employed surveyors has until now been maintained.

The tasks of the Geodetic Institute were geodetic surveying, topographical mapping, seismological registrations, and research in geodesy and seismology. The activities of the Geodetic Institute call for the production of maps in relatively small scales with many details. The question of current updating of the maps is less urgent than for the cadastral mapping.

The purpose of the Nautical Archives was to produce and communicate nautical charts and information. Improved methods of hydrographical surveying and charting, natural changes in the sea bed, increased draft of the ships and growing attention to environmental problems have meant that surveying and charting have become permanent activities. Hydrographic charts are thus updated daily, and corrected charts are issued once or twice a year.

All three organizations can trace their roots as professional bodies many years back. Although the National Land Registry in the form it had at the time of the merger was established as late as in 1919, concurrently with a major land reform, its roots go back to the first and second cadastre of 1664 and 1844, respectively. Similarly the Geodetic Institute was set up in 1928, but the first systematic geodetic measurements were commenced in 1757 under the auspices of the Royal Danish Society of Sciences and Letters (Videnskabernes Selskab) which remained responsible for the activities until 1816. At that time the tasks were taken over by the newly established Institute for Measurement of Degrees (Den Danske Gradmåling) which in 1928 was merged with a military body, viz the Topographical Department of the General Staff (Generalstabens Topografiske Afdeling). The Nautical Archives was established in 1784 as a permanent institute to maintain nautical records and charts. It remained an independent body until 1973 when it was integrated into the newly formed Authority of the Danish Waters (Farvandsdirektoratet) which also came to include the national life saving service and the authorities of lighthouses and pilotage.

As a result of this development with long periods of basically unchanged responsibility all three bodies had cultivated their own organizational cultures. Common characteristics of these cultures are a high degree of professionalism with commitment to do thorough work, an awareness to utilize the most effective technical tools, and a consciousness about being part of a long chain of professional endeavours to produce information of great importance to the Danish society. On the other hand, the three organizations also had important cultural differences. The National Land Registry was mainly oriented towards a legalistic way of thinking, while the staff of the Geodetic Institute was characterized by scientific ideals in their approach to the work—and partly also a military approach, although the latter has been of declining importance over the last few decades. The Nautical Archives was distinguished by a marine cultural influence with great awareness towards safety in navigation and preventing accidents at sea. The Nautical Archives and the Geodetic Institute were clearly internationally oriented while the National Land Registry was nationally oriented with an open and collaborative attitude towards its many partners and customers in the Danish society. The Geodetic Institute was more self-contained, and the Nautical Archives primarily related to the marine milieus. The National Land Registry maintained a hierarchical and bureaucratic tradition, but was open to changes. The Geodetic Institute was characterized by a more individualistic or elitist tradition, although the military part of the institute was hierarchically organized. The personnel of the Nautical Archives was a much smaller group of people which had maintained a feeling of belonging to the same "family."

Of course, these remarks about the cultural differences are very general and many important aspects and individual or group related circumstances have been left out. It remains, however, that the three organizations had strongly developed and different organizational cultures, with some common characteristics. The high degree of professionalism in all the three organizations has probably served as an important background for establishing the mutual respect among each other. This state of mutual respect might be essential to succeed in bringing strong organizational cultures together.

Setting the Stage

Background and Perspectives for a Merger

The differences in the working conditions between the three institutions have tended to overshadow the one thing they have in common, namely that the results of their work are typically presented on geographical maps. In the early 1970's this was the point in a report from the National Audit Department. Closer investigations, however, seemed to prove that a merger would bring neither technical nor economic benefits. But the investigations threw light on the problems from a new angle.

Following the general development of the society, maps were increasingly being used to assist and prepare the large investments in the technical and physical infrastructure of the country, e.g. for natural gas distribution and for high capacity telecommunication networks. Furthermore, there was an increased demand for maps to support the work with environmental problems. This demand had in particular been directed towards so-called thematic maps, i.e. large scale maps with detailed information about specific phenomena only, e.g. the position of buried telecommunication cables in a densely built-over area.

The number of map producers had grown extensively to about one thousand. Out of this number half were private cable owners, building contractors, municipalities and counties, who produced maps for internal use. The total turn-over of the mapping and geodata sector in 1985 was estimated at 750-800 million DKK (one DKK compares to 1/6 US dollar) out of which different governmental institutions covered 34 percent, counties and municipalities 26 percent, and the private sector thus 40 percent. The large number of map producers called for better standardization and coordination of the production. As a result the Council for Denmark's Geographical Reference Network (Rådet for Danmarks Geografiske Referencenet) was established in 1986 on a voluntary basis.

A further aspect of the development was the increased use of geodata for planning and administrative purposes. In an application to the Finance Committee of the Parliament in December 1985 for means to begin the construction of a digital national system of cadastral maps, the National Land Registry noted that one of the important perspectives of this digitalization was to give a geographical reference to the geodata units, registered also in other nation wide information systems. This would make it possible to produce a variety of new thematic presentations in maps quicker and cheaper than before, for the benefit of many public and private enterprises as well as for citizens and the society as a whole. This was seen as a major step towards the realization of the vision about a coherent Body of Danish Maps and Charts Year 2000 (Danmarks Kortværk 2000), which would form the basis in a geographical-administrative information system, called GIS (for Geodata or Geographical/administrative Information System), see figure 1. This perspective preliminarily treated in a cross departmental committee under the Board of Coordination of Public Data Systems (Frøkjær 1985; Frøkjær and Korsbæk 1992).

The total costs of the digitalization project, i.e. the conversion of the cadastral and the topographic maps from analog to digital form, were estimated at 684 million DKK in January 1985 prices. The project includes the renewal of the system of pivot points of control (the fix point network) and the production of ortho-photos of the entire country. The expenditures, to follow over a period of 20 years, would be covered by savings and proceeds from new products. The first four years the project would demand about 400 people per year.

It is not possible here to give an appropriate review of the history and status of the geodata technology as it has developed generally or more specifically in Denmark. Readers interested in this important, but also complicated background information are referred to the basic literature, e.g. the general introduction to the concepts and techniques of GIS given by Burrough (1986). Balstrøm et al. (1994) give a thorough account of the technical and organizational status of the geodata sector in Denmark. In a following section 'Current Status of the Case' we shall report briefly about the shift in technology within the new merged geodata institution.

Preparatory Committee Work

Against the background outlined above the Minister of Agriculture, under whom the National Land Registry was placed, the Minister of Defense, under whom the Geodetic Institute and the Nautical Archives were placed, and the Minister of Finance decided to set up a committee to discuss

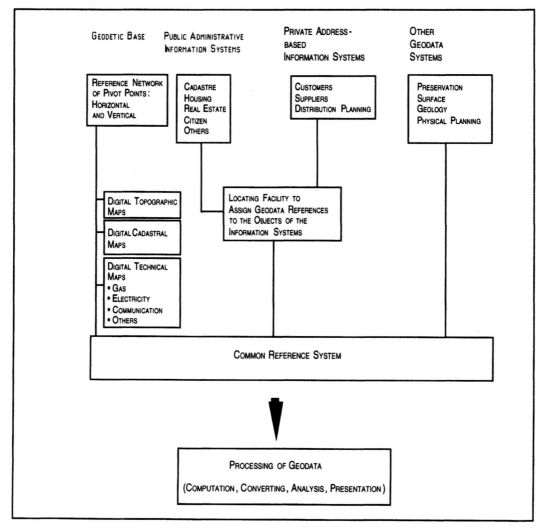

Figure 1. Schematic presentation of the Danish Geodata Information System. After Georegistergruppen (1984), see Frøkjær (1985).

and report on the following issues:

- the appropriateness of a merger of the three institutions into one new state-enterprise to be financed, as far as possible, by user payments;
- which of the present tasks should be continued by a possible new state-enterprise;
- the economic and administrative consequences of a merger, as well as the consequences for the personnel involved;
- under which field of responsibility should such an enterprise belong;
- the administrative and economic consequences of increased user payments for topographical products delivered by a government institution;
- the way of financing and the time perspective in the construction of a digitalized national system of cadastral maps; and finally,

• how the influence of the users on such a system could be ensured.

The committee submitted its report to the ministers in May 1986 (Kortudvalget 1986). Here, it is pointed out that the large number of map producers implies an unstructured distribution of tasks and authority. The total expenditure for a digitalization of the sector's information systems over the coming 15 years was estimated at 4,500 million DKK of which about 25 percent would be wasted under the present arrangement due to double administration and parallel product development (Kortudvalget 1986; p. 13). Through adequate coordination half of this misinvestment could be avoided. An uncoordinated transition to digital techniques would probably lead to a lasting inhomogenity within the entire system. This would add up to considerable misinvestments and sharply increased costs for maintenance and development because of the large variety of products. Further, it would bring difficulties for the communication between the individual systems and their interplay with other geodata related information systems.

A clear placing of the responsibility for public sector policies in the field was, however, considered to be a precondition for an efficient future coordination. Important tasks for the central government institutions were (a) to complete the building of the national reference network, (b) to computerize certain national geodata systems, e.g. the land and real estate registry, (c) to pay more attention to other public map producers, e.g. by establishing linkage facilities between public administrative information systems and the map producing systems, and, finally, (d) to promote research and development and education and guidance.

To handle these tasks the committee recommended a complete merger of the three institutions in a state-enterprise as soon as possible. The choice of ministry to be responsible for the new state-enterprise was seen as secondary compared to the more practical questions, e.g. to facilitate the integration of the different groups of personnel and the creation of a common enterprise culture. Finally, the choice of ministry should not give rise to organizational restructuring elsewhere in the ministry chosen. In the same way the appropriateness of introducing user payments would depend on a number of considerations. For instance, the total public expenditure would not be affected, if the expenditure for the priced products were to be financed, directly or indirectly, by central or local government. Another problem followed from the fact that the costs in some cases would come at a much earlier time than the revenues from the sale of products.

Case Description

The Decision of a Merger

The proposals of the committee were, by and large, followed by the government. In the autumn of 1987 the three mapping institutions were transferred to the Ministry of Housing, which was a new ministry to all the merging institutions. Peter Jakobsen, Director General of the National Land Registry, was appointed head of all three. In January 1988 the government introduced a bill on the proposed merger in Parliament, and on the first of January 1989 the new institution called the National Survey and Cadastre (Kort & Matrikelstyrelsen) was established as a state-enterprise.

As mentioned, the purpose of the merger was not to obtain direct savings, but rather to avoid excess-expenditures in the longer run. According to the comments accompanying the bill, the purpose was to strengthen the efforts of central government in the field of national surveying and cadastre, because the use of computing for surveying, production of maps and registration of information would imply that essential advantages could only be obtained through common development and use of standardized computing methods and equipment.

The new enterprise would have the following groups of tasks:

• The official functions so far executed by the three central government institutions.
• Promotion of efficiency in the field of surveying and mapping, in part to be financed by user payments.
• Coordination and development of central government research and training.
• Coordination of the total production and use of maps and geodata products in Denmark.

Referring to the status of the new organization as state-enterprise, the comments of the bill stress that its activities, as far as possible, should be based on user payments. Becoming a 'state-enterprise' in Denmark finds an economic and legal expression by introducing a net budgeting mechanism. This gives the enterprise more freedom to adjust to market needs, for instance by increasing or decreasing staff, or by cooperating with private companies without asking for approval in the ministry as long as the external budget boundaries of the state-enterprise are respected.

A considerable part of the expenditure for the new organization's official functions, as well as for research, training, and other basic societal activities, would also in the future be covered by annual government appropriations. Conversely, the new organization should be at liberty to develop and deliver special products on markets with free competition, e.g., thematic surveying and analyses based upon linkages to geodata of own or a partners' registers. Also participation in systems export activities were anticipated, because the Danish mapping and geodata sector is among the most advanced in the world.

Goals and Conditions for the New Organization

In order to form a clear opinion of the possibilities of a total digitalization of the maps used by the National Survey and Cadastre, the Ministry of Housing in 1990 set up a committee, the so-called Ten-year Committee, composed of representatives from the Ministry of Housing, the National Survey and Cadastre, and the Ministry of Finance. The committee should look into the scope for modernization and the economic prospects for the National Survey and Cadastre for the period until year 2000. In November 1991 the representatives of the Ministry of Housing presented a proposal for a four year agreement with the Ministry of Finance. This agreement had precise objectives for the period 1992-95, and more sketchy plans for the years until 2000 when the basic national system of digital maps should be ready for use.

The main objectives in the plan were:

• to adapt the organization, production, and market orientation of the National Survey and Cadastre in a manner which would comply with the needs of the users and further the coordination within the field of mapping and geodata;
• to enter agreements with other parties within the sector on future cooperation;
• to finish the reorganization of production and production methods from analog to digital form;
• to develop a new map and register concept to be the core of the future geographical-administrative information system, called GIS (see figure 1) taking into account the experiences gained from a pilot project of the county of Funen;
• to concentrate the effort in research and development on methods that would further the technological reorganization and the coordination within the sector.

According to the agreement, the fulfilment of these objectives would require the National Survey and Cadastre:

- to make the necessary investments in technical equipment and training to allow the reorganization to be technically completed before 1997,
- to finish the new map and data representation concepts to allow the digital map and geodata products of the agency and of the external users to be integrated into one coherent system of maps before year 2000 (Danmarks Kortværk 2000),
- to reduce its staff by the equivalent of 125 full time employees, i.e., about 20 percent, during the period 1992-95,
- to increase the amount of outsourcing from 28 million DKK in 1991 to 42 million DKK in 1995,
- to improve the profitability of the agency's businesslike activities by a growth in the yearly proceeds from about 50 million DKK in 1991 to about 75 million DKK in 1995, and
- to intensify the development activities, as well as the agency's statutory tasks, regarding the coordination of the public production of maps and geodata.

Further, a reorganization of the cadastral administration in the southern part of Jutland should be stepped up with a view to a privatization in 1997.

To the agreement was attached some freedom of action, primarily by virtue of the status as state-enterprise. The agency would also be exempted from general or specific savings, and the repayment of a loan granted for a pilot project was postponed till after 1995.

Current Status of the Case

The Realization of the Merger

Each of the three institutions that were merged into the state-enterprise were at the time of the merger highly specialized and their functions thus not overlapping. The natural point of departure for the new organization was therefore the establishment of three divisions matching the essential tasks of the original institutions, viz:

- a cadastral division, to be responsible for cadastral registrations and for the authorization of the licensed surveyors,
- a geodetic division, to be responsible for the overall geodetic reference network and for research in geodesy and seismology, and
- a map and chart division, to be responsible for topographic and hydrographic surveys and cartographic production.

But also three new units were set up:

- a market division, to be responsible for the coordination of marketing and pricing policy, a function necessitated by the status as state-enterprise,
- an information technology division, to be responsible for the overall computing strategy, planning, and functions,
- a finance and staff division, to be responsible for the overall financing, staffing, and planning.

The purpose of the transformations under way since the mid eighties was, as mentioned above, to save money by state and local authorities in the forthcoming process of introducing digital products and computer-based production methods in the field of geographical and cadastral information. Now, a decade later, the merger is almost completed in the sense that the identity of the old founding institutions is almost gone, and a new one is established. But great changes had taken place during the process:

- reduction of personnel by about 25%, i.e., from 717 man-years at the time of the merger in 1989 to 534 in 1994—a great part was terminated through involuntary retirement,
- several changes of the organizational structure,
- moving into one common location from 8 different locations in the Copenhagen area, proceeded by a long debate lasting almost two years, involving even the Parliament, the main point being whether or not the National Survey and Cadastre should be moved from Copenhagen to the province. The new institution stayed in Copenhagen, but moved to a new building.
- change of government pricing policy concerning maps and other geodata from no or relatively small fees for use by public authorities, to increased user financing,
- widely increased use of subcontractors in the production of maps and geodata.

The targets set up for the new organization, mentioned in the previous section have been controlled as part of the yearly planning and budgeting procedure of the National Survey and Cadastre and their fulfilment have so far been documented in the specifications to the National Budgets from 1991 until 1996. It should be emphasized that it is very unusual that targets about reducing the number of employees are actually fulfilled within the Danish public administration, although this condition very often has been stated when large investments in new information systems were granted (Frøkjær and Korsbæk 1992; pp. 42-45)

The Status of Information Technology in the National Survey and Cadastre

The merger of the three mapping institutions and the development, implementation and use of new technology within the National Survey and Cadastre might have taken place as processes independent of each other, but in practice the two processes have grown together and have supported each other. Only a few decades ago the collection, the data processing, the storage and the presentation of data with geographical information were mainly accomplished by means of paper, pencil, tape measure and tables of logarithms. The records were protocols, charts, plastic sheets, topographical maps in large scales, air photographs, notebooks and so forth. Since the sixties, the products and the production methods have been radically transformed by utilizing digitalized techniques everywhere. Satellite technology (by means of the global positioning system GPS) is used to determine the geographical coordinates of objects or of areas on or at the Earth with still higher precision obtained at reduced costs.

An essential and critical side effect of the complete computerization within the National Survey and Cadastre is that the highly complex computer systems are only understood in depth by very few people within the organization. The staff can only work when the systems and the computer networks are functioning. This situation is completely different to previously when many of the experts within the organization knew all details and limitations in every step of the data processing performed, and nearly anyone of the staff were able to find information within the manually stored records whenever needed.

Another important source of geodata information is the large, or small, information systems that public or private companies have built up in the same period of time. Many of these systems can offer new and useful information if combined and presented in thematic maps. The access to and utilization of these information systems are often complicated or made impossible because of either technical difficulties stemming from incoherent data formats and updating frequencies, or because of administrative, economic and ownership boundaries.

As a general characteristic of the technology development within the National Survey and Cadastre in the mid nineties, it might be emphasized that the organization is trying to move from the specialized and rather expensive dedicated cartographic work stations and software packages to solutions based upon personal computers and more generic standard software.

In the eighties and the nineties, a large part of the National Survey and Cadastre's resources have been directed towards the combination of the geographical data in new ways, in accordance with the ideas of GIS. An experience from this effort is that the problems with the implementation of GIS are mainly of an administrative and organizational nature and less of a technical nature. The GIS concept has demanded a higher level of interdependence among the parties involved in the specific GIS projects, and the parties have had to learn to live with more standardized solutions and accept compromises. Although GIS-products typically do not contain sensitive personal data, questions are raised about how far to go before the citizens' expectations of respect of their personal integrity will be threatened. For instance, it has been discussed whether information about the size and the facilities of people's dwellings should be made available for commercial use.

Successes and Failures

Experiences to be Learned According to the Director General

In a speech to an international audience of managers within the field of surveying and geographical mapping, Peter Jakobsen, the General Director of the new National Survey and Cadastre and the leading personality behind this merger, has given an account of the conclusions of a more general nature to be drawn from the process, without emphasizing the numerous problems and solutions that were determined by the actual Danish context which cannot be covered here (Jakobsen 1994).

What Were the Problems?

Apart from appointing a new director general, the management of the new organization consisted from the start of the combined management of the three old institutions. This management had very little experience in merging organizations and in running rather big organizations with well over 800 employees.

'The personnel was well motivated people with a large number of highly qualified professionals who took great pride in their work. However, not all were motivated for change, nor were they happy about the planned merger. The creation of the new organization meant that we all had to make changes in almost everything, and that many of these had to occur simultaneously. This created a very high degree of insecurity. However, this insecurity is a necessity when you want to change something, but you must not forget to give everybody a new sense of purpose as soon as possible, else they soon become very unmotivated.' (Jakobsen 1994)

The main areas of change were:

• Creating the new organization, the merger.
• Technological change.
• Market orientation and increased user payments.

- Outsourcing and use of subcontractors.
- Creating the tools to run a business.
- Learning about management.

Creating the New Organization, the Merger

The first task for the new organization was to create a new sense of belonging to a common organization, among both management and personnel, and to make everybody see their own efforts as being part of a common effort.

'It has taken a long time to achieve this, and it has not yet been fully accomplished. This is a very important aspect of a merger. If different parts of an organization are competing with each other rather than supporting each other, it drains the organization of its strength. In this context, it is most important that management stands united.' (Jakobsen, 1994).

What was helpful in the process was:

- to move to new locations (new buildings) even if it demanded a lot of work;
- to change 'owners' by moving to a new ministry, here from the Ministries of Agriculture and Defense to the Ministry of Housing;
- to get a possibility to assert yourself in common, vis-à-vis your surroundings, i.e. users / customers.

What prolonged this process was the long established and quite separate enterprise cultures of the original organizations, each of them positive and good in their own ways, but very different, making joint action quite difficult. As mentioned earlier, Geodetic Institute was in many ways still characterized by a combination of a military culture and an academic approach, while the National Survey and Cadastre was very close to agriculture and to a legalistic way of thinking, the nautical culture being again a quite different one. All cultures were strong and should only be replaced by one that was superior, and to create this takes time.

Another confusing issue was whether the new organization should be understood mostly as a "government authority" or whether it was better off being "a state-enterprise." *This created something of an identity crisis were the advocates for the one or the other line of thinking looked for a new "security" in promoting their views. The best thing to do in this situation is to establish new common goals for the whole organization as soon as possible. This should be done by making the whole organization participate in the process of creating these goals,'* Peter Jakobsen recommends and emphasizes the importance of making an over-all long term plan, or a *vision* of what the management want to achieve with and within the organization.

'As a manager you must dare to want to do something, and discuss it with everyone in your organization. Try to convince them of your ideas and make them believe in them too. But listen carefully to all suggestions you get and see if you can improve your vision by using them. Consider the people you are responsible for as your prime resource to reach your goals and treat them accordingly' (Jakobsen 1994).

Technological Change

As explained in the section "Setting the Stage," the driving motive for creating the new organization was the need to prepare for an ordered transformation from mainly analog to mainly digital techniques in both products and production methods within the sector. This part of the process was not so difficult, according to Peter Jakobsen. Fortunately, the National Survey and Cadastre was in a position where the financing of this change was not the main problem. *"By and large, we can say that the whole organization benefited quickly from the high level of technological knowledge and experience in its different parts,"* says Peter Jakobsen (1994).

But also here there were lessons to be learnt.

'One part of the organization had long experience in making everything themselves, not relying on standard solutions to problems. They had not much experience in co-operating with others in doing their jobs, i.e. using subcontractors. Other parts held quite opposite views. A more open mind for co-operating with others while still maintaining ones basic expertise was the result of the learning process.'

'Another problem area was to learn to live with the fact that the "best possible technical solution" is not necessarily the "best possible overall solution." The customers and even the owners, i.e. the government, can justly interfere with the decision of what "technical solutions" should be found.'

One way to handle the problem of making your maps and other products not as good as they could be is to confront "producer" and "customer" directly, making them understand the "real needs" and make the map-producer understand that he plays a part in solving a real problem for someone.'

'When changing from traditional to new technology one should realize that some skills are lost and the *concept of quality* changes with the new production methods. Changing from analog to digital methods often implies that the sense of "when things go wrong," obtained through years of experience with the traditional methods, is sometimes totally lost and has to be reinvented and understood' (Jakobsen 1994).

Market Orientation and Increased User Payments

When the National Survey and Cadastre was created, it was the intention of the government that the new organization should co-ordinate the activities of the other official producers and users of maps and geodata in order to save money for the taxpayers, and at the same time should finance more of its own activities with income from the market. The National Survey and Cadastre would have:

• to make other public authorities pay for maps and other geodata instead of supplying them almost free of charge as before;
• to make a considerable effort to familiarize all parts of the organization with the actual requirements of the customer and adapt the products in such a way that they fulfil the demand of the customer as much as possible;
• to accept the fact that you are in a competitive situation (Jakobsen 1994).

The new situation to be created was to make the organization "fight for the customer." Peter Jakobsen says:

'Here you fight with other potential suppliers of the same service, or with the customer himself if he is in a position of doing the job himself instead of paying you to do it.'

He emphazises *"that a government enterprise, even competing in a market where there are only 'potential' private competitors, is very vulnerable to accusations of unfair competition and must behave more cautiously than a private company."'* (Jakobsen 1994)

Outsourcing and Use of Subcontractors

The merging partners of the National Survey and Cadastre had always used subcontractors, but as mentioned, not with the same enthusiasm in the entire organization, and generally with very little economic consideration behind the decision of whether or not you should do the job yourself or make use of others.

As part of the general administrative reform and modernization in Denmark since the mid eighties, governmental organizations are generally obliged from time to time to evaluate whether they should still do whatever they do, by themselves, or subject the whole or part of it to public tender, in order to ascertain whether you or somebody else offer the best value for money.

The National Survey and Cadastre has subcontracted much more than before the merger. They have chosen to do so in areas where they would not compete for the job, for instance converting analog data to digital form. Also, the use of consultants, external computer programmers and systems developers was increased.

'This process has given the organization new knowledge. For instance when doing a job in-house, this is very seldom specified correctly, nor is it clarified why it is necessary and what it costs. Buying a service from somebody else will require a definition of the service so that others can understand it. The service will get a price, and its quality will be controlled. In this way, the organization can create new possibilities for using its resources more effectively. On the other hand, the organization has to accept that it might educate an external supplier to do a certain job and thereby turning him into a potential competitor' (Jakobsen 1994).

Creating the Tools to Run a Business

The National Survey and Cadastre being a state-enterprise is partly a commercial enterprise and partly a government institution. Many of the administrative tools for running such an organization have not been available in an proper form in the general governmental budgeting and accounting system, for instance tools for project planning, project budgeting and accounting, pricing etc. The commercially available tools for the private sector are not very applicable either. The National Survey and Cadastre had to develop their own internal activity planning system to support the planning of objectives, tasks and resources in a way convenient for current follow-up.

Peter Jakobsen argues that adequate management tools for private sector businesses are not the same as adequate tools for handling the demands of the political environment. The political system is often more interested in guarding the 'legality' of actions than in securing its "profitability."

When you try to manage a governmental enterprise controlled by politicians, your "best plans" will often be turned into "official demands", and you have to explain afterwards why another route of action was followed, and why slightly different goals were reached than the ones foreseen in the plan. When you are planning for the future, it is important that you realize that all planning has to adapt to changing circumstances and that continuous changes in planning are as necessary as the initial planning itself. You must therefore try to make both your colleagues and your "owners" understand that to deviate from the planned goals and routes of action can also be regarded as a success. These considerations make planning and managing of both "business" and politics at the same time very difficult, but it is important to establish some kind of system that permits you to monitor what you do to realize the goals you have set for yourself, and to establish the costs of different alternative routes of action' (Jakobsen 1994).

Learning About Management

Management in the classical governmental tradition was often understood as being a guarantee of the legality of the actions of others, and/or to oversee the quality of the process. It seldom meant setting goals, controlling efficiency, competing with others, running economic risks, or other aspects of management that are normal within the private sector. Further, he points to problems because of different management ideals in organizational cultures dominated by professionalism and cultures dominated by classical bureaucracy ideals.

'Another aspect of management in a professional world of technicians and scientists as in the National Survey and Cadastre, is that management is often considered as something inferior to the essential activities of the organization, i.e. production or research. Management is often termed "administration", partly meaning "unwanted interference" and thus taking quality out of the real work. In such cases, it is necessary to improve the art of management and make it more respectable' (Jakobsen 1994).

Epilogue and Lessons Learned

We can conclude that the modernization of the Danish mapping and geodata sector, which was planned and initiated in the mid eighties, has been successful in the sense that the strategic goals set up for the technical and organizational transformations by Parliament and the responsible ministries have been fulfilled.

It is striking both when following the actual changes through the decade, and when reading the account from the Director General of the National Survey and Cadastre, that nearly all aspects characterizing the sector, and its key enterprises, have been markedly changed. The crucial point has been the merger of the original, main mapping institutions into a new enterprise, the National Survey and Cadastre. The development of an overall understanding of the necessity of this merger within the government and the relevant ministries was an important basis for the break through.

The merged enterprise was given new departmental relations and new modes of operation as a "state-enterprise." This meant much more freedom to find the proper means to reach the overall goals. By virtue of the net budgeting procedure the National Survey and Cadastre has obtained a considerable freedom to hire the personnel they find adequate, to use subcontractors, and to engage in various commercial activities. Extensive rationalizations implied a 25 percent reduction of staff, but in the coming years a small increase is expected.

The technological changes have made it necessary to develop a new understanding of the essential quality aspects of the products and production methods. New products have been developed, for instance a variety of thematic maps and a CD-ROM based topographical information system. In this process of new thinking the customers' requirements, it was pivotal to establish a close dialog and direct collaboration between the product developers and the end-users in order to develop a mutual learning process necessary to really understand the new technical possibilities and requirements. This is in accordance with recommendations by Gould and Lewis (1985).

The process of change in this case confirms the classical understanding of technological changes in organizations expressed by for instance Leavitt (1964) and Beer (1966). According to this, development and implementation of technological changes in an enterprise require a coherent new thinking of the tasks, the organization of work, and the education and training of the people of the enterprise. In a strengthened form the same way of thinking permeates the topical ideas about business process reengineering (BPR) which can be studied from a variety of perspectives for instance in the book by Grover & Kettinger (1995). Chapter 20 of that book "Public Sector Reengineering: Applying Lessons Learned in Private Sector to the U.S. Department of Defense" by Gulledge et al. (1995) as well as Lenk (1994) is of interest for a broader discussion about the relevance and difficulties of business process reengineering within the public sector. But this is beyond the scope of the present discussion. Only it should be emphasized that, albeit this case contains ideas intimately intertwined with those found within the conceptual framework of business process reengineering, the managers of the transformation of the involved institutions have not in any way made use of specific systems or organizations development methods.

In the National Survey and Cadastre, the process of change was treated as a learning, communication, and negotiation process, both internally in the organization and externally in relation to customers, subcontractors and owners. Similar observations have been made by Curtis et al. (1988) in the study of 17 large projects involving major technological changes. These conclusions underline that the human sides of the process of change in large projects typically are the most decisive. In the present context of public administration, the relation to the political owners, viz the government represented by the Ministry of Housing and the Ministry of Finance, seems to cause special difficulties because the political system is often more interested in looking after "legality of action" and less in "profitability."

The last, and maybe the most important lesson to be elicited from the present study, is that the guiding vision of successful, large technological and organizational projects rests upon a few highly motivated people with a striking talent for leadership of people and with comprehensive professional insight in the application area of concern. These leaders have a demanding task in pushing and establishing the desired changes in a coherent and balanced way. Whether this observation is commonly accepted in the management and organization literature may be questioned, although already Schumpeter (1934) stressed the indispensability of leadership and innovative visions for economic development. More recently, this has been emphasized in some of the literature about business process reengineering, for example by Davenport (1993). Also Smith & Willcocks (1995) seem to support the lessons of our case, e.g. by emphasizing the necessity of a strategic thrust and a vision of the future. Their study also demonstrates that *'business process reengineering raises political issues that are inherent, not marginal to business process reengineering activity'* and *'IT-driven business process reengineering programmes are likely to marginalize attention to human, social and political processes, despite that these may be strong determinants of success or failure.'*

In the literature on large systems development similar conclusions about the importance of a coherent overall vision of changes and individual talent and experience can be found in works by Naur (1985), Brooks (1987), Curtis (1988) and Boehm (1991). Large technological and organizational projects are highly complex activities often on the edge of what humans can comprehend. Further, the development tasks change during their solution, partly because requirements determined by the surroundings inevitably alter in substance and priority, implying that the development processes cannot be foreseen in all essentials and therefore cannot be planned in a rational sense. Plans have to change to keep the vision in sight.

Manoeuvring in such a space of changeability requires managers and system developers with a living understanding of the vision of change. To succeed in reaching the strategic goals of the vision, managers and system developers must be given some freedom of action. Otherwise, the responsibility and commitment will soon be undermined, and it will become impossible to create what was desired. Such freedom of action does not mean freedom of external and critical evaluation of results or fulfilment of milestones, on the contrary. The present study shows many examples where Peter Jakobsen and the National Survey and Cadastre have exposed themselves actively to sharp evaluation of clearly defined milestones, especially those defined in the specifications to the National Budgets, see the section "Goals and Conditions for the New Organization."

These sides of IT projects do not seem to be sufficiently emphasized in most of the text books and in much of the research literature about systems development and management of information technology. Much of the literature leaves the reader with the erroneous impression that the success of IT projects is basically a question of following some kind of method in a systematic way. In the present case guidance from specific systems or organizations development methods has played no role in the process of change, and the study suggests that such guidance is of minor importance compared to professional insight, visions and leadership.

In conclusion, it seems to be crucial to engage leaders with a living vision about the strategic goals of large IT projects. These projects are highly complex and cannot be planned and managed in a strictly rational sense. The responsible managers must possess thorough professional insight, intuition and a striking talent for leading people. Managers with these qualities are extremely rare. This might be an important factor when trying to explain why so many large IT projects in practice have failed.

Questions for Discussion

1. Identify three conditions or factors, external to the three merging mapping institutions, that seem to have been essential for maturing the setting within which the accomplishment of the merger could take place?

2. The leading personality in creating the merger of the three national mapping institutions, Peter Jacobsen, identifies a variety of managerial tasks which he finds most crucial, for instance 'to create a sense of belonging to a common organization.' Select three of these tasks and: (a) discuss the content of the task, and how the task might manifest itself within the organization or might be expressed by individuals or groups of people; (b) identify the person or the group of persons that you consider to be mainly responsible for the fulfilment of the task; (c) discuss possibilities to find support in solving the tasks through external sources.

3. In this case we have emphasized that the vision about the objectives and the organization of the new geodata enterprise was possessed by a small number of people with one person, the general director, Peter Jacobsen, as the primary carrier of the vision. Examine whether you find similarities in other IT cases that you know of or find described in the present book.

4. Discuss which managerial tasks are emphasized in one of the text books about systems development, which is well known to you and your fellow students. Compare these tasks to those stressed in this case. Find the reference Curtis et al. (1988) at your library. Compare the conclusions from Curtis et al's empirical study of the design process for large information systems with the descriptions and the advice given in the selected text book, and the experiences described in this case. Similarly, read Smith & Willcocks (1995) and compare their guidelines for business process reengineering activity revealed from their case studies with the "lessons learned" from this case.

5. This case is primarily based upon official documents, viz governmental reports, the National Budget and public accounts, and a transcript of a speech given by the Director General Peter Jacobsen to an international audience of managers from the geodata sector. The selection and interpretation of

this material, as well as the presentation given in this case description, has been made by the two authors. They both have backgrounds in the civil service and have until the mid eighties been involved in the creation of the governmental conditions of the subsequent transformation of the geodata sector described in the case. Further, they have experience with development and evaluation of many large information systems. Discuss possible sources of misinterpretations and biases in this case description and point out ways to uncover and counterbalance the shortcomings you expect to be most critical.

References

Balstrøm, T., Jacobi, O., and Sørensen, E.M. 1994. *GIS i Danmark*, Teknisk Forlag, Danmark. In Danish.

Beer, Stafford 1966. *Decision and Control*, New York: Wiley.

Boehm, Barry W. 1991. Software Risk Management: Principles and Practices, *IEEE Software*, January.

Brooks, Jr., Frederick P. 1987. No Silver Bullet: Essence and Accidents of Software Engineering, *Computer*, IEEE, April.

Burrough, P.A. 1986. *Principles of Geographical Information Systems for Land Resources Assessment*, Claredon, Oxford.

Curtis, B., Krasner, H., and Iscoe, N. 1988. A field study of the software design process for large systems, *Communications ACM* 31, 11, 1268-1287.

Davenport, T.H. 1993. *Process Innovation: Reengineering Work through Information Technology*, Harvard Business School Press, Boston, Massachusetts.

Frøkjær, E. 1985. Om georegistergruppens forslag til opbygning af i Danmark, *Tidsskrift for Dansk Kartografisk Selskab*, nr. 5, pp. 22-29.

Frøkjær, E. and Korsbæk, H. 1992. Informatization Policies in Denmark, Chapter 3 in P.H.A. Frissen et al (eds): *European Public Administration and Informatization*, IOS Press, Elsevier, Amsterdam, 1992.

Georegistergruppen 1984. *Forslag til fælles geografisk basisregister*, Edb-samordningsrådet, Administrationsdepartementet, Finansministeriet.

Gould, John D. and Lewis, Clayton 1985. Designing for Usability: Key Principles and What Designers Think, *Communications of the ACM*, Vol. 28, No. 3, pp. 300-311.

Grover, V. & Kettinger, W.J. 1995. *Business Process Change: Concepts, Methods and Technologies*, Idea Group Publishing, Harrisburg, USA.

Gulledge, T.R., Hill, D.H., Sibley, E.H. 1995. Public Sector Reengineering: Applying Lessons Learned in Private Sector to the U.S. Department of Defense. Chapter 20 in: Grover, V. & Kettinger, W.J. 1995. *Business Process Change: Concepts, Methods and Technologies*, Idea Group Publishing, Harrisburg, USA.

Jakobsen, Peter 1994. An Experience in the Pursuit of Stability and Long Term Security through Change, speech by the Director General of the National Survey and Cadastre, unpublished, Kort- og Matrikelstyrelsen, København.

Kortudvalget 1986. Betænkning vedrørende den statslige kort- og geodataproduktion, *Betænkning nr. 1073*, København.

Leavitt, H.J. 1964. Applied organizational change in industry: structural, technical, and human approaches. In W.W. Cooper & H.J. Leavitt, eds., *New Perspectives in Organization Research*, pp. 55-71, New York.

Lenk, K. 1994. "Business Process Re-engineering": Sind die Ansätze der Privatwirtschaft auf die öffentliche Verwaltung übertragbar?, pp 27-43. In Roland Traunmüller (Hrsg), *Geschäftsprozesse in öffentlichen Verwaltungen*, Neugestaltung mit Informationstechnik, *Schriftenreihe Verwaltungsinformatik 13*, R.v. Decker's Verlag, G. Schenck, 1994.

Naur, P. 1985. Programming as theory building. *Microprocessing and Microprogramming*, 15: 253-261. Also in P. Naur, *Computing: a human activity*, section 1.4, ACM Press/Addison-Wesley, New York, 1992.

Schumpeter, Joseph A. 1934. *The Theory of Economic Development*, The Department of Economics of Harvard University, *Harvard Economic Studies Series*, Vol. XLVI, 1934. Reprinted as A Galaxy Book by Oxford University Press, 1961.

Smith, G. & Willcocks, L. 1995. Business Process Reengineering, Politics and Management: From Methodologies and Processes. Chapter 19 in: Grover, V. & Kettinger, W.J. 1995. *Business Process Change:*

Concepts, Methods and Technologies, Idea Group Publishing, Harrisburg, USA.

Sveistrup, P., Naur, P., Hansen, H.B., and Gram, Chr. [eds.] 1976. *Niels Ivar Bech - en epoke i edb-udviklingen i Danmark*, Data, Danmark. In Danish with summaries in English.

Basic documentation:

Anmærkninger II til forslag til finanslov, and Tillægsbevillingslov for the fiscal years 1989-1996.

Finansudvalgets aktstykke nr. 93, Folketingsåret 1985-86, and Finansudvalgets aktstykke nr. 296, 1991-92.

Finansministeriet, Årsberetning 1979, Administrationsdepartementet, April 1980, pp. 13-14.

Folketingstidende 1975-76. Tillæg A, column 2541-2560, København 1977.

Folketingstidende. Tillæg B, 1. samling, column 705-718, København 1989.

Folketingstidende 1988-89. Tillæg A, column 461-486, and column 487-496, København 1990.

Kort-og Matrikelstyrelsen, National Reports from the National Survey and Cadastre, København, 1992-1994.

Glossary

application - Business task or process to which an information system is or can be applied. Also refers to the information system for a particular business application.

Assembler/Assembly code - Program code written in assembly language, usually hard to understand and maintain.

backup - a copy of programs and/or files made for archival and safety purposes. The backup can represent a historical record of files/programs and be used in times of emergency to re-establish a working copy of a file or program. Backup copies should be kept in a secure, off-site location.

BPS/I coordinator - The person responsible for coordinating and facilitating BPS/I projects by working with instructor/facilitators, team members, and top managers. The BPS/I coordinator is the champion of the entire process improvement effort at Caterpillar.

business process reengineering (BPR) - A philosophy of redesigning existing business processes and activities to enhance product quality and customer satisfaction.

Business Process Simplification and Improvement (BPS/I) - A systematic methodology for analysis, design, and implementation of reengineering principles. The methodology provides the structure, techniques, and new job roles to effectively implement redesigned business processes.

Business systems planning (BSP) - A business information systems planning technique developed by IBM that defines a technology plan.

Central processing unit (CPU) - The main computational unit from which a computer derives much of its speed and power.

CGI - Common Gateway Interface; the protocol for specifying remotely invoking programs on World Wide Web servers.

Champion - Champions are transformational leaders, espousing ideologies and beliefs different than the established order, i.e., advocates of change in the organization. Champions contribute to ideological and belief reorientation of individuals in the organization. Championing processes in the organization can be rationally based, participatively based, or, alternatively, a renegade process. Further reading: Howell and Higgins (1990); Klempa (1995a, 1995b)

Change Control - The management process put in place to help manage changing requirements in the course of the Application Development Life Cycle (ADLC) process for an application. (The ADLC is the time-line describing various events in the ïbirthî of an application, from conception to implementation; this cycle is part of the five stage, top-down approach to information systems development described under Requirements Analysis.) It is rarely the case in the real world that all business needs and related applications requirements can be accurately and completely pre-specified. Business needs may change. Technology may change (usually does, and quite rapidly). Applications that must harness changing technology to meet changing business needs must necessarily change. Also, application requirements may have been insufficiently or inaccurately articulated in the first place and must be revised. Changes of any type, once a direction is agreed upon, should go through this change management process to ascertain the cost of instituting or not instituting the change so that sound business decisions about the change can be made.

Cicero - a World Wide Web based UNIX software distribution system developed at NASA Langley Research Center.

Client/server - an information system architecture that divides an application into components, placing the components on the machines that are best able to run them. For example, a client/server system might use PCs to manage user interfaces, and a mainframe for database processing. The two might be linked via a local area network.

Client-Server Application - A type of information systems application in which application processing workload is distributed between a relatively more powerful central (server) computer and multiple smaller (client) computers that can communicate with the server. Thus, the application is made up of a set of server processes that only run on the server and a set of client processes that run on the individual client stations. This strategy may be thought of as a via-media between fully centralized processing (all processing workload is performed by one central, host machine; attached stations merely act as terminals) and full decentralization (replicate all processing capability on each workstation; essentially, each station is fully functional on its own).

Computer–aided software engineering (CASE) - A set of tools to hep application developers complete the software development process more quickly and more accurately.

connectivity - the degree to which a given computer or piece of software can function in a networked setting.

Critical Success Factor (CSF) method - A business information system planning technique that identifies key business goals and strategies that must be addressed with information technology.

Customer service representative (CSR) - A Frontier employee who works directly with customers to resolve any problems with service, billing, etc.

Customer service workstation (CSWS) - A PC running software that CSRs use to perform their jobs.

Data Base Server - A kind of server in a networked computer processing environment that is solely dedicated to data base management tasks. In some circumstances, having a dedicated Data Base Server alleviates the processing burden on the Network Server ñ the latter can focus solely on applications and file sharing tasks and leave all data base processing tasks to the former. Often, a Data Base server is used as a back-end processor to a Network Server. Data base related requests are passed on by the Network Server to the Data Base Server for processing. Subsequently, the Data Base Server passes on its output to the Network Server for passing on to a client.

Data flow diagram - A graphic diagramming tool which uses a few simple symbols to illustrate the flow of data among external entities, processing activities, and data storage elements.

Data model - A conceptual framework which defines the logical relationships among the data elements needed to support a basic business or other process.

DRIVES - DRIver and VEhicle System

Dumb terminals - Typically a keyboard and screen for interacting with a computer, it does not have any computing power of its own. Dumb terminals rely on other machines, such as mainframes, to run programs.

Easel - a tool for developing GUI programs.

Electronic Commerce (EC) - The use of electronic media such as telecommunication networks for commercial transactions.

Electronic Data Interchange (EDI) - A specific type of electronic commerce which involves the exchange of electronic documents.

end-user - Person who benefits directly or indirectly from information systems and information technology. End-users use IS/IT to aid them in the conduct of the professional, managerial and technical tasks associated with their work. Some end-users have sufficient technical expertise to administer local area networks, develop programs in fourth generation languages and do some maintenance and troubleshooting.

end-user computing - computing by end-users.

Ends/means analysis - A method of determining management information requirements. Ends–means analysis uses effectiveness criteria to define outputs and specifies efficiency criteria for processes used to generate outputs.

ergonomics - the science of designing and arranging machines and tools (e.g., computer hardware) and work areas so that people find them easy and healthful to use.

Gantt chart - A diagramming tool showing the entire set of project tasks, people assigned, and estimated completion times.

Gateway - a device for connecting dissimilar networks.

Graphical user interface - an interface that allows the user to manipulate graphical objects using a pointing device. Microsoft Windows and IBM's OS/2 are examples. They are easier to use than text interfaces.

Gross military deficit - The number of personnel that do not have adequate housing on an Army post or in the private market surrounding the installation.

Groupware - Computer–based systems that support groups of people engaged in a common task (or goal) and that provide an interface to a shared environment.

GIS - Geographic Information Systems; a collection of databases, information systems, and techniques for managing and modeling the state of a physical location, such as a building, county, roads, etc.

Housing Analysis Decision Technology System (HADTS) - An information system that delivers database management, mapping, and decision science technologies in support of the Armyís construction or leasing management process.

Housing Analysis System (HANS) - An information system that helps Army managers to forecast available private market supplies and predict housing deficits.

Housing Market Area (HMA) - A predefined geographic area in the vicinity of an Army installation.

IBM 4381 - A now outdated IBM mainframe computer

ICE - Integrated Computing Environment; a NASA Langley project aimed at presenting computer users with a uniform and extensible interface to their environment and resources while decreasing the system administration effort required to manage remote systems.

Informal Organization - The informal organization often serves to foster and nature creativity in an organization. The members' collective core values may foster innovation. The informal organization may have reward mechanisms that encourage risk, communication networks that facilitate innovation, and role mechanisms promoting innovation, e.g., champions.

instructor/facilitators (I/F) - Managers responsible for training and facilitating all team members involved in a BPS/I project.

inter-operability - The ability of different pieces of hardware or software to communicate with each other.

Intranet - A term describing using TCP/IP and Internet tools and techniques primarily for internal organizational communications usage.

Internet - A global network of interconnected networks that all use the TCP/IP communications protocol.

Interorganizational Systems (IOS) - Computer applications that span multiple organizations.

Joint application development/design (JAD) - A special form of structured meeting during which user representatives, application developers, and a facilitator meet continuously over several days to define the functional requirements of an application.

LANTERN - The name of NASA Langley Research Center's intranet.

Licensing - Government process for authorising individuals to drive specific classes of motor vehicle in return for payment. Captures data about drivers which can be used for regulatory and policing purposes.

Local area network (LAN) - a network connecting computers in a small geographic region, such as within a single building.

LSS - Langley Software Server; an experimental World Wide Web technology transfer resource at NASA Langley for customers to receive or order NASA software available for distribution.

MACOM - A major Army command.

macro process teams - Cross–functional work teams who actually perform the process. Team composition consists of six to eight members, including a supervisor or mid–level manager.

management review team (MRT) - The MRT is the governing body that consists of the General Manager, department heads, BPS/I coordinator, and invited guests depending on the process being considered. The MRT selects and authorizes business processes to be examined that have critical links to Caterpillar business strategies. The MRT also guides projects by interacting with the PRT and macro process teams.

Masculine organization - A masculine organization is "assertive", less concerned about people. A performance orientation is associated with high masculinity. Organization units characterized by low masculinity would generally be more cooperative and less competitive, i.e., performance oriented. For further reading Keon, Vazzana & Slocum (1992)

Master Plan - The canonical reference document describing the state of all NASA Langley buildings, and surrounding resources.

Minicomputer-A now outdated term for a computer which is smaller, cheaper, and more compact than a mainframe but which performs similar functions. Larger and more powerful than a personal computer.

Motor registry-A shopfront based in local centres at which members of the public can register their vehicles, take driving tests and obtain driving licences.

Multi-processor-Computer architecture with more than one processor for processing multiple programs simultaneously.

Multi-skilling-Providing employees with an extended skill set so that they can undertake more elements of a single task or more tasks.

MVS-An IBM proprietary operating system for its mainframe computers.

NTRS - NASA Technical Report Server; a NASA-wide digital library for receiving unclassified NASA technical publications

ODBC (Open Database connectivity) - A common language definition and a set of protocols that allow a client to interactively determine a server's capabilities and adapt the processing to work within the functions supported by the server.

Offsetting - The formal processing of using surpluses in some housing categories to reduce or eliminate deficits in other categories in accordance with Department of Defense policies.

OLE (Object Linking and Embedding) - A standard model for creating and communicating between objects. It is the glue that binds together different applications.

Open systems - Computer systems that permit the use of a wide range of software and hardware supplied by many vendors.

Organizational transformation - Substantial organizational change with the effect of changing the way the organization does business.

Outsource - The elimination of part of the internal IS organization by hiring an outside organization to perform these functions.

Outsourcing - the use of an external organization or freelance workers/consultants to provide all or part of an organization's information systems needs.

Point–of–sale (POS) systems - hardware and software designed to capture transactions through the use of scannable bar codes, simultaneously updating various internal and external data files.

potential problem analysis (PPA) - An analytical technique that helps teams identify potential problems associated with an alternative and anticipate the impact of changes required by an alternative on the existing process and other processes along the process path.

process implementation - The fifth and final step of BPS/I. It involves figuring out how to implement the new process.

process improvement - The third step of BPS/I. It involves analysis of existing processes and suggestions for change.

process mapping - The second step of BPS/I. The goal of process mapping is to understand the current process or set of processes and associated problems. Project limitations and the process mission are also established at this step. Process mapping is the most important step as it provides a full view of the process in its entirety, both upstream and downstream along the process path.

process selection - The first step of BPS/I. The MRT selects critical business processes based on their potential to add value to Caterpillar businesses.

process verification - The fourth step of BPS/I. The team determines the impact of eachalternative on the company as a whole.

project review team (PRT) - The PRT consists of mid–to–upper–level managers familiar with the specific process being improved. The PRT sets stretch improvement goals and selects macro process team members. The PRT also facilitates macro process team activities and communicates the importance of the project to the company.

Prototype - a partially-functioning version of an information system used to test a design.

Prototyping - An abbreviated system development life cycle that uses advanced development tools to create a prototype system in a very short period of time.

Quick Response (QR) - refers to the ability of organizations to rapidly react to changing business conditions (example: demand).

Reengineering - The radical redesign of broad, cross–functional business processes with the objective of order–of–magnitude performance gains, often with the aid of information technology.

repetitive stress (strain) injury (RSI) - a serious, painful and potentially debilitating occupational illness caused by prolonged repetitive hand and arm movements that can damage and inflame the nerves of the hands, arms, shoulders and neck. There has been a major increase in such injuries with the widespread use of computers. Many computer input devices (e.g., keyboards and point-and-click devices) are being designed with ergonomics in mind. Poor design of work areas as well as hardware contributes to RSI.

Requirements Analysis - The process of determining what features and capabilities an information systems application must possess and specifying financial and temporal restrictions on its development. The analysis is usually part of a top-down approach to information systems (IS) development in modern organizations. This approach consists of the following stages: determining business needs, identifying appropriate IS application needs (and their specifications) to satisfy these business needs, determining data distribution, storage, and processing requirements for each application (i.e., logical data base design), determining network architecture and performance criteria (logical network design), and finally, physical design and implementation (i.e., physical data base design, physical network design, and applications implementation). The last three stages usually proceed concurrently. Requirements Analysis is a term that encompasses the first two of the five stages mentioned and is a preliminary step to the design and development of any information system application.

Response times - The time taken from a user transmitting a transaction from a terminal or work station to receiving a response from a *mainframe* computer.

RTA - Roads and Traffic Authority of the state of New South Wales in Australia.

Safe-T-Cam - A system, enabled by *DRIVES*, for electronically collecting data on heavy vehicles.

Screen map - a specification showing where data entry fields are displayed on a terminal.

security: the protection of hardware, software and/or data so that unauthorized individuals cannot access, modify, copy or steal it.

Segmented Housing Market Analysis (SHMA) - The formal analysis required to economically justify an Armyís housing construction or leasing request.

sneaker net - the comically term used to refer to inter-computer communication prior to the installation of a local area network (LAN). In Sneaker Net, an individual would copy a file onto a diskette and literally walk it to another machine where it was then loaded; thus the name "Sneaker Net".

Systems development - (1) Conceiving, designing, and implementing a system. (2) Developing information systems by a process of investigation, analysis, design, implementation, and maintenance. Also called the systems development life cycle (SDLC).

TCP/IP - Transmission Control Protocol/Internet Protocol; the primary communications protocol that allows computers on the Internet to communicate with each other.

Technology platform - Combination of computer hardware, software and networks which provide the basis for running *applications*.

Text interface - a user interface that relies solely on letters, digits and a few special characters. It does not have any graphical components. Text interfaces are more difficult to use than graphical interfaces.

TIGER files - United States Census Bureau topologically integrated geographic encoding and referencing files used to locate housing within a housing market area.

TOPS - Technology Opportunities Showcase; a technology transfer conference held at NASA Langley Research Center that was later converted to a World Wide Web database.

Trading Partners are the customers or suppliers of a business organization.

Transaction processing system - an information system that handles day-to-day operations of a firm, such as accounts payable and shipping.

UNIX - A complex, multi-user operating system frequently employed in academic departments, scientific laboratories, and other areas of intensive use.

URL - Uniform Resource Locator; an address that specifies a unique location of a resource on the Internet.

USENET - A global news system arranged in subject hierarchies. Allows submission and reading of articles over a nearly unlimited breadth of topics.

User interface - That part of an operating system or other program that allows users to communicate with it to load programs, access files, and accomplish other computing tasks.

User requirements - information inputs/outputs deemed necessary by the people who will interact with, and use outputs of, the information system.

UTS/M - Fujitsu's proprietary version of *UNIX*.

Wide area network (LAN) - a network connecting computers dispersed over a large geographic region, such as a country.

X–command - A x–command enables unconditional branching, to a self–contained routine, with program control returned to the original branching point. Inappropriate use of this capability generally results in very "nested" coding.

X.500 - An international standard for implementing directory services for organizations. Often used to look up people's e-mail addresses, telephone numbers, and other public attributes.

Authors

EDITORS OF THE BOOK

Jay Liebowitz held the Chaired Professorship in Artificial Intelligence at the U.S. Army War College, and is Professor of Management Science at George Washington University. He has published 18 books and over 200 journal articles, mostly in expert systems and information technology. He is the editor-in-chief of the international journal, Expert Systems With Applications and the associate editor of the international journal, Telematics and Informatics. He is the founder of The World Congress on Expert Systems and he has lectured in over 20 countries.

Dr. Liebowitz has a Doctor of Science in Systems Analysis and Management (minor in Operations Research), MBA in Finance and Investments, and B.B.A. in Accounting, all from George Washington University. He has served as president of the GWU chapters of Sigma Xi (Scientific Research Honor Society) and Omega Rho (Operations Research Honor Society). He has also served as president of the College of AI in Management Science of TIMS (The Institute for Management Science, now called INFORMS). He has consulted for industry, universities and government (e.g., Navy, Army, etc.) on many expert system-related projects. He has also just started his role as editor-in-chief of a new international journal, titled Failures and Lessons Learned in Information Technology Management: An International Journal. He was recently selected as the Computer Educator of the Year 1996 by the International Association for Computer Information Systems.

Mehdi Khosrowpour is currently an Associate Professor of Information Systems at Penn State Harrisburg. He is the editor-in-charge of the Information Resources Management Journal, the Journal of Database Management and Information Management and consulting editor of the Information Technology Newsletter. In addition, he also serves on the editorial review boards of six other international information systems journals.

Dr. Khosrowpour is the author/editor of 10 books and more than 30 articles published in various scholarly and professional journals, such as the Journal of Information Systems Management, Business Review, Journal of Systems Management, Journal of Applied Business Research, Computing Review, Journal of Computer Information Systems, Journal of Education Technology Systems and Journal of Microcomputer Systems Management. He is a frequent speaker at many international meetings and organizations, such as the Association of Federal Information Resources Management, Contract Management Association, Financial Women Association, National Association of States Information Resources Executives and IBM.

CONTRIBUTORS TO THE BOOK

Lieutenant Commander Virginia Callaghan Bayer received a MS in Information Technology Management from the Naval Postgraduate School in 1995 and a MBA from the University of Redlands in 1993. She is currently serving on active duty in the United States Navy and pursuing a career subspecialty in corporate information systems management. By virtue of experience, her core competency is in naval manpower, personnel, education, and training. LCDR Bayer's key academic interests include development of training technologies, organizational change, and information systems analysis, design, and implementation strategies.

Tom Beckman After completing graduate studies in Artificial Intelligence and Management Science at MIT in 1986, Mr. Beckman spent the next seven years in the AI lab developing business applications of expert systems. For the past three years, Tom has overseen and contributed to the development of handbooks for business reengineering and process improvement. Currently, Mr. Beckman is the chief methodologist for business reengineering and process improvement at the Internal Revenue Service. Tom specializes in designing visionary business systems, identifying and applying innovative IT; and integrating diverse, but complementary, methodologies such as strategic planning, reengineering, process improvement, performance management, and work systems design. Mr. Beckman also teaches graduate courses in AI, Expert Systems, Knowledge Acquisition, and Reengineering in the Management Science Department at The George Washington University.

John Benamati is an independent information technology consultant and a Ph.D. candidate in Decision Science and Information Systems at the Carol Martin Gatton College of Business and Economics, University of Kentucky. He is a University of Kentucky Presidential Fellow since 1994 and is a Richard D. Irwin Dissertation Fellowship recipient for 1996-97. His research investigates the effects of rapidly changing IT on the management of information from an IT providers' perspective. Prior to beginning his doctoral work, Mr. Benamati was an information systems professional for over 12 years and has held positions in internal IS organizations, IT technical marketing, and IT consulting and services. His experience includes extensive work on large-scale application development efforts from both the technical and the managerial perspectives. Mr. Benamati is a member of the Association for Information Systems, the Decision Sciences Institute, and the Institute for Operations Research and the Management Sciences.

David J. Bianco <d.j.bianco@larc.nasa.gov> began working for Computer Sciences Corporation in November of 1993. David has assisted NASA Langley's Information Systems and Services Division in many areas, including standards-based computing environments, distributed information systems, cryptography, the Distributed Computing Environment / Distributed File Service (DCE/DFS), and his work on the Integrated Computing Environment team. David has previously held positions at the Old Dominion University and iTRiBE.

Dr. Connie Crook is an Assistant Professor within the Department of Management Information Systems and Operations Management at the University of North Carolina At Charlotte, where she teaches undergraduate and graduate courses in management information systems, data communications, database, and information resource management. She received a M.Ed. in Mathematics and M.S. in Industrial Engineering from North Carolina State University, and a Ph.D. in Business Administration with a major in Management Information Systems from the University of South Carolina. Prior to her employment at the University, she held positions in industry. Her research has appeared or is forthcoming in the Journal of Management Information Systems, Journal of Systems Management, Computer Personnel, and Popular Government , book chapters, and several conference proceedings. Her current research interests involve career paths of information systems professionals, electronic commerce, and communication support systems.

Gurpreet Dhillon, BSc (Hons), MBA, MSc (Econ), Ph.D., is with the Information Systems Group at the Cranfield School of Management. He has a Ph.D. in Information Systems from the London School of Economics. His doctoral research on the management of information systems security has been extended to encompass other issues including risk management, economic crime, computer related fraud and business ethics. Recently he has been researching in the area of information technology-related organizational competencies and implications for business change. He has published numerous academic and refereed papers, and has produced several research reports for major government and private sector organizations.

Steve Dickinson is the Venture Support Manager at the Caterpillar Inc. Engine Division located near Peoria, Illinois. Mr. Dickinson developed, and for the past five years, has coordinated, his division's methodology for process improvement known as Business Process Simplification and Improvement (BPS/I). His organization's methods have served as a pattern for business process improvement throughout much of the Caterpillar organization. His company's achievements in the process improvement arena have been published in Managing

Automation magazine and was the subject of a series of college instruction videos published by the Richard D. Irwin Company. Beyond process improvement, his interests include information technologies, competitive intelligence and organizational communication techniques.

Guisseppi A. Forgionne is Professor of Information Systems at the University of Maryland Baltimore County (UMBC). Professor Forgionne holds a B.S. in Commerce and Finance, an M.A. in Econometrics, an M.B.A. and a Ph.D. in Management Science and Econometrics. He has published 20 books and approximately 100 research articles and consulted for a variety of public and private organizations on decision support systems theory and applications. Dr. Forgionne also has served a department chair at UMBC, Mount Vernon College and Cal Poly Pomona. He has received several national and international awards for his work.

Erik Frøkjær is associate professor in computing at the University of Copenhagen. He received MSc degrees in Mathematical Engineering and in Electrical Engineering from the Technical University of Denmark in 1973, and in 1977 a Bachelor degree in Business Administration. Areas of research have been methods and techniques for systems design and implementation, interface design for information retrieval systems, evaluation methods of interactive information systems, understanding of computing as a human activity inspired by Peter Naur's approach, and computer support for learning and problem solving. He joined the University of Copenhagen in 1985 after twelve years as a systems developer and project manager. He has maintained a special interest in the development and use of information technology in large organizations, especially public, as well as for IT policy issues. In 1983-84 Erik Frøkjær was chairman of the Geodata Group, the cross departmental committee under the Board of Coordination of Public Data Systems who initially proposed to develop the Danish Geodata Information System, see Georegistergruppen (1984) and Frøkjær (1985).

Barry Frew is an Associate Professor of Information Systems, Naval Postgraduate School (NPS). He received a MS in Computer Systems Management from Naval Postgraduate School. Before joining the NPS faculty in 1984, he spent several years as an information resource management practitioner involved with software development, technology acquisition and integration, and computer operations. In 1989, he was named Dean of Computer and Information Services at NPS managing the school's IT budget, the library, centralized academic computing, administrative computing, and computer information security. His primary research and teaching interests include the political and organizational impacts of information technology, the use of information technology to support process improvement, and measuring the value added aspects of a firm's use of information technologies.

Gretchen L. Gottlich <ggottlich@fruit.com> received a M.L.S. in library and information science from Indiana University in 1991, and a B.S. in geography & urban affairs in 1985 from the University of Arkansas. Gretchen's principal contributions at NASA included digital library work and World Wide Web team management. The latter involved such projects as the implementation of the NASA Langley intranet, the organizing of two NASA Langley Internet Fairs, the design of World Wide Web training modules, insuring computer access to over 800 NASA Langley technicians, and numerous internal and external presentations about NASA Langley Internet resources. In July 1996, Gretchen joined Fruit of the Loom as a senior information technology analyst.

Susan Page Hocevar received her Ph.D. in Business Administration from the University of Southern California. She is currently an Assistant Professor in the Department of Systems Management at the Naval Postgraduate School in Monterey, California. There she teaches courses in organization and management to military officers earning a graduate degree. Her research and publications are in the areas of organization change, high involvement organizations, organizational reward systems, self–managed teams, organizational culture, quality of work life, and corporate social responsibility.

David L. Jordan, MBA is CEO of CompuTec Consulting in Royston, GA. After graduating from The Citadel in 1990 with a BSBA, Mr. David L. Jordan worked as an Information Systems Administrator and Controller in private industry. He obtained his MBA from The Citadel in 1996 where he provided support and supervision for the campus network of computers. He is currently CEO of CompuTec Consulting of Georgia where he continues to research information systems implementation issues while consulting with various business and industry clients.

Sherif Kamel is an assistant professor in the management department, School of Business, Economics and Mass Communication, the American University in Cairo. He holds a bachelor of arts degree in business administration and a master of business administration degree from the American University in Cairo; and a Ph.D. degree from London School of Economics and Political Science. His research focuses on management information systems, decision support systems, organizational restructuring, crisis management and information technology transfer into developing countries. He has published a number of publications and has conducted several information systems management consulting and workshops related to information technology and management theories and applications and their implications in developing countries.

Mathew J. Klempa is a consultant in the application of computer information systems. He has taught at the University of Southern California and the California State University. He holds a B.S. in Mathematics/ Economics from Allegheny College, M.S. degree in Management Science, M.B.A. degree in International Business, and Ph.D. degree in Business Administration from the University of Southern California. His doctoral majors were Decision Support Systems and Corporate Policy and Strategy. He was formerly a corporate planning officer for a major bank holding company, systems analyst at IBM and operations research analyst at McDonnell™ Douglas. His research interests include business process reengineering; business process change; organization impacts of information technology; the interaction among information technology and organizational structures, control mechanisms, culture, learning, work processes, and performance; information technology diffusion; and cognitive and individual differences in DSS use. E-mail: mklempa@delphi.com

Helge Korsbæk, M.A. in economics from Aarhus University, now retired, has served as a Deputy Secretary in the Ministry of Finance, Department of Administration, primarily concerned with questions regarding the organization and the efficiency of the central government administration. He has been chairman of a number of working groups among others the so-called 'Korsbæk-committee' which in 1970 made proposals for general changes of the organization of the Danish central administration (Official Report no. 629) and a working group on the coordination of central government map producing institutions (1980-82). He has been Danish contact officer to the International Institute of Administrative Sciences (IIAS) in Brussels an d a member of the board of the European Institute of Public Administration (EIPA) in Maastricht.

Dr. Ram L. Kumar is Assistant Professor in the Department of MIS and Operations at the Belk College of Business Administration , the University of North Carolina, Charlotte. He has worked for five years in information systems development and management. He received his Ph.D. from the University of Maryland in 1993, where he was the recipient of the Frank T. Paine Award for Academic Merit. His research interests include management of information and manufacturing technology, security and control in information systems, and the interface between MIS and Operations Management. His research has appeared or is forthcoming in Computers & Operations Research, International Journal of Production Economics, Journal of MIS, Journal of Systems Management, book chapters, and several conference proceedings. His work has been funded by organizations such as the US Department of Commerce, the Maryland Industrial Partnerships Scheme, and Barclays American. He is a member of AIS, DSI, and INFORMS.

Kieran Mathieson is Associate Professor of MIS at Oakland University in Rochester, Michigan. He received his doctorate from Indiana University. His research focuses on the manner in which beliefs about information systems are formed, the factors individuals consider when deciding whether to use information systems, and the implementation of GUI and client/server systems.

Nina McGarry is a Senior Principal Consultant at PRC Inc. a large, international management consulting firm headquartered near Washington, DC. Ms. McGarry develops and facilitates human resource programs for organizations. She teaches Management Information Systems at The George Washington University. Ms. McGarry holds a Masters of Science in Management Information Systems.

John M. Meyer <j.m.meyer@larc.nasa.gov> received a B.S. in electrical engineering from Virginia Tech in 1985. John has been active in numerous areas at NASA Langley, including CADD, design of real-time video and data acquisition systems, geographic information systems both with NASA and the United States Air Force, and network information systems.

Kathleen Moffitt is a professor of information systems at California State University, Fresno. She received her Ph.D. in Computer Information Systems from Arizona State University, M.A. from the University of Arizona, and B.A. from the University of Colorado. She has published in IEEE Expert, Decision Sciences, Transportation Research and Human Factors in Information Systems. Her current research interests include, end-user computing, global information systems, Internet application and strategy, IS/IT management and innovative education.

William H. Money, Ph.D., Associate Professor of Information Systems, School of Business and Public Management, joined the George Washington University faculty September, 1992. His present publications and recent research interests focus on information system development tools and methodologies, workflow and expert systems, and the impacts of Group Support Systems (GSSs) on organization memory, individual learning and project planning. Prior to his appointment to the GWU faculty he supported the Government acquisition of the Reserve Component Automation System (RCAS); served as the Program Manager, and the Deputy Program Manager for the Baxter Healthcare Systems' Composite Healthcare System Program; and served as a Product Manager for Technicon Data Systems. His previous teaching background (1976-80) includes one year at the Purdue University, Graduate School of Industrial Administration, and four years at the Kent State University, Graduate School of Business. Dr. Money also has extensive healthcare research experience. He was a research assistant for the Northwestern University Health Services Research Center for four years, and completed an analysis of the impact of mergers and acquisitions on the integration of Multi-hospital Systems for his doctoral dissertation. Dr. Money's academic training includes the Ph.D., Organizational Behavior/Systems Engineering, 1977, Northwestern University, Graduate School of Management; the M.B.A., Management, 1969, Indiana University; and a B.A., Political Science, 1968, University of Richmond.

Prior to becoming a professor of MIS and accounting, **Dr. Jeanette Moody** acquired extensive corporate experience with major organizations such as General Telephone and Electronics, Eastern Airlines and Jack Eckerd Corporation, and was a practicing CPA with Price Waterhouse, CPA's in Florida. Her research has been published in *MIS Quarterly, Expert Systems with Applications,* and *The Journal of Systems Management.* Dr. Moody's research interests are in the area of information requirements determination, communication aspects of systems development, and end–user training issues. Dr. Moody obtained her MBA and Ph. D. in MIS from the University of South Florida and her BSBA from the University of Florida.

Martin Müller is a Ph.D. student at the AI-Lab of the Department of Computer Science at the University of Zurich, Switzerland. 'Situated Design', a software development methodology which takes the situational and social nature of human conduct into account, will be his dissertational subject. In 1992 he received his Master of Science in engineering of informatics (computer science) at the Federal Institute for Technology of Switzerland (ETH Zurich). He enhanced his engineering background with additional studies in work psychology during his study, by studying psychology for one year at the University of Zurich, and a visit at the Institute for Research on Learning (IRL) in Palo Alto (USA) for two months during 1996.

Michael L. Nelson <m.l.nelson@larc.nasa.gov> graduated with a B.S. in computer science from Virginia Tech and is a graduate student in computer science at Old Dominion University. Since coming to work for NASA Langley Research Center's Information Systems Division in September of 1991, Michael has worked on a variety of projects in the distributed and parallel computing, distributed information systems, and computing environments areas. He is the "webmaster" for NASA Langley Research Center and has worked with others to implement report servers, software servers, technology transfer databases and other World Wide Web services. He has over 20 technical publications and presentations about distributed and parallel computing and information systems.

Dr. Ram Pakath is an Associate Professor of Decision Science and Information Systems at the University of Kentucky. He received the PhD degree in Management from Purdue University in 1988. Professor Pakath's teaching interests and experience are in the a reas of data base management, business telecommunications, business computing systems, applied artificial intelligence, and management science. His current research focuses on hybrid and adaptive problem processors and multimedia systems. Dr. Pakath's work has appeared in such forums as Decision Sciences, Decision Support Systems, European Journal of Operational Research, IEEE Transactions on Systems, Man, and Cybernetics, Information and Management, and Information Systems Research. He is author of the book Computerized Support Systems for Business: A Concise Introduction (Copley) and several refereed book chapters. Dr. Pakath is an Associate Editor of Decision Support Systems and an Editorial Board Member of Journal of End User Computing and Management. His research has been funded by IBM, Ashland Oil, and the University of Kentucky. He is currently a member of the Institute for Operations Research and the Management Sciences and the Information Resources Management Association.

David Paper is an assistant professor at Utah State University, teaching in the Business Information Systems and Education Department. He has several refereed publications appearing in journals such as Accounting Management and Information Technologies, Journal of Computer Information Systems, Information Strategy: The Executive's Journal, Journal of High Technology Management Research, and Malaysian Management Review. His teaching and research interests include business process reengineering, total quality management, worker empowerment, and strategic management of information technologies.

Rolf Pfeifer is a full professor of computer science and heads the AI Lab at the Computer Science Department of the University of Zurich in Switzerland. After receiving his M.S. in physics and mathematics and his Ph.D. in computer science at the Swiss Federal Institute of Technology (ETH), he spent three years in the US at CMU in Herb Simon's group and at Yale in Bob Abelson and Roger Schank's cognitive science lab. In 1990/91 he was visiting professor on the Swift AI Chair of the Free University of Brussel (VUB). His main research interests are foundations of AI and cognitive science, autonomous agents, adaptive behavior, and "situated design".

Dr. Sorel Reisman is Professor of Management Information Systems in the Department of Management Science/Information Systems at Cal State Fullerton, and University Extended Education Director of Information Systems and Services. In addition to his MIS educational responsibilities, Dr. Reisman is actively involved in the development, implementation and management of client/server software and systems, multimedia systems and applications, the Internet, intranets, and the World Wide Web. Dr. Reisman is a member of the editorial boards of The Journal of End User Computing and the Journal of Global Information Management as well as IEEE Software and IEEE Multimedia in which he serves as a referee, product reviewer, and writes regular editorial columns concerning contemporary issues in computing. Dr. Reisman's book "Multimedia Computing, Preparing for the 21st Century" was published in 1994 and reprinted in 1996. Dr. Reisman confers with a variety of US and foreign multinational corporations in the fields of management consulting, information systems management, and multimedia computing.

Chris Sauer is currently Senior Research Fellow at the Fujitsu Centre for Managing Information Technology in Organisations at the Australian Graduate School of Management in Sydney. He researches general management issues in IT-based organizational transformation. His first book *Why Information Systems Fail: a Case Study Approach* was published in 1993. He is co-editor with Philip Yetton of *Steps to the Future: Fresh Thinking in the Dynamics of IT-Based Organizational Transformation* to be published by Jossey-Bass in 1997. In addition he has published various papers on his research and on IT educational issues. He is Secretary to the International Federation for Information Processing (IFIP) Working Group 8.6 on Technology Transfer and Diffusion. He is a member of the editorial boards of the Information Systems Journal and the Australian Journal of Management. Dr. Sauer is a graduate of Oxford University and the University of Western Australia.

Tim Toland is a programmer for the ITSS Applications and Development group at Allnet Communications in Birmingham, Michigan. He is a graduate of the Oakland University MIS program.

Lucy Wegner is Interim Assistant Dean for Information Technology and Director of the Center for Scholarly Technology in the University Libraries at the University of Southern California. She holds MBA and

MLS degrees from the University of California (Los Angeles), and a MA degree (Music) from the California State University (Northridge). Ms. Wegner's career has focused on developing systems to access and organize electronic information resources. She is a frequent writer and speaker on the library of the twenty-first century, the future of librarianship, and technology innovation in libraries.

Vincent C. Yen is associate professor of management science and information systems at Wright State University College of Business Administration. He received his Ph.D. from the Ohio State University in operations research. His research interests include strategic information systems planning, determination of systems requirements, systems development processes, decision support systems, fuzzy control, and fuzzy decision–making. He and Prof. H. Li co–published a book in 1995 entitled "fuzzy sets and fuzzy decision-making" by CRC Press.

Dr. Ira Yermish is currently an Assistant Professor of Management and Information Systems at St. Joseph's University in Philadelphia. His teaching and research areas include systems analysis and design, data base management, data communications, information resource management, decision support and expert systems, and business policy and strategic management. In addition to designing the undergraduate and graduate curricula in Management Information Systems he has been active in the executive MBA program and the executive programs in Food Marketing and Pharmaceutical Marketing. He was the designer of the College of Business microcomputer network and has provided continuing technical support for microcomputer applications in the College. Dr. Yermish is the advisor to the student Information Systems Society and was awarded a certificate for Excellence in Teaching in 1988. In addition to his current academic activities, Dr. Yermish is an active management and information systems consultant with clients in manufacturing, wholesale/distribution, banking, law and other service industries. He has been active in project management seminars with such firms as AT&T, Johnson & Johnson, and Bristol–Myers/Squibb. Dr. Yermish earned a B.S. in Management Science from Case Western Reserve University, an M.S. in Operations Research from Stanford University, and a Ph.D. in Computer and Information Sciences from the University of Pennsylvania. His early professional experience included positions with Sperry Rand, Control Data, RCA Corporation and the Institute for Scientific Information. At these firms he held positions as a systems analyst, operations research analyst and computer scientist. Prior to coming to St. Joseph's University in 1984, Dr. Yermish owned and operated a software development firm specializing in wholesale-distribution and manufacturing systems.

Index

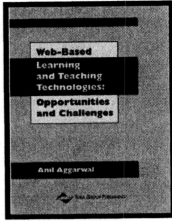